Juliet

Volume 5

Story & Art by Emura

W Juliet
Volume 5

Story and Art by Emura

Translation & English Adaptation/William Flanagan
Touch-up Art & Lettering/Mark McMurray
Graphic Design/Hidemi Sahara
Editor/Megan Bates

Managing Editor/Annette Roman
Director of Production/Noboru Watanabe
Vice President of Publishing/Alvin Lu
Sr. Director of Acquisitions/Rika Inouye
Vice President of Sales & Marketing/Liza Coppola
Publisher/Hyoe Narita

W Juliet by Emura © Emura 2000. All rights reserved.
First published in Japan in 2000 by HAKUSENSHA, Inc., Tokyo. English language
translation rights in America and Canada arranged with HAKUSENSHA, Inc., Tokyo.
The W JULIET logo is a trademark of VIZ, LLC. All rights reserved.
The stories, characters and incidents mentioned in this publication are entirely fictional.

Printed in Canada.

Published by VIZ, LLC
P.O. Box 77010
San Francisco, CA 94107

10 9 8 7 6 5 4 3 2 1
First printing, June 2005

www.viz.com

store.viz.com

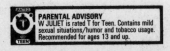

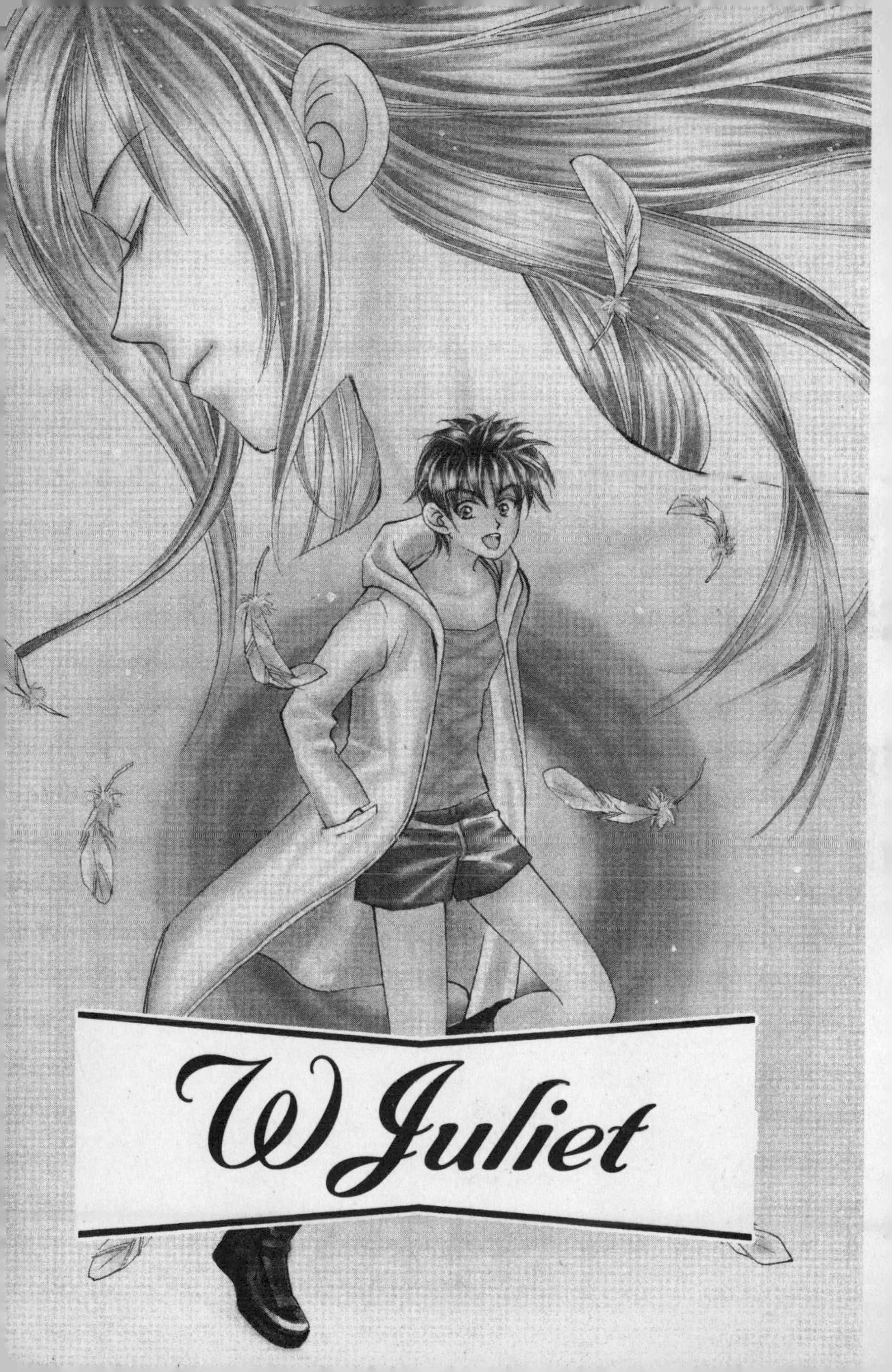
W Juliet

Pencils (on tracing paper) Size: B4

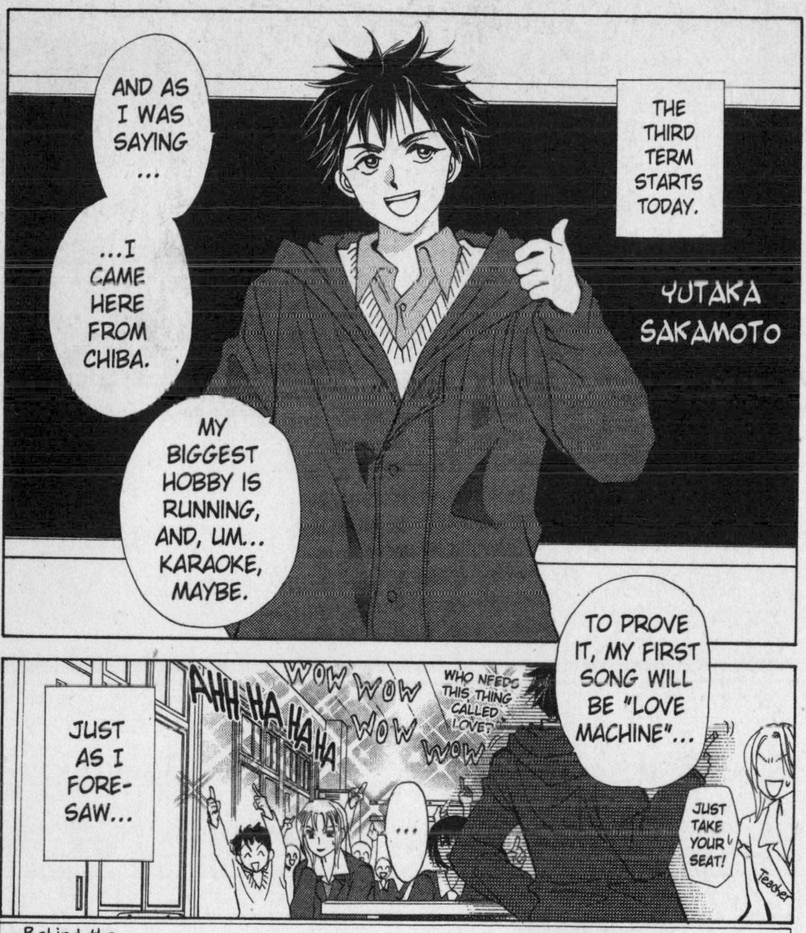
THE THIRD TERM STARTS TODAY.
YUTAKA SAKAMOTO
AND AS I WAS SAYING ...
...I CAME HERE FROM CHIBA.
MY BIGGEST HOBBY IS RUNNING, AND, UM... KARAOKE, MAYBE.
TO PROVE IT, MY FIRST SONG WILL BE "LOVE MACHINE"...
JUST TAKE YOUR SEAT!
Teacher
WHO NEEDS THIS THING CALLED LOVE?
WOW WOW WOW WOW WOW
AHH HA HA HA HA
...
JUST AS I FORESAW...

-Behind the Scenes Story- ①

Sakamoto transferred in! People sure don't like him! Well, I like him a whole lot! But it's okay! They like him a lot better than Takashi! And among the readers, there are a few Sakamoto fans!

There are a lot of people who knew without hearing it from me, but I had Romeo and Juliet in mind when I drew the veranda scene. ♡ But if I really wanted to convey the feeling, I probably should have drawn in more flowers (and plants). What do you think?

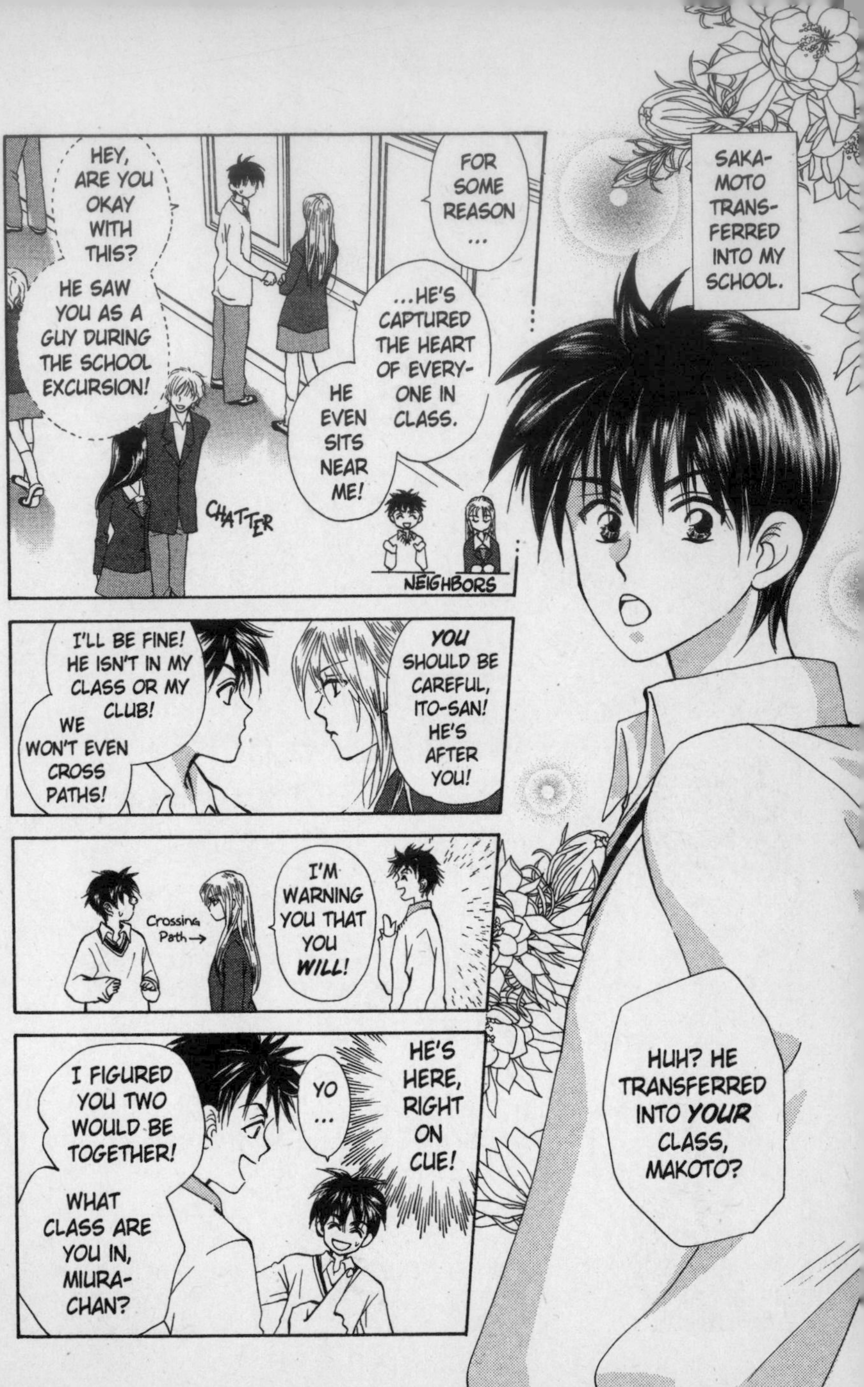
SAKA-MOTO TRANS-FERRED INTO MY SCHOOL.
HUH? HE TRANSFERRED INTO YOUR CLASS, MAKOTO?
FOR SOME REASON ...
...HE'S CAPTURED THE HEART OF EVERY-ONE IN CLASS.
HE EVEN SITS NEAR ME!
NEIGHBORS
HEY, ARE YOU OKAY WITH THIS?
HE SAW YOU AS A GUY DURING THE SCHOOL EXCURSION!
CHATTER
YOU SHOULD BE CAREFUL, ITO-SAN! HE'S AFTER YOU!
I'LL BE FINE! HE ISN'T IN MY CLASS OR MY CLUB!
WE WON'T EVEN CROSS PATHS!
I'M WARNING YOU THAT YOU WILL!
Crossing Path →
HE'S HERE, RIGHT ON CUE!
YO ...
I FIGURED YOU TWO WOULD BE TOGETHER!
WHAT CLASS ARE YOU IN, MIURA-CHAN?

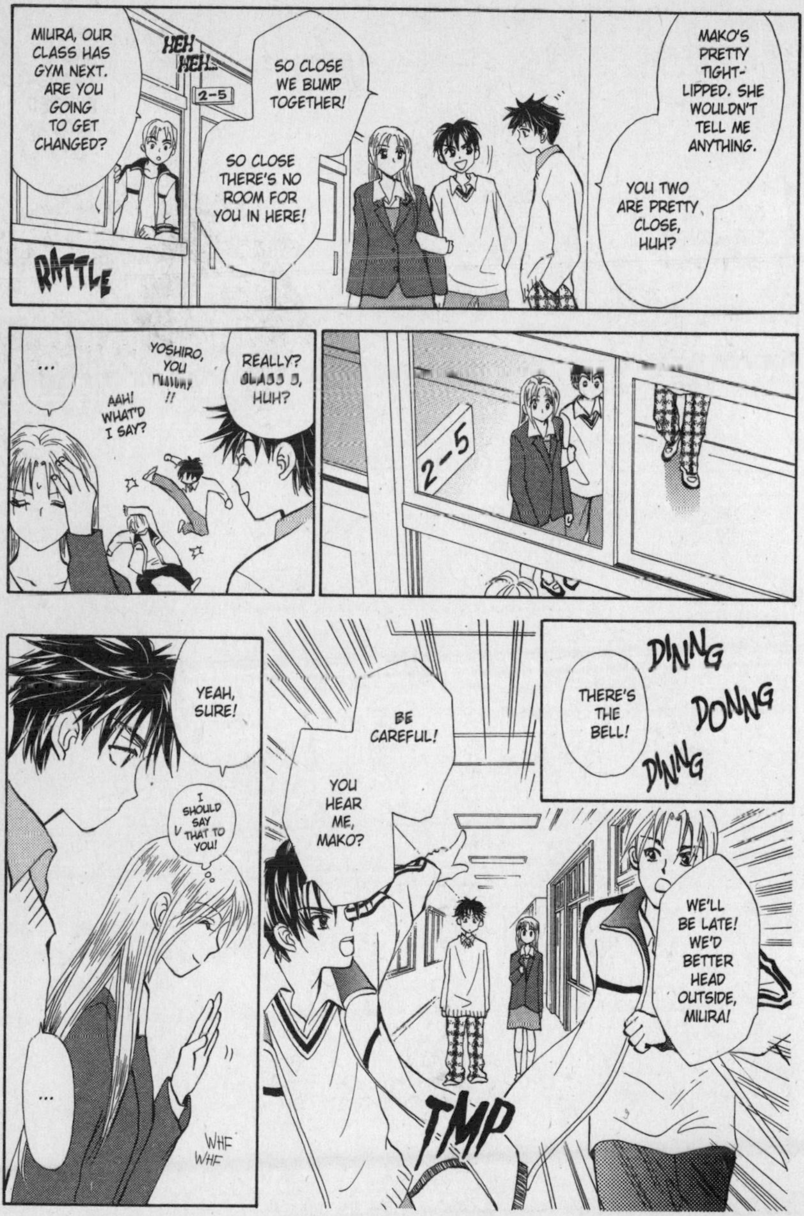
MAKO'S PRETTY TIGHT-LIPPED. SHE WOULDN'T TELL ME ANYTHING.
YOU TWO ARE PRETTY CLOSE, HUH?
SO CLOSE WE BUMP TOGETHER!
SO CLOSE THERE'S NO ROOM FOR YOU IN HERE!
HEH HEH...
MIURA, OUR CLASS HAS GYM NEXT. ARE YOU GOING TO GET CHANGED?
RATTLE
REALLY? CLASS 5, HUH?
YOSHIRO, YOU
!!
AAH! WHAT'D I SAY?
...
DINNG
DONNG
DINNG
THERE'S THE BELL!
WE'LL BE LATE! WE'D BETTER HEAD OUTSIDE, MIURA!
BE CAREFUL!
YOU HEAR ME, MAKO?
TMP
YEAH, SURE!
I SHOULD SAY THAT TO YOU!
...
WHF WHF

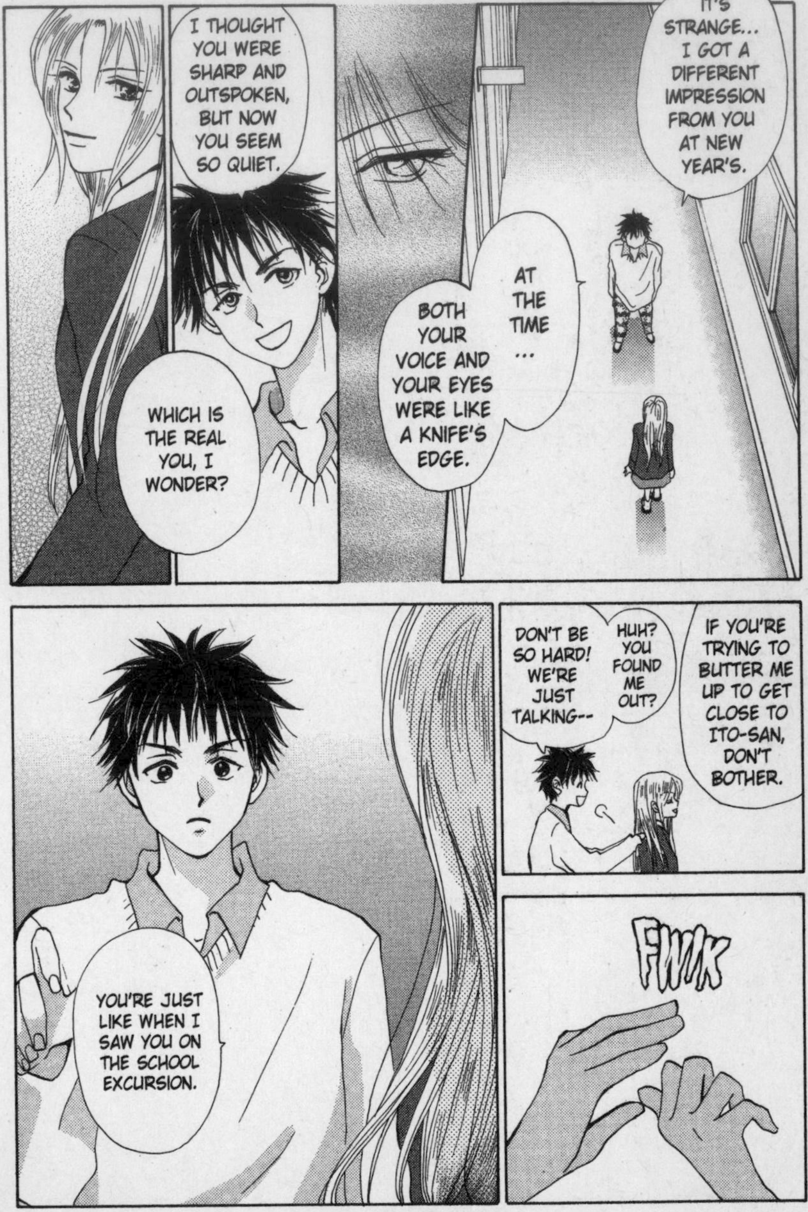
IT'S STRANGE... I GOT A DIFFERENT IMPRESSION FROM YOU AT NEW YEAR'S.
AT THE TIME...
BOTH YOUR VOICE AND YOUR EYES WERE LIKE A KNIFE'S EDGE.
I THOUGHT YOU WERE SHARP AND OUTSPOKEN, BUT NOW YOU SEEM SO QUIET.
WHICH IS THE REAL YOU, I WONDER?
IF YOU'RE TRYING TO BUTTER ME UP TO GET CLOSE TO ITO-SAN, DON'T BOTHER.
HUH? YOU FOUND ME OUT?
DON'T BE SO HARD! WE'RE JUST TALKING--
FWIK
YOU'RE JUST LIKE WHEN I SAW YOU ON THE SCHOOL EXCURSION.

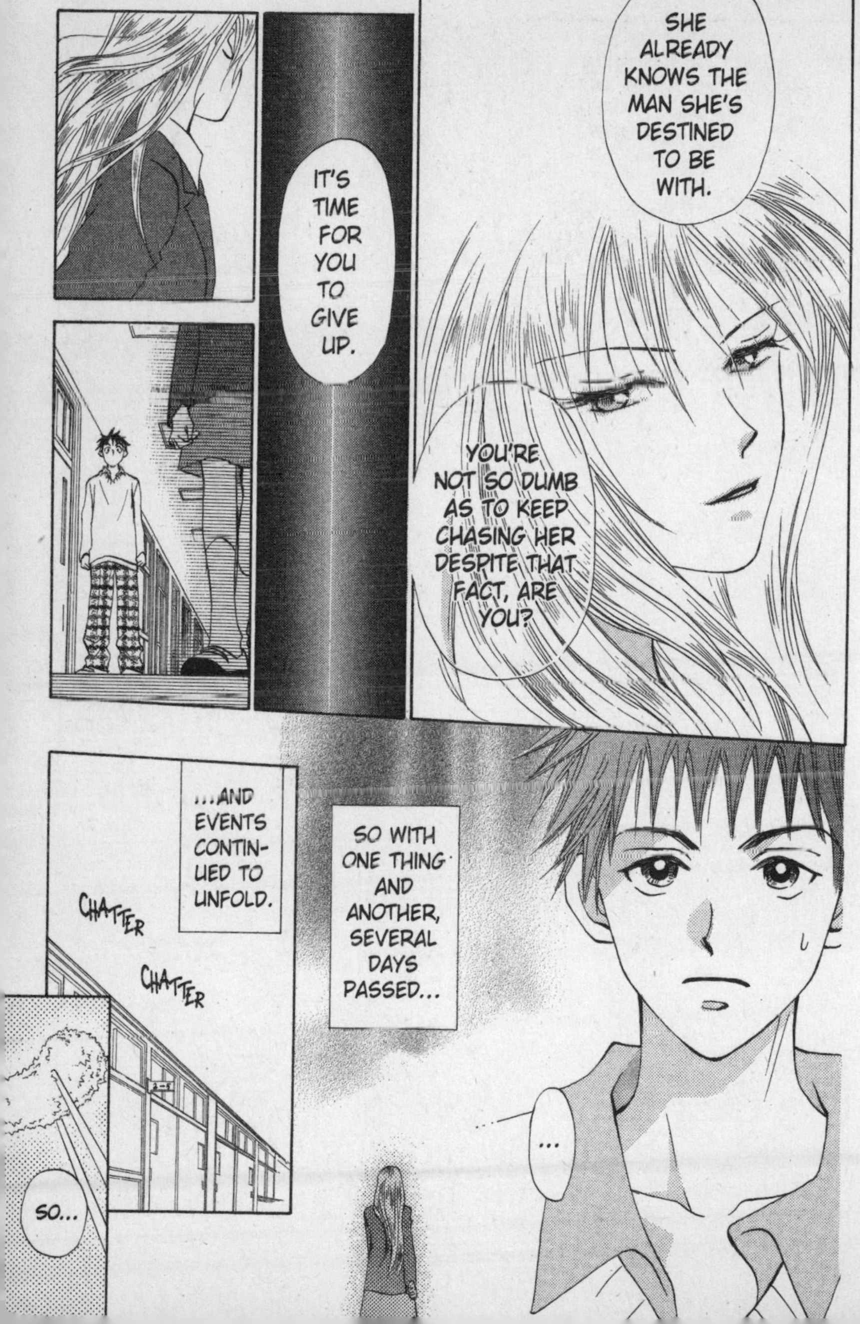
SHE ALREADY KNOWS THE MAN SHE'S DESTINED TO BE WITH.
YOU'RE NOT SO DUMB AS TO KEEP CHASING HER DESPITE THAT FACT, ARE YOU?
IT'S TIME FOR YOU TO GIVE UP.
SO WITH ONE THING AND ANOTHER, SEVERAL DAYS PASSED...
...
...AND EVENTS CONTIN-UED TO UNFOLD.
CHATTER
CHATTER
SO...

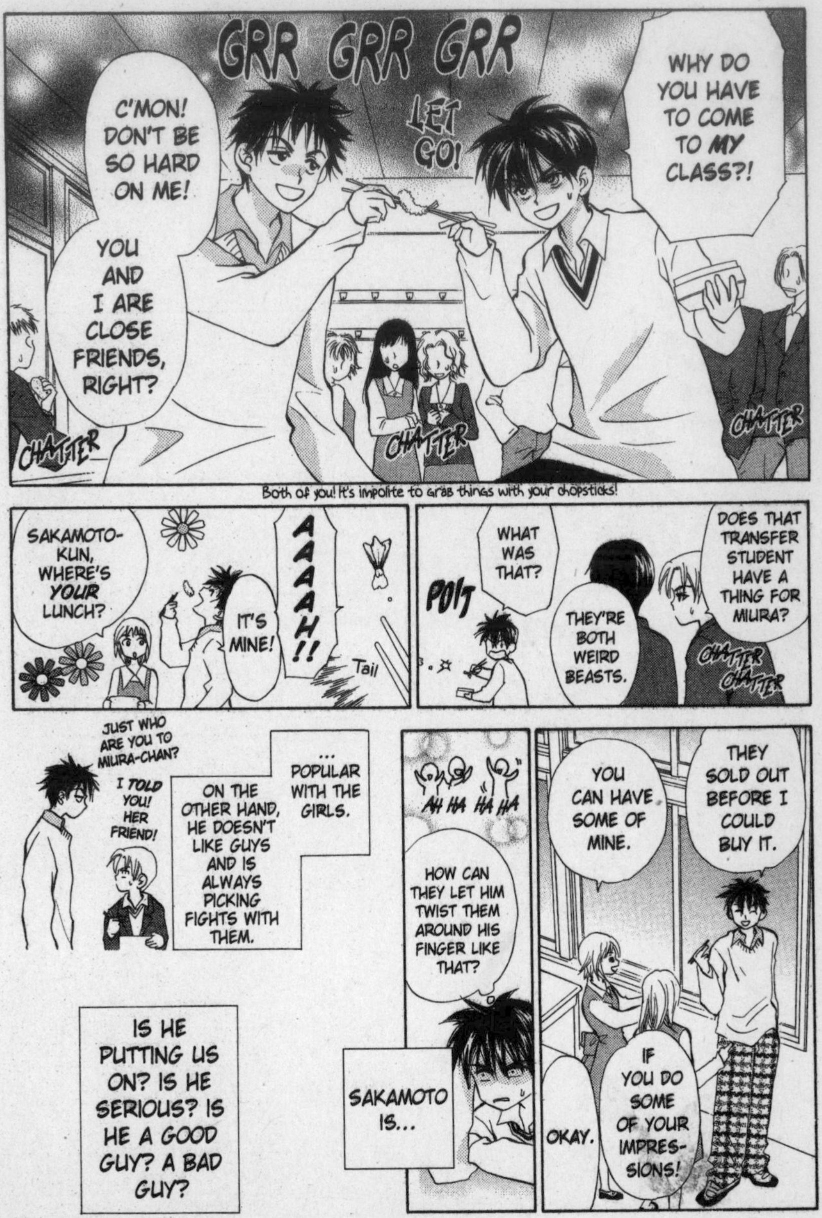
WHY DO YOU HAVE TO COME TO MY CLASS?!
GRR GRR GRR
LET GO!
C'MON! DON'T BE SO HARD ON ME!
YOU AND I ARE CLOSE FRIENDS, RIGHT?
CHATTER
CHATTER
CHATTER
Both of you! It's impolite to grab things with your chopsticks!
DOES THAT TRANSFER STUDENT HAVE A THING FOR MIURA?
CHATTER CHATTER
WHAT WAS THAT?
THEY'RE BOTH WEIRD BEASTS.
POIT
AAAAAH!!
IT'S MINE!
Tail
SAKAMOTO-KUN, WHERE'S YOUR LUNCH?
THEY SOLD OUT BEFORE I COULD BUY IT.
YOU CAN HAVE SOME OF MINE.
IF YOU DO SOME OF YOUR IMPRESSIONS!
OKAY.
AH HA HA HA
HOW CAN THEY LET HIM TWIST THEM AROUND HIS FINGER LIKE THAT?
SAKAMOTO IS...
... POPULAR WITH THE GIRLS.
ON THE OTHER HAND, HE DOESN'T LIKE GUYS AND IS ALWAYS PICKING FIGHTS WITH THEM.
JUST WHO ARE YOU TO MIURA-CHAN?
I TOLD YOU! HER FRIEND!
IS HE PUTTING US ON? IS HE SERIOUS? IS HE A GOOD GUY? A BAD GUY?

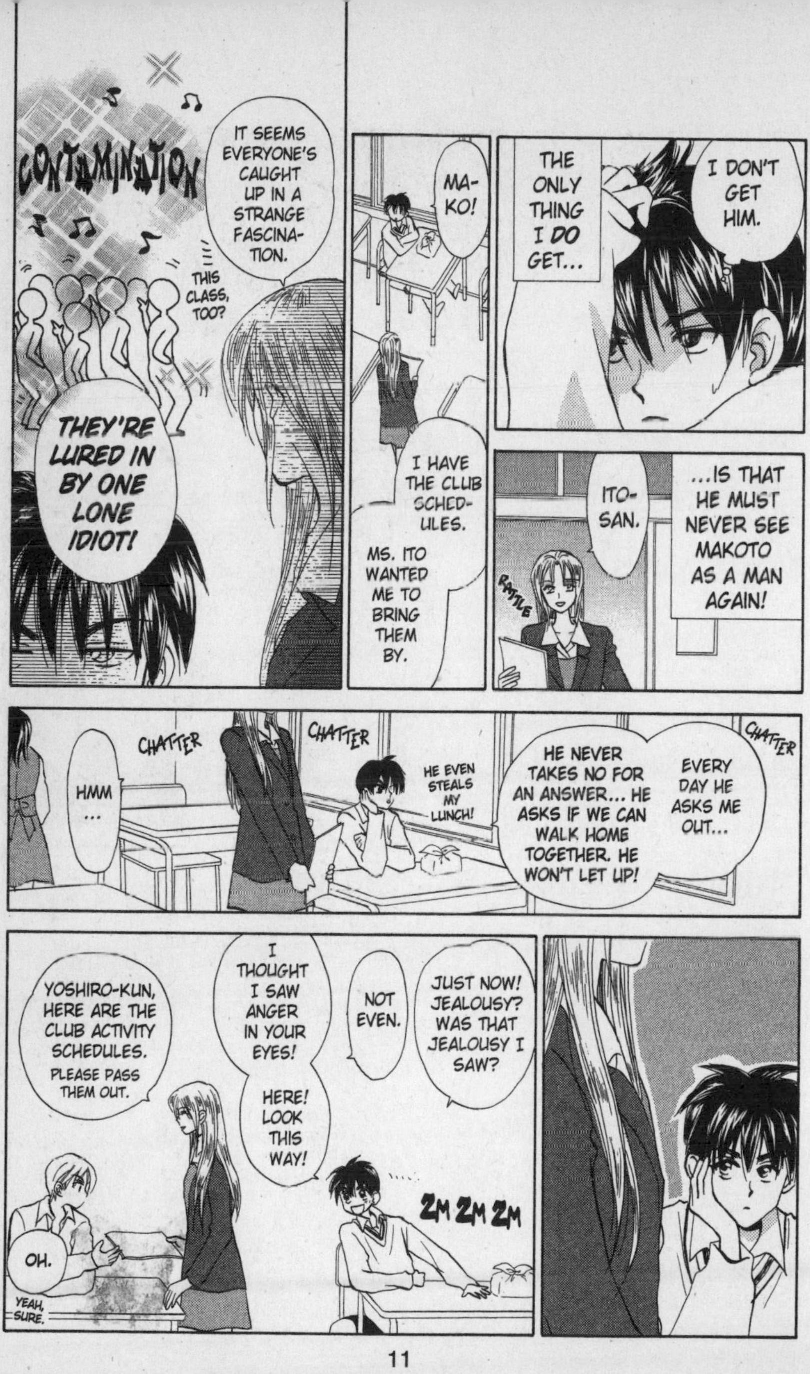
I DON'T GET HIM.
THE ONLY THING I *DO* GET...
...IS THAT HE MUST NEVER SEE MAKOTO AS A MAN AGAIN!
ITO-SAN.
RAMBLE
MA-KO!
I HAVE THE CLUB SCHEDULES.
MS. ITO WANTED ME TO BRING THEM BY.
IT SEEMS EVERYONE'S CAUGHT UP IN A STRANGE FASCINATION.
THIS CLASS, TOO?
CONTAMINATION
THEY'RE LURED IN BY ONE LONE IDIOT!
CHATTER
EVERY DAY HE ASKS ME OUT...
HE NEVER TAKES NO FOR AN ANSWER... HE ASKS IF WE CAN WALK HOME TOGETHER. HE WON'T LET UP!
HE EVEN STEALS MY LUNCH!
CHATTER
HMM...
CHATTER
JUST NOW! JEALOUSY? WAS THAT JEALOUSY I SAW?
NOT EVEN.
I THOUGHT I SAW ANGER IN YOUR EYES!
HERE! LOOK THIS WAY!
ZM ZM ZM
....
YOSHIRO-KUN, HERE ARE THE CLUB ACTIVITY SCHEDULES.
PLEASE PASS THEM OUT.
OH.
YEAH, SURE.

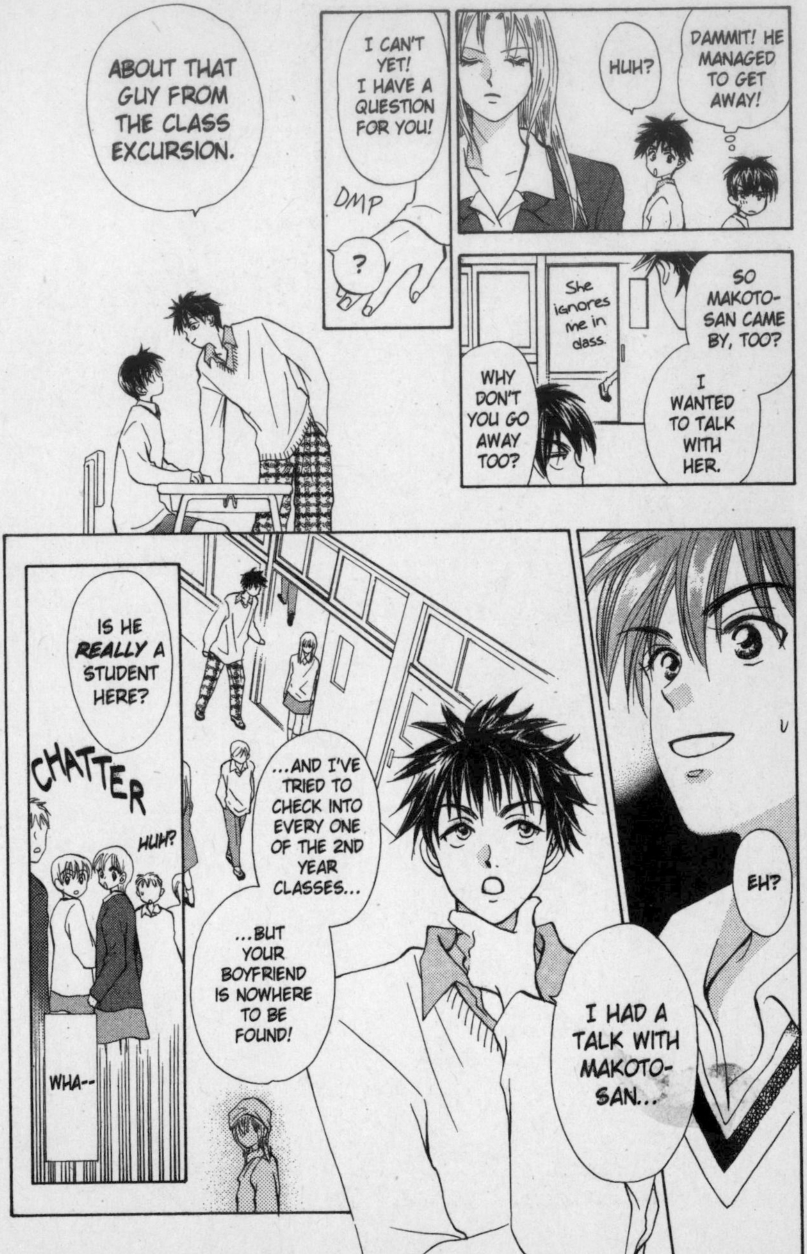

DAMMIT! HE MANAGED TO GET AWAY!
HUH?
I CAN'T YET! I HAVE A QUESTION FOR YOU!
DMP
?
ABOUT THAT GUY FROM THE CLASS EXCURSION.
SO MAKOTO-SAN CAME BY, TOO?
I WANTED TO TALK WITH HER.
She ignores me in class.
WHY DON'T YOU GO AWAY TOO?
EH?
I HAD A TALK WITH MAKOTO-SAN...
...AND I'VE TRIED TO CHECK INTO EVERY ONE OF THE 2ND YEAR CLASSES...
...BUT YOUR BOYFRIEND IS NOWHERE TO BE FOUND!
IS HE *REALLY* A STUDENT HERE?
CHATTER
HUH?
WHA--

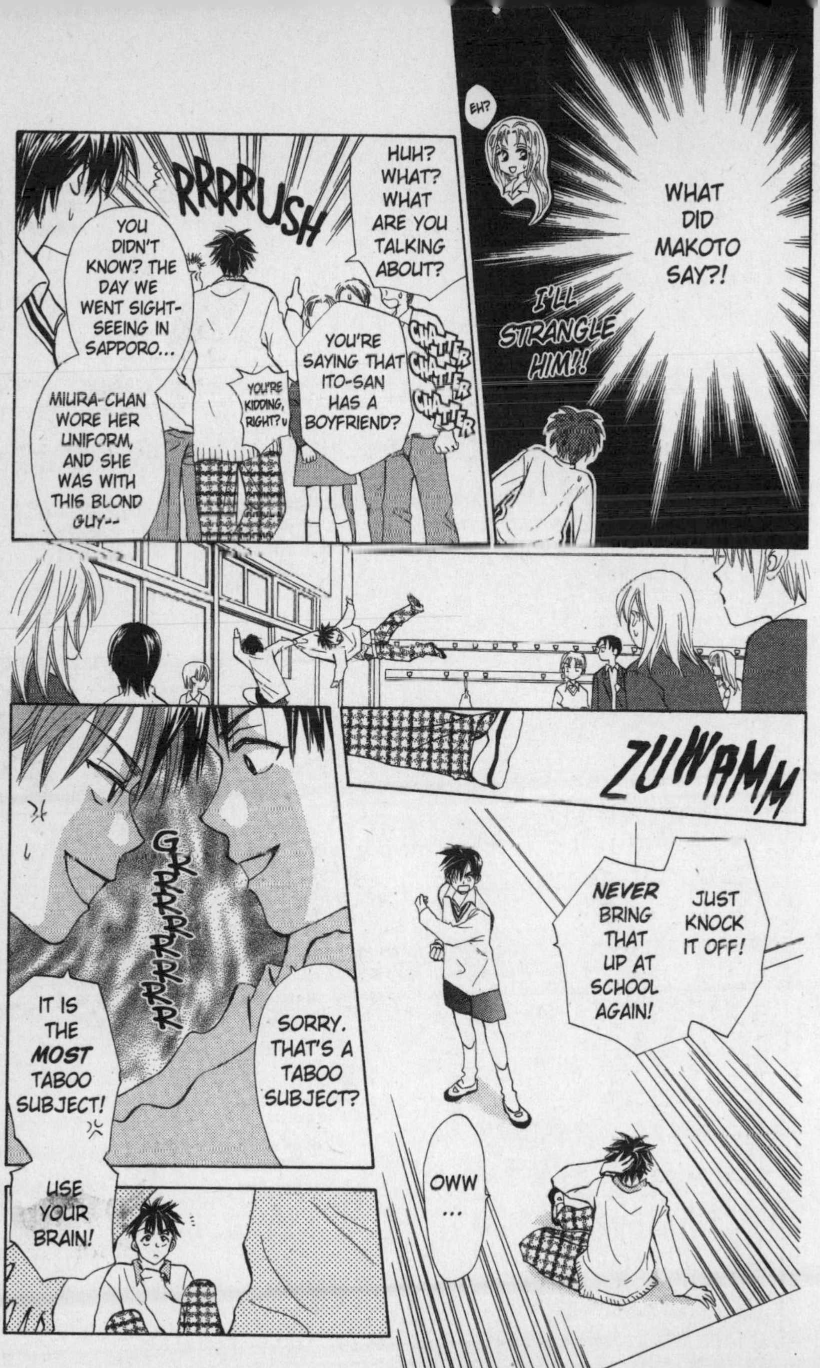
EH?
WHAT DID MAKOTO SAY?!
I'LL STRANGLE HIM!!
HUH? WHAT? WHAT ARE YOU TALKING ABOUT?
RRRRUSH
YOU DIDN'T KNOW? THE DAY WE WENT SIGHT-SEEING IN SAPPORO...
YOU'RE SAYING THAT ITO-SAN HAS A BOYFRIEND?
CHATTER CHATTER CHATTER
YOU'RE KIDDING, RIGHT?
MIURA-CHAN WORE HER UNIFORM, AND SHE WAS WITH THIS BLOND GUY--
ZUWAMM
JUST KNOCK IT OFF!
NEVER BRING THAT UP AT SCHOOL AGAIN!
OWW...
GRRRRRRRR
SORRY. THAT'S A TABOO SUBJECT?
IT IS THE MOST TABOO SUBJECT!
USE YOUR BRAIN!

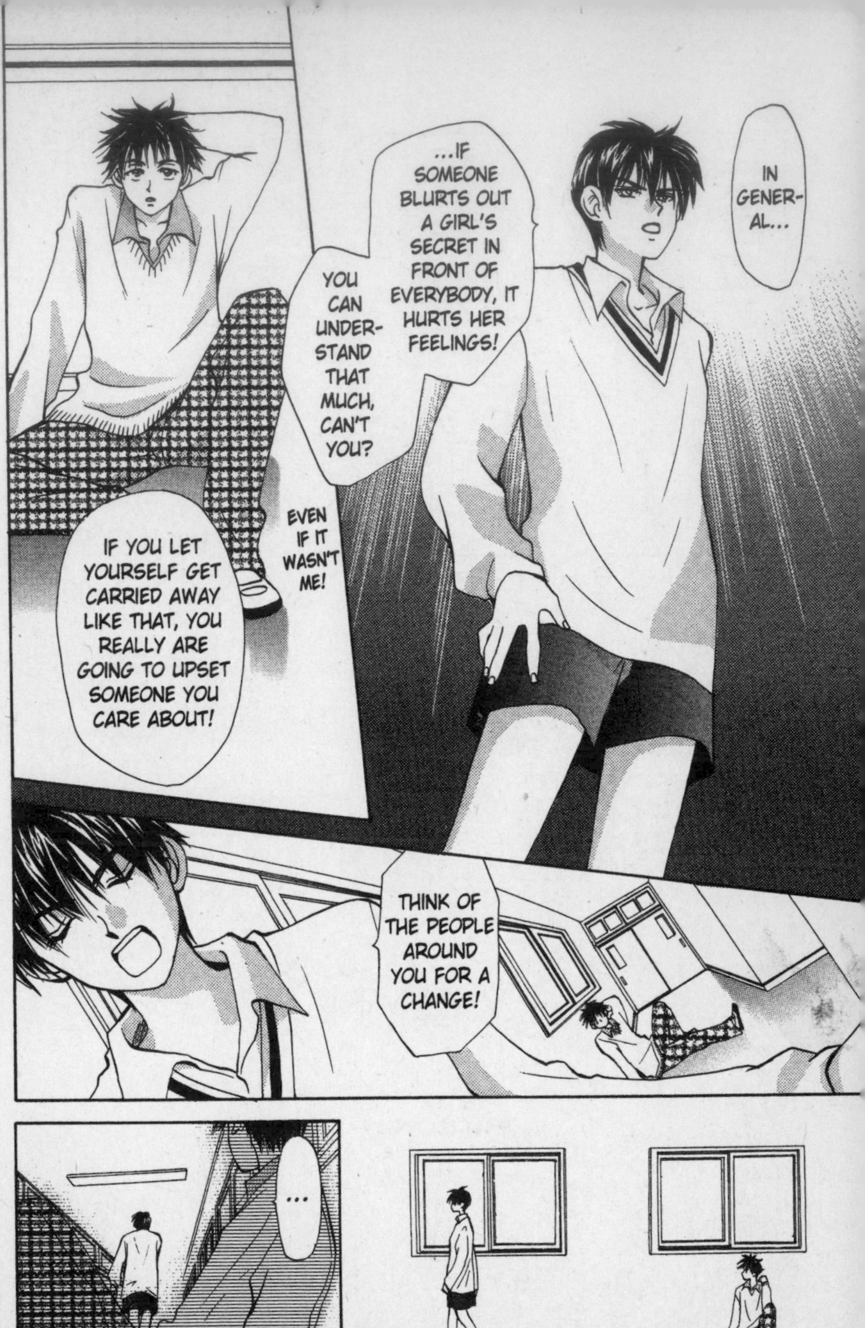
IN GENERAL...
...IF SOMEONE BLURTS OUT A GIRL'S SECRET IN FRONT OF EVERYBODY, IT HURTS HER FEELINGS!
YOU CAN UNDERSTAND THAT MUCH, CAN'T YOU?
EVEN IF IT WASN'T ME!
IF YOU LET YOURSELF GET CARRIED AWAY LIKE THAT, YOU REALLY ARE GOING TO UPSET SOMEONE YOU CARE ABOUT!
THINK OF THE PEOPLE AROUND YOU FOR A CHANGE!
...

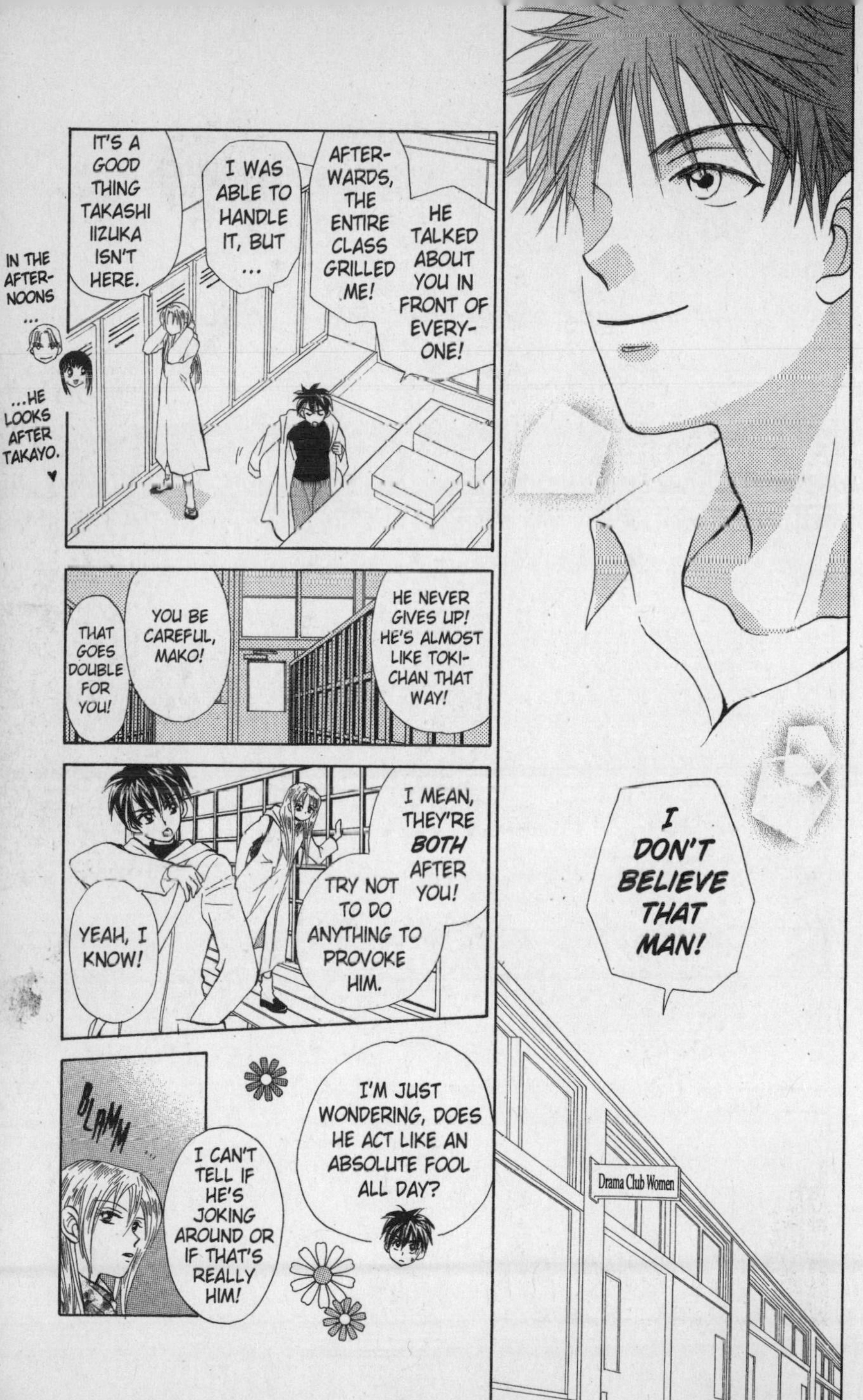
I DON'T BELIEVE THAT MAN!
Drama Club Women
HE TALKED ABOUT YOU IN FRONT OF EVERYONE!
AFTERWARDS, THE ENTIRE CLASS GRILLED ME!
I WAS ABLE TO HANDLE IT, BUT ...
IT'S A GOOD THING TAKASHI IIZUKA ISN'T HERE.
IN THE AFTERNOONS ...
...HE LOOKS AFTER TAKAYO. ♥
HE NEVER GIVES UP! HE'S ALMOST LIKE TOKI-CHAN THAT WAY!
YOU BE CAREFUL, MAKO!
THAT GOES DOUBLE FOR YOU!
I MEAN, THEY'RE BOTH AFTER YOU!
TRY NOT TO DO ANYTHING TO PROVOKE HIM.
YEAH, I KNOW!
I'M JUST WONDERING, DOES HE ACT LIKE AN ABSOLUTE FOOL ALL DAY?
BLAMM
I CAN'T TELL IF HE'S JOKING AROUND OR IF THAT'S REALLY HIM!

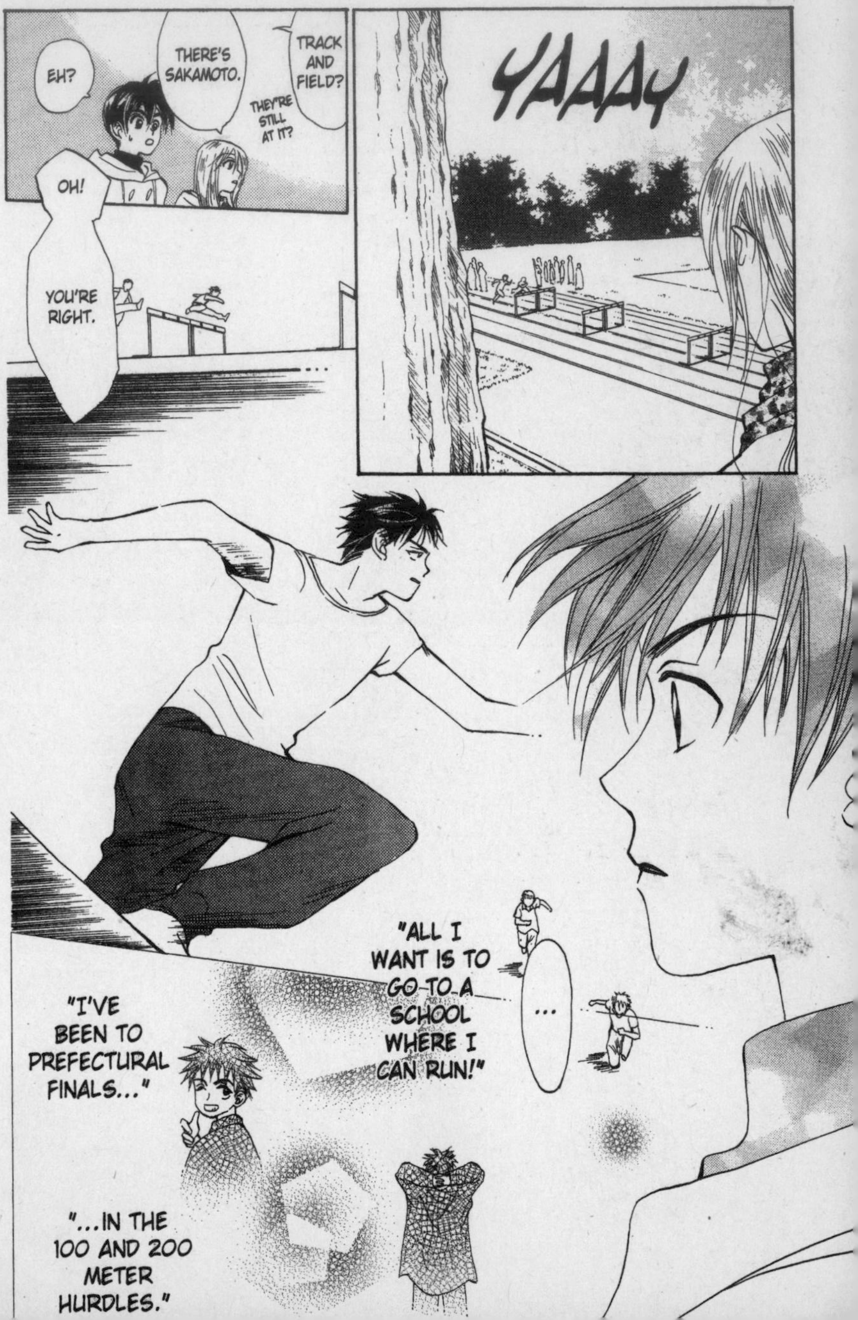
YAAAY
TRACK AND FIELD?
THEY'RE STILL AT IT?
THERE'S SAKAMOTO.
EH?
OH!
YOU'RE RIGHT.
...
"ALL I WANT IS TO GO TO A SCHOOL WHERE I CAN RUN!"
"I'VE BEEN TO PREFECTURAL FINALS..."
"...IN THE 100 AND 200 METER HURDLES."

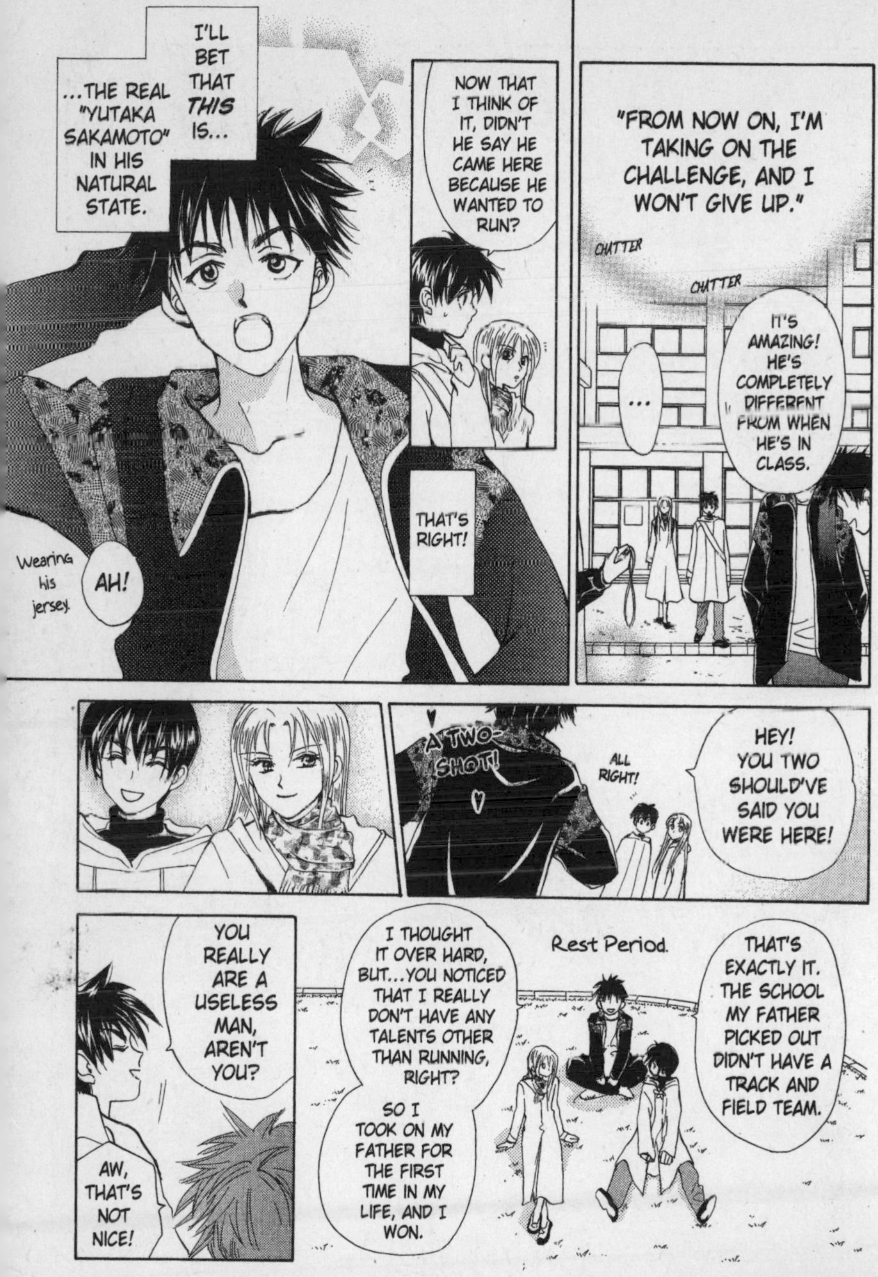
"FROM NOW ON, I'M TAKING ON THE CHALLENGE, AND I WON'T GIVE UP."
CHATTER
CHATTER
IT'S AMAZING! HE'S COMPLETELY DIFFERENT FROM WHEN HE'S IN CLASS.
...
NOW THAT I THINK OF IT, DIDN'T HE SAY HE CAME HERE BECAUSE HE WANTED TO RUN?
THAT'S RIGHT!
I'LL BET THAT *THIS* IS...
...THE REAL "YUTAKA SAKAMOTO" IN HIS NATURAL STATE.
AH!
Wearing his jersey.
HEY! YOU TWO SHOULD'VE SAID YOU WERE HERE!
ALL RIGHT!
A TWO-SHOT!
Rest Period.
THAT'S EXACTLY IT. THE SCHOOL MY FATHER PICKED OUT DIDN'T HAVE A TRACK AND FIELD TEAM.
I THOUGHT IT OVER HARD, BUT...YOU NOTICED THAT I REALLY DON'T HAVE ANY TALENTS OTHER THAN RUNNING, RIGHT?
SO I TOOK ON MY FATHER FOR THE FIRST TIME IN MY LIFE, AND I WON.
YOU REALLY ARE A USELESS MAN, AREN'T YOU?
AW, THAT'S NOT NICE!

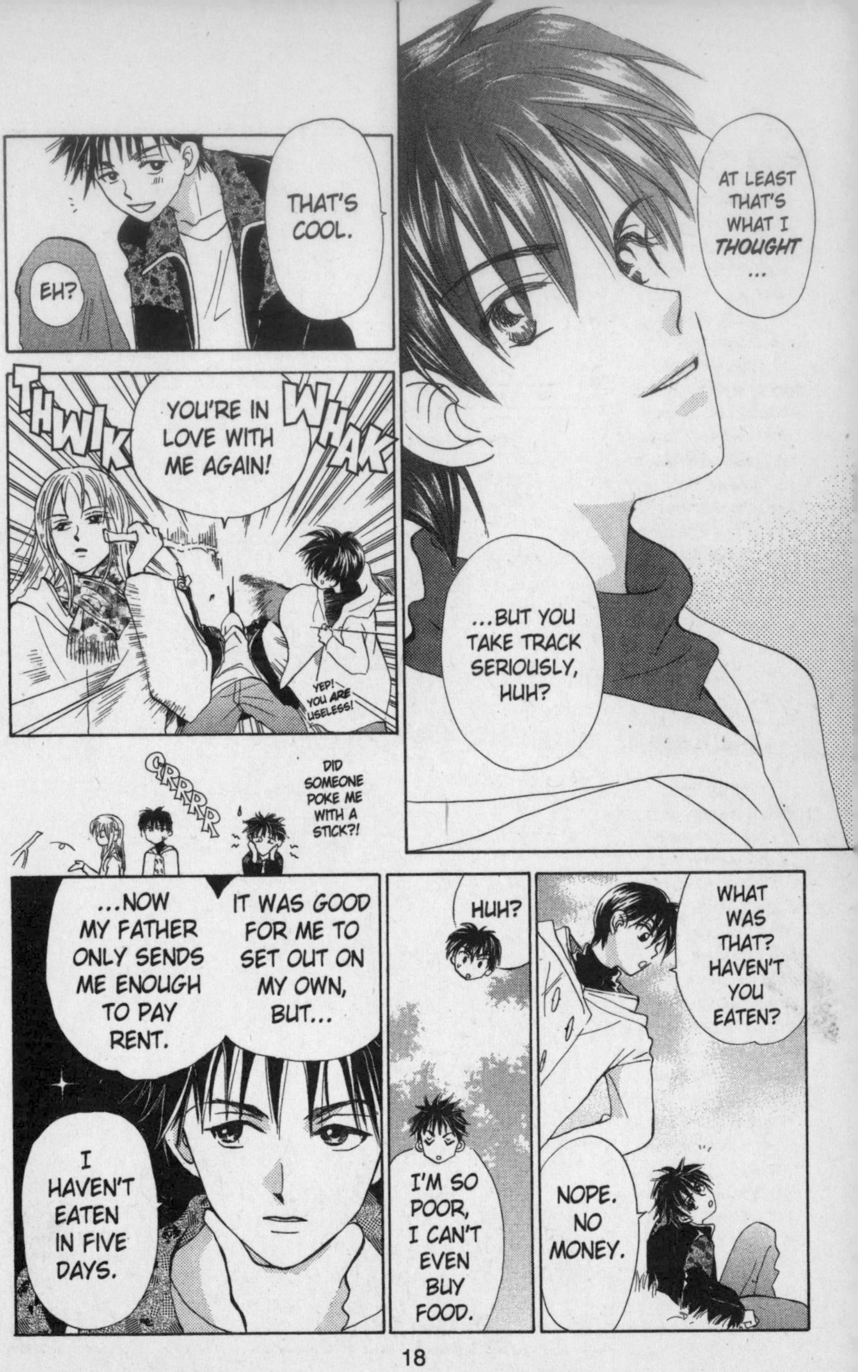

AT LEAST THAT'S WHAT I *THOUGHT* ...
...BUT YOU TAKE TRACK SERIOUSLY, HUH?
THAT'S COOL.
EH?
THWIK
WHAK
YOU'RE IN LOVE WITH ME AGAIN!
YEP! YOU *ARE* USELESS!
GRRRRR
DID SOMEONE POKE ME WITH A STICK?!
WHAT WAS THAT? HAVEN'T YOU EATEN?
NOPE. NO MONEY.
HUH?
I'M SO POOR, I CAN'T EVEN BUY FOOD.
IT WAS GOOD FOR ME TO SET OUT ON MY OWN, BUT...
...NOW MY FATHER ONLY SENDS ME ENOUGH TO PAY RENT.
I HAVEN'T EATEN IN FIVE DAYS.

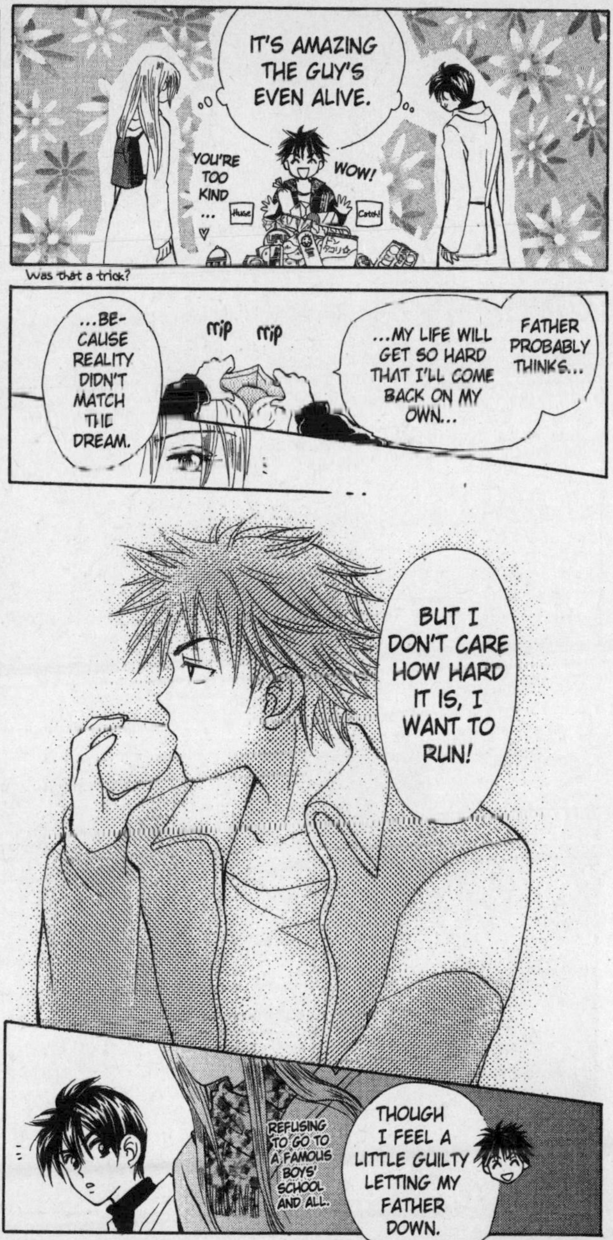
WOW!
IT'S AMAZING THE GUY'S EVEN ALIVE.
YOU'RE TOO KIND...
Catch!
Huse
Was that a trick?
FATHER PROBABLY THINKS...
...MY LIFE WILL GET SO HARD THAT I'LL COME BACK ON MY OWN...
rrip rrip
...BE-CAUSE REALITY DIDN'T MATCH THE DREAM.
BUT I DON'T CARE HOW HARD IT IS, I WANT TO RUN!
THOUGH I FEEL A LITTLE GUILTY LETTING MY FATHER DOWN.
REFUSING TO GO TO A FAMOUS BOYS' SCHOOL AND ALL.

HELLO! IT'S EMURA!

W Juliet has gone into its fifth volume! I want to thank you for all your support! Recently I've noticed that there are a lot of readers who get the impression that this manga is "sweet" or "heartwarming." Really? I'm drawing "heartwarming" manga? (I never noticed.) "Heart-warming"?! Is that how you see it?? Maybe "didn't notice" is too light a phrase. I should've said: "I don't see it at all!!" I'll concede that my manga gives the impression that the two of them will be okay at the end of each episode. But that's because they're both happy, optimistic people! I think W-J stories have to be fun! (The next volume may have a few low points though...) But putting in peaks and valleys is the only way to write a good story, right?!

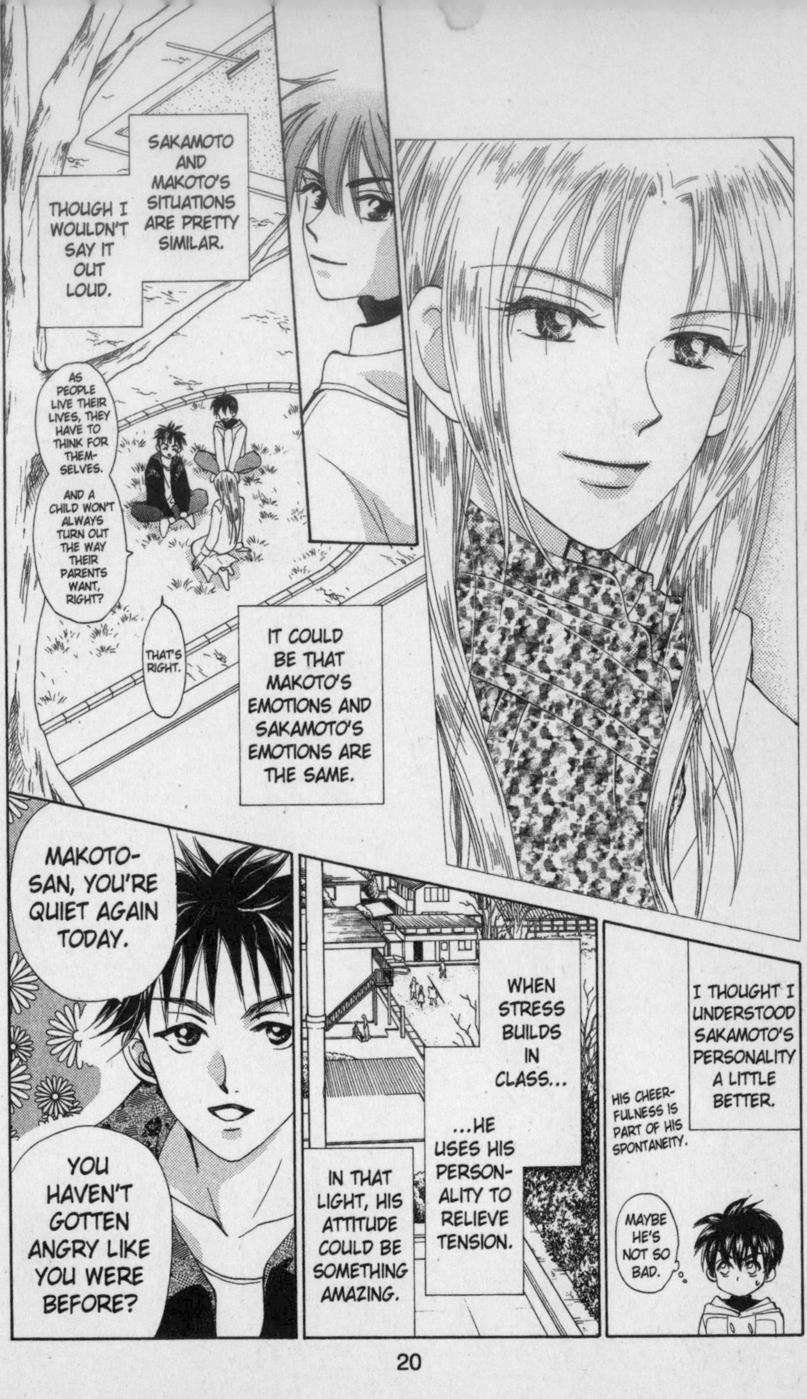
SAKAMOTO AND MAKOTO'S SITUATIONS ARE PRETTY SIMILAR.
THOUGH I WOULDN'T SAY IT OUT LOUD.
AS PEOPLE LIVE THEIR LIVES, THEY HAVE TO THINK FOR THEM-SELVES.
AND A CHILD WON'T ALWAYS TURN OUT THE WAY THEIR PARENTS WANT, RIGHT?
THAT'S RIGHT.
IT COULD BE THAT MAKOTO'S EMOTIONS AND SAKAMOTO'S EMOTIONS ARE THE SAME.
I THOUGHT I UNDERSTOOD SAKAMOTO'S PERSONALITY A LITTLE BETTER.
HIS CHEER-FULNESS IS PART OF HIS SPONTANEITY.
MAYBE HE'S NOT SO BAD.
WHEN STRESS BUILDS IN CLASS...
...HE USES HIS PERSON-ALITY TO RELIEVE TENSION.
IN THAT LIGHT, HIS ATTITUDE COULD BE SOMETHING AMAZING.
MAKOTO-SAN, YOU'RE QUIET AGAIN TODAY.
YOU HAVEN'T GOTTEN ANGRY LIKE YOU WERE BEFORE?

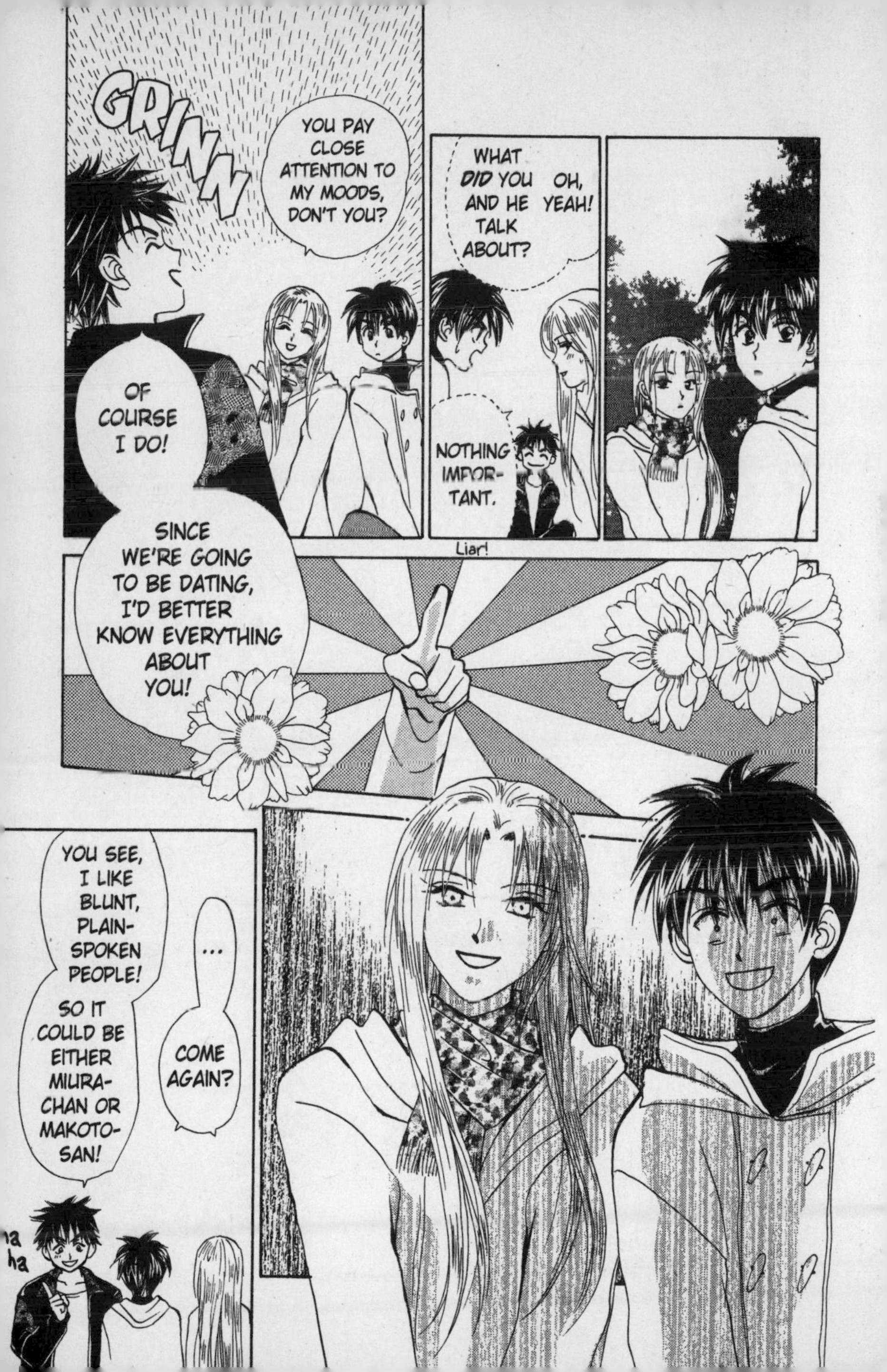
OH, YEAH!
WHAT DID YOU AND HE TALK ABOUT?
NOTHING IMPORTANT.
Liar!
GRINN
YOU PAY CLOSE ATTENTION TO MY MOODS, DON'T YOU?
OF COURSE I DO!
SINCE WE'RE GOING TO BE DATING, I'D BETTER KNOW EVERYTHING ABOUT YOU!
YOU SEE, I LIKE BLUNT, PLAIN-SPOKEN PEOPLE!
SO IT COULD BE EITHER MIURA-CHAN OR MAKOTO-SAN!
...
COME AGAIN?
ha ha

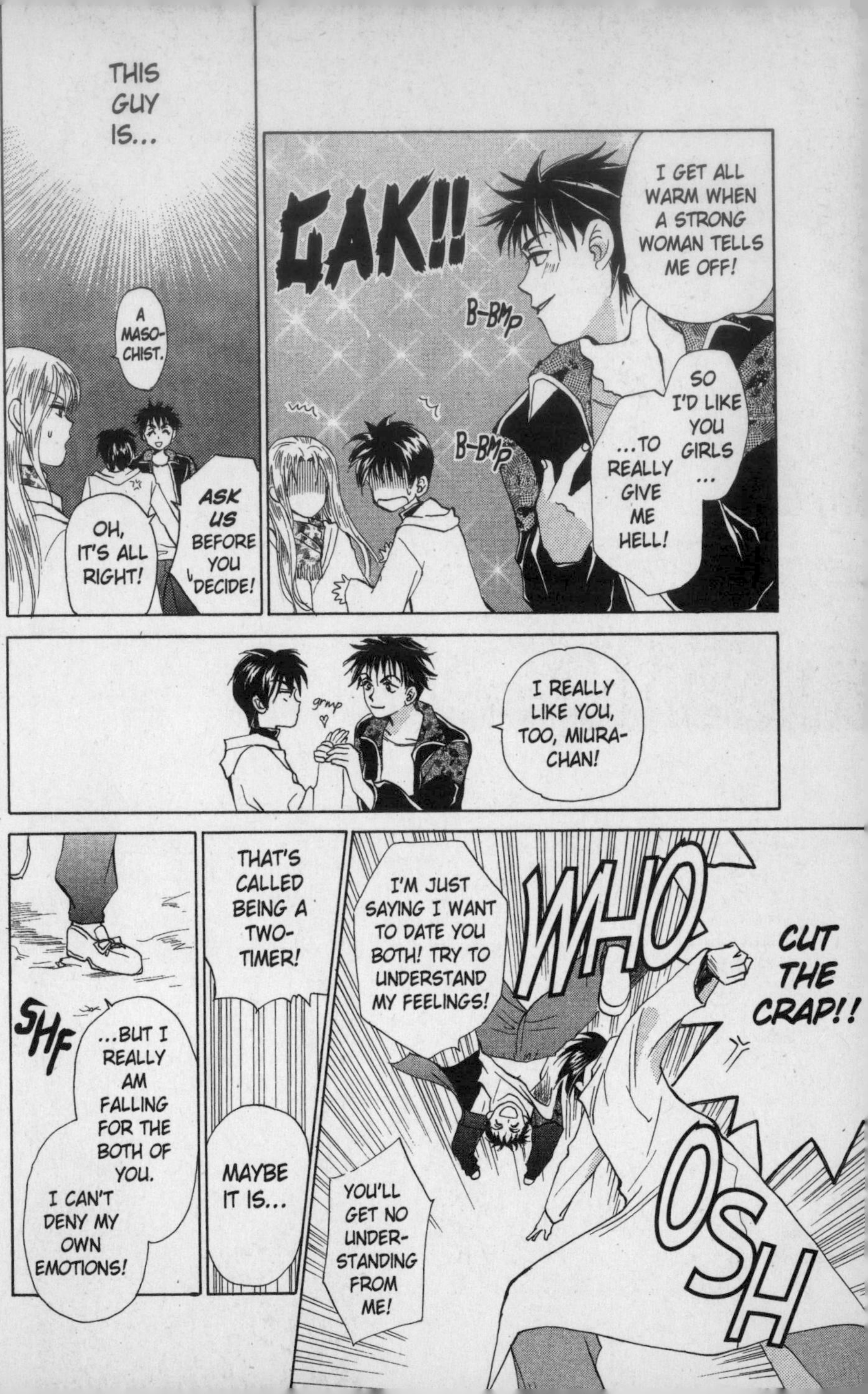
GAK!!
I GET ALL WARM WHEN A STRONG WOMAN TELLS ME OFF!
B-BMP
B-BMP
SO I'D LIKE YOU GIRLS ...
...TO REALLY GIVE ME HELL!
THIS GUY IS...
A MASO-CHIST.
ASK US BEFORE YOU DECIDE!
OH, IT'S ALL RIGHT!
I REALLY LIKE YOU, TOO, MIURA-CHAN!
grmp
I'M JUST SAYING I WANT TO DATE YOU BOTH! TRY TO UNDERSTAND MY FEELINGS!
WHOOSH
CUT THE CRAP!!
YOU'LL GET NO UNDER-STANDING FROM ME!
THAT'S CALLED BEING A TWO-TIMER!
MAYBE IT IS...
SHF
...BUT I REALLY AM FALLING FOR THE BOTH OF YOU.
I CAN'T DENY MY OWN EMOTIONS!

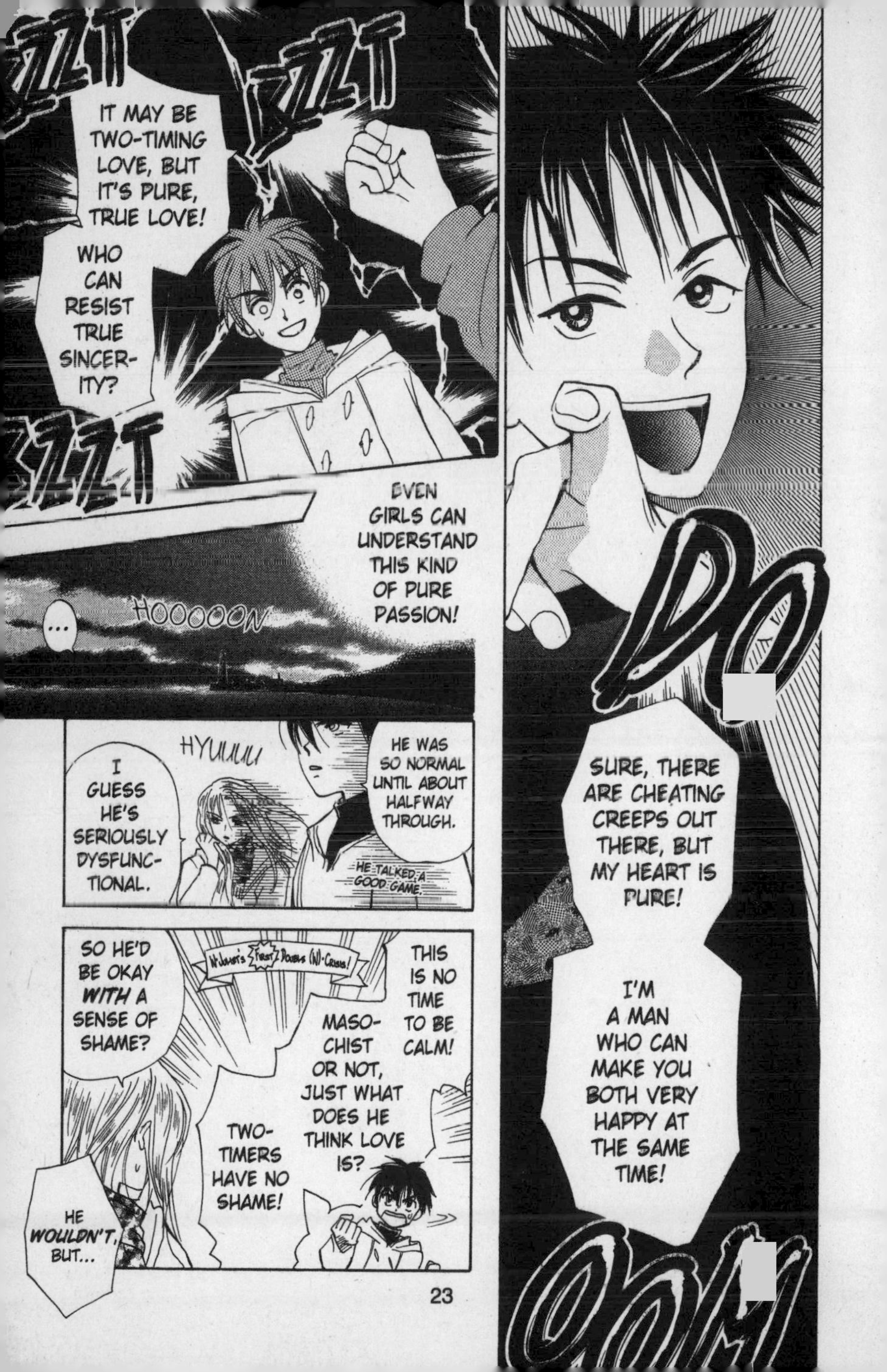
DO
SURE, THERE ARE CHEATING CREEPS OUT THERE, BUT MY HEART IS PURE!
I'M A MAN WHO CAN MAKE YOU BOTH VERY HAPPY AT THE SAME TIME!
OOM
ZZZT
ZZZT
IT MAY BE TWO-TIMING LOVE, BUT IT'S PURE, TRUE LOVE!
WHO CAN RESIST TRUE SINCERITY?
ZZZT
EVEN GIRLS CAN UNDERSTAND THIS KIND OF PURE PASSION!
HOOOOON
...
HE WAS SO NORMAL UNTIL ABOUT HALFWAY THROUGH.
HE TALKED A GOOD GAME.
HYUUUU
I GUESS HE'S SERIOUSLY DYSFUNCTIONAL.
THIS IS NO TIME TO BE CALM!
N-JULIET'S FIRST DOUBLES (N)-CRISIS!
MASOCHIST OR NOT, JUST WHAT DOES HE THINK LOVE IS?
TWO-TIMERS HAVE NO SHAME!
SO HE'D BE OKAY *WITH* A SENSE OF SHAME?
HE *WOULDN'T*, BUT...

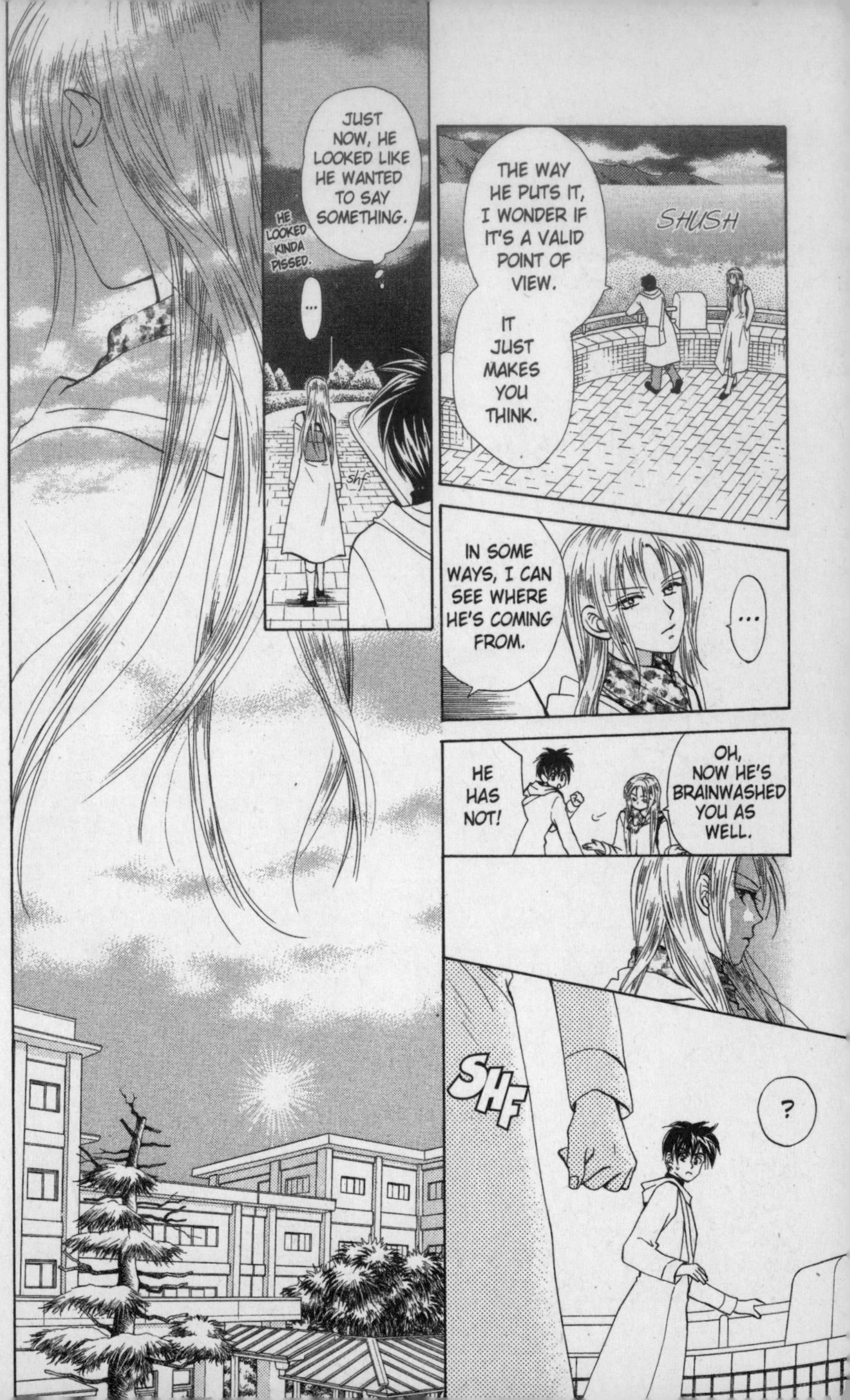
THE WAY HE PUTS IT, I WONDER IF IT'S A VALID POINT OF VIEW.
IT JUST MAKES YOU THINK.
SHUSH
...
IN SOME WAYS, I CAN SEE WHERE HE'S COMING FROM.
OH, NOW HE'S BRAINWASHED YOU AS WELL.
HE HAS NOT!
SHF
?
JUST NOW, HE LOOKED LIKE HE WANTED TO SAY SOMETHING.
HE LOOKED KINDA PISSED.
...
shf

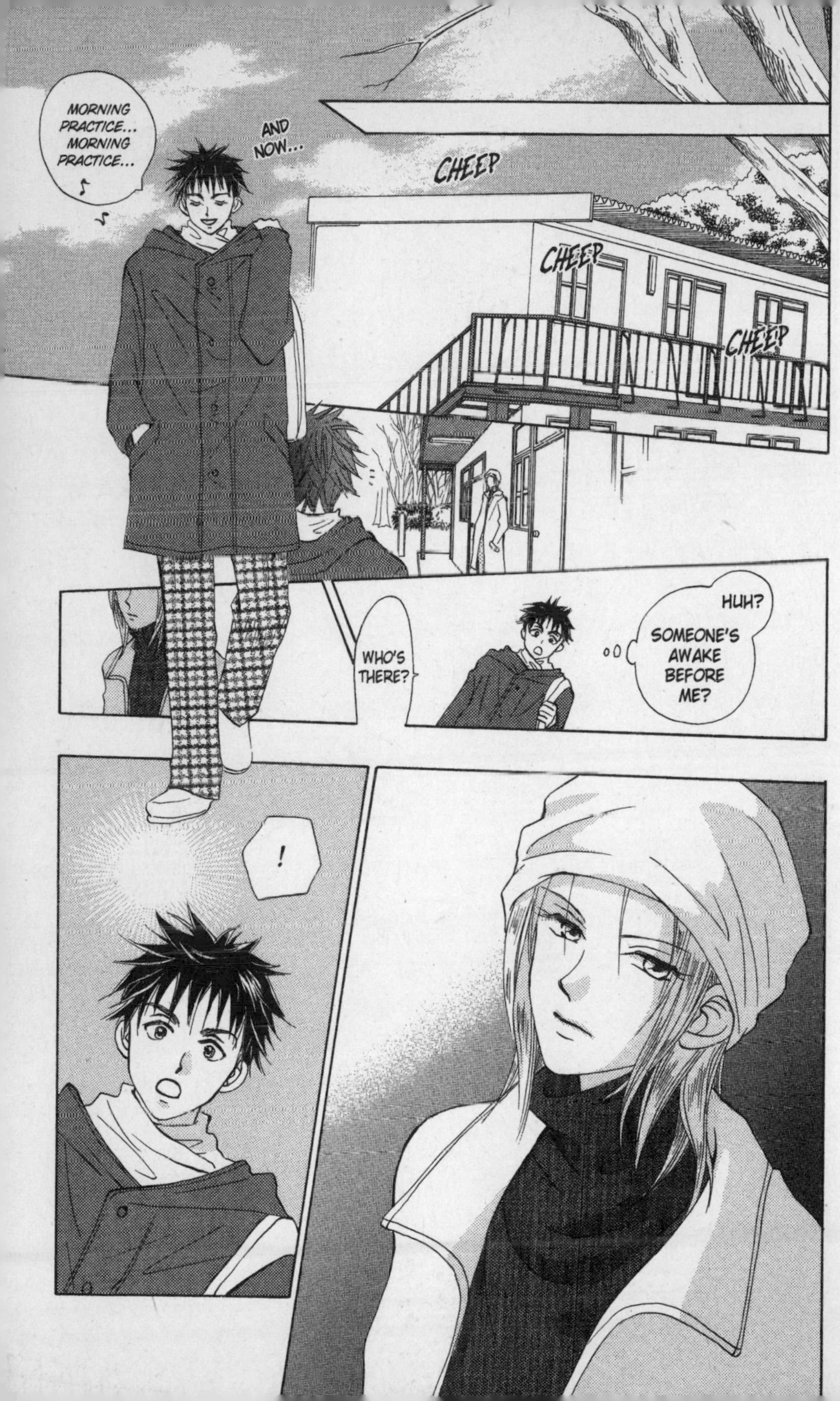

CHEEP
CHEEP
CHEEP
MORNING PRACTICE... MORNING PRACTICE...
AND NOW...
HUH?
SOMEONE'S AWAKE BEFORE ME?
WHO'S THERE?
!

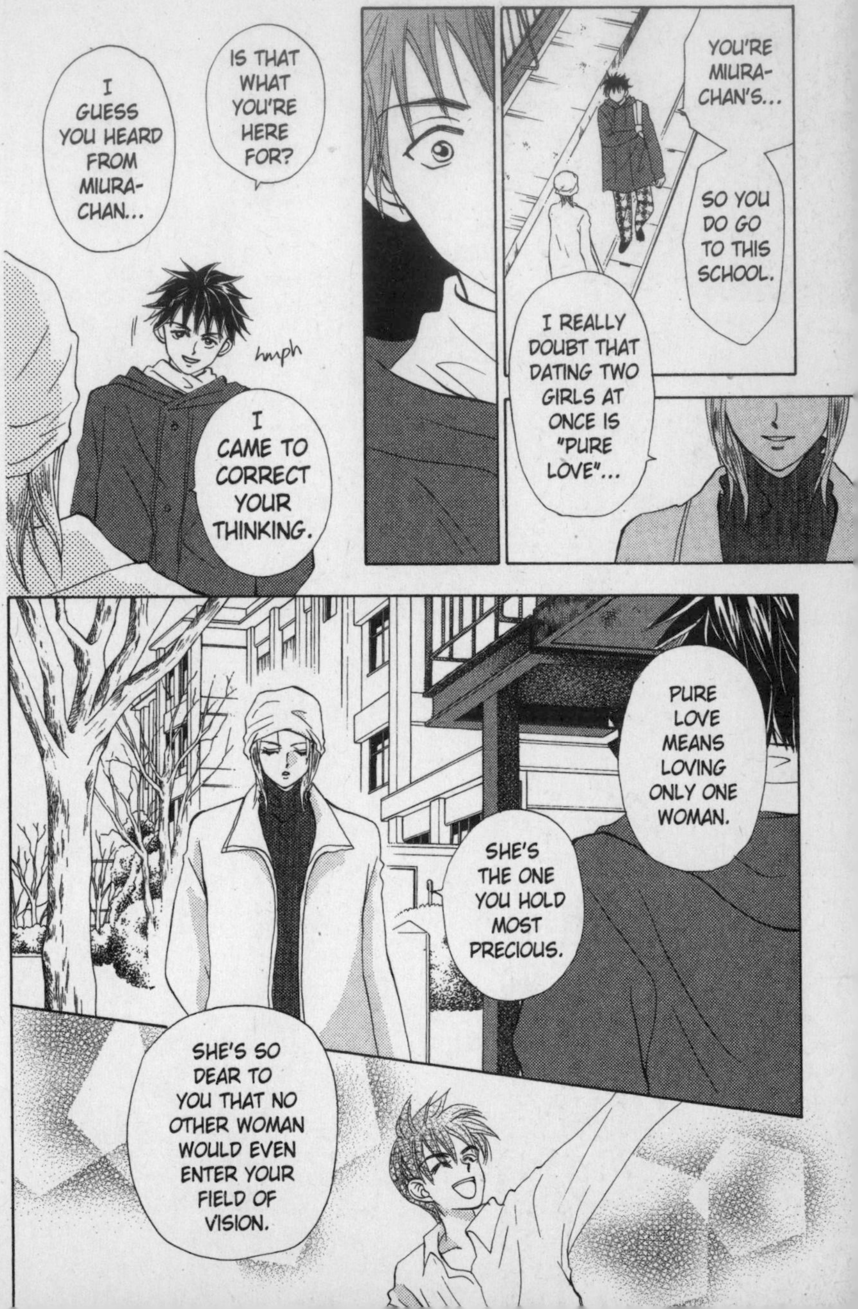
YOU'RE MIURA-CHAN'S...
SO YOU DO GO TO THIS SCHOOL.
I REALLY DOUBT THAT DATING TWO GIRLS AT ONCE IS "PURE LOVE"...
IS THAT WHAT YOU'RE HERE FOR?
I GUESS YOU HEARD FROM MIURA-CHAN...
hmph
I CAME TO CORRECT YOUR THINKING.
PURE LOVE MEANS LOVING ONLY ONE WOMAN.
SHE'S THE ONE YOU HOLD MOST PRECIOUS.
SHE'S SO DEAR TO YOU THAT NO OTHER WOMAN WOULD EVEN ENTER YOUR FIELD OF VISION.

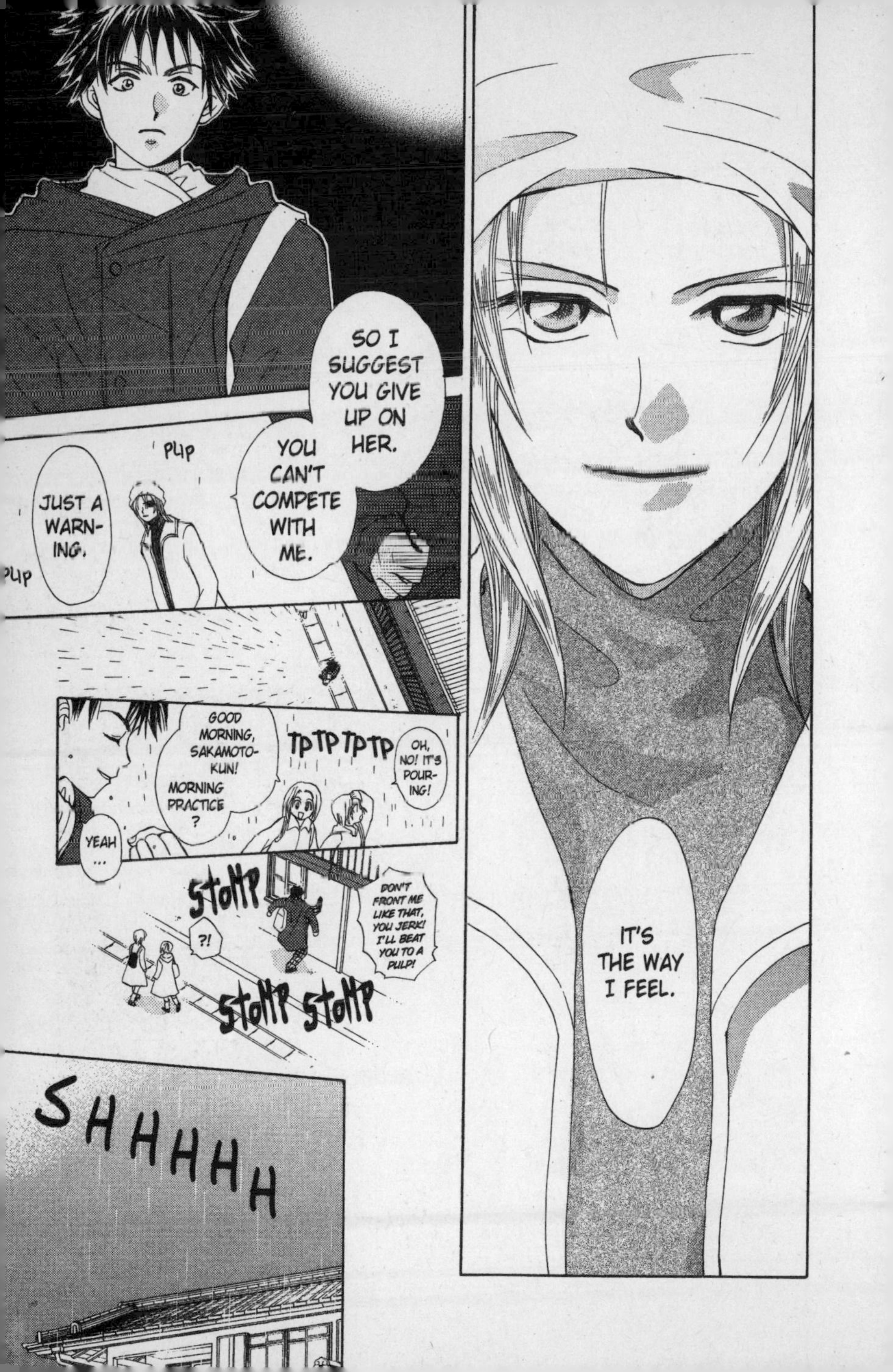
IT'S THE WAY I FEEL.
SO I SUGGEST YOU GIVE UP ON HER.
YOU CAN'T COMPETE WITH ME.
PLIP
JUST A WARNING.
PLIP
OH, NO! IT'S POURING!
TPTPTPTP
GOOD MORNING, SAKAMOTO-KUN! MORNING PRACTICE?
YEAH...
DON'T FRONT ME LIKE THAT, YOU JERK! I'LL BEAT YOU TO A PULP!
STOMP
?!
STOMP STOMP
SHHHHH

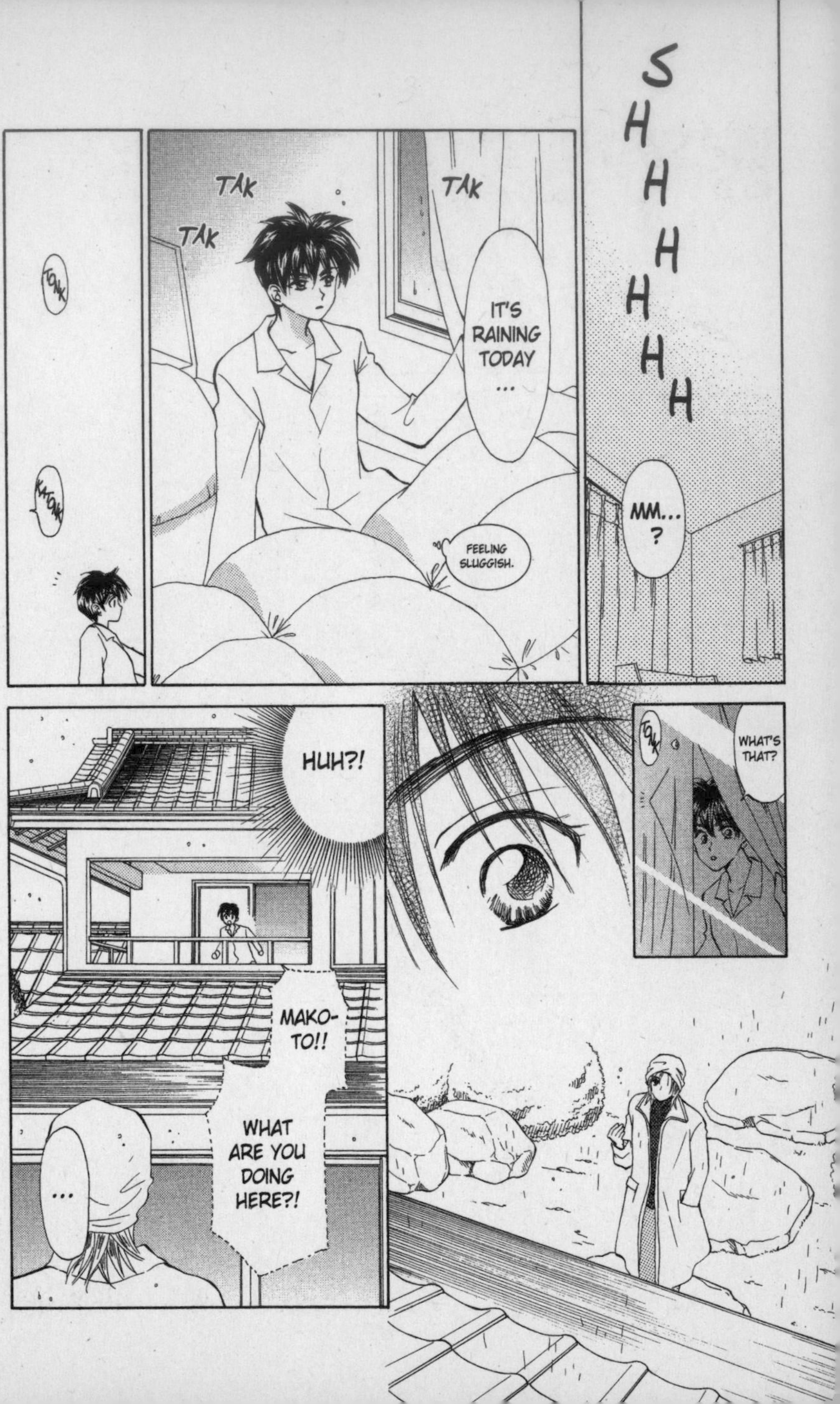
SHHHHHH
MM... ?
TAK
TAK
TAK
IT'S RAINING TODAY ...
FEELING SLUGGISH.
TONK
KATONK
TONK
WHAT'S THAT?
HUH?!
MAKO-TO!!
WHAT ARE YOU DOING HERE?!
...

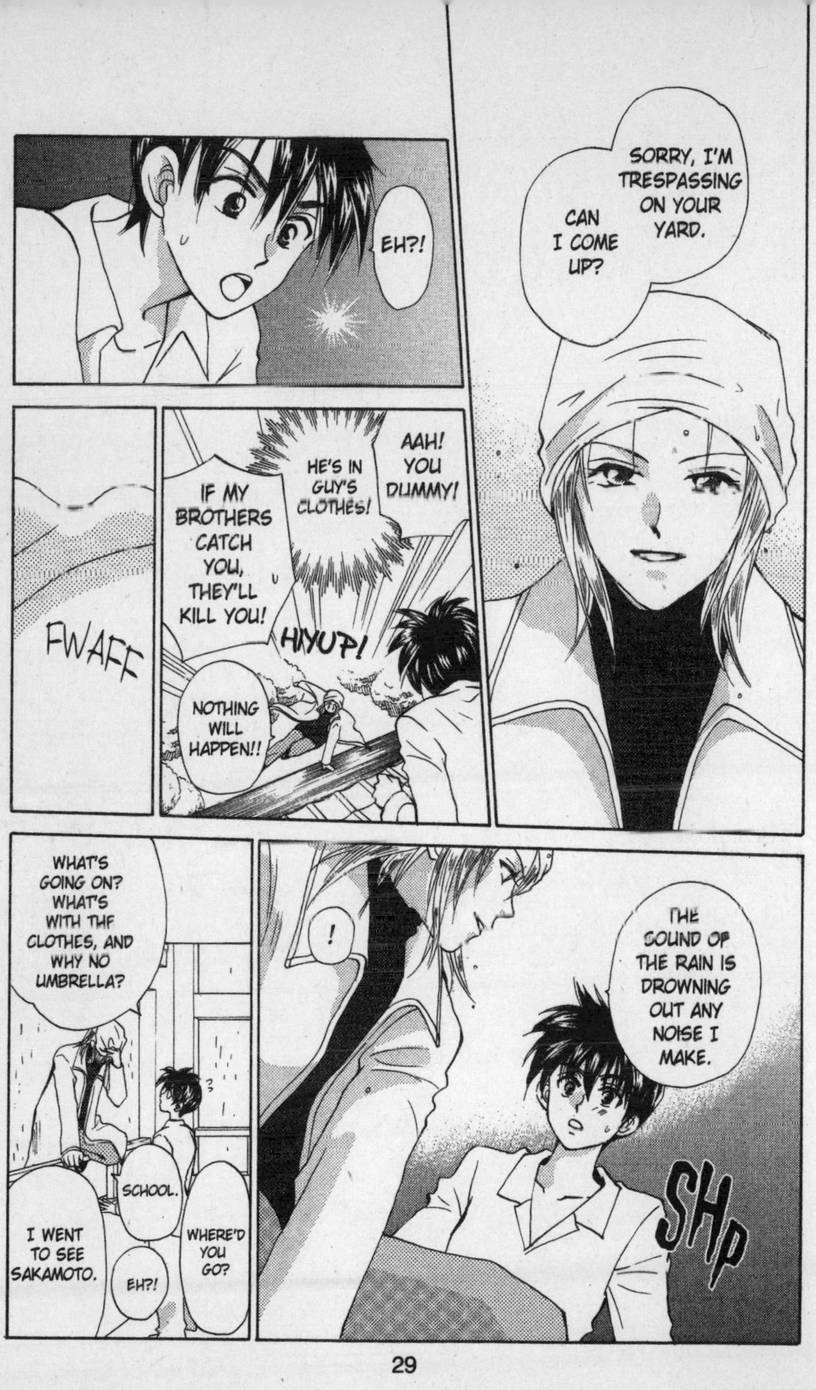
SORRY, I'M TRESPASSING ON YOUR YARD.
CAN I COME UP?
EH?!
AAH! YOU DUMMY!
HE'S IN GUY'S CLOTHES!
IF MY BROTHERS CATCH YOU, THEY'LL KILL YOU!
HIYUP!
NOTHING WILL HAPPEN!!
FWAFF
!
THE SOUND OF THE RAIN IS DROWNING OUT ANY NOISE I MAKE.
SHP
WHAT'S GOING ON? WHAT'S WITH THE CLOTHES, AND WHY NO UMBRELLA?
WHERE'D YOU GO?
SCHOOL.
I WENT TO SEE SAKAMOTO.
EH?!

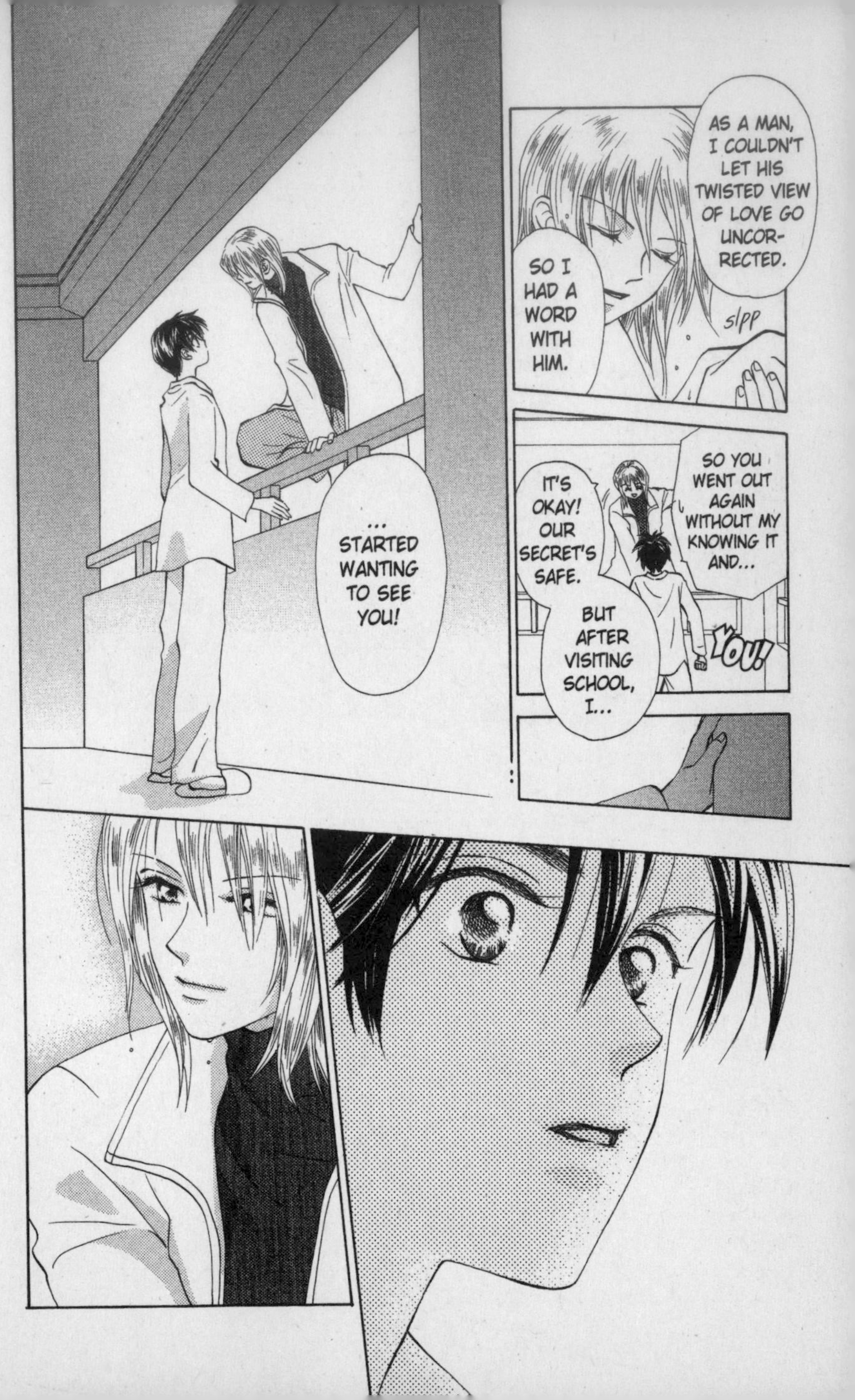
AS A MAN, I COULDN'T LET HIS TWISTED VIEW OF LOVE GO UNCORRECTED.
SO I HAD A WORD WITH HIM.
slpp
SO YOU WENT OUT AGAIN WITHOUT MY KNOWING IT AND...
YOU!
IT'S OKAY! OUR SECRET'S SAFE.
BUT AFTER VISITING SCHOOL, I...
... STARTED WANTING TO SEE YOU!

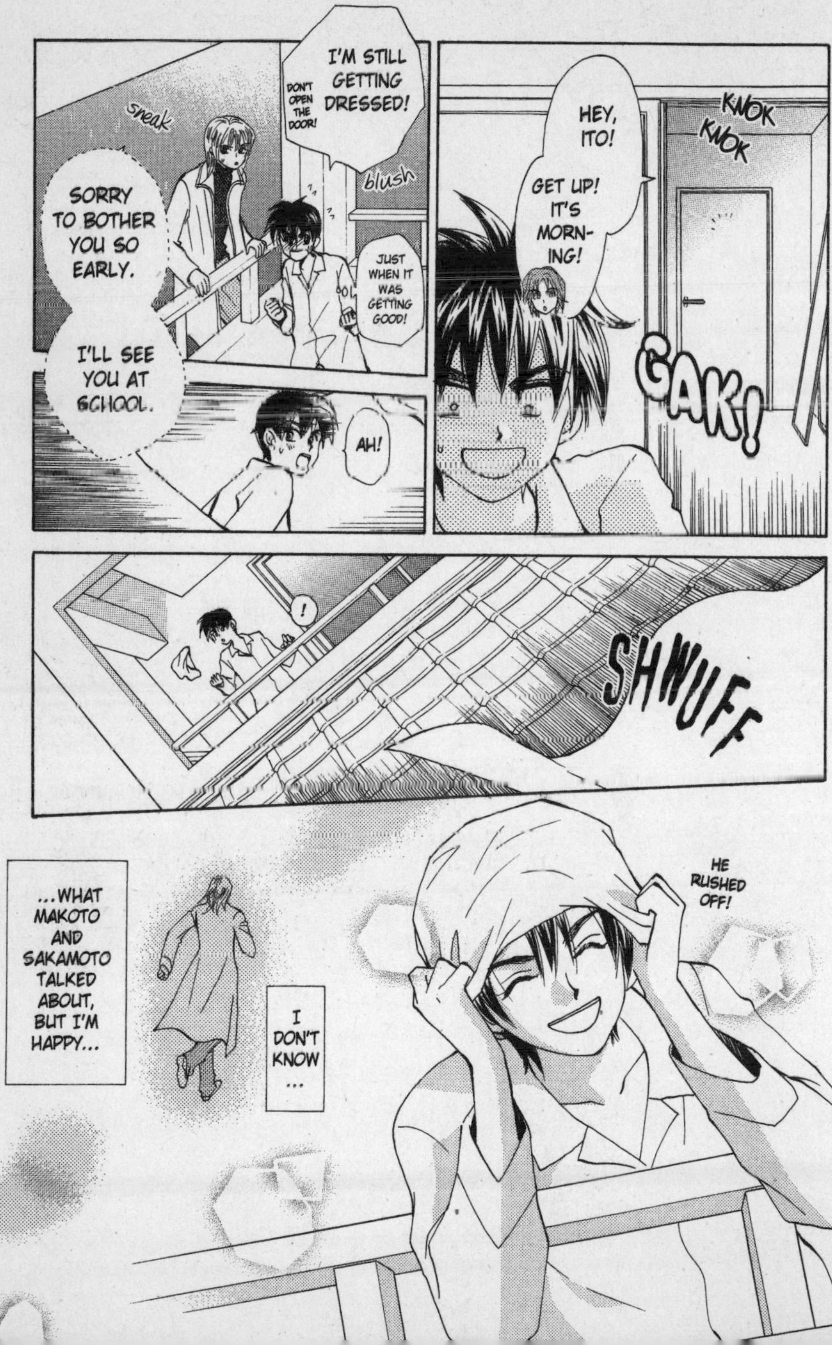
KNOK KNOK
HEY, ITO!
GET UP! IT'S MORNING!
GAK!
I'M STILL GETTING DRESSED!
DON'T OPEN THE DOOR!
blush
sneak
JUST WHEN IT WAS GETTING GOOD!
SORRY TO BOTHER YOU SO EARLY.
I'LL SEE YOU AT SCHOOL.
AH!
SHWUFF
!
HE RUSHED OFF!
I DON'T KNOW ...
...WHAT MAKOTO AND SAKAMOTO TALKED ABOUT, BUT I'M HAPPY...

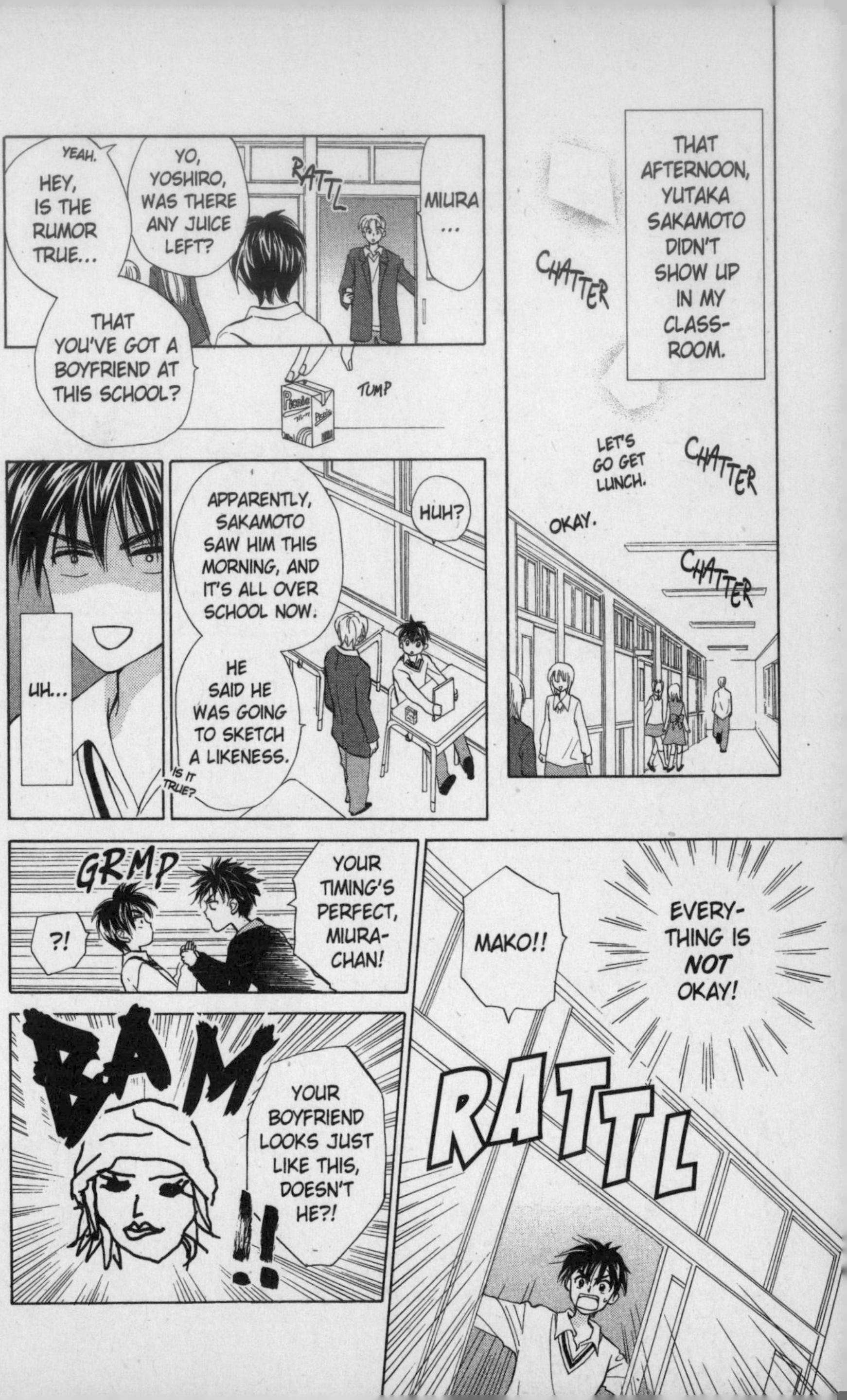
THAT AFTERNOON, YUTAKA SAKAMOTO DIDN'T SHOW UP IN MY CLASS-ROOM.
CHATTER
CHATTER
LET'S GO GET LUNCH.
OKAY.
CHATTER
MIURA...
RATTL
YO, YOSHIRO, WAS THERE ANY JUICE LEFT?
YEAH.
HEY, IS THE RUMOR TRUE...
THAT YOU'VE GOT A BOYFRIEND AT THIS SCHOOL?
TUMP
HUH?
APPARENTLY, SAKAMOTO SAW HIM THIS MORNING, AND IT'S ALL OVER SCHOOL NOW.
HE SAID HE WAS GOING TO SKETCH A LIKENESS.
IS IT TRUE?
UH...
EVERY-THING IS *NOT* OKAY!
MAKO!!
RATTL
YOUR TIMING'S PERFECT, MIURA-CHAN!
GRMP
?!
BAM
YOUR BOYFRIEND LOOKS JUST LIKE THIS, DOESN'T HE?!
!!

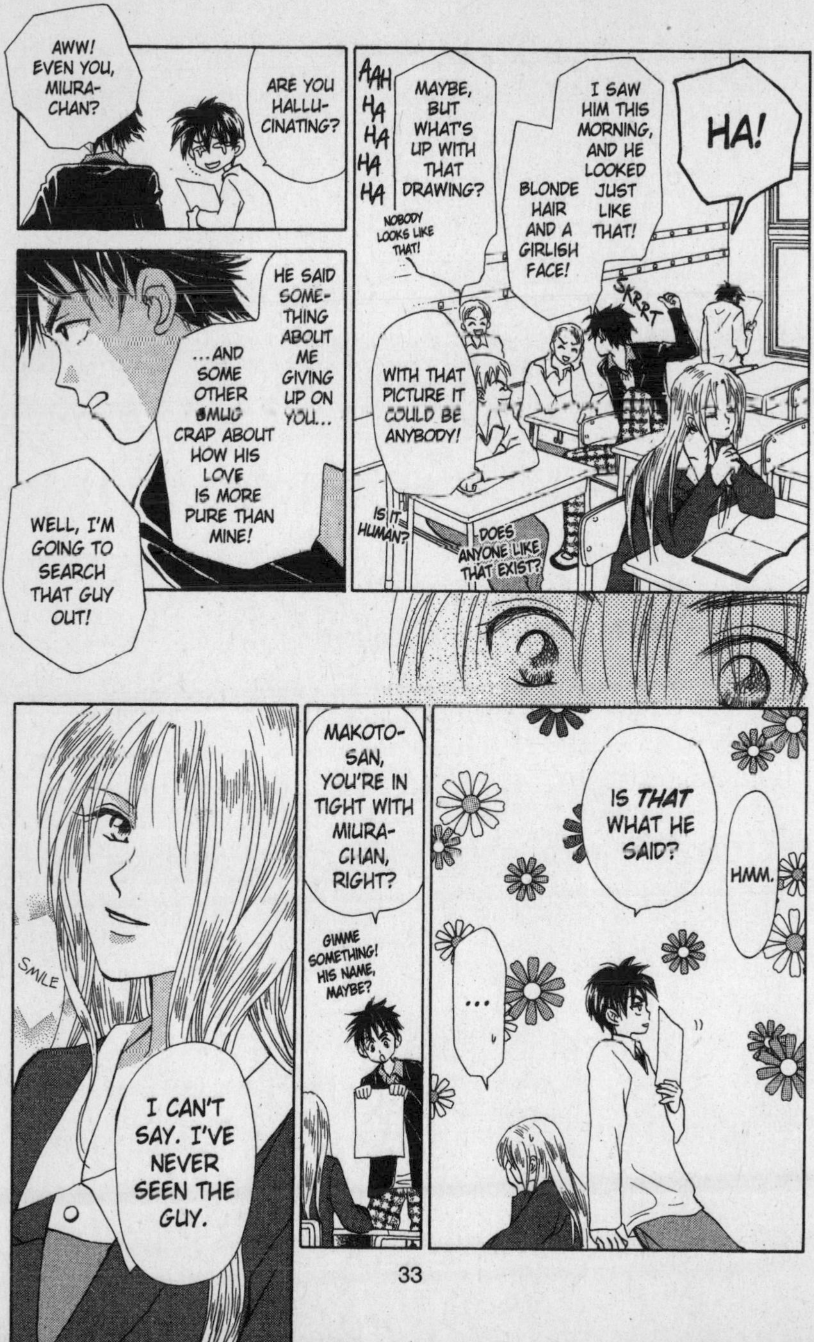
HA!
I SAW HIM THIS MORNING, AND HE LOOKED JUST LIKE THAT!
BLONDE HAIR AND A GIRLISH FACE!
MAYBE, BUT WHAT'S UP WITH THAT DRAWING?
AAH HA HA HA HA
NOBODY LOOKS LIKE THAT!
SKRRT
WITH THAT PICTURE IT COULD BE ANYBODY!
DOES ANYONE LIKE THAT EXIST?
IS IT HUMAN?
ARE YOU HALLUCINATING?
AWW! EVEN YOU, MIURA-CHAN?
HE SAID SOMETHING ABOUT ME GIVING UP ON YOU...
...AND SOME OTHER SMUG CRAP ABOUT HOW HIS LOVE IS MORE PURE THAN MINE!
WELL, I'M GOING TO SEARCH THAT GUY OUT!
IS THAT WHAT HE SAID?
HMM.
...
MAKOTO-SAN, YOU'RE IN TIGHT WITH MIURA-CHAN, RIGHT?
GIMME SOMETHING! HIS NAME, MAYBE?
SMILE
I CAN'T SAY. I'VE NEVER SEEN THE GUY.

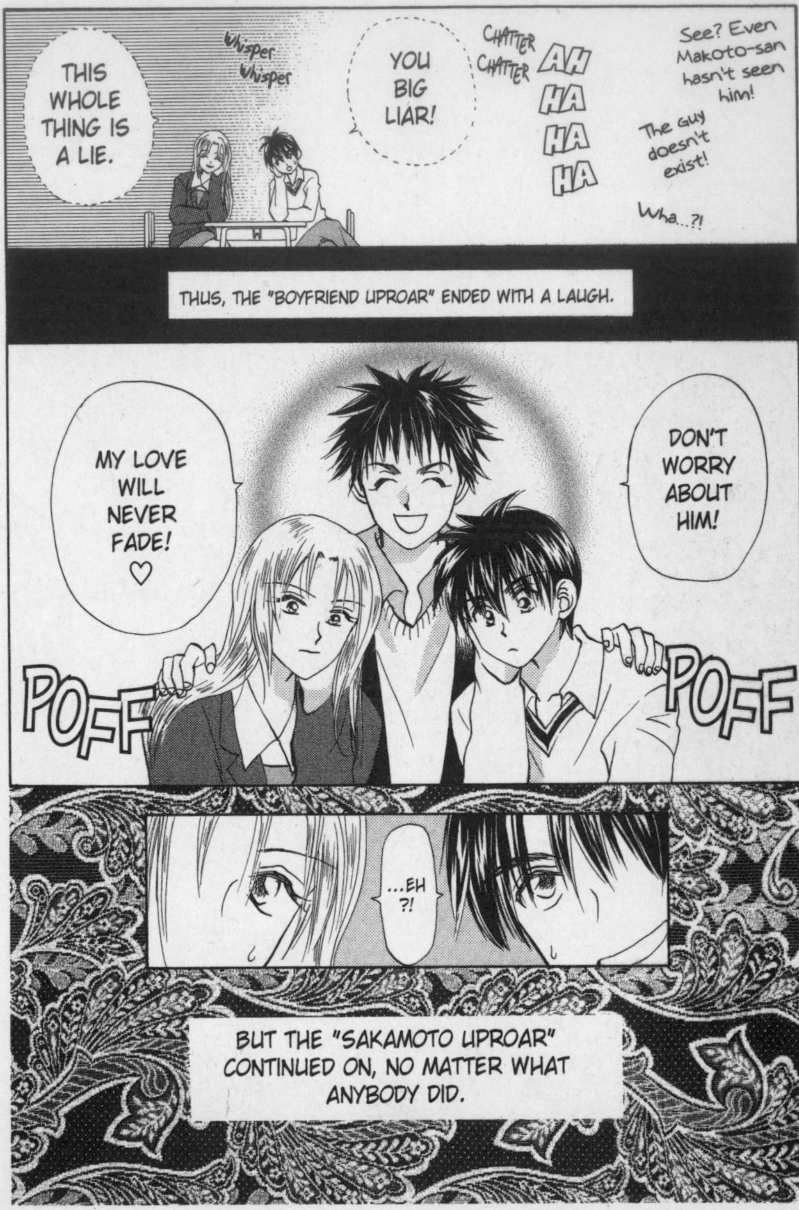
See? Even Makoto-san hasn't seen him!
The guy doesn't exist!
Wha...?!
AH HA HA HA
CHATTER CHATTER
YOU BIG LIAR!
Whisper Whisper
THIS WHOLE THING IS A LIE.
THUS, THE "BOYFRIEND UPROAR" ENDED WITH A LAUGH.
DON'T WORRY ABOUT HIM!
POFF
MY LOVE WILL NEVER FADE! ♡
POFF
...EH ?!
BUT THE "SAKAMOTO UPROAR" CONTINUED ON, NO MATTER WHAT ANYBODY DID.

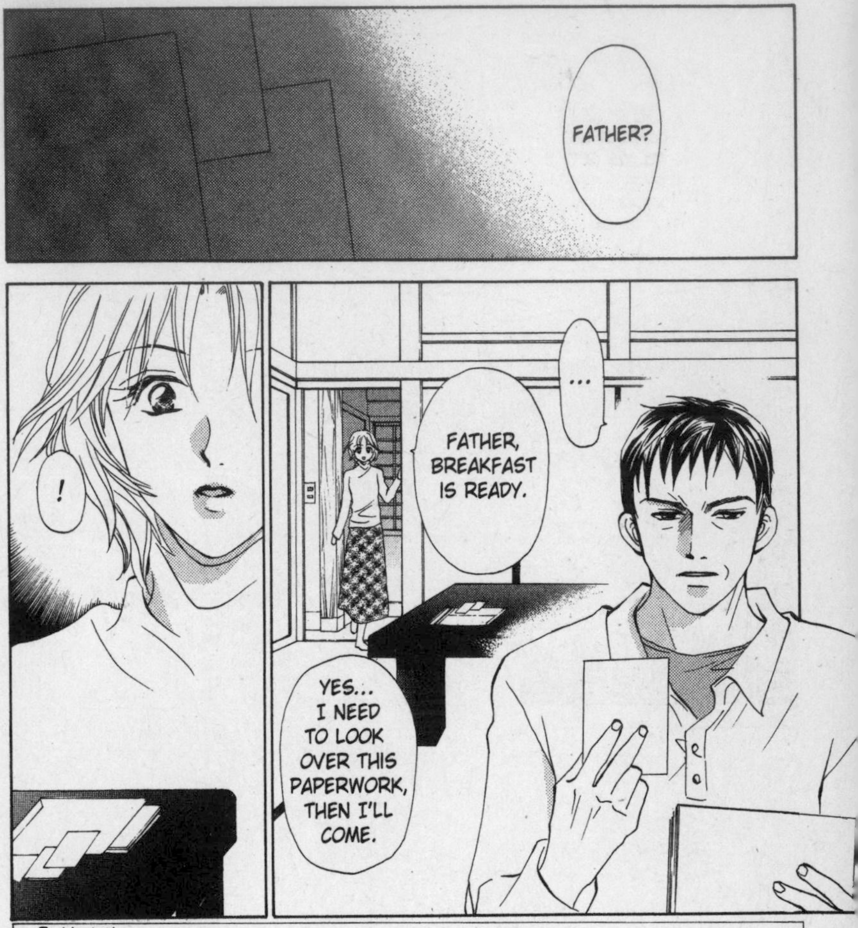
FATHER?
...
FATHER, BREAKFAST IS READY.
YES... I NEED TO LOOK OVER THIS PAPERWORK, THEN I'LL COME.
!

-Behind the Scenes Story- ②

I thought I'd talk a little about the origin of the name "Ito."* I had a friend in high school named Ito. Well, I guess that's not much of an origin story. But I wanted a name with just that kind of feel, so when it was time to come up with the story, that's what I went with. By the way, it was my mother who kept saying "That name is a bad omen!" Hey, hey!! That's rude! Especially to all the Itos in the nation of Japan! I always thought it was a cute name... What do you all think?

I learned the characters to write it after I was already used to saying the name.

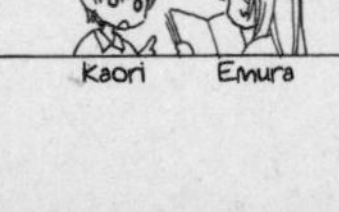
YUP!
Kaori
Emura

Is this really the character you use to write "Ito"?

* Ito means "thread" in Japanese. -Ed.

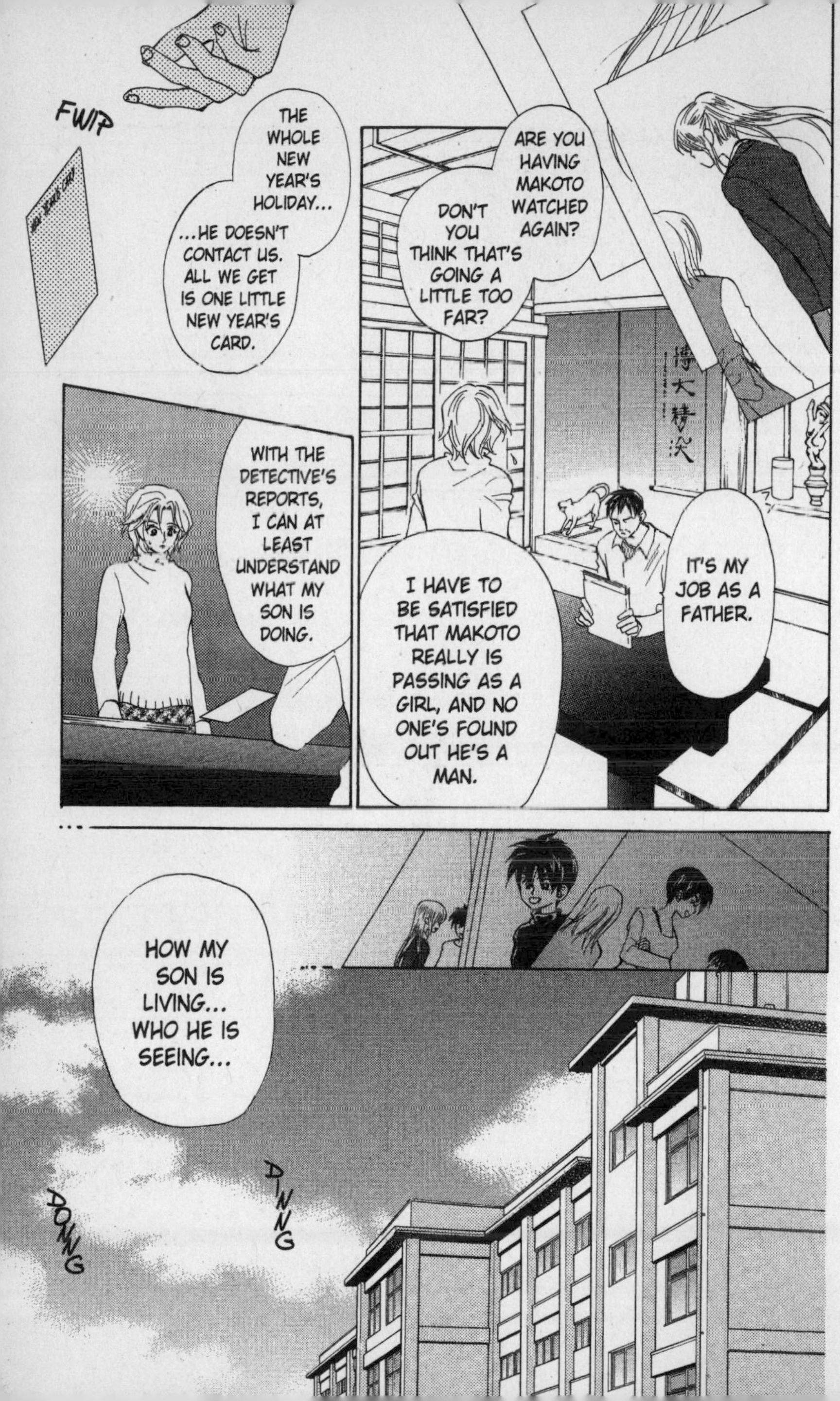
ARE YOU HAVING MAKOTO WATCHED AGAIN?
DON'T YOU THINK THAT'S GOING A LITTLE TOO FAR?
THE WHOLE NEW YEAR'S HOLIDAY...
...HE DOESN'T CONTACT US. ALL WE GET IS ONE LITTLE NEW YEAR'S CARD.
FWIP
IT'S MY JOB AS A FATHER.
I HAVE TO BE SATISFIED THAT MAKOTO REALLY IS PASSING AS A GIRL, AND NO ONE'S FOUND OUT HE'S A MAN.
WITH THE DETECTIVE'S REPORTS, I CAN AT LEAST UNDERSTAND WHAT MY SON IS DOING.
HOW MY SON IS LIVING... WHO HE IS SEEING...
DINNG
DONNG

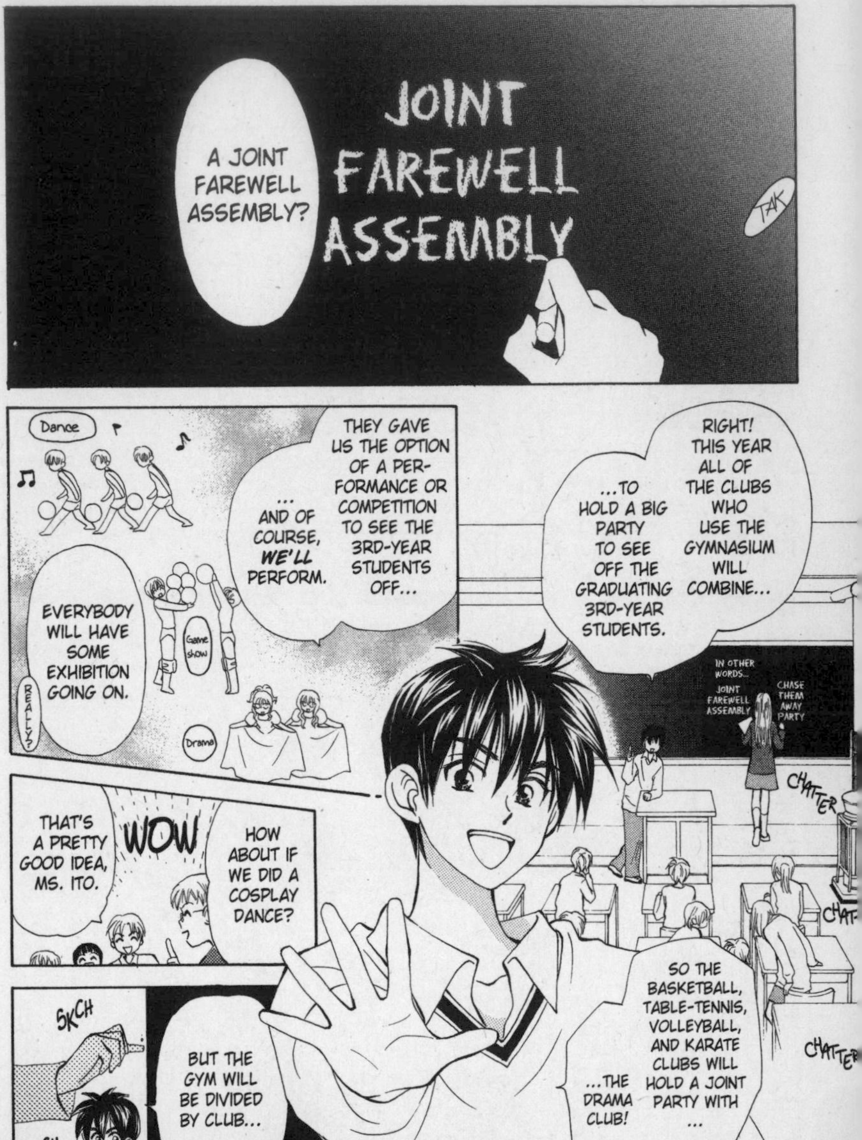
TAK
JOINT FAREWELL ASSEMBLY
A JOINT FAREWELL ASSEMBLY?
RIGHT! THIS YEAR ALL OF THE CLUBS WHO USE THE GYMNASIUM WILL COMBINE...
...TO HOLD A BIG PARTY TO SEE OFF THE GRADUATING 3RD-YEAR STUDENTS.
IN OTHER WORDS... JOINT FAREWELL ASSEMBLY
CHASE THEM AWAY PARTY
CHATTER
CHAT-
SO THE BASKETBALL, TABLE-TENNIS, VOLLEYBALL, AND KARATE CLUBS WILL HOLD A JOINT PARTY WITH ...
...THE DRAMA CLUB!
CHATTER
THEY GAVE US THE OPTION OF A PER-FORMANCE OR COMPETITION TO SEE THE 3RD-YEAR STUDENTS OFF...
... AND OF COURSE, ***WE'LL*** PERFORM.
Dance
Game show
EVERYBODY WILL HAVE SOME EXHIBITION GOING ON.
REALLY?
Drama
HOW ABOUT IF WE DID A COSPLAY DANCE?
WOW
THAT'S A PRETTY GOOD IDEA, MS. ITO.
BUT THE GYM WILL BE DIVIDED BY CLUB...
SKCH
SKCH

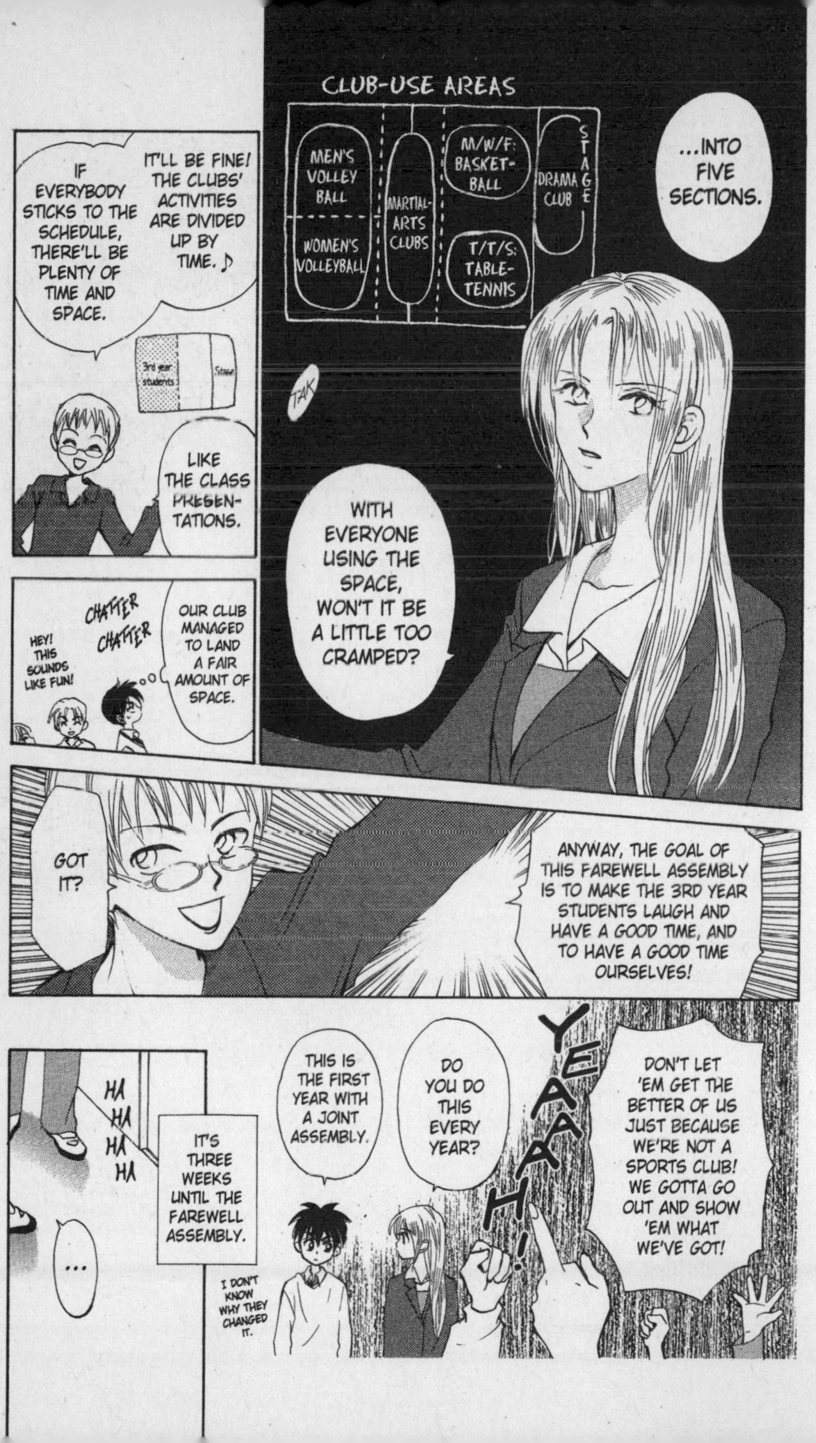
CLUB-USE AREAS
MEN'S VOLLEY BALL
WOMEN'S VOLLEYBALL
MARTIAL-ARTS CLUBS
M/W/F: BASKET-BALL
T/T/S: TABLE-TENNIS
DRAMA CLUB
STAGE
...INTO FIVE SECTIONS.
TAK
WITH EVERYONE USING THE SPACE, WON'T IT BE A LITTLE TOO CRAMPED?
IT'LL BE FINE! THE CLUBS' ACTIVITIES ARE DIVIDED UP BY TIME. ♪
IF EVERYBODY STICKS TO THE SCHEDULE, THERE'LL BE PLENTY OF TIME AND SPACE.
3rd year students
Stage
LIKE THE CLASS PRESENTATIONS.
OUR CLUB MANAGED TO LAND A FAIR AMOUNT OF SPACE.
CHATTER CHATTER
HEY! THIS SOUNDS LIKE FUN!
ANYWAY, THE GOAL OF THIS FAREWELL ASSEMBLY IS TO MAKE THE 3RD YEAR STUDENTS LAUGH AND HAVE A GOOD TIME, AND TO HAVE A GOOD TIME OURSELVES!
GOT IT?
DON'T LET 'EM GET THE BETTER OF US JUST BECAUSE WE'RE NOT A SPORTS CLUB! WE GOTTA GO OUT AND SHOW 'EM WHAT WE'VE GOT!
YEAAAH!
DO YOU DO THIS EVERY YEAR?
THIS IS THE FIRST YEAR WITH A JOINT ASSEMBLY.
I DON'T KNOW WHY THEY CHANGED IT.
IT'S THREE WEEKS UNTIL THE FAREWELL ASSEMBLY.
HA HA HA HA
...

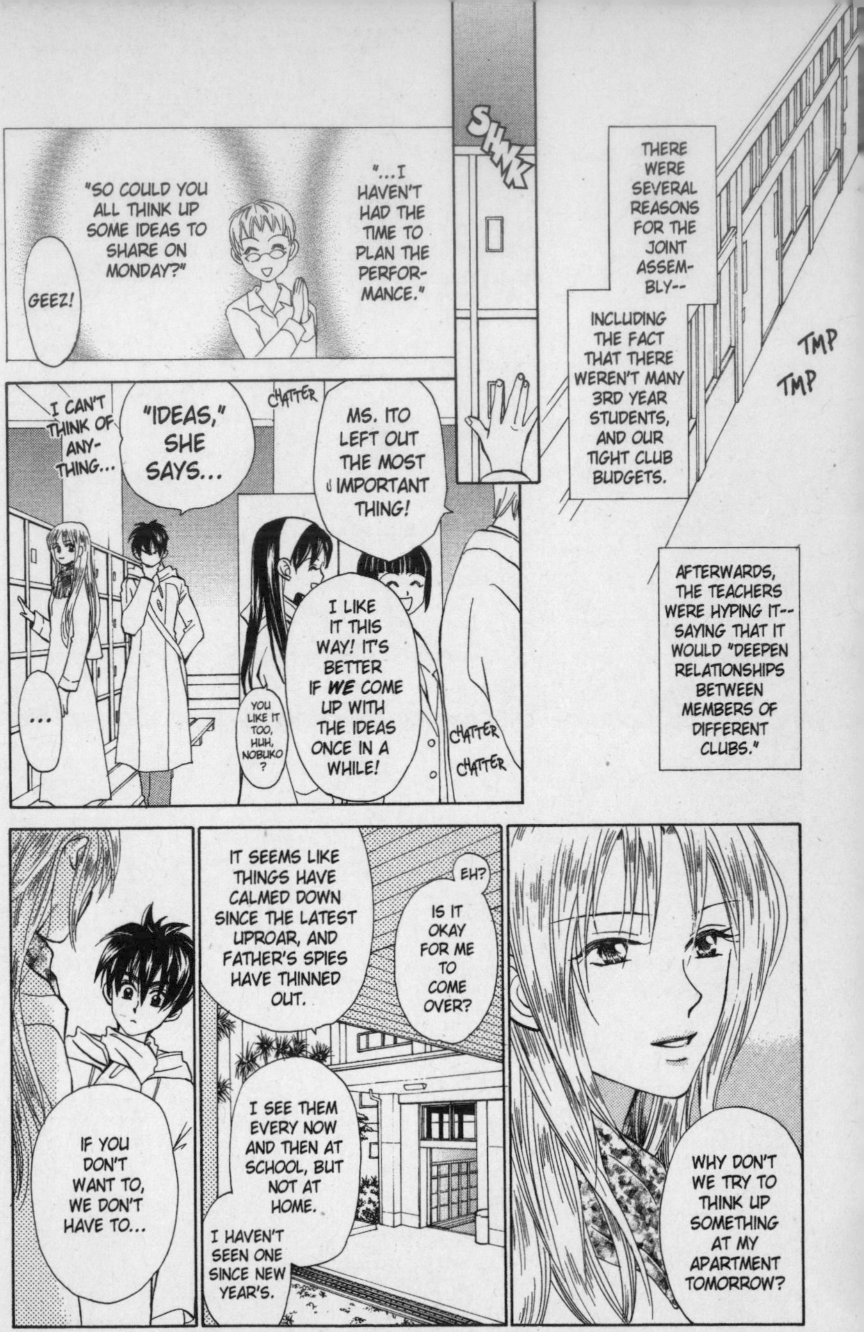
THERE WERE SEVERAL REASONS FOR THE JOINT ASSEMBLY--
INCLUDING THE FACT THAT THERE WEREN'T MANY 3RD YEAR STUDENTS, AND OUR TIGHT CLUB BUDGETS.
TMP
TMP
AFTERWARDS, THE TEACHERS WERE HYPING IT-- SAYING THAT IT WOULD "DEEPEN RELATIONSHIPS BETWEEN MEMBERS OF DIFFERENT CLUBS."
SHWK
"...I HAVEN'T HAD THE TIME TO PLAN THE PERFORMANCE."
"SO COULD YOU ALL THINK UP SOME IDEAS TO SHARE ON MONDAY?"
GEEZ!
CHATTER
MS. ITO LEFT OUT THE MOST IMPORTANT THING!
"IDEAS," SHE SAYS...
I CAN'T THINK OF ANY-THING...
I LIKE IT THIS WAY! IT'S BETTER IF WE COME UP WITH THE IDEAS ONCE IN A WHILE!
YOU LIKE IT TOO, HUH, NOBUKO?
CHATTER
CHATTER
...
WHY DON'T WE TRY TO THINK UP SOMETHING AT MY APARTMENT TOMORROW?
EH?
IS IT OKAY FOR ME TO COME OVER?
IT SEEMS LIKE THINGS HAVE CALMED DOWN SINCE THE LATEST UPROAR, AND FATHER'S SPIES HAVE THINNED OUT.
I SEE THEM EVERY NOW AND THEN AT SCHOOL, BUT NOT AT HOME.
I HAVEN'T SEEN ONE SINCE NEW YEAR'S.
IF YOU DON'T WANT TO, WE DON'T HAVE TO...

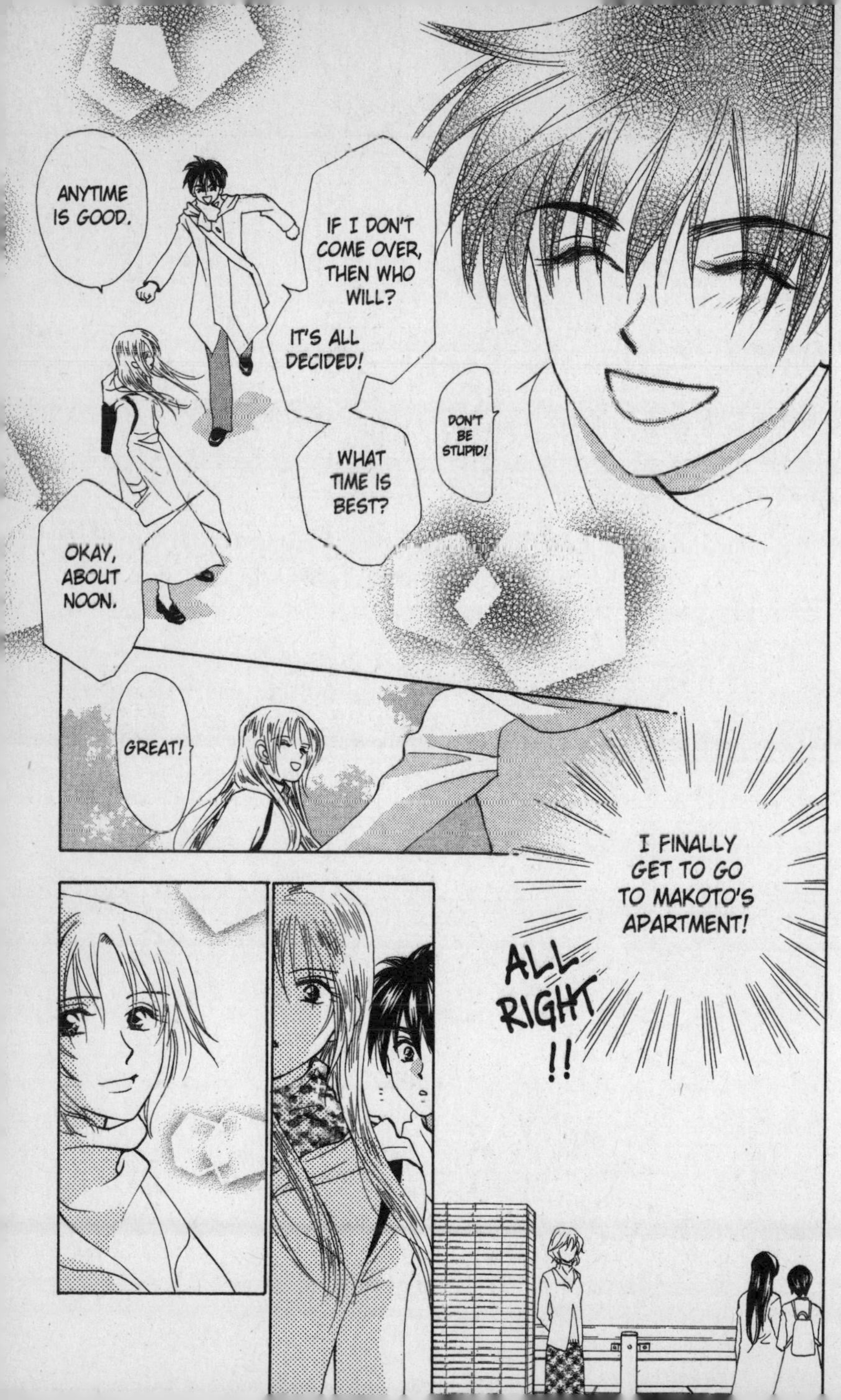
IF I DON'T COME OVER, THEN WHO WILL?
IT'S ALL DECIDED!
DON'T BE STUPID!
WHAT TIME IS BEST?
ANYTIME IS GOOD.
OKAY, ABOUT NOON.
GREAT!
I FINALLY GET TO GO TO MAKOTO'S APARTMENT!
ALL RIGHT !!

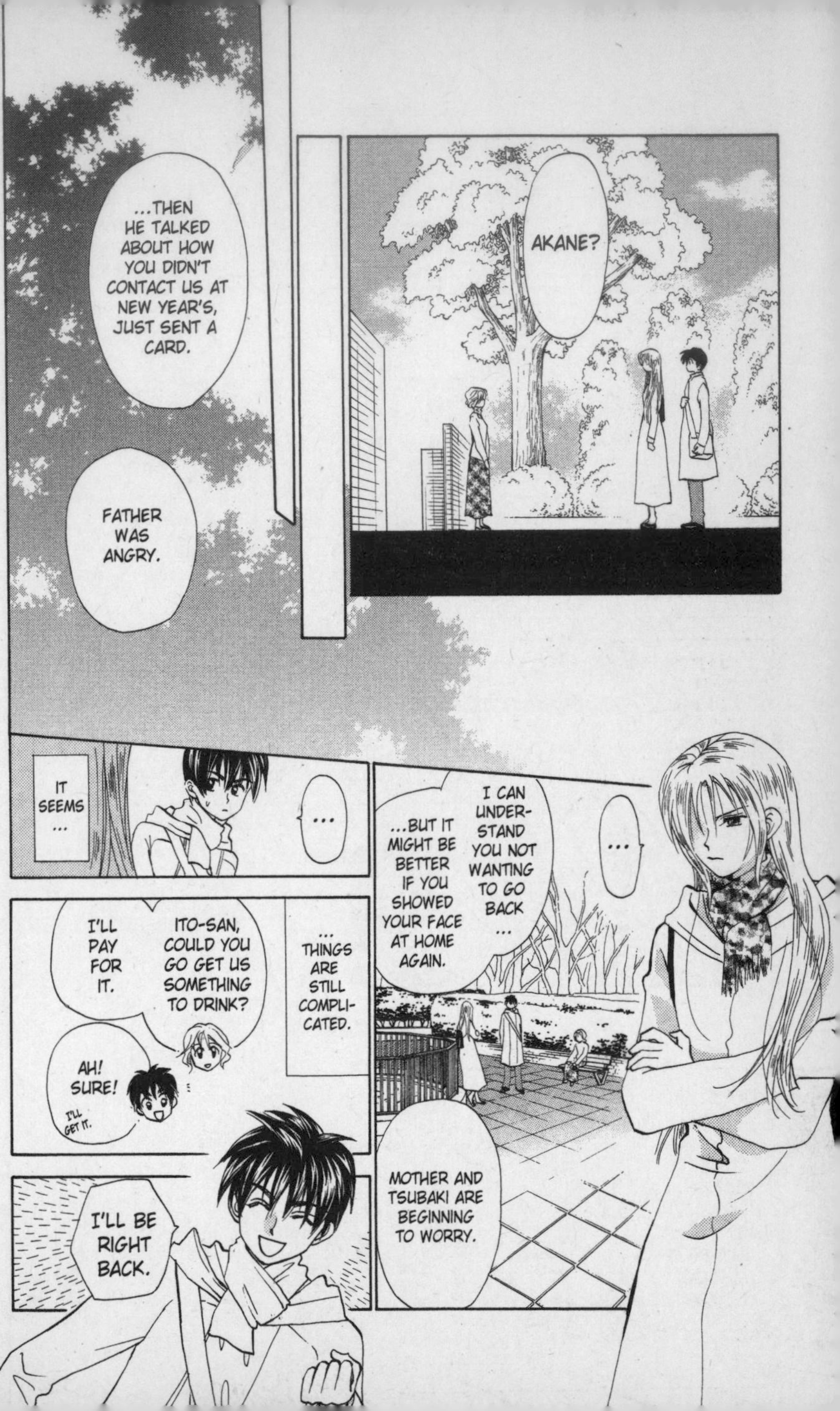
AKANE?
...THEN HE TALKED ABOUT HOW YOU DIDN'T CONTACT US AT NEW YEAR'S, JUST SENT A CARD.
FATHER WAS ANGRY.
...
I CAN UNDER-STAND YOU NOT WANTING TO GO BACK ...
...BUT IT MIGHT BE BETTER IF YOU SHOWED YOUR FACE AT HOME AGAIN.
MOTHER AND TSUBAKI ARE BEGINNING TO WORRY.
...
IT SEEMS ...
... THINGS ARE STILL COMPLI-CATED.
ITO-SAN, COULD YOU GO GET US SOMETHING TO DRINK?
I'LL PAY FOR IT.
AH! SURE!
I'LL GET IT.
I'LL BE RIGHT BACK.

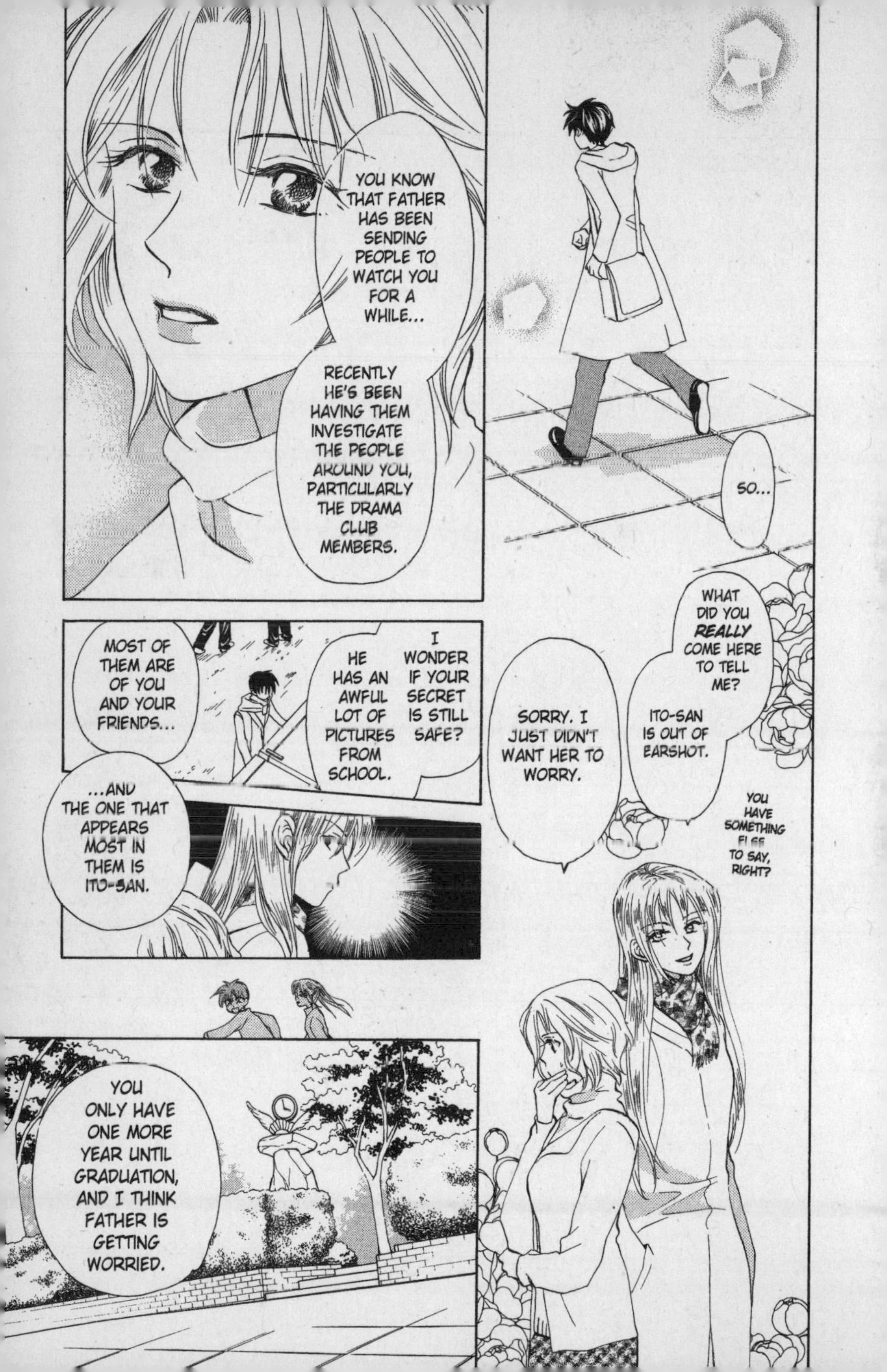
SO...
WHAT DID YOU REALLY COME HERE TO TELL ME?
ITO-SAN IS OUT OF EARSHOT.
SORRY. I JUST DIDN'T WANT HER TO WORRY.
YOU HAVE SOMETHING ELSE TO SAY, RIGHT?
YOU KNOW THAT FATHER HAS BEEN SENDING PEOPLE TO WATCH YOU FOR A WHILE...
RECENTLY HE'S BEEN HAVING THEM INVESTIGATE THE PEOPLE AROUND YOU, PARTICULARLY THE DRAMA CLUB MEMBERS.
I WONDER IF YOUR SECRET IS STILL SAFE?
HE HAS AN AWFUL LOT OF PICTURES FROM SCHOOL.
MOST OF THEM ARE OF YOU AND YOUR FRIENDS...
...AND THE ONE THAT APPEARS MOST IN THEM IS ITO-SAN.
YOU ONLY HAVE ONE MORE YEAR UNTIL GRADUATION, AND I THINK FATHER IS GETTING WORRIED.

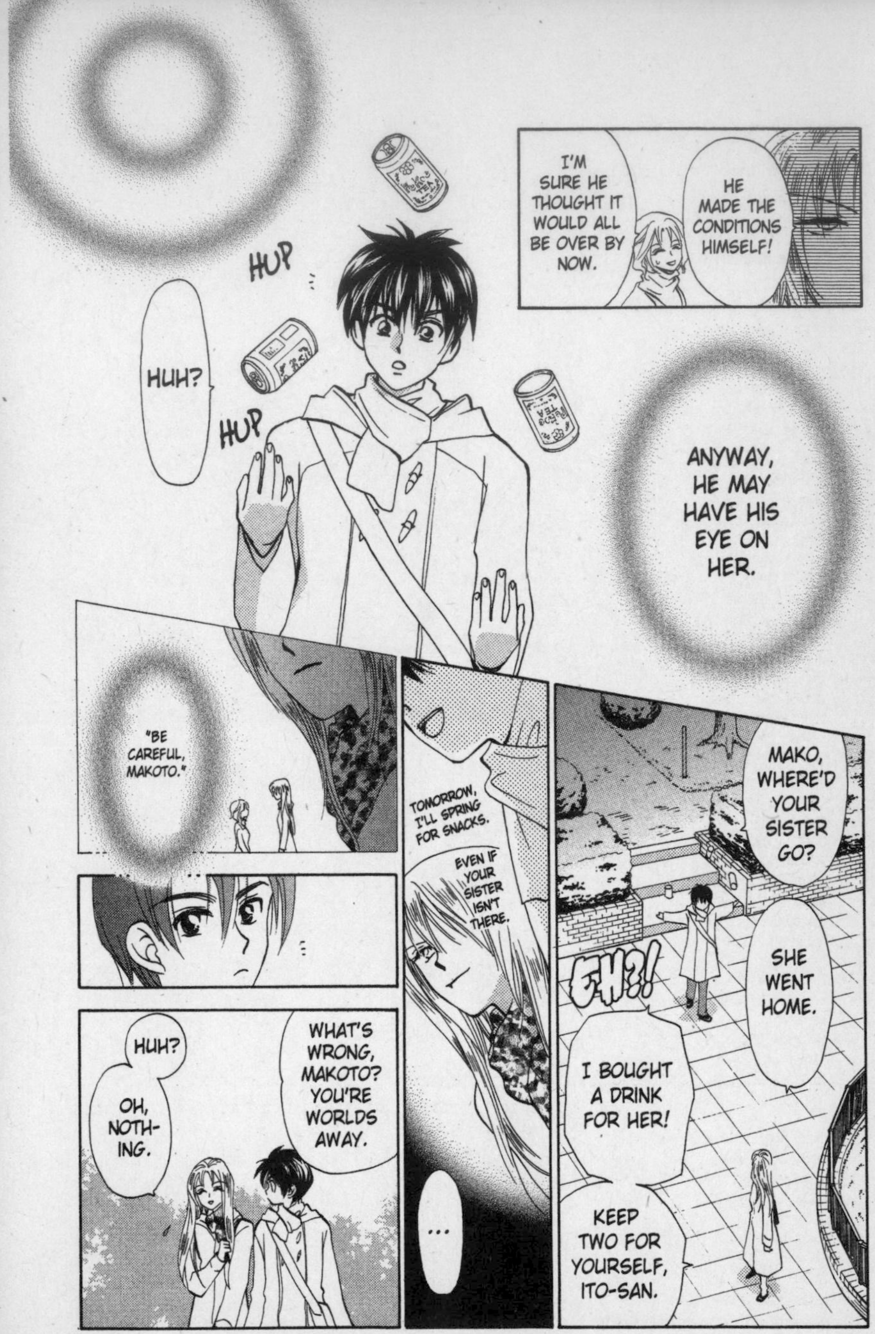
HE MADE THE CONDITIONS HIMSELF!
I'M SURE HE THOUGHT IT WOULD ALL BE OVER BY NOW.
ANYWAY, HE MAY HAVE HIS EYE ON HER.
HUP
HUH?
HUP
MAKO, WHERE'D YOUR SISTER GO?
SHE WENT HOME.
EH?!
I BOUGHT A DRINK FOR HER!
KEEP TWO FOR YOURSELF, ITO-SAN.
TOMORROW, I'LL SPRING FOR SNACKS.
EVEN IF YOUR SISTER ISN'T THERE.
...
"BE CAREFUL, MAKOTO."
WHAT'S WRONG, MAKOTO? YOU'RE WORLDS AWAY.
HUH?
OH, NOTHING.

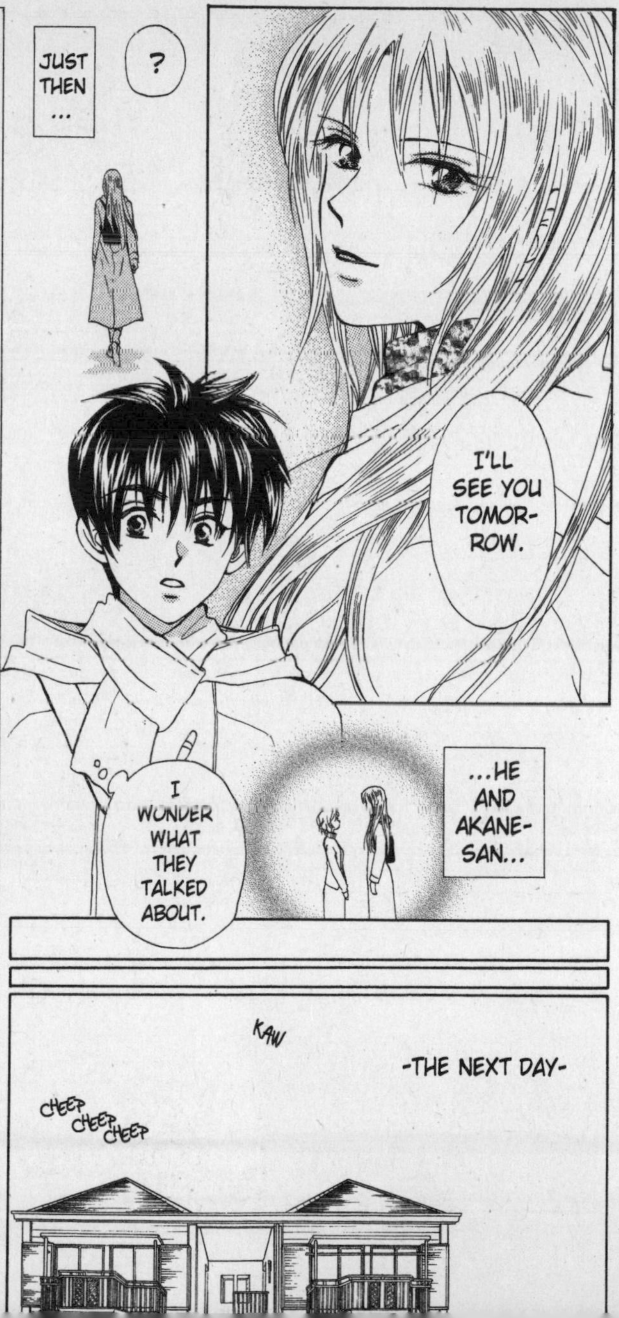
I'LL SEE YOU TOMOR-ROW.
?
JUST THEN ...
...HE AND AKANE-SAN...
I WONDER WHAT THEY TALKED ABOUT.
KAW
-THE NEXT DAY-
CHEEP CHEEP CHEEP

QUESTION CORNER

Last volume I wasn't able to do Question Corner, so this time you'll have lots of it!

- Isn't Ito ever going to grow her hair out?

Ⓔ No, not yet. Maybe in the future the time will come.

- About the graphic novel covers... I can't figure out what plays the costumes on the cover of Volumes Three & Four came from.

Ⓔ Right. The covers for Vols. One & Two came from the plays put on inside the books. But from Vol. Three on, I'm just doing covers that I feel like doing. The covers I'm doing from now on have images of clothes from all different countries.

- How tall is Makoto at the moment? And will there be a time when he overtakes Ito in height?

Ⓔ We'll update the heights in the next volume, so look forward to that. And we'll just have to see when and if he outgrows her!

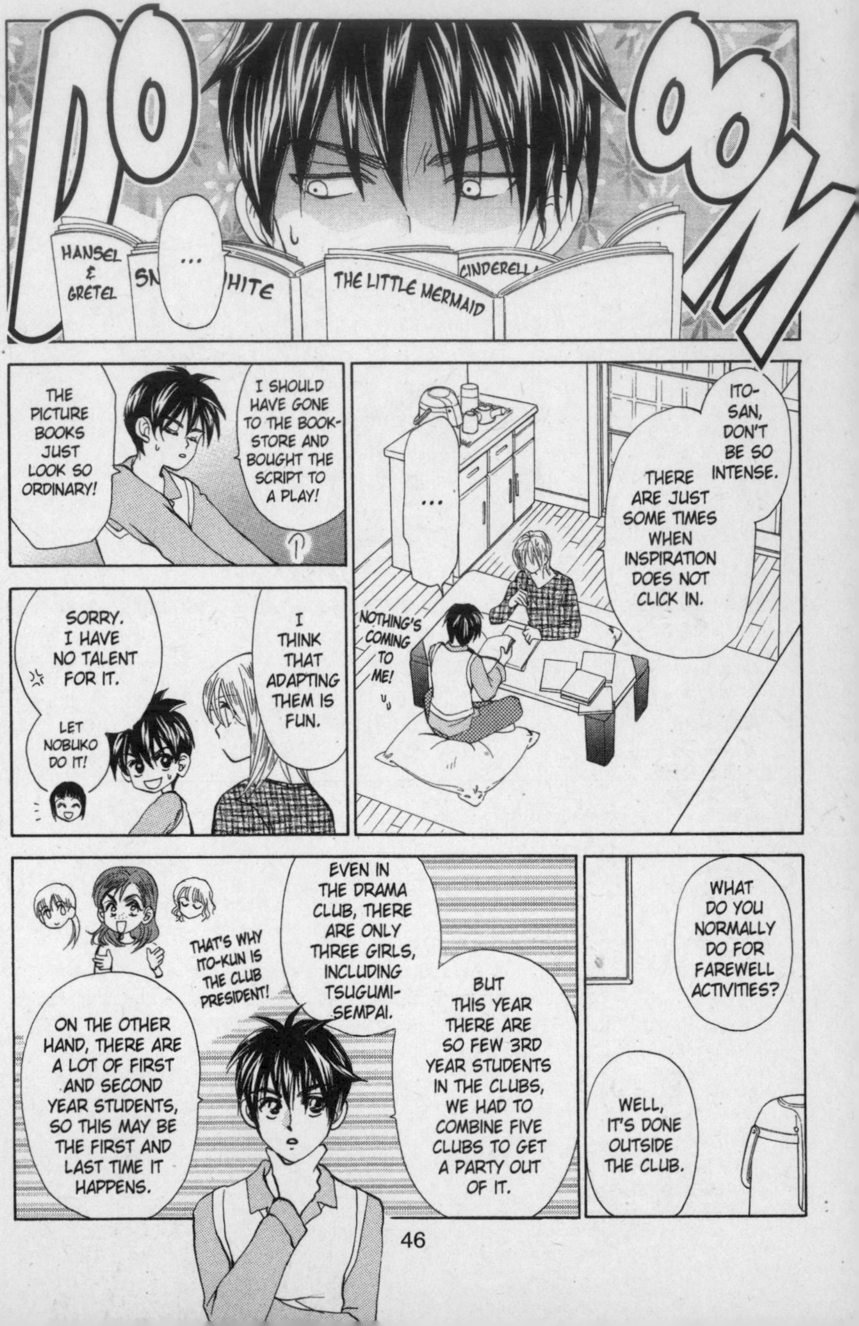
DOOOM
...
HANSEL & GRETEL
SN WHITE
THE LITTLE MERMAID
CINDERELL
ITO-SAN, DON'T BE SO INTENSE.
THERE ARE JUST SOME TIMES WHEN INSPIRATION DOES NOT CLICK IN.
...
NOTHING'S COMING TO ME!
I SHOULD HAVE GONE TO THE BOOK-STORE AND BOUGHT THE SCRIPT TO A PLAY!
THE PICTURE BOOKS JUST LOOK SO ORDINARY!
I THINK THAT ADAPTING THEM IS FUN.
SORRY. I HAVE NO TALENT FOR IT.
LET NOBUKO DO IT!
WHAT DO YOU NORMALLY DO FOR FAREWELL ACTIVITIES?
WELL, IT'S DONE OUTSIDE THE CLUB.
EVEN IN THE DRAMA CLUB, THERE ARE ONLY THREE GIRLS, INCLUDING TSUGUMI-SEMPAI.
BUT THIS YEAR THERE ARE SO FEW 3RD YEAR STUDENTS IN THE CLUBS, WE HAD TO COMBINE FIVE CLUBS TO GET A PARTY OUT OF IT.
THAT'S WHY ITO-KUN IS THE CLUB PRESIDENT!
ON THE OTHER HAND, THERE ARE A LOT OF FIRST AND SECOND YEAR STUDENTS, SO THIS MAY BE THE FIRST AND LAST TIME IT HAPPENS.

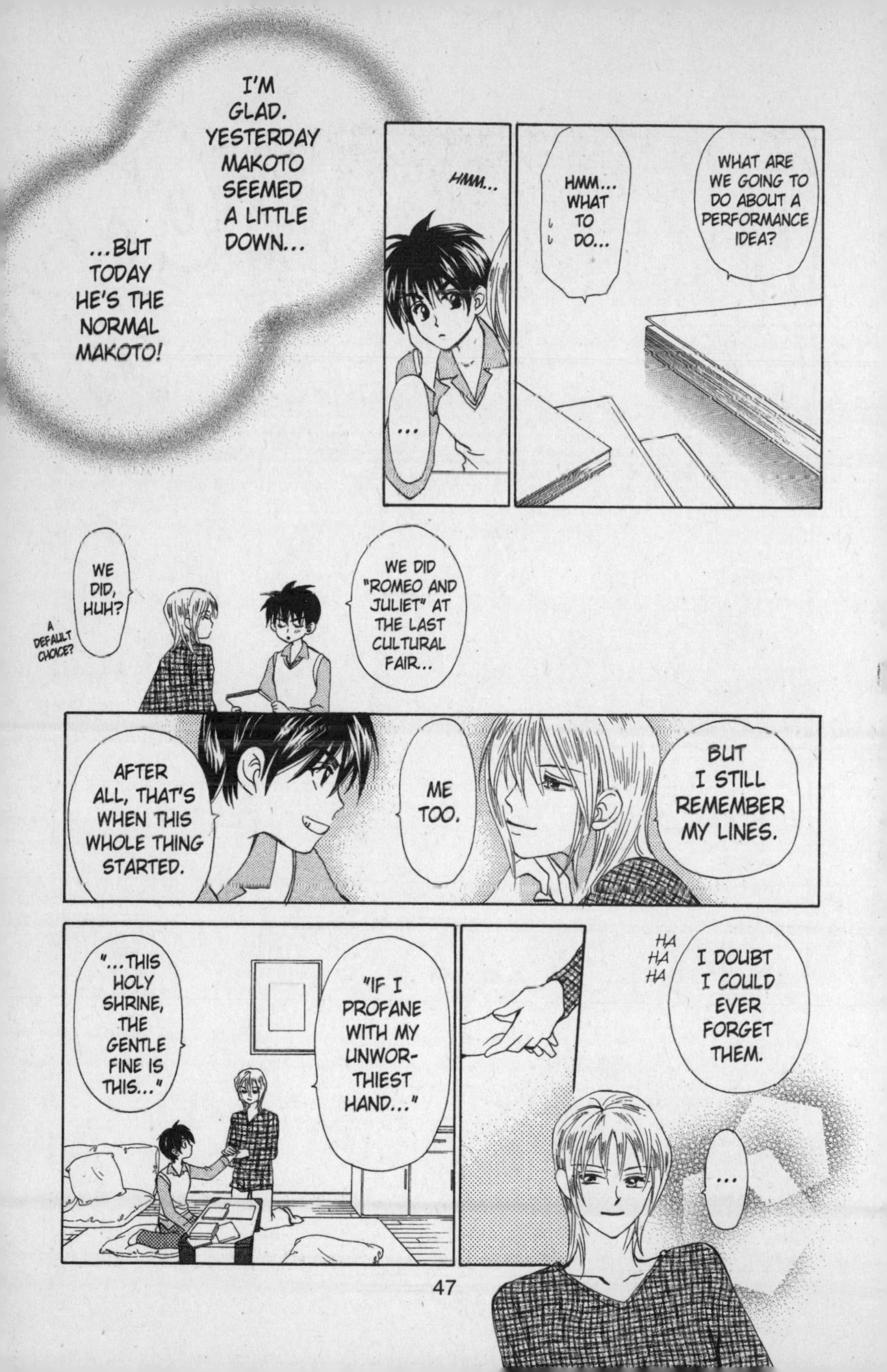
WHAT ARE WE GOING TO DO ABOUT A PERFORMANCE IDEA?
HMM... WHAT TO DO...
HMM...
...
I'M GLAD. YESTERDAY MAKOTO SEEMED A LITTLE DOWN...
...BUT TODAY HE'S THE NORMAL MAKOTO!
WE DID "ROMEO AND JULIET" AT THE LAST CULTURAL FAIR...
WE DID, HUH?
A DEFAULT CHOICE?
BUT I STILL REMEMBER MY LINES.
ME TOO.
AFTER ALL, THAT'S WHEN THIS WHOLE THING STARTED.
HA HA HA
I DOUBT I COULD EVER FORGET THEM.
...
"IF I PROFANE WITH MY UNWOR-THIEST HAND..."
"...THIS HOLY SHRINE, THE GENTLE FINE IS THIS..."

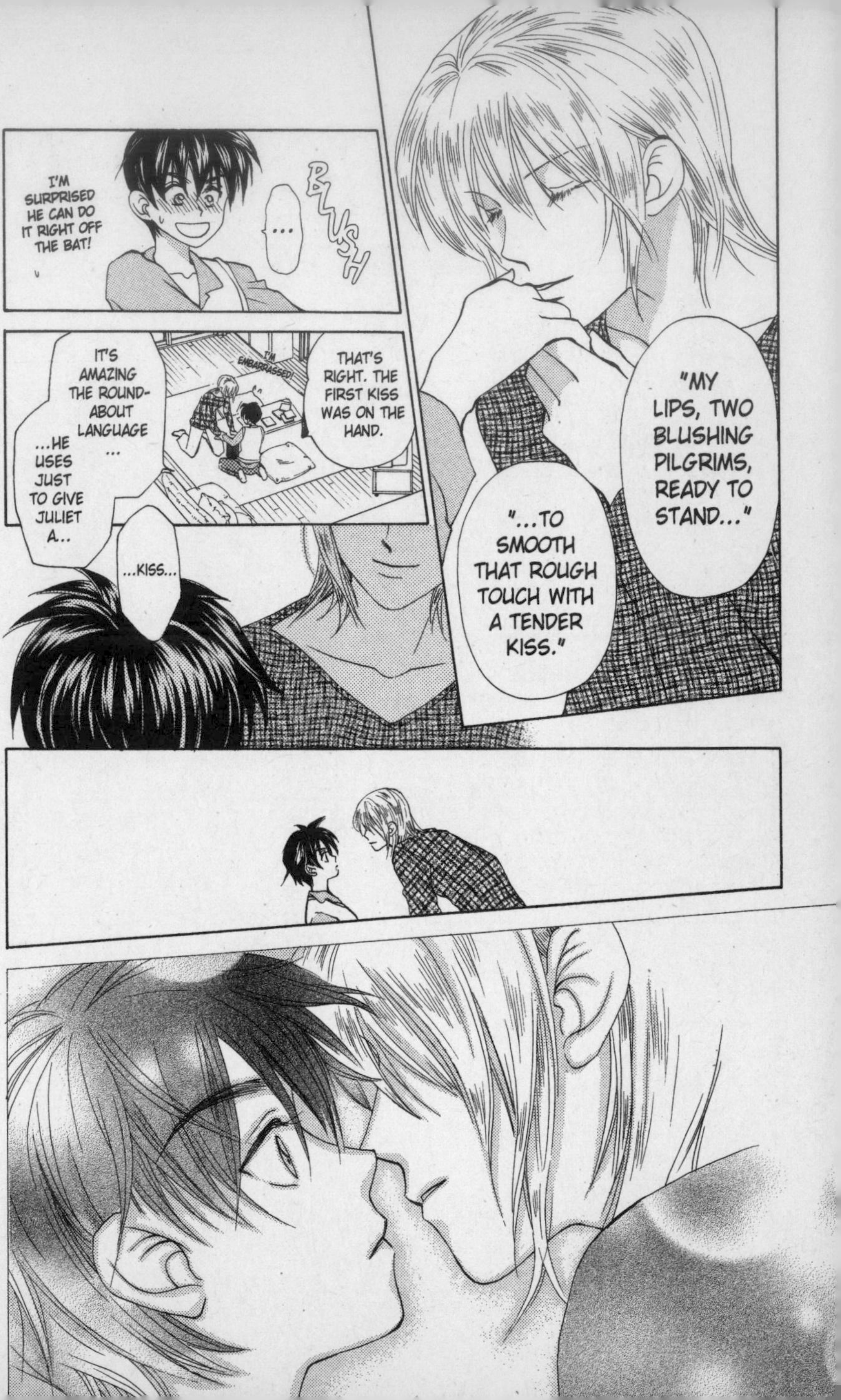
"MY LIPS, TWO BLUSHING PILGRIMS, READY TO STAND..."
"...TO SMOOTH THAT ROUGH TOUCH WITH A TENDER KISS."
...
BLUSH
I'M SURPRISED HE CAN DO IT RIGHT OFF THE BAT!
THAT'S RIGHT. THE FIRST KISS WAS ON THE HAND.
I'M EMBARRASSED!
IT'S AMAZING THE ROUND-ABOUT LANGUAGE ...
...HE USES JUST TO GIVE JULIET A...
...KISS...

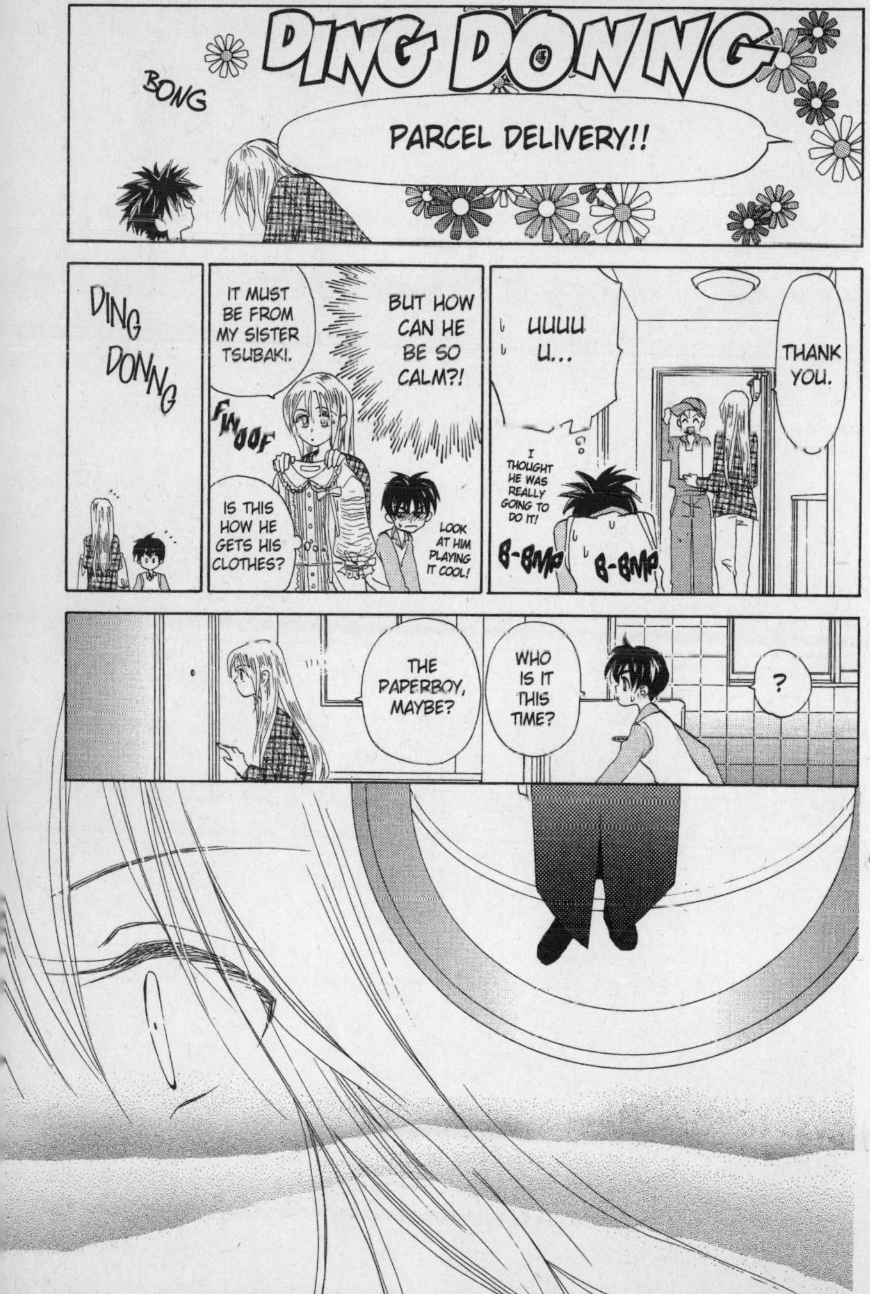
DING DONNG
BONG
PARCEL DELIVERY!!
THANK YOU.
UUUU U...
I THOUGHT HE WAS REALLY GOING TO DO IT!
B-BMP
B-BMP
BUT HOW CAN HE BE SO CALM?!
IT MUST BE FROM MY SISTER TSUBAKI.
FWOOF
IS THIS HOW HE GETS HIS CLOTHES?
LOOK AT HIM PLAYING IT COOL!
DING DONNG
?
WHO IS IT THIS TIME?
THE PAPERBOY, MAYBE?

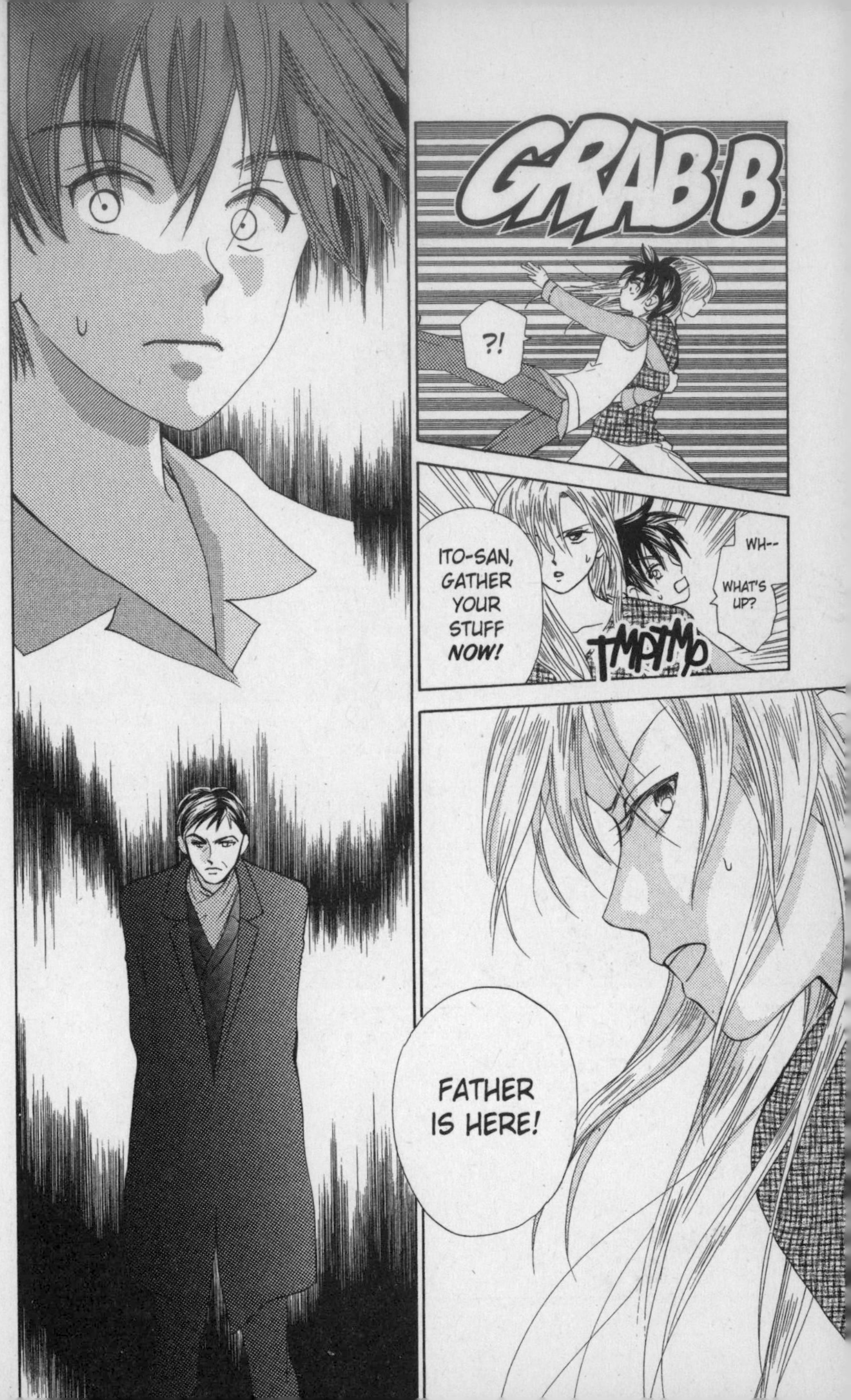
GRAB B
?!
WH--
WHAT'S UP?
ITO-SAN, GATHER YOUR STUFF NOW!
TMPTMP
FATHER IS HERE!

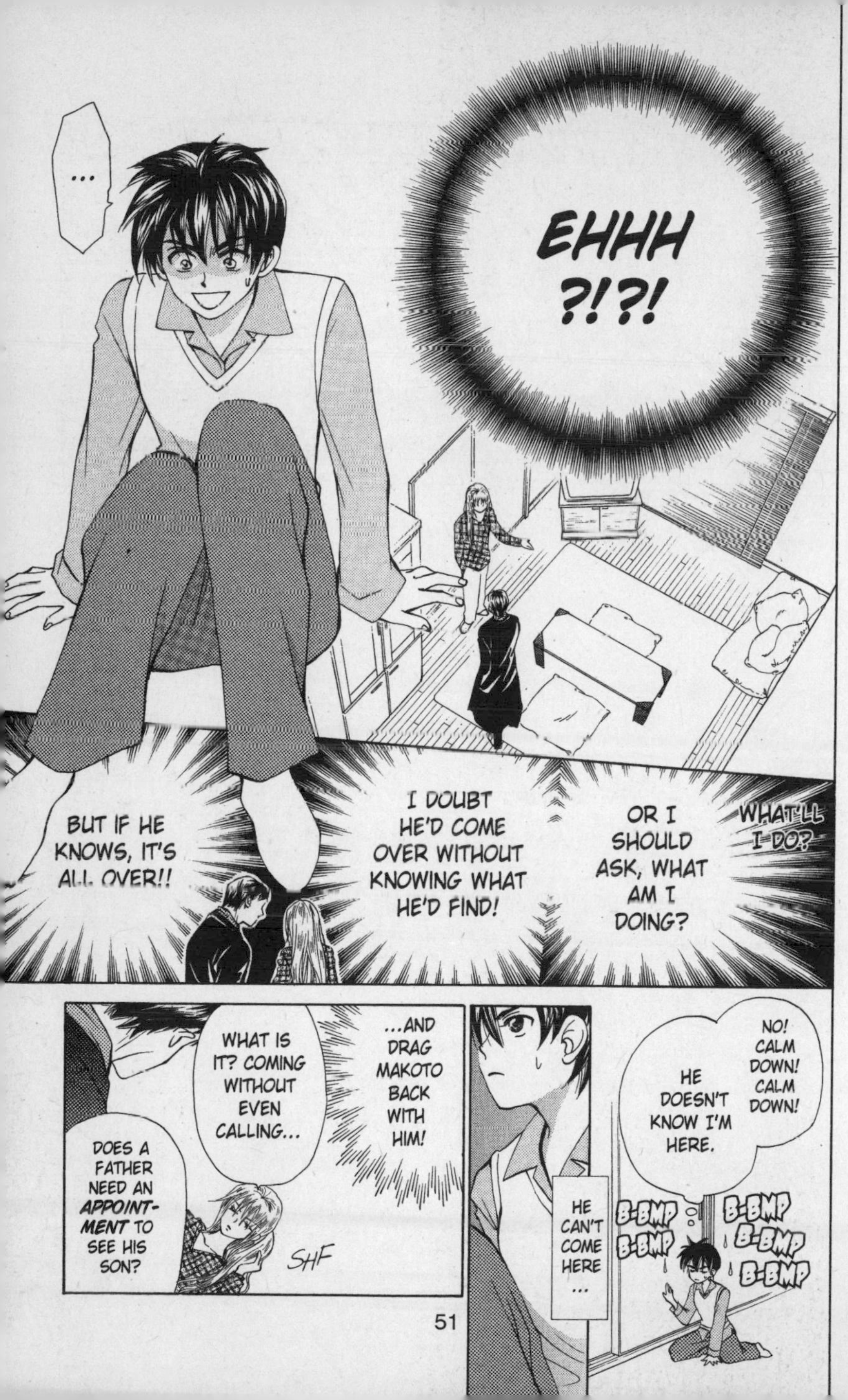
EHHH ?!?!
...
WHAT'LL I DO?
OR I SHOULD ASK, WHAT AM I DOING?
I DOUBT HE'D COME OVER WITHOUT KNOWING WHAT HE'D FIND!
BUT IF HE KNOWS, IT'S ALL OVER!!
NO! CALM DOWN! CALM DOWN!
HE DOESN'T KNOW I'M HERE.
B-BMP B-BMP
B-BMP B-BMP B-BMP
HE CAN'T COME HERE ...
...AND DRAG MAKOTO BACK WITH HIM!
WHAT IS IT? COMING WITHOUT EVEN CALLING...
DOES A FATHER NEED AN *APPOINTMENT* TO SEE HIS SON?
SHF

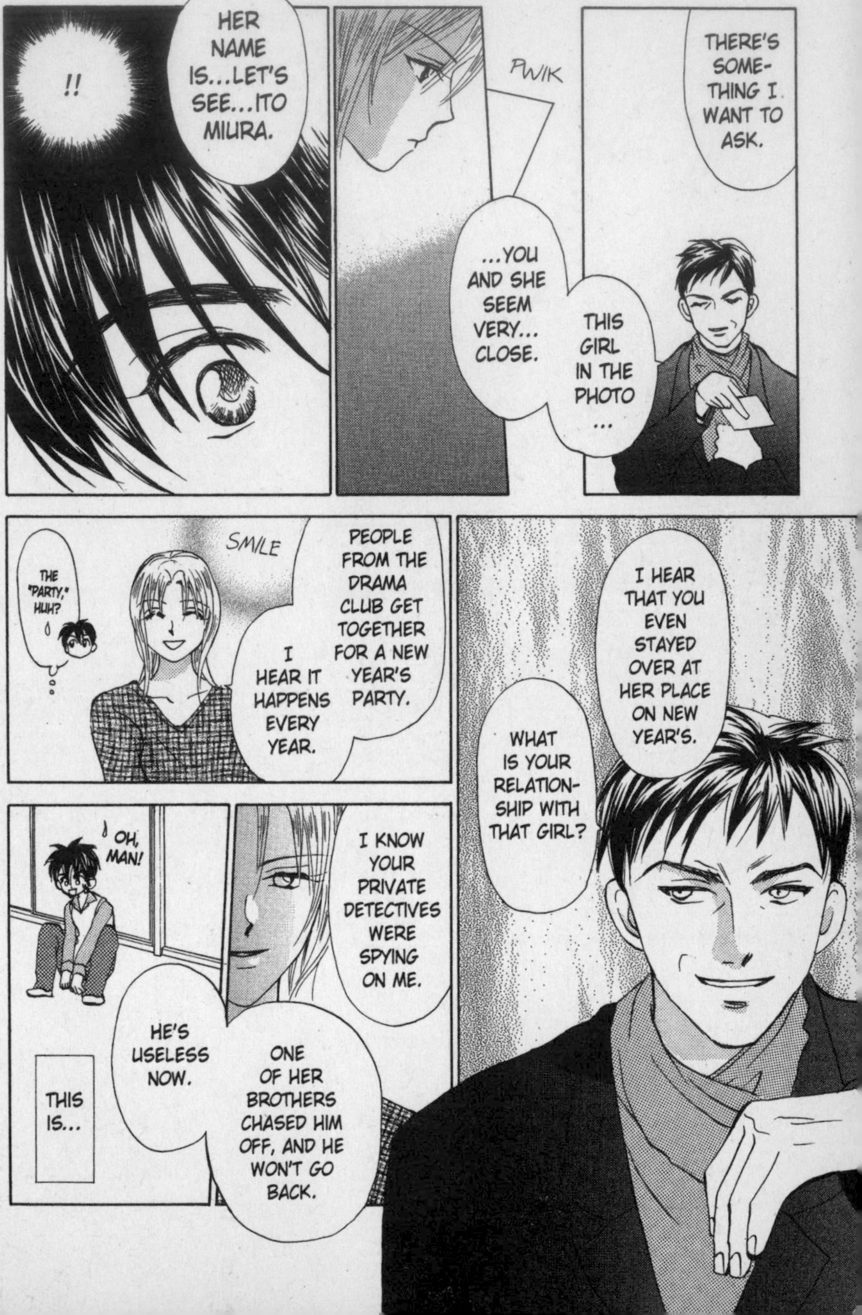
THERE'S SOME-THING I WANT TO ASK.
THIS GIRL IN THE PHOTO...
PWIK
...YOU AND SHE SEEM VERY... CLOSE.
HER NAME IS...LET'S SEE...ITO MIURA.
!!
I HEAR THAT YOU EVEN STAYED OVER AT HER PLACE ON NEW YEAR'S.
WHAT IS YOUR RELATION-SHIP WITH THAT GIRL?
PEOPLE FROM THE DRAMA CLUB GET TOGETHER FOR A NEW YEAR'S PARTY.
SMILE
I HEAR IT HAPPENS EVERY YEAR.
THE "PARTY," HUH?
I KNOW YOUR PRIVATE DETECTIVES WERE SPYING ON ME.
ONE OF HER BROTHERS CHASED HIM OFF, AND HE WON'T GO BACK.
HE'S USELESS NOW.
OH, MAN!
THIS IS...

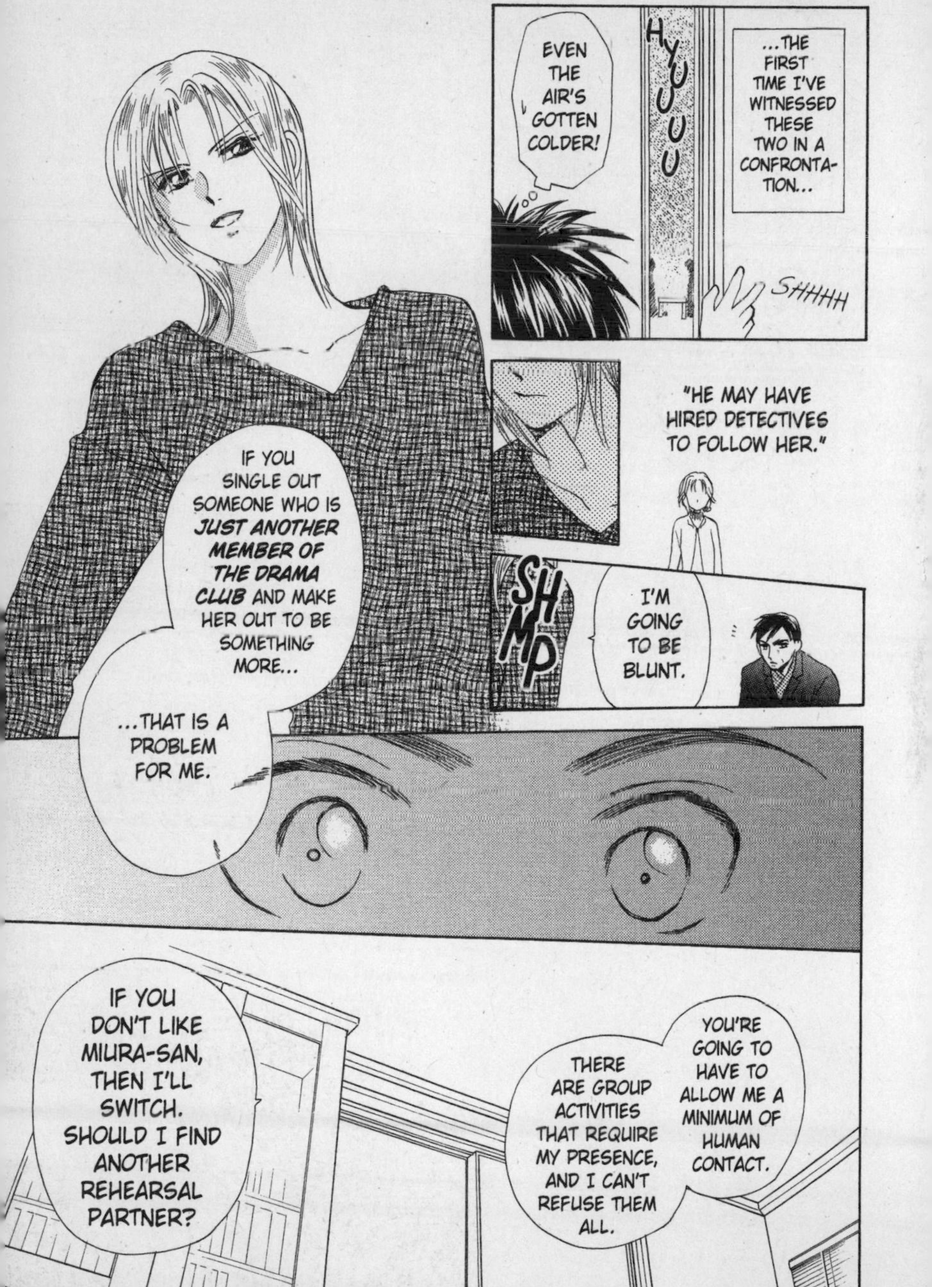
...THE FIRST TIME I'VE WITNESSED THESE TWO IN A CONFRONTATION...
HYUUUU
EVEN THE AIR'S GOTTEN COLDER!
SHHHH
"HE MAY HAVE HIRED DETECTIVES TO FOLLOW HER."
SHMP
I'M GOING TO BE BLUNT.
IF YOU SINGLE OUT SOMEONE WHO IS ***JUST ANOTHER MEMBER OF THE DRAMA CLUB*** AND MAKE HER OUT TO BE SOMETHING MORE...
...THAT IS A PROBLEM FOR ME.
YOU'RE GOING TO HAVE TO ALLOW ME A MINIMUM OF HUMAN CONTACT.
THERE ARE GROUP ACTIVITIES THAT REQUIRE MY PRESENCE, AND I CAN'T REFUSE THEM ALL.
IF YOU DON'T LIKE MIURA-SAN, THEN I'LL SWITCH. SHOULD I FIND ANOTHER REHEARSAL PARTNER?

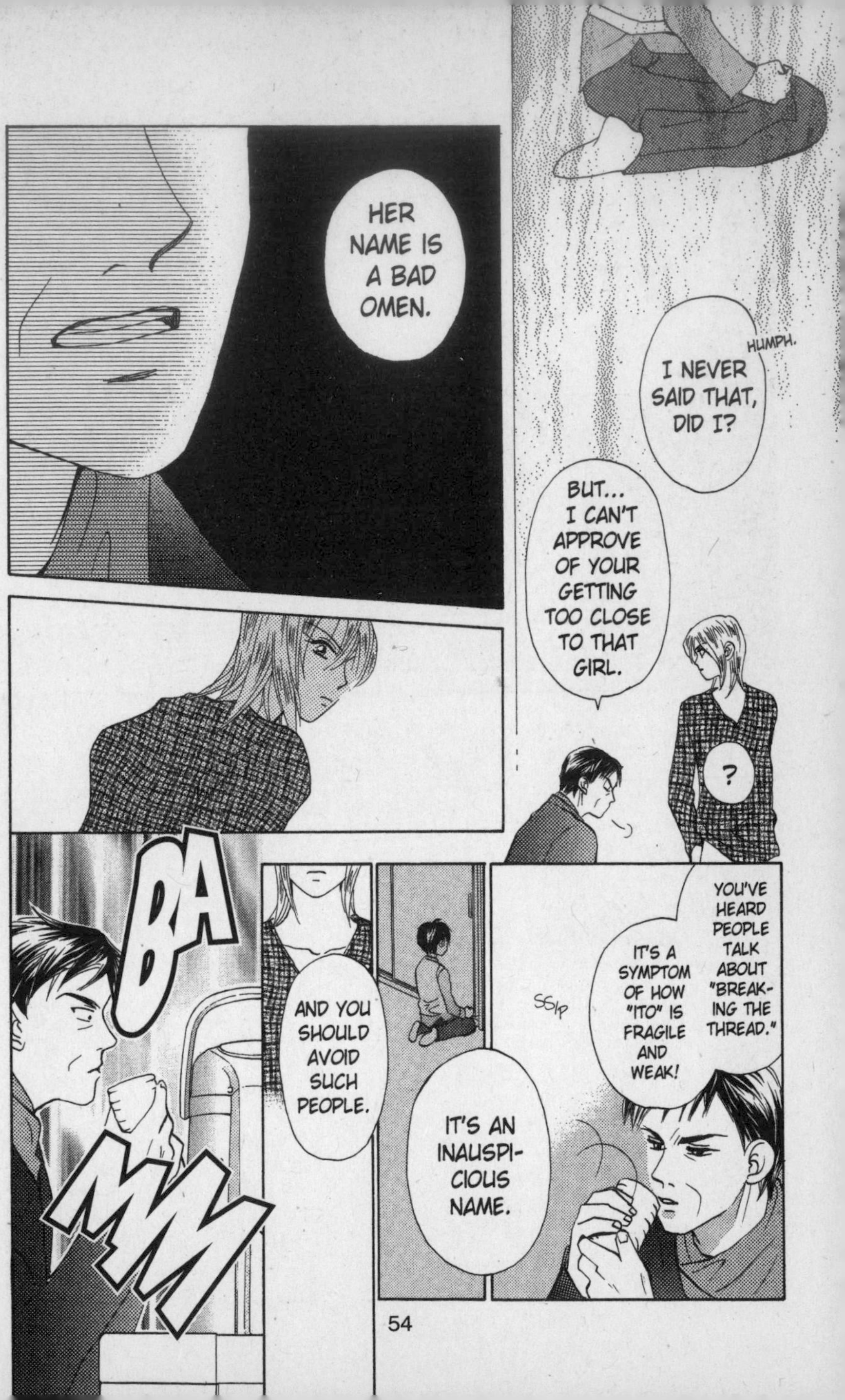
HUMPH.
I NEVER SAID THAT, DID I?
BUT... I CAN'T APPROVE OF YOUR GETTING TOO CLOSE TO THAT GIRL.
?
HER NAME IS A BAD OMEN.
YOU'VE HEARD PEOPLE TALK ABOUT "BREAKING THE THREAD."
IT'S A SYMPTOM OF HOW "ITO" IS FRAGILE AND WEAK!
SSIP
IT'S AN INAUSPICIOUS NAME.
AND YOU SHOULD AVOID SUCH PEOPLE.
BAMM

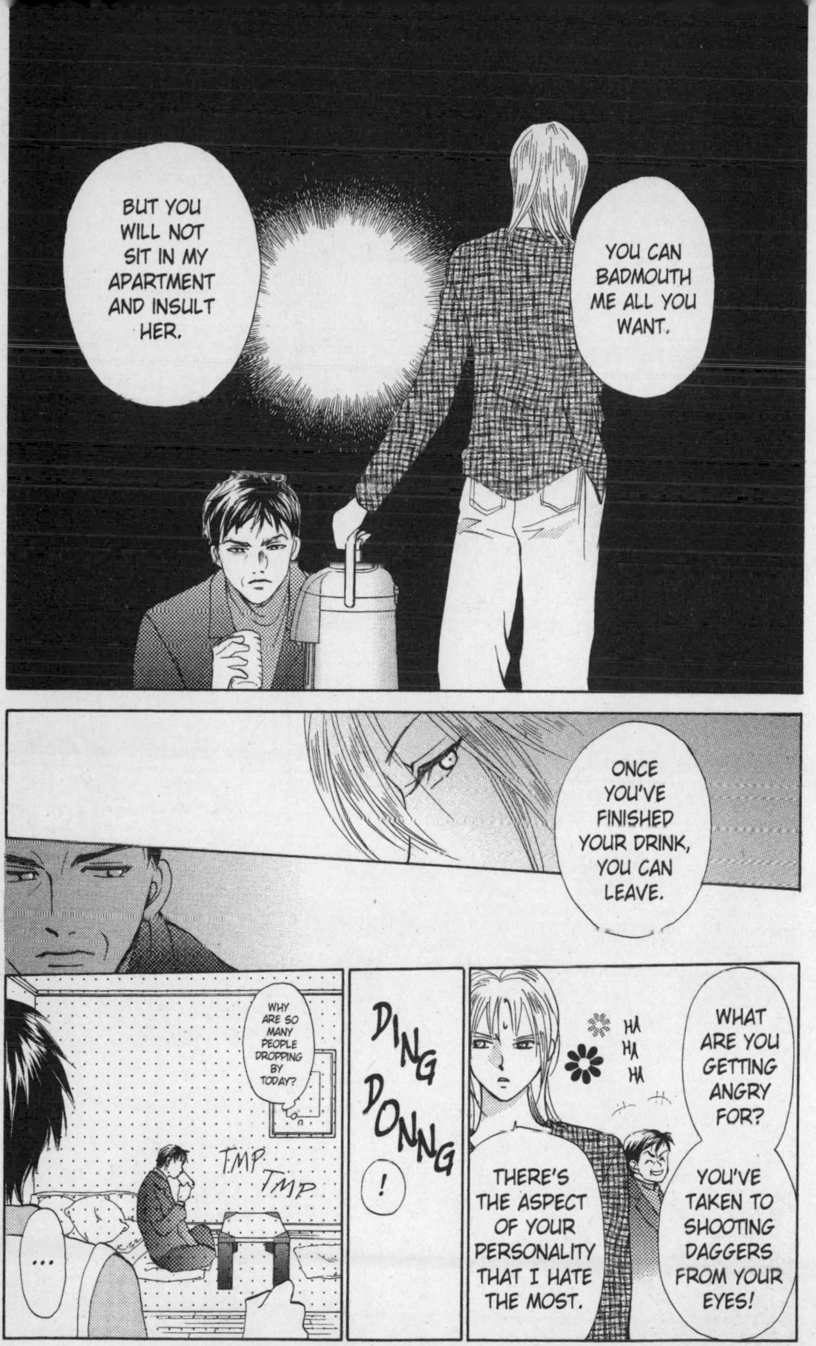
YOU CAN BADMOUTH ME ALL YOU WANT.
BUT YOU WILL NOT SIT IN MY APARTMENT AND INSULT HER.
ONCE YOU'VE FINISHED YOUR DRINK, YOU CAN LEAVE.
WHAT ARE YOU GETTING ANGRY FOR?
HA HA HA
YOU'VE TAKEN TO SHOOTING DAGGERS FROM YOUR EYES!
THERE'S THE ASPECT OF YOUR PERSONALITY THAT I HATE THE MOST.
DING DONNG
!
WHY ARE SO MANY PEOPLE DROPPING BY TODAY?
TMP TMP
...

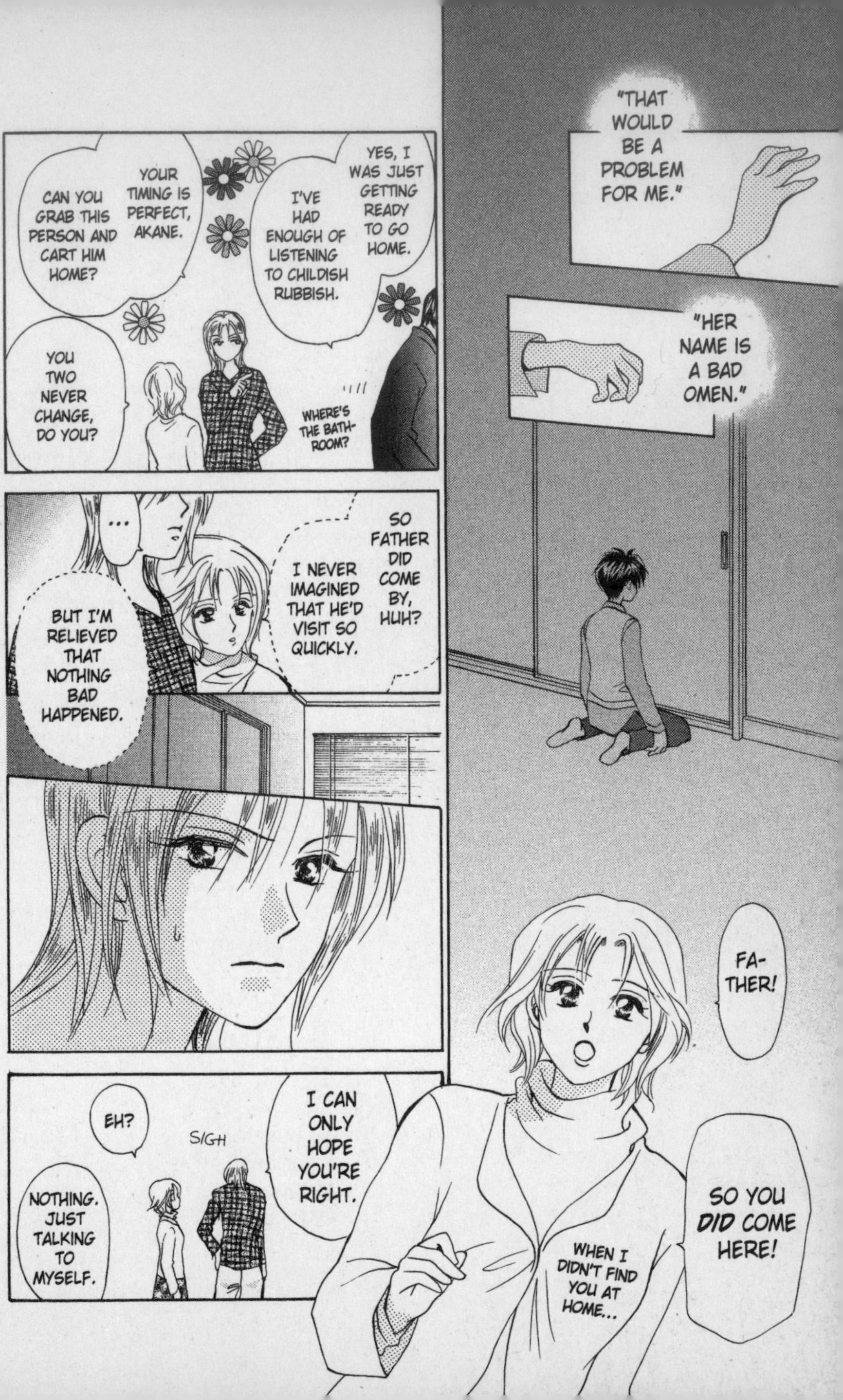
"THAT WOULD BE A PROBLEM FOR ME."
"HER NAME IS A BAD OMEN."
FA-THER!
SO YOU *DID* COME HERE!
WHEN I DIDN'T FIND YOU AT HOME...
YES, I WAS JUST GETTING READY TO GO HOME.
I'VE HAD ENOUGH OF LISTENING TO CHILDISH RUBBISH.
YOUR TIMING IS PERFECT, AKANE.
CAN YOU GRAB THIS PERSON AND CART HIM HOME?
YOU TWO NEVER CHANGE, DO YOU?
WHERE'S THE BATH-ROOM?
SO FATHER DID COME BY, HUH?
I NEVER IMAGINED THAT HE'D VISIT SO QUICKLY.
...
BUT I'M RELIEVED THAT NOTHING BAD HAPPENED.
I CAN ONLY HOPE YOU'RE RIGHT.
SIGH
EH?
NOTHING. JUST TALKING TO MYSELF.

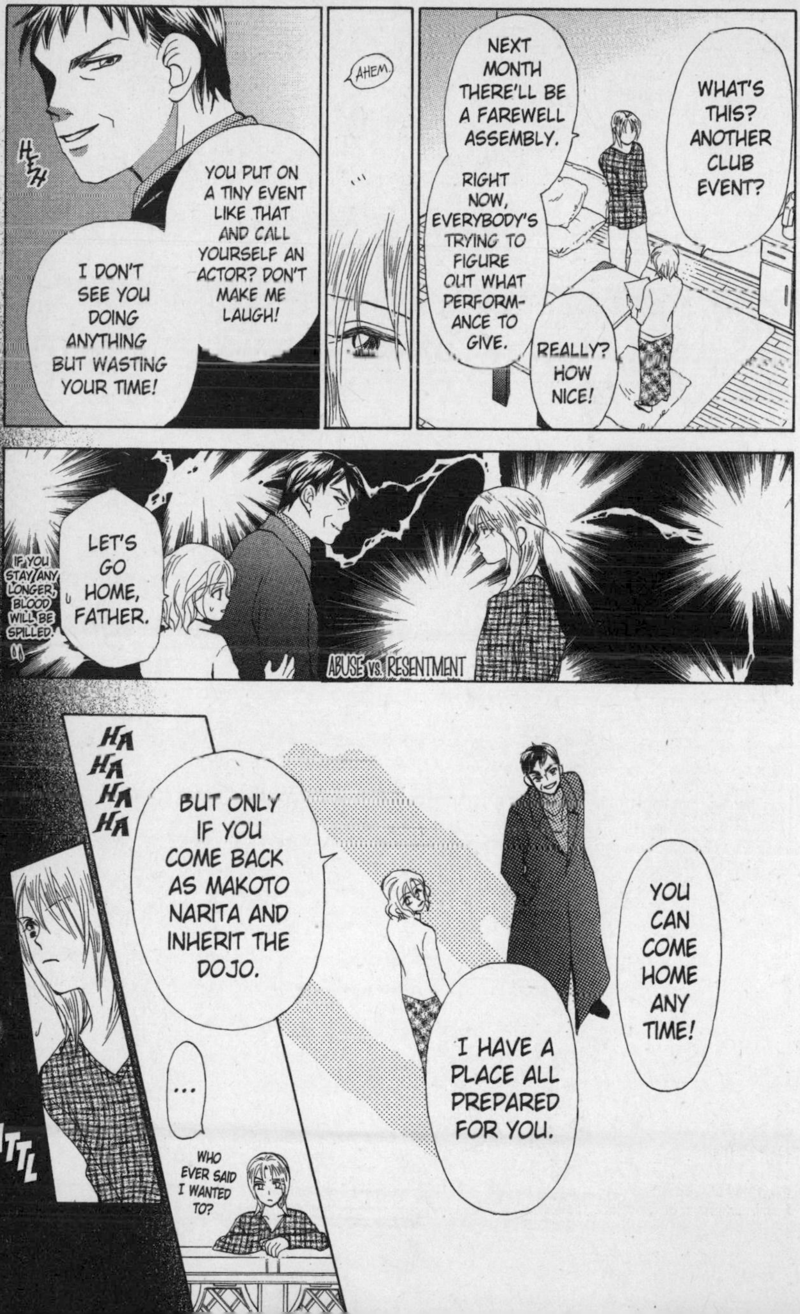

WHAT'S THIS? ANOTHER CLUB EVENT?
NEXT MONTH THERE'LL BE A FAREWELL ASSEMBLY.
RIGHT NOW, EVERYBODY'S TRYING TO FIGURE OUT WHAT PERFORMANCE TO GIVE.
REALLY? HOW NICE!
AHEM.
...
HEH
YOU PUT ON A TINY EVENT LIKE THAT AND CALL YOURSELF AN ACTOR? DON'T MAKE ME LAUGH!
I DON'T SEE YOU DOING ANYTHING BUT WASTING YOUR TIME!
LET'S GO HOME, FATHER.
IF YOU STAY ANY LONGER, BLOOD WILL BE SPILLED.
ABUSE vs. RESENTMENT
YOU CAN COME HOME ANY TIME!
I HAVE A PLACE ALL PREPARED FOR YOU.
BUT ONLY IF YOU COME BACK AS MAKOTO NARITA AND INHERIT THE DOJO.
HA HA HA HA
...
WHO EVER SAID I WANTED TO?
RATTL

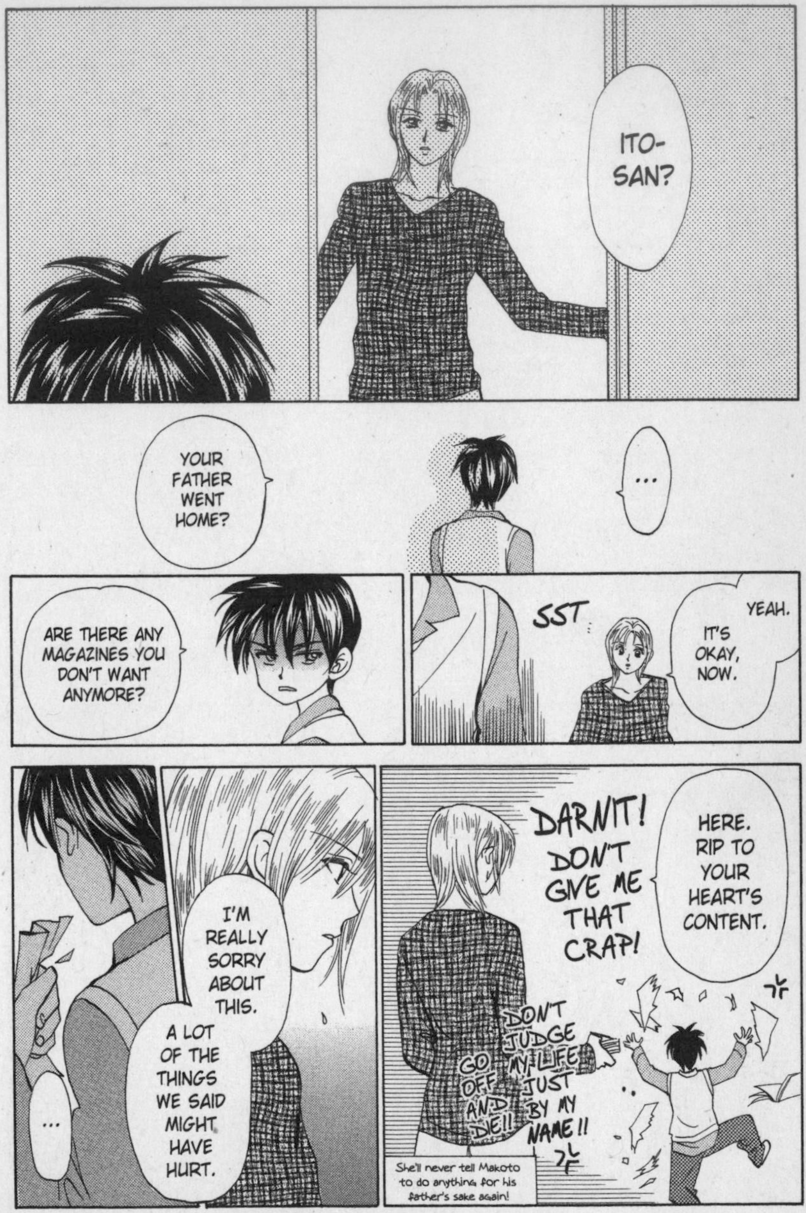
ITO-SAN?
...
YOUR FATHER WENT HOME?
SST
YEAH. IT'S OKAY, NOW.
ARE THERE ANY MAGAZINES YOU DON'T WANT ANYMORE?
HERE. RIP TO YOUR HEART'S CONTENT.
DARNIT! DON'T GIVE ME THAT CRAP!
DON'T JUDGE MY LIFE JUST BY MY NAME!!
GO OFF AND DIE!!
She'll never tell Makoto to do anything for his father's sake again!
I'M REALLY SORRY ABOUT THIS.
A LOT OF THE THINGS WE SAID MIGHT HAVE HURT.
...

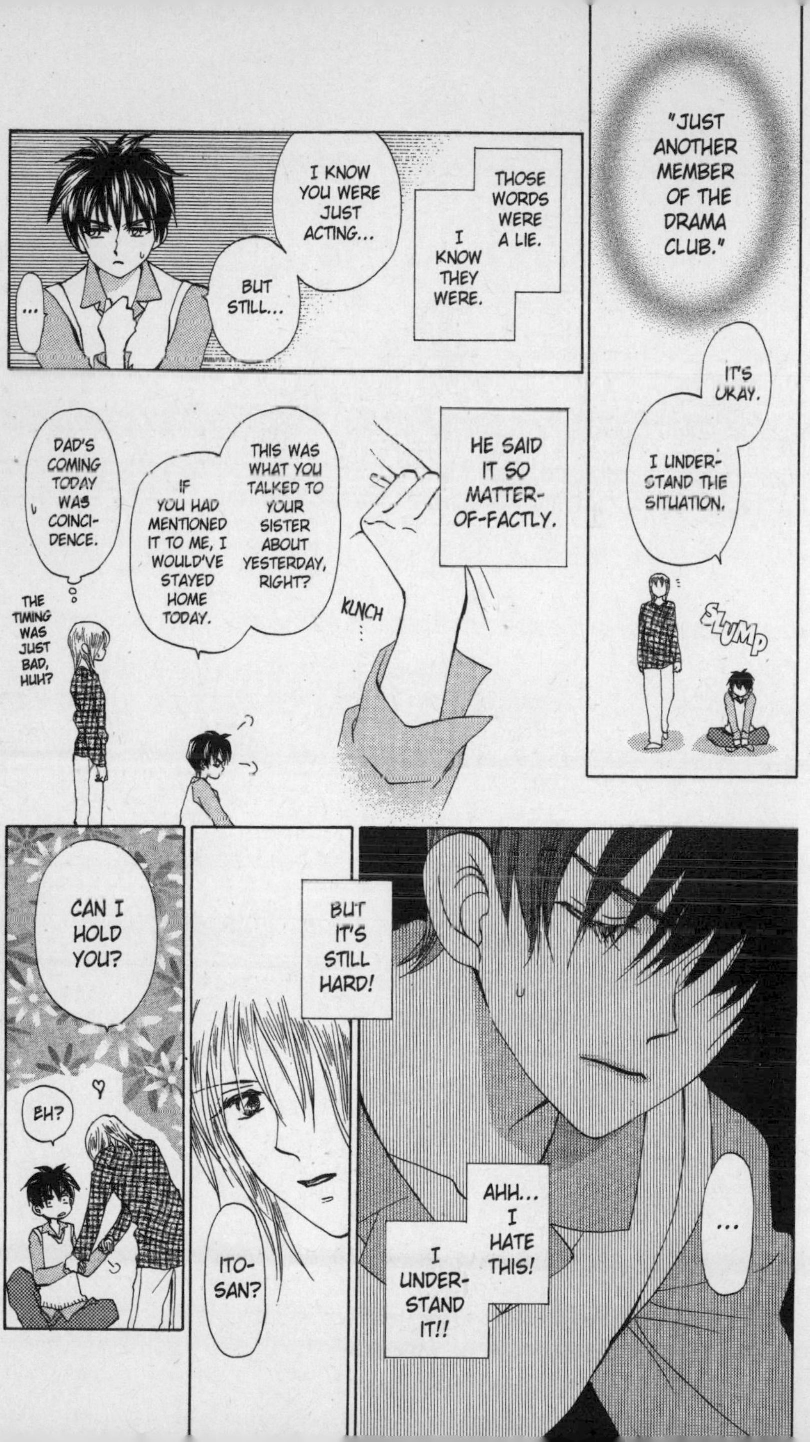
"JUST ANOTHER MEMBER OF THE DRAMA CLUB."
IT'S OKAY.
I UNDERSTAND THE SITUATION.
SLUMP
THOSE WORDS WERE A LIE.
I KNOW THEY WERE.
I KNOW YOU WERE JUST ACTING...
BUT STILL...
...
HE SAID IT SO MATTER-OF-FACTLY.
KUNCH...
THIS WAS WHAT YOU TALKED TO YOUR SISTER ABOUT YESTERDAY, RIGHT?
IF YOU HAD MENTIONED IT TO ME, I WOULD'VE STAYED HOME TODAY.
DAD'S COMING TODAY WAS COINCIDENCE.
THE TIMING WAS JUST BAD, HUH?
...
AHH... I HATE THIS!
I UNDERSTAND IT!!
BUT IT'S STILL HARD!
ITO-SAN?
CAN I HOLD YOU?
EH?

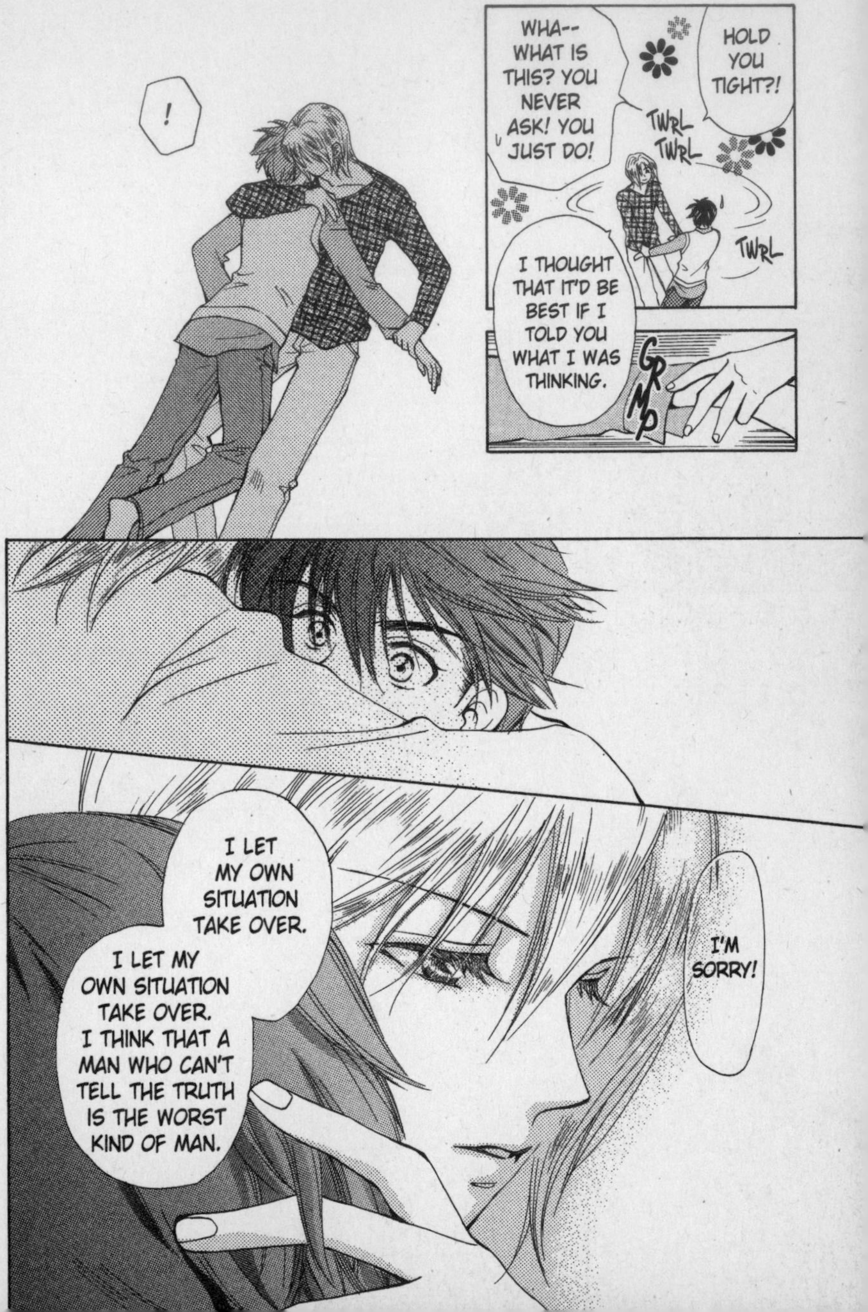
HOLD YOU TIGHT?!
WHA-- WHAT IS THIS? YOU NEVER ASK! YOU JUST DO!
TWRL TWRL
TWRL
I THOUGHT THAT IT'D BE BEST IF I TOLD YOU WHAT I WAS THINKING.
GRMP
!
I'M SORRY!
I LET MY OWN SITUATION TAKE OVER.
I LET MY OWN SITUATION TAKE OVER. I THINK THAT A MAN WHO CAN'T TELL THE TRUTH IS THE WORST KIND OF MAN.

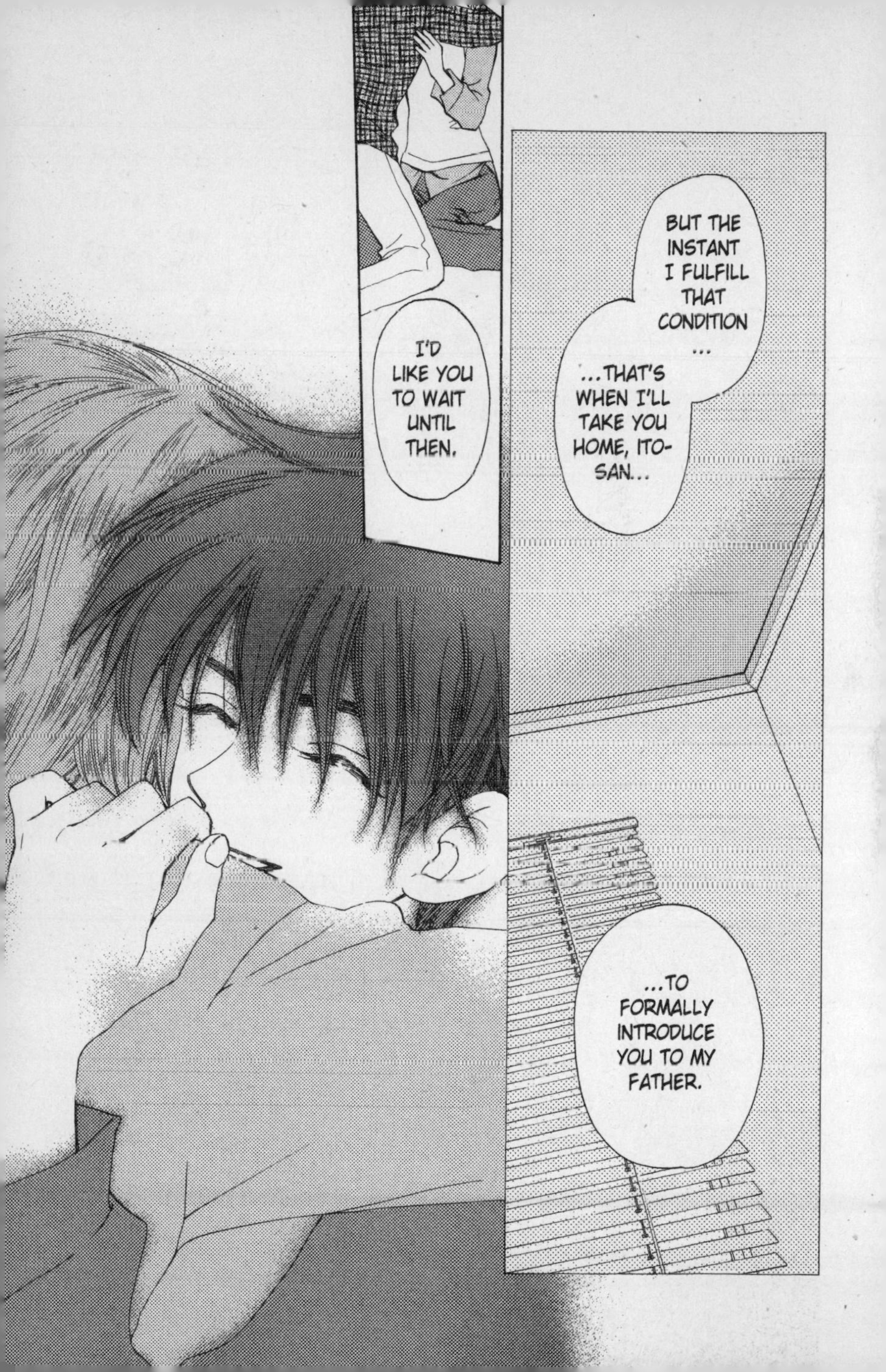
BUT THE INSTANT I FULFILL THAT CONDITION...
...THAT'S WHEN I'LL TAKE YOU HOME, ITO-SAN...
...TO FORMALLY INTRODUCE YOU TO MY FATHER.
I'D LIKE YOU TO WAIT UNTIL THEN.

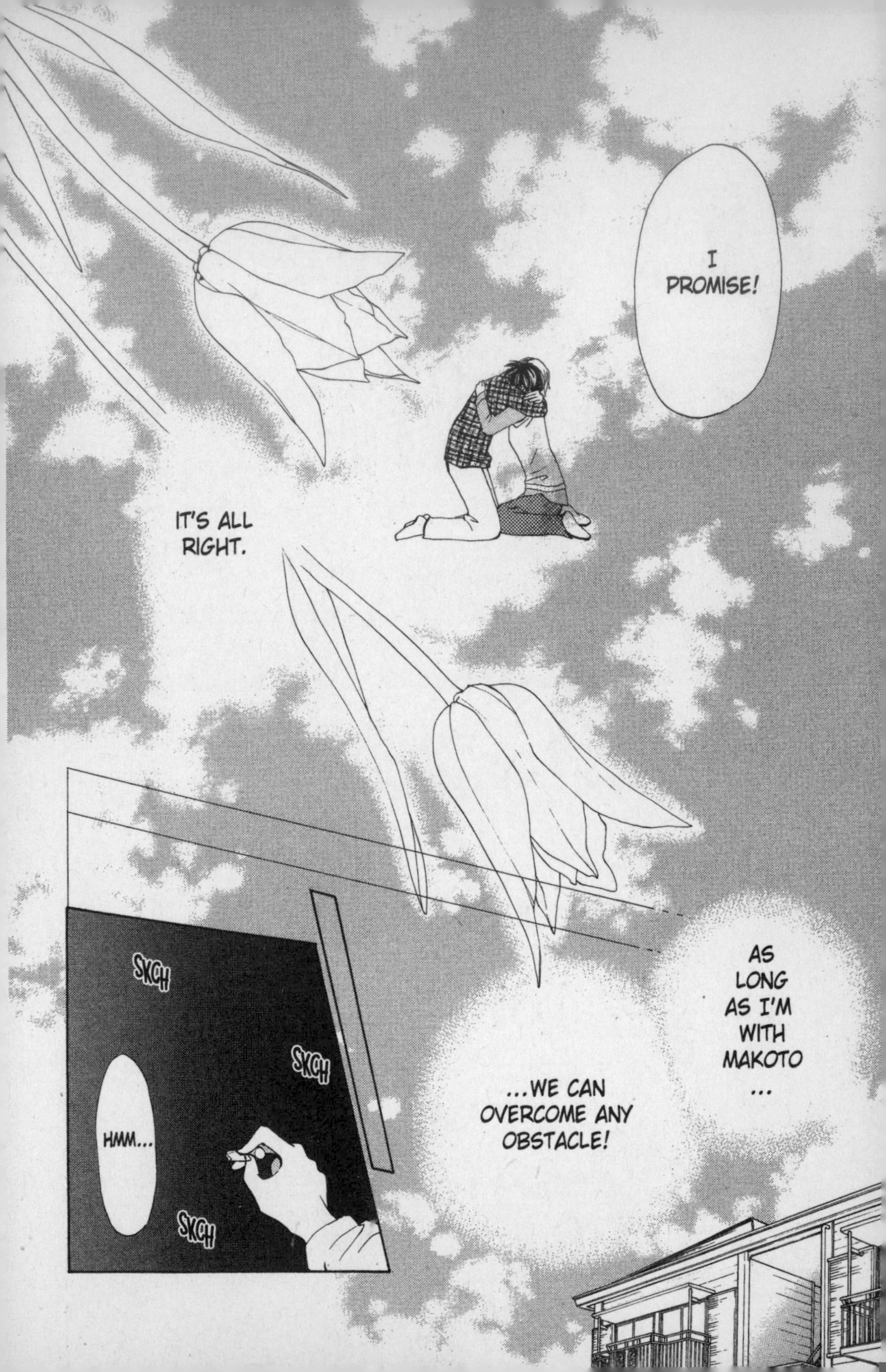
I PROMISE!
IT'S ALL RIGHT.
AS LONG AS I'M WITH MAKOTO ...
...WE CAN OVERCOME ANY OBSTACLE!
SKCH
SKCH
HMM...
SKCH

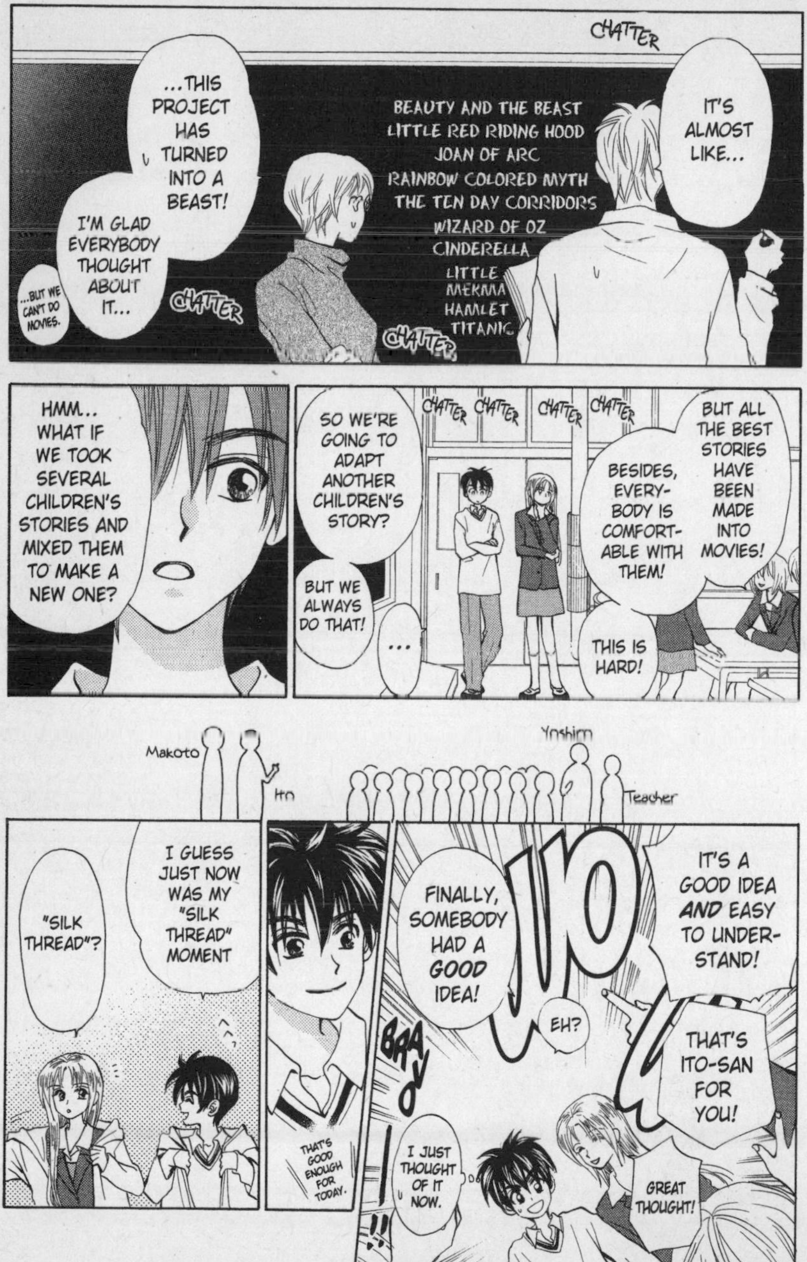
CHATTER
IT'S ALMOST LIKE...
BEAUTY AND THE BEAST
LITTLE RED RIDING HOOD
JOAN OF ARC
RAINBOW COLORED MYTH
THE TEN DAY CORRIDORS
WIZARD OF OZ
CINDERELLA
LITTLE MERMA
HAMLET
TITANIC
...THIS PROJECT HAS TURNED INTO A BEAST!
I'M GLAD EVERYBODY THOUGHT ABOUT IT...
CHATTER
...BUT WE CAN'T DO MOVIES.
CHATTER
CHATTER CHATTER CHATTER CHATTER
BUT ALL THE BEST STORIES HAVE BEEN MADE INTO MOVIES!
BESIDES, EVERYBODY IS COMFORTABLE WITH THEM!
SO WE'RE GOING TO ADAPT ANOTHER CHILDREN'S STORY?
THIS IS HARD!
BUT WE ALWAYS DO THAT!
...
HMM.. WHAT IF WE TOOK SEVERAL CHILDREN'S STORIES AND MIXED THEM TO MAKE A NEW ONE?
Makoto
Ito
Yoshiro
Teacher
IT'S A GOOD IDEA AND EASY TO UNDERSTAND!
FINALLY, SOMEBODY HAD A GOOD IDEA!
EH?
THAT'S ITO-SAN FOR YOU!
BRAVO
GREAT THOUGHT!
I JUST THOUGHT OF IT NOW.
THAT'S GOOD ENOUGH FOR TODAY.
I GUESS JUST NOW WAS MY "SILK THREAD" MOMENT
"SILK THREAD"?

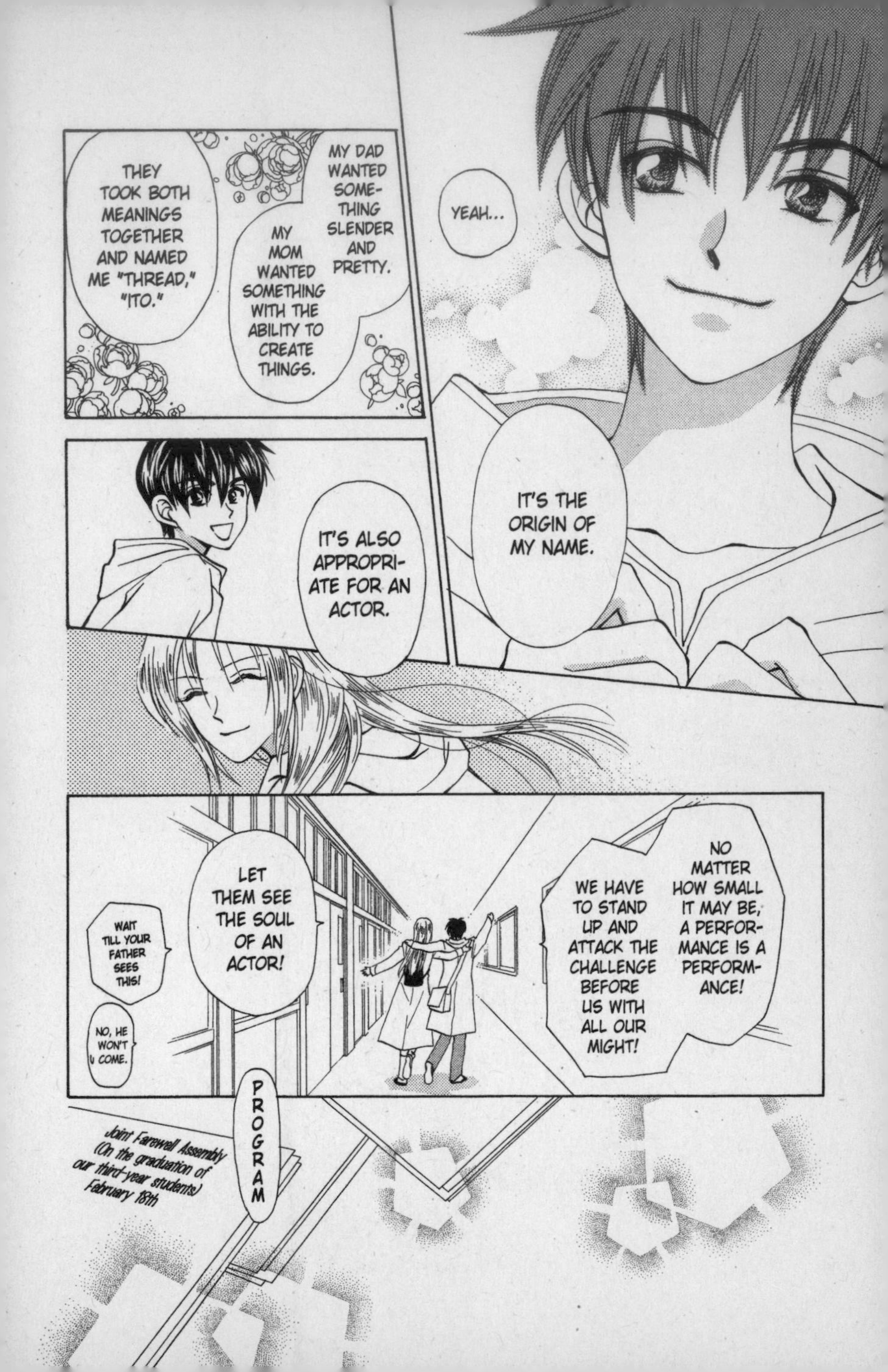
YEAH...
IT'S THE ORIGIN OF MY NAME.
MY DAD WANTED SOME-THING SLENDER AND PRETTY.
MY MOM WANTED SOMETHING WITH THE ABILITY TO CREATE THINGS.
THEY TOOK BOTH MEANINGS TOGETHER AND NAMED ME "THREAD," "ITO."
IT'S ALSO APPROPRI-ATE FOR AN ACTOR.
NO MATTER HOW SMALL IT MAY BE, A PERFOR-MANCE IS A PERFORM-ANCE!
WE HAVE TO STAND UP AND ATTACK THE CHALLENGE BEFORE US WITH ALL OUR MIGHT!
LET THEM SEE THE SOUL OF AN ACTOR!
WAIT TILL YOUR FATHER SEES THIS!
NO, HE WON'T COME.
PROGRAM
Joint Farewell Assembly (On the graduation of our third-year students) February 18th

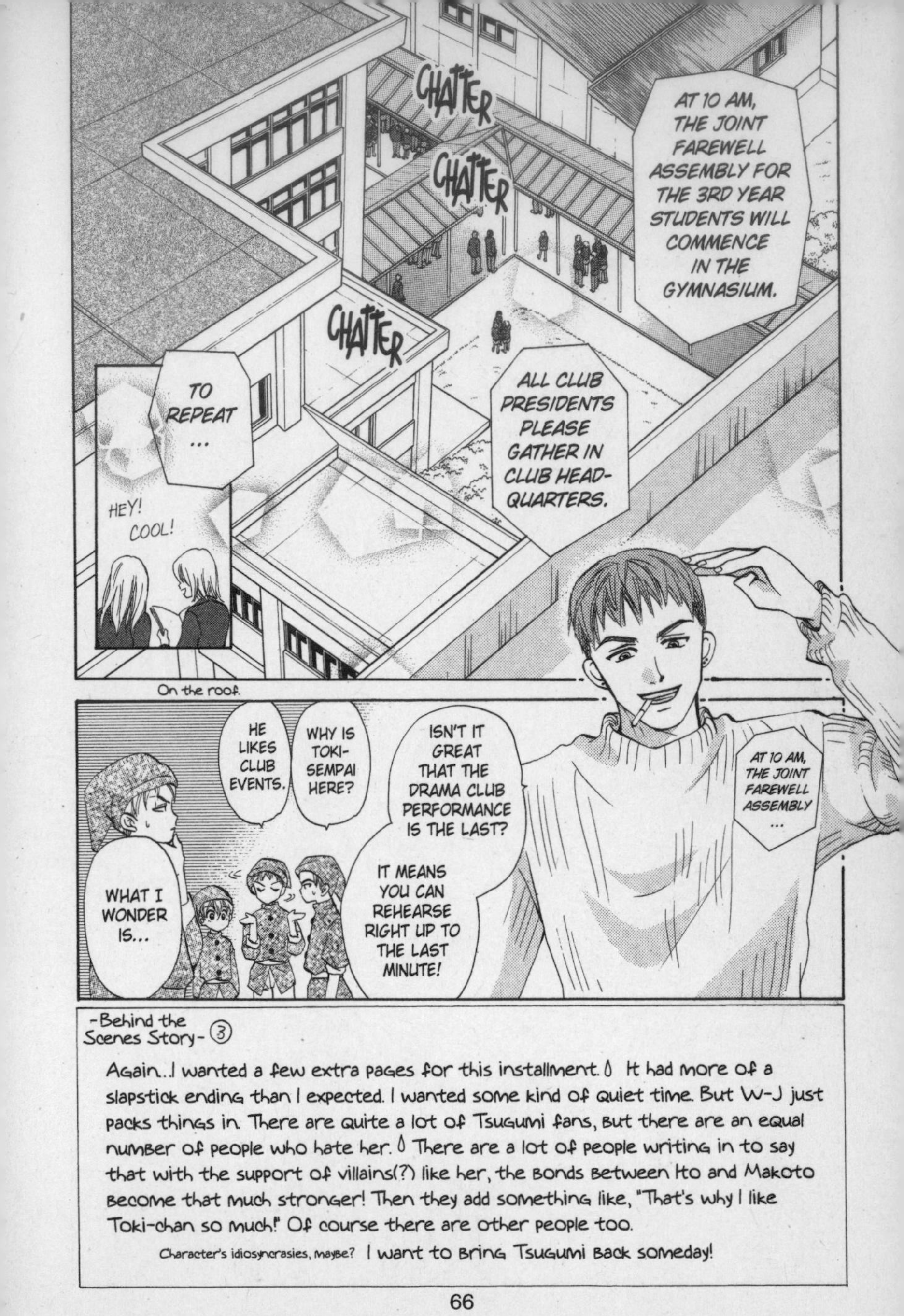
CHATTER
CHATTER
CHATTER
AT 10 AM, THE JOINT FAREWELL ASSEMBLY FOR THE 3RD YEAR STUDENTS WILL COMMENCE IN THE GYMNASIUM.
ALL CLUB PRESIDENTS PLEASE GATHER IN CLUB HEAD-QUARTERS.
TO REPEAT ...
HEY! COOL!
On the roof.
AT 10 AM, THE JOINT FAREWELL ASSEMBLY ...
ISN'T IT GREAT THAT THE DRAMA CLUB PERFORMANCE IS THE LAST?
IT MEANS YOU CAN REHEARSE RIGHT UP TO THE LAST MINUTE!
WHY IS TOKI-SEMPAI HERE?
HE LIKES CLUB EVENTS.
WHAT I WONDER IS...

-Behind the Scenes Story- ③

Again...I wanted a few extra pages for this installment. It had more of a slapstick ending than I expected. I wanted some kind of quiet time. But W-J just packs things in. There are quite a lot of Tsugumi fans, but there are an equal number of people who hate her. There are a lot of people writing in to say that with the support of villains(?) like her, the bonds between Ito and Makoto become that much stronger! Then they add something like, "That's why I like Toki-chan so much!" Of course there are other people too.

Character's idiosyncrasies, maybe? I want to bring Tsugumi back someday!

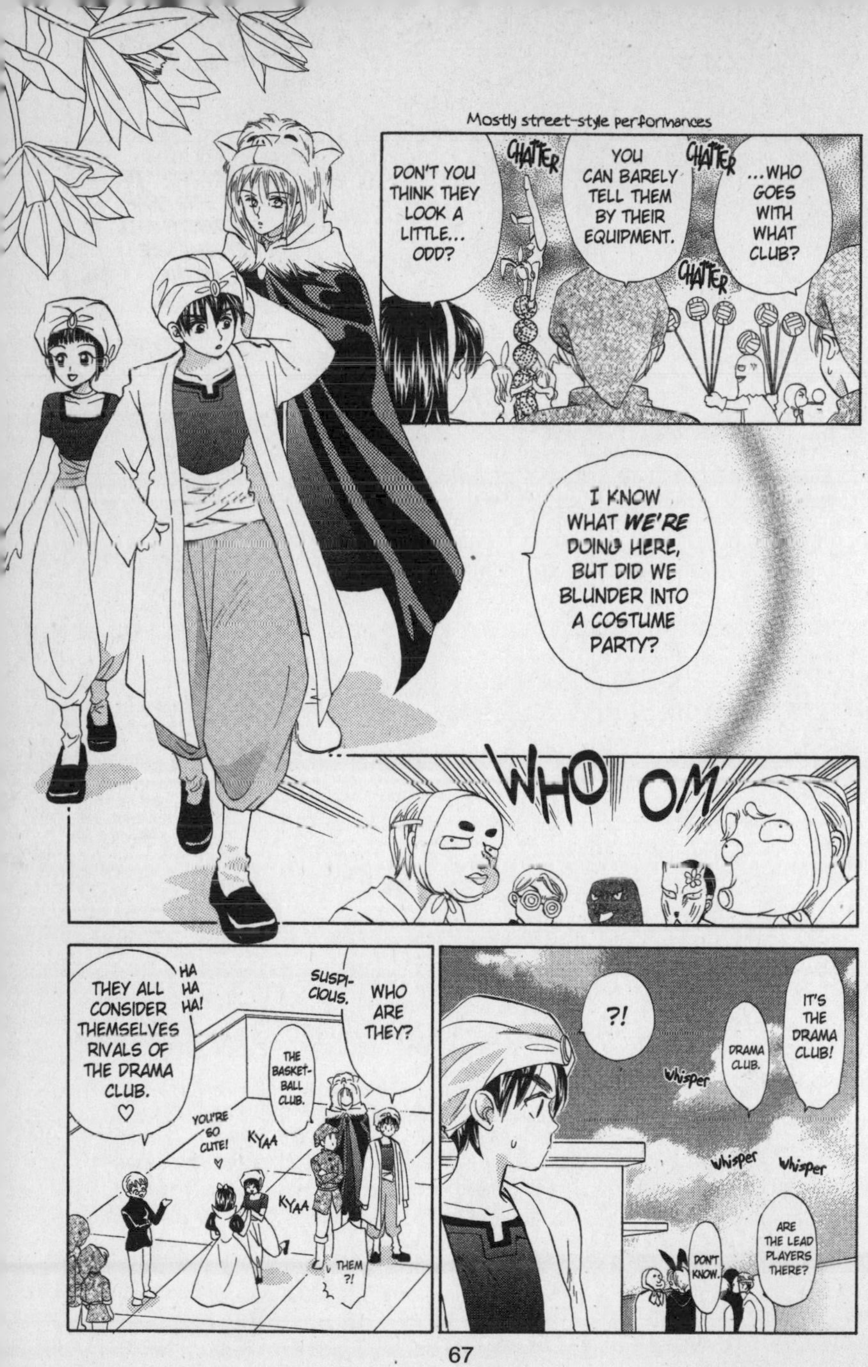
Mostly street-style performances
...WHO GOES WITH WHAT CLUB?
CHATTER
YOU CAN BARELY TELL THEM BY THEIR EQUIPMENT.
CHATTER
DON'T YOU THINK THEY LOOK A LITTLE... ODD?
CHATTER
I KNOW WHAT *WE'RE* DOING HERE, BUT DID WE BLUNDER INTO A COSTUME PARTY?
WHOOM
IT'S THE DRAMA CLUB!
DRAMA CLUB.
?!
Whisper
ARE THE LEAD PLAYERS THERE?
Whisper
Whisper
DON'T KNOW.
WHO ARE THEY?
SUSPI-CIOUS.
THE BASKET-BALL CLUB.
HA HA HA!
THEY ALL CONSIDER THEMSELVES RIVALS OF THE DRAMA CLUB. ♡
KYAA
YOU'RE SO CUTE! ♡
KYAA
THEM ?!

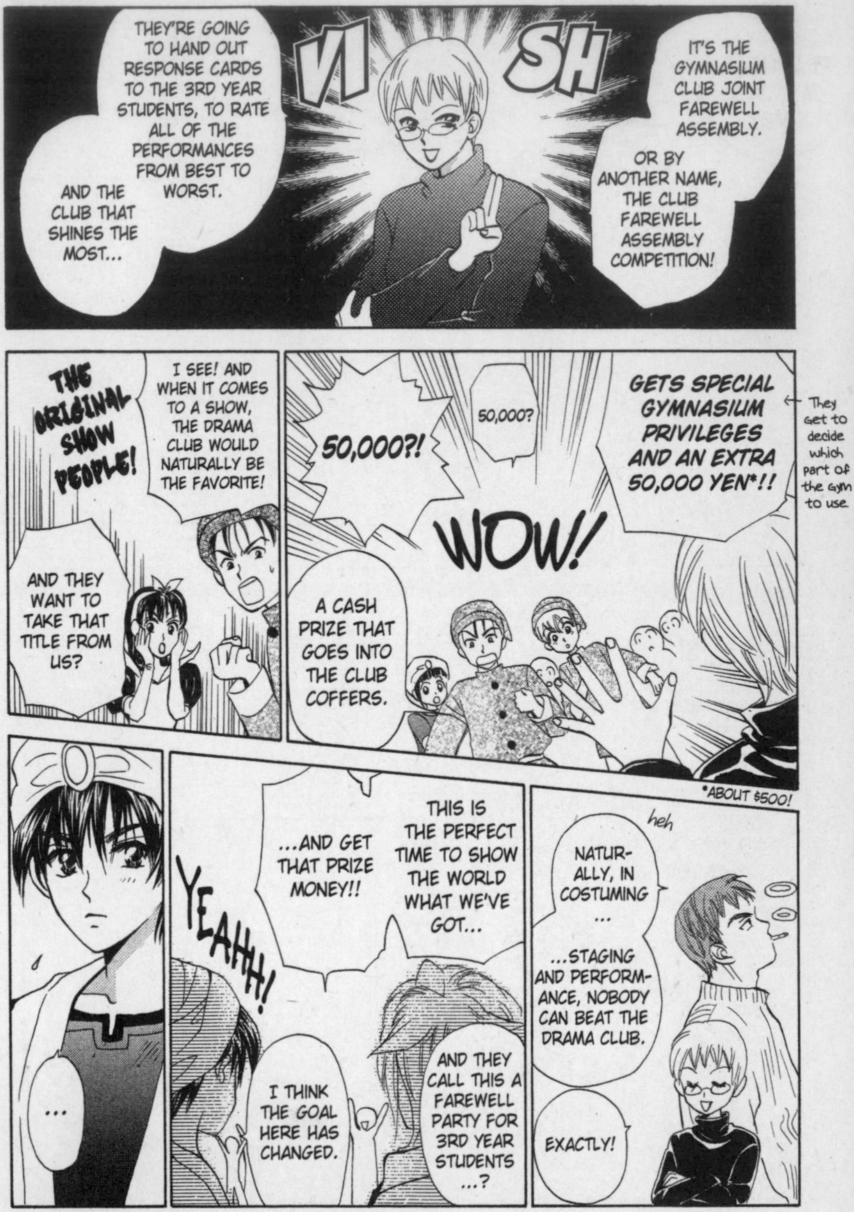
IT'S THE GYMNASIUM CLUB JOINT FAREWELL ASSEMBLY.
OR BY ANOTHER NAME, THE CLUB FAREWELL ASSEMBLY COMPETITION!
SH
VI
THEY'RE GOING TO HAND OUT RESPONSE CARDS TO THE 3RD YEAR STUDENTS, TO RATE ALL OF THE PERFORMANCES FROM BEST TO WORST.
AND THE CLUB THAT SHINES THE MOST...
GETS SPECIAL GYMNASIUM PRIVILEGES AND AN EXTRA 50,000 YEN*!!
They get to decide which part of the Gym to use.
50,000?
50,000?!
WOW!
A CASH PRIZE THAT GOES INTO THE CLUB COFFERS.
I SEE! AND WHEN IT COMES TO A SHOW, THE DRAMA CLUB WOULD NATURALLY BE THE FAVORITE!
THE ORIGINAL SHOW PEOPLE!
AND THEY WANT TO TAKE THAT TITLE FROM US?
*ABOUT $500!
heh
NATURALLY, IN COSTUMING ...
...STAGING AND PERFORMANCE, NOBODY CAN BEAT THE DRAMA CLUB.
EXACTLY!
THIS IS THE PERFECT TIME TO SHOW THE WORLD WHAT WE'VE GOT...
...AND GET THAT PRIZE MONEY!!
YEAHHH!
AND THEY CALL THIS A FAREWELL PARTY FOR 3RD YEAR STUDENTS ...?
I THINK THE GOAL HERE HAS CHANGED.
...

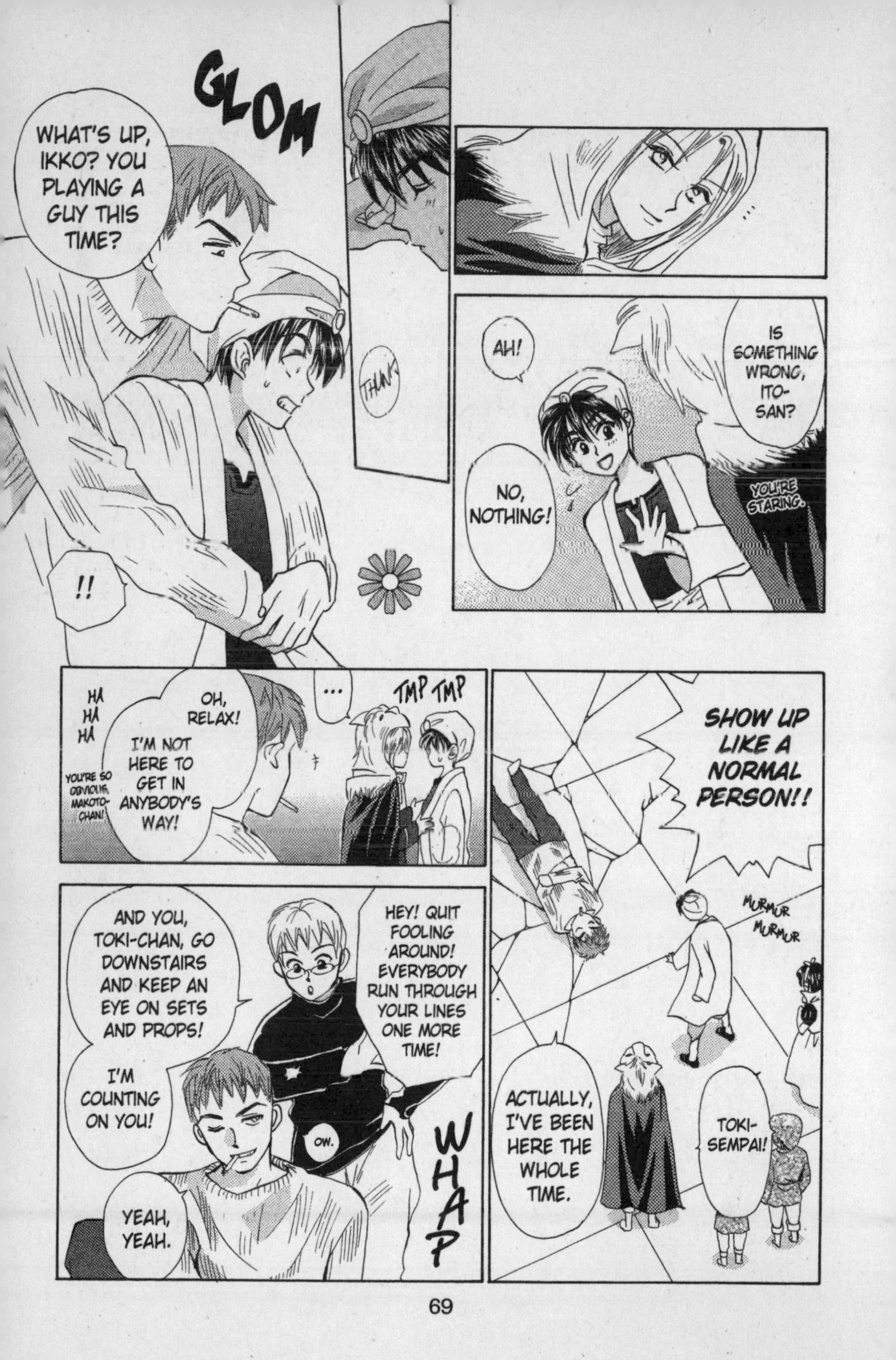
...
IS SOMETHING WRONG, ITO-SAN?
AH!
NO, NOTHING!
YOU'RE STARING.
THUNK
GLOM
WHAT'S UP, IKKO? YOU PLAYING A GUY THIS TIME?
!!
SHOW UP LIKE A NORMAL PERSON!!
MURMUR MURMUR
TOKI-SEMPAI!
ACTUALLY, I'VE BEEN HERE THE WHOLE TIME.
TMP TMP
...
OH, RELAX! I'M NOT HERE TO GET IN ANYBODY'S WAY!
HA HA HA
YOU'RE SO OBVIOUS, MAKOTO-CHAN!
HEY! QUIT FOOLING AROUND! EVERYBODY RUN THROUGH YOUR LINES ONE MORE TIME!
AND YOU, TOKI-CHAN, GO DOWNSTAIRS AND KEEP AN EYE ON SETS AND PROPS!
I'M COUNTING ON YOU!
OW.
WHAP
YEAH, YEAH.

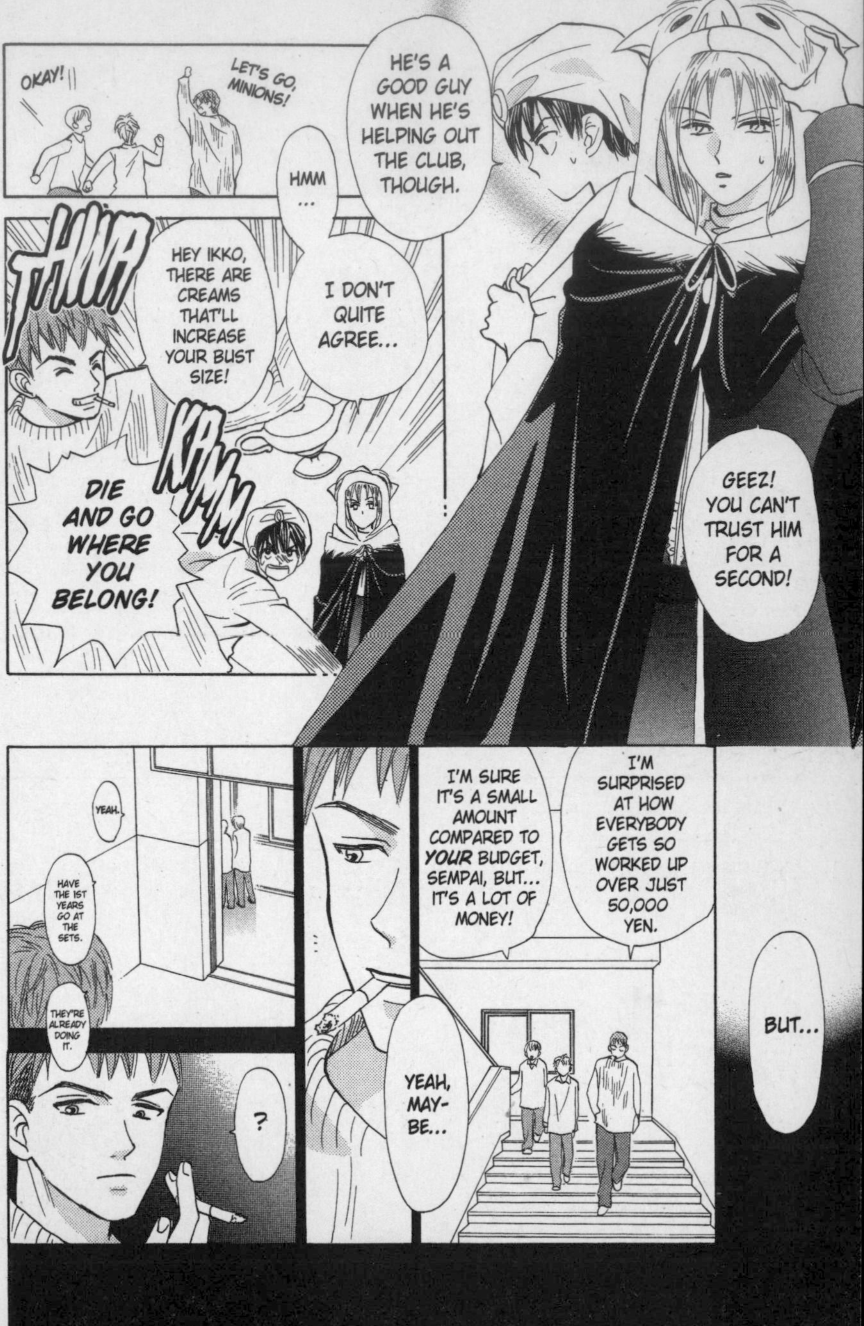
GEEZ! YOU CAN'T TRUST HIM FOR A SECOND!
HE'S A GOOD GUY WHEN HE'S HELPING OUT THE CLUB, THOUGH.
HMM...
I DON'T QUITE AGREE...
LET'S GO, MINIONS!
OKAY!
HEY IKKO, THERE ARE CREAMS THAT'LL INCREASE YOUR BUST SIZE!
THWAP
KRAM
DIE AND GO WHERE YOU BELONG!
I'M SURPRISED AT HOW EVERYBODY GETS SO WORKED UP OVER JUST 50,000 YEN.
I'M SURE IT'S A SMALL AMOUNT COMPARED TO *YOUR* BUDGET, SEMPAI, BUT... IT'S A LOT OF MONEY!
YEAH, MAY-BE...
BUT...
YEAH.
HAVE THE 1ST YEARS GO AT THE SETS.
THEY'RE ALREADY DOING IT.
?

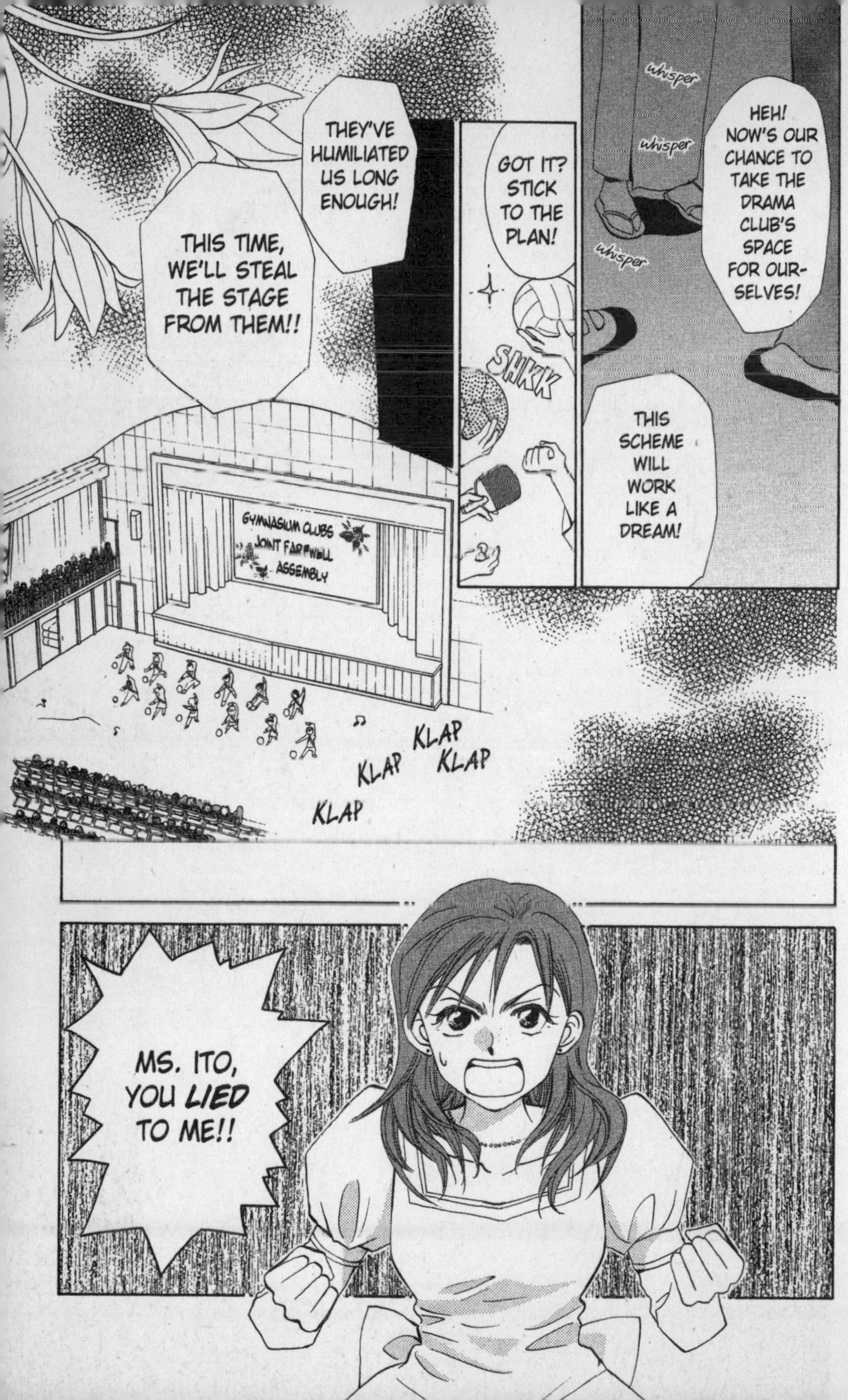
whisper
whisper
whisper
HEH! NOW'S OUR CHANCE TO TAKE THE DRAMA CLUB'S SPACE FOR OUR-SELVES!
THIS SCHEME WILL WORK LIKE A DREAM!
GOT IT? STICK TO THE PLAN!
SHKK
THEY'VE HUMILIATED US LONG ENOUGH!
THIS TIME, WE'LL STEAL THE STAGE FROM THEM!!
GYMNASIUM CLUBS JOINT FAREWELL ASSEMBLY
KLAP
KLAP
KLAP
KLAP
MS. ITO, YOU *LIED* TO ME!!

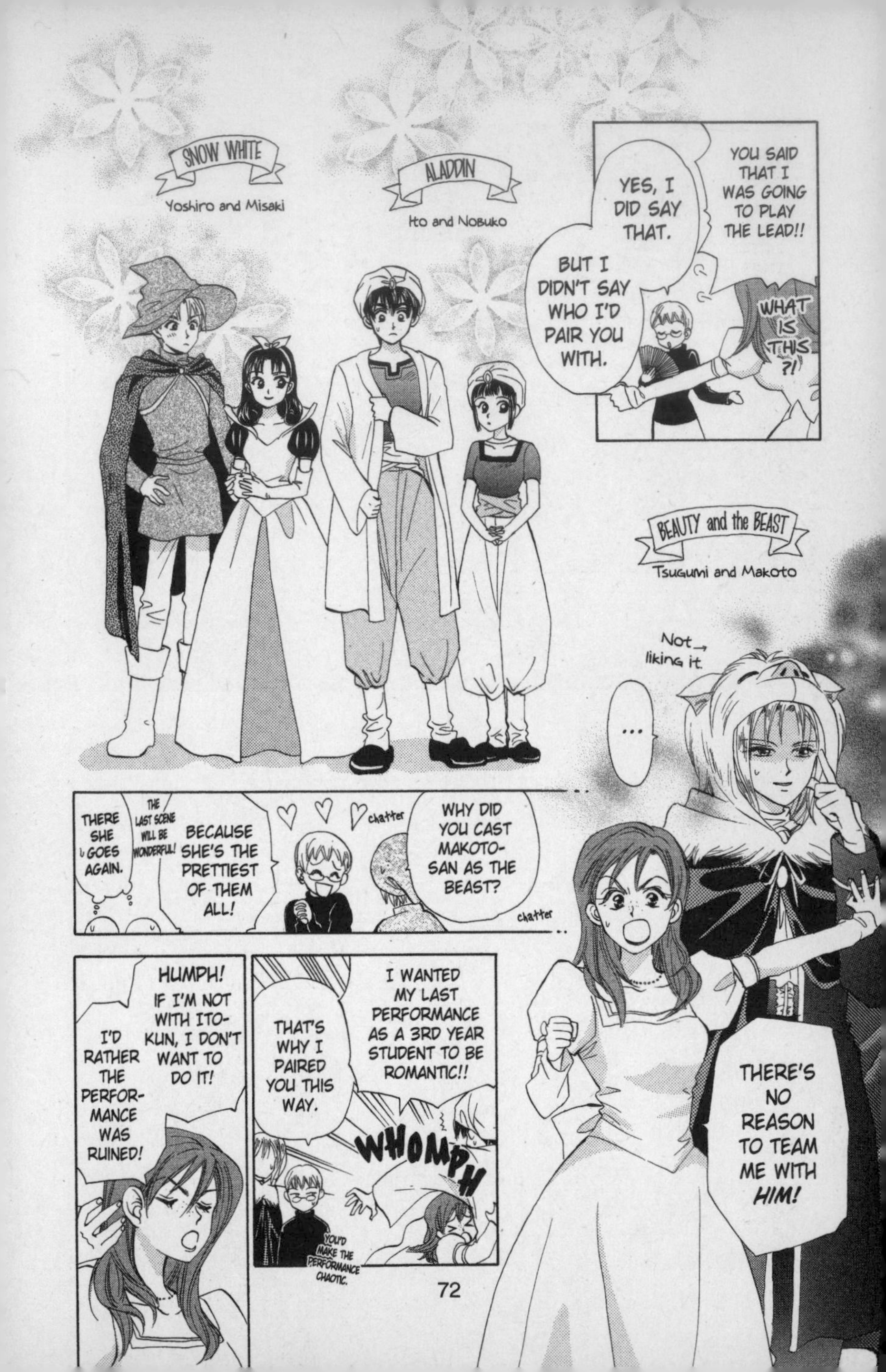

YOU SAID THAT I WAS GOING TO PLAY THE LEAD!!
WHAT IS THIS?!
YES, I DID SAY THAT.
BUT I DIDN'T SAY WHO I'D PAIR YOU WITH.
SNOW WHITE
Yoshiro and Misaki
ALADDIN
Ito and Nobuko
BEAUTY and the BEAST
Tsugumi and Makoto
Not liking it
...
THERE'S NO REASON TO TEAM ME WITH *HIM!*
WHY DID YOU CAST MAKOTO-SAN AS THE BEAST?
chatter
chatter
BECAUSE SHE'S THE PRETTIEST OF THEM ALL!
THE LAST SCENE WILL BE WONDERFUL!
THERE SHE GOES AGAIN.
I WANTED MY LAST PERFORMANCE AS A 3RD YEAR STUDENT TO BE ROMANTIC!!
THAT'S WHY I PAIRED YOU THIS WAY.
WHOMPH
YOU'D MAKE THE PERFORMANCE CHAOTIC.
HUMPH! IF I'M NOT WITH ITO-KUN, I DON'T WANT TO DO IT!
I'D RATHER THE PERFORMANCE WAS RUINED!

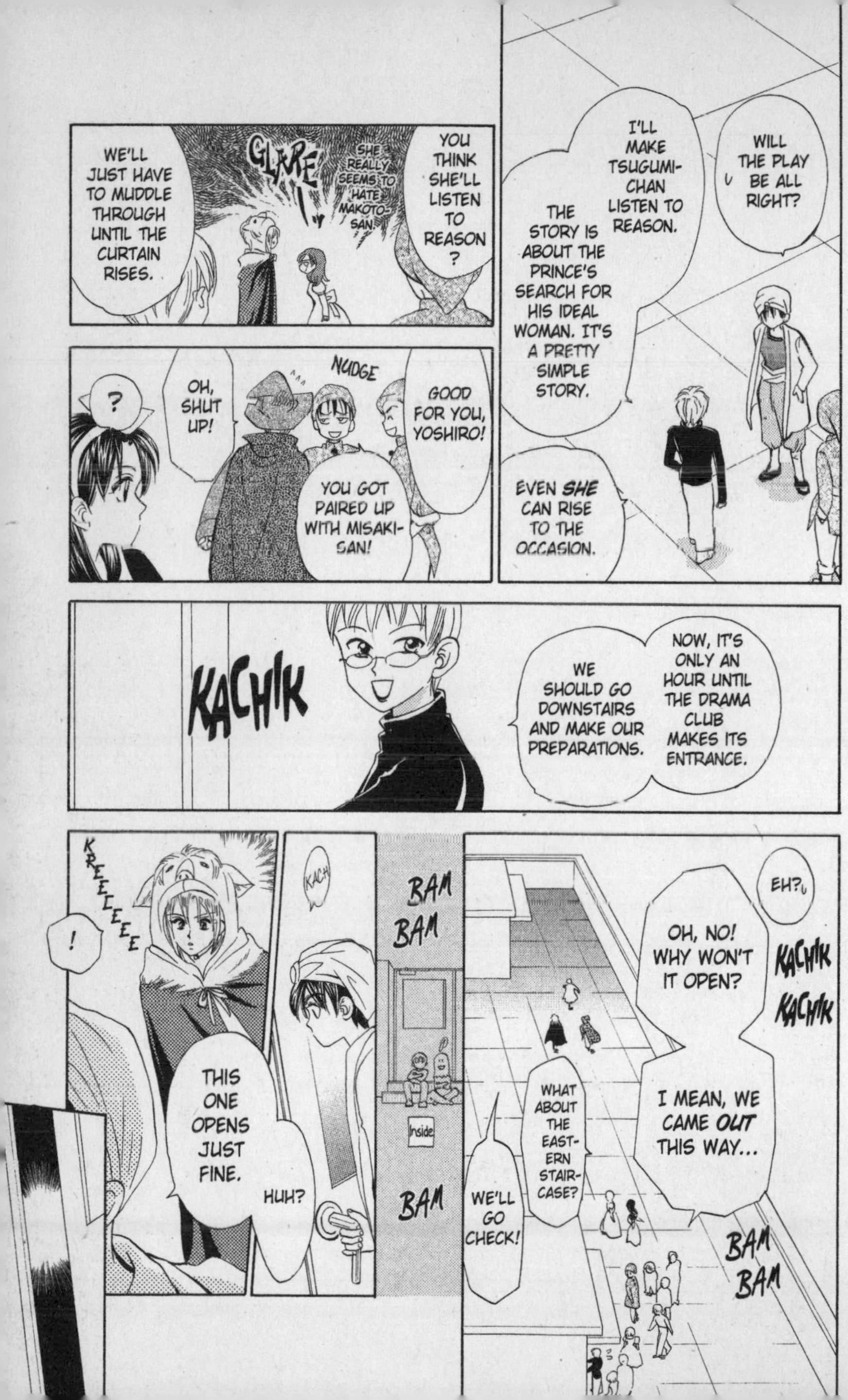
WILL THE PLAY BE ALL RIGHT?
I'LL MAKE TSUGUMI-CHAN LISTEN TO REASON.
THE STORY IS ABOUT THE PRINCE'S SEARCH FOR HIS IDEAL WOMAN. IT'S A PRETTY SIMPLE STORY.
EVEN SHE CAN RISE TO THE OCCASION.
YOU THINK SHE'LL LISTEN TO REASON?
SHE REALLY SEEMS TO HATE MAKOTO-SAN.
GLARE
WE'LL JUST HAVE TO MUDDLE THROUGH UNTIL THE CURTAIN RISES.
GOOD FOR YOU, YOSHIRO!
YOU GOT PAIRED UP WITH MISAKI-SAN!
NUDGE
OH, SHUT UP!
?
NOW, IT'S ONLY AN HOUR UNTIL THE DRAMA CLUB MAKES ITS ENTRANCE.
WE SHOULD GO DOWNSTAIRS AND MAKE OUR PREPARATIONS.
KACHIK
EH?
OH, NO! WHY WON'T IT OPEN?
KACHIK KACHIK
I MEAN, WE CAME OUT THIS WAY...
WHAT ABOUT THE EASTERN STAIRCASE?
WE'LL GO CHECK!
BAM BAM
BAM BAM
Inside
BAM
KACH
THIS ONE OPENS JUST FINE.
HUH?
KREEEEEE
!

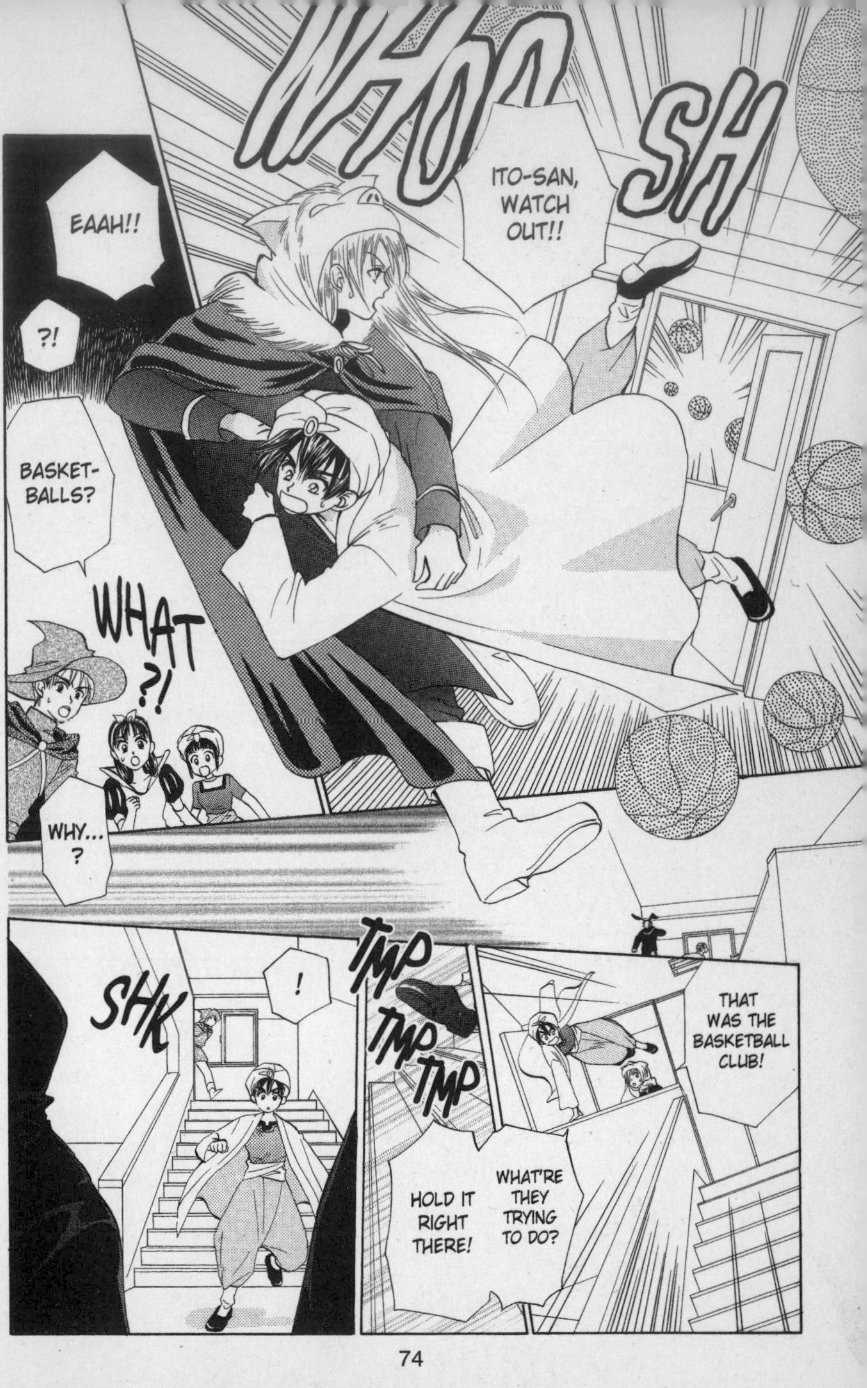
WHOOSH
ITO-SAN, WATCH OUT!!
EAAH!!
?!
BASKET-BALLS?
WHAT?!
WHY...?
THAT WAS THE BASKETBALL CLUB!
TMP TMP TMP
WHAT'RE THEY TRYING TO DO?
HOLD IT RIGHT THERE!
!
SHK

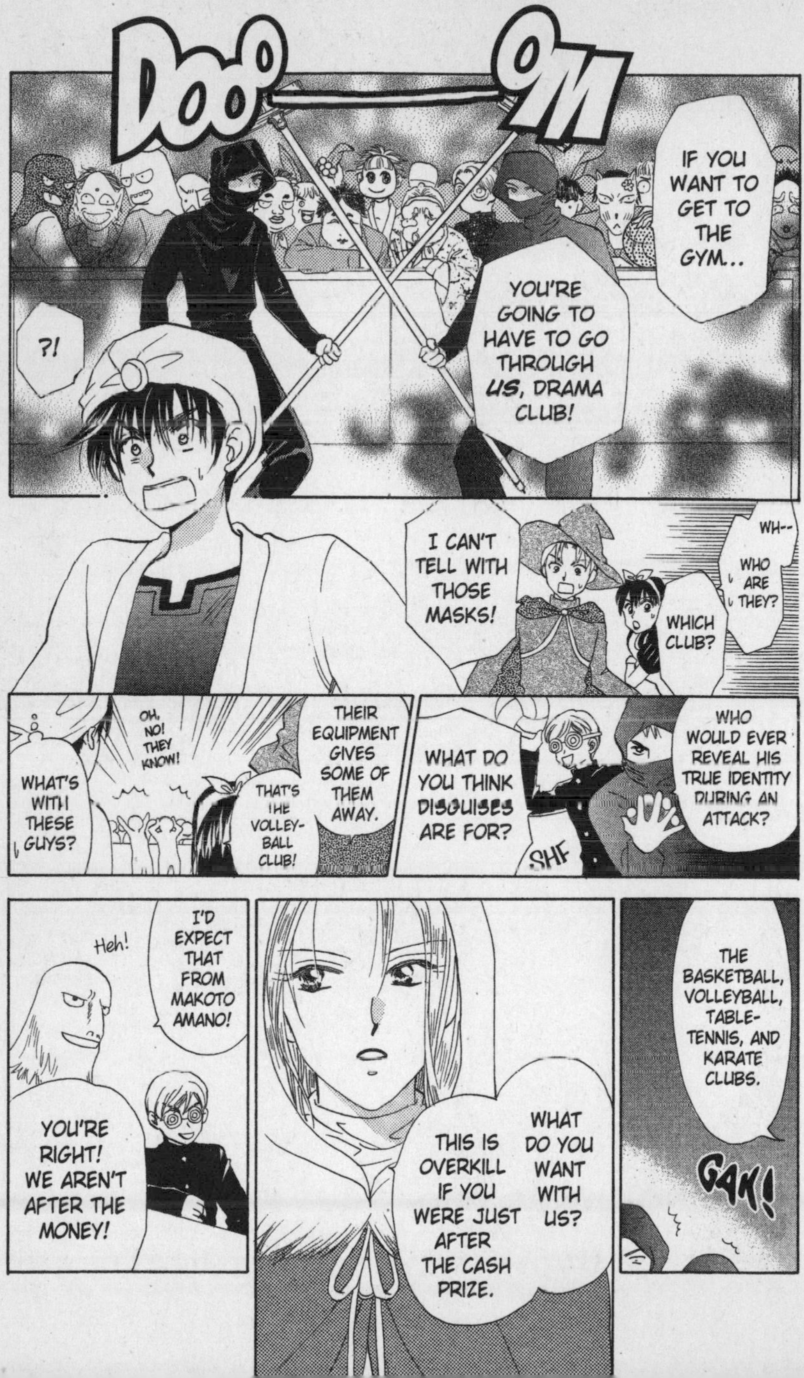
DOOOOM
IF YOU WANT TO GET TO THE GYM..
YOU'RE GOING TO HAVE TO GO THROUGH US, DRAMA CLUB!
?!
WH-- WHO ARE THEY?
WHICH CLUB?
I CAN'T TELL WITH THOSE MASKS!
WHO WOULD EVER REVEAL HIS TRUE IDENTITY DURING AN ATTACK?
WHAT DO YOU THINK DISGUISES ARE FOR?
SHF
THEIR EQUIPMENT GIVES SOME OF THEM AWAY.
THAT'S THE VOLLEY-BALL CLUB!
OH, NO! THEY KNOW!
WHAT'S WITH THESE GUYS?
THE BASKETBALL, VOLLEYBALL, TABLE-TENNIS, AND KARATE CLUBS.
GAK!
WHAT DO YOU WANT WITH US?
THIS IS OVERKILL IF YOU WERE JUST AFTER THE CASH PRIZE.
I'D EXPECT THAT FROM MAKOTO AMANO!
Heh!
YOU'RE RIGHT! WE AREN'T AFTER THE MONEY!

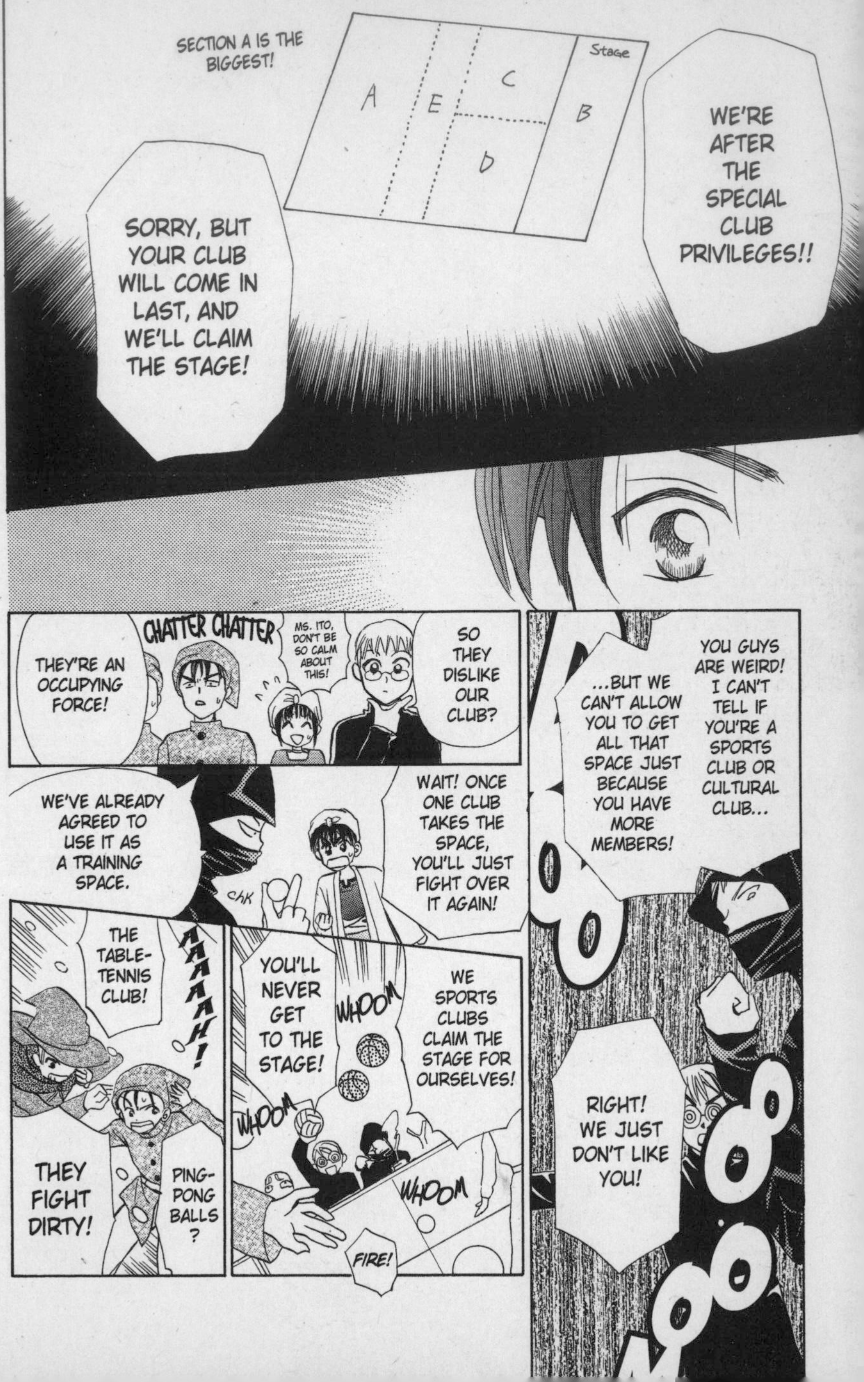
SECTION A IS THE BIGGEST!
Stage
C
A
E
B
D
WE'RE AFTER THE SPECIAL CLUB PRIVILEGES!!
SORRY, BUT YOUR CLUB WILL COME IN LAST, AND WE'LL CLAIM THE STAGE!
YOU GUYS ARE WEIRD! I CAN'T TELL IF YOU'RE A SPORTS CLUB OR CULTURAL CLUB...
...BUT WE CAN'T ALLOW YOU TO GET ALL THAT SPACE JUST BECAUSE YOU HAVE MORE MEMBERS!
RIGHT! WE JUST DON'T LIKE YOU!
SO THEY DISLIKE OUR CLUB?
MS. ITO, DON'T BE SO CALM ABOUT THIS!
CHATTER CHATTER
THEY'RE AN OCCUPYING FORCE!
WAIT! ONCE ONE CLUB TAKES THE SPACE, YOU'LL JUST FIGHT OVER IT AGAIN!
WE'VE ALREADY AGREED TO USE IT AS A TRAINING SPACE.
ChK
WE SPORTS CLUBS CLAIM THE STAGE FOR OURSELVES!
YOU'LL NEVER GET TO THE STAGE!
WHOOM
WHOOM
WHOOM
FIRE!
AAAAAAH!
THE TABLE-TENNIS CLUB!
PING-PONG BALLS?
THEY FIGHT DIRTY!

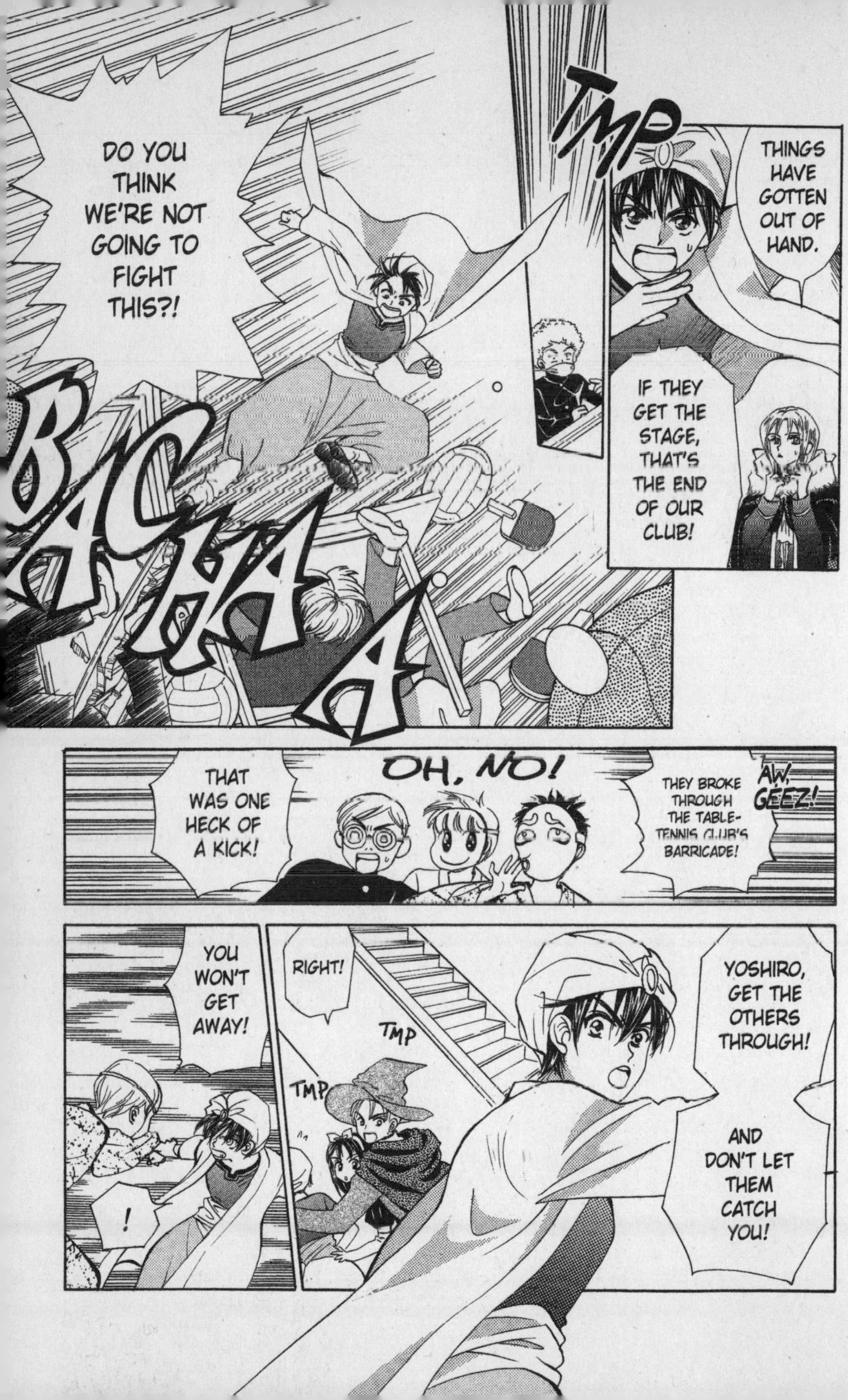
TMP
THINGS HAVE GOTTEN OUT OF HAND.
IF THEY GET THE STAGE, THAT'S THE END OF OUR CLUB!
DO YOU THINK WE'RE NOT GOING TO FIGHT THIS?!
BACHAA
AW, GEEZ!
THEY BROKE THROUGH THE TABLE-TENNIS CLUB'S BARRICADE!
OH, NO!
THAT WAS ONE HECK OF A KICK!
YOSHIRO, GET THE OTHERS THROUGH!
AND DON'T LET THEM CATCH YOU!
TMP
TMP
RIGHT!
YOU WON'T GET AWAY!
!

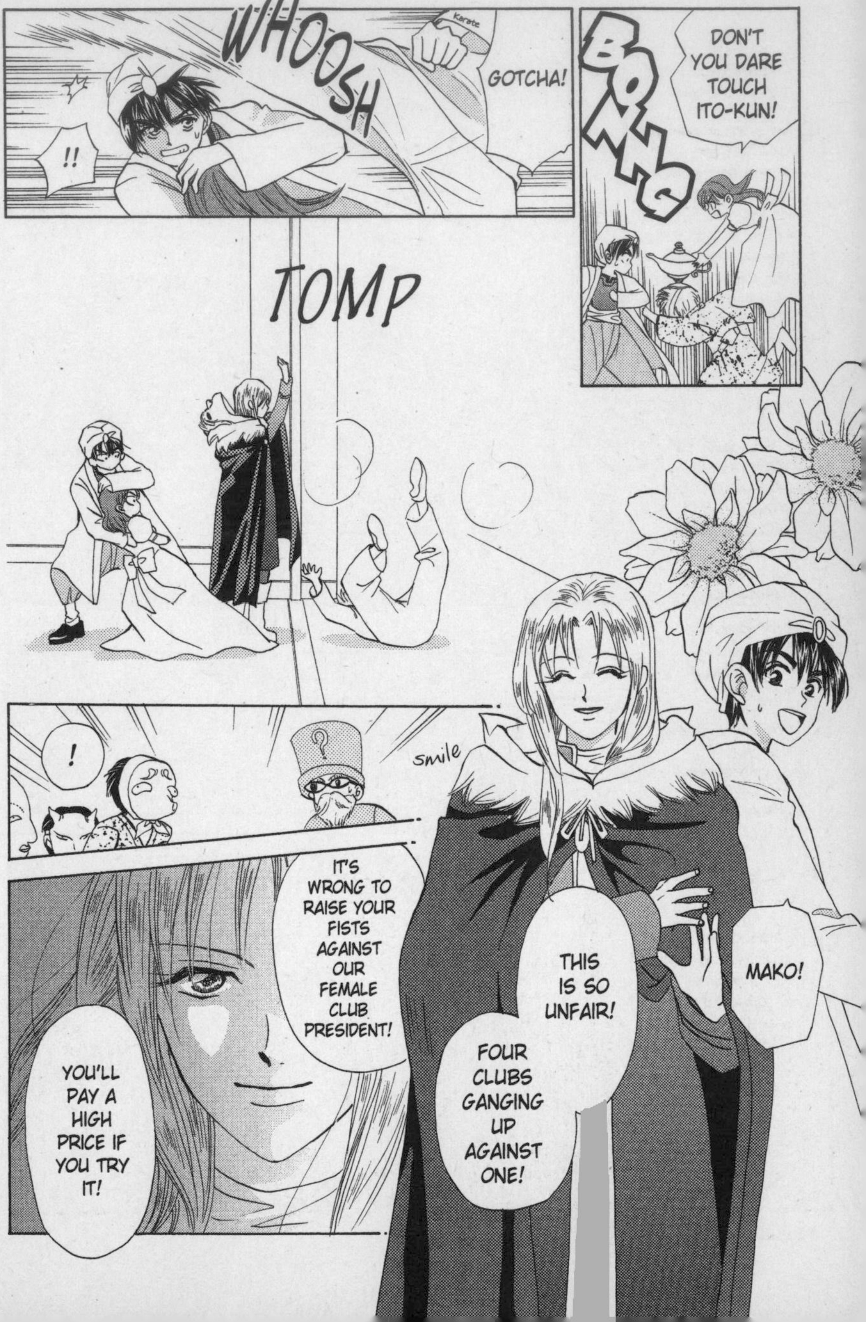
BONG
DON'T YOU DARE TOUCH ITO-KUN!
Karate
WHOOSH
GOTCHA!
!!
TOMP
smile
MAKO!
THIS IS SO UNFAIR!
FOUR CLUBS GANGING UP AGAINST ONE!
!
IT'S WRONG TO RAISE YOUR FISTS AGAINST OUR FEMALE CLUB PRESIDENT!
YOU'LL PAY A HIGH PRICE IF YOU TRY IT!

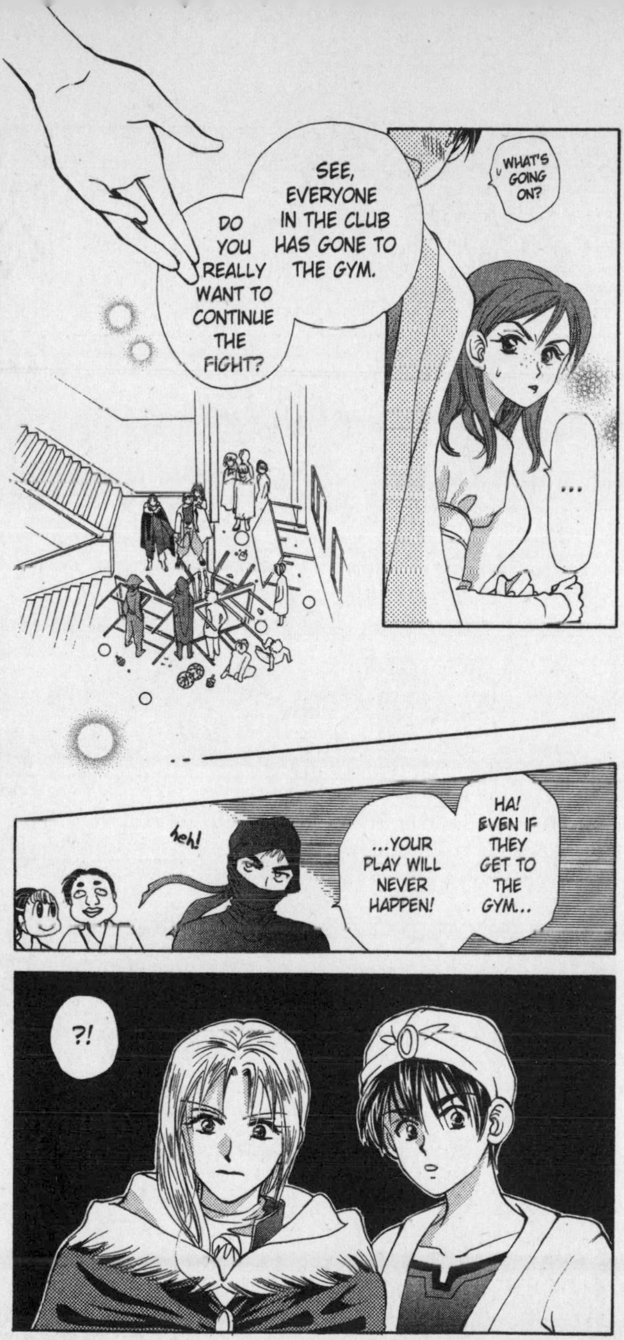
WHAT'S GOING ON?
...
SEE, EVERYONE IN THE CLUB HAS GONE TO THE GYM.
DO YOU REALLY WANT TO CONTINUE THE FIGHT?
HA! EVEN IF THEY GET TO THE GYM...
...YOUR PLAY WILL NEVER HAPPEN!
heh!
?!

- Emura-sensei, when did you first start to draw?

Ⓔ I've been drawing as long as I can remember. I first thought I wanted to be a manga artist in about the second year of elementary school. The first time that I remember my parents getting mad at me for drawing manga in my class notebooks was... a long time ago... The first time I officially (?) sent a manga in to a magazine was toward the end of my first year of high school.

- How long has it been since you became a manga-ka?

Ⓔ Although I dabbled before... It'll officially be four years this spring. (Written in fall of 2000.)

- Are you and your sister close?

Ⓔ We're close. I never would have imagined how close we'd become back when I was middle-school age. It could be that our hearts matured since high school. At least my friends tell me that.

There are a lot of people I disliked long ago and like now.

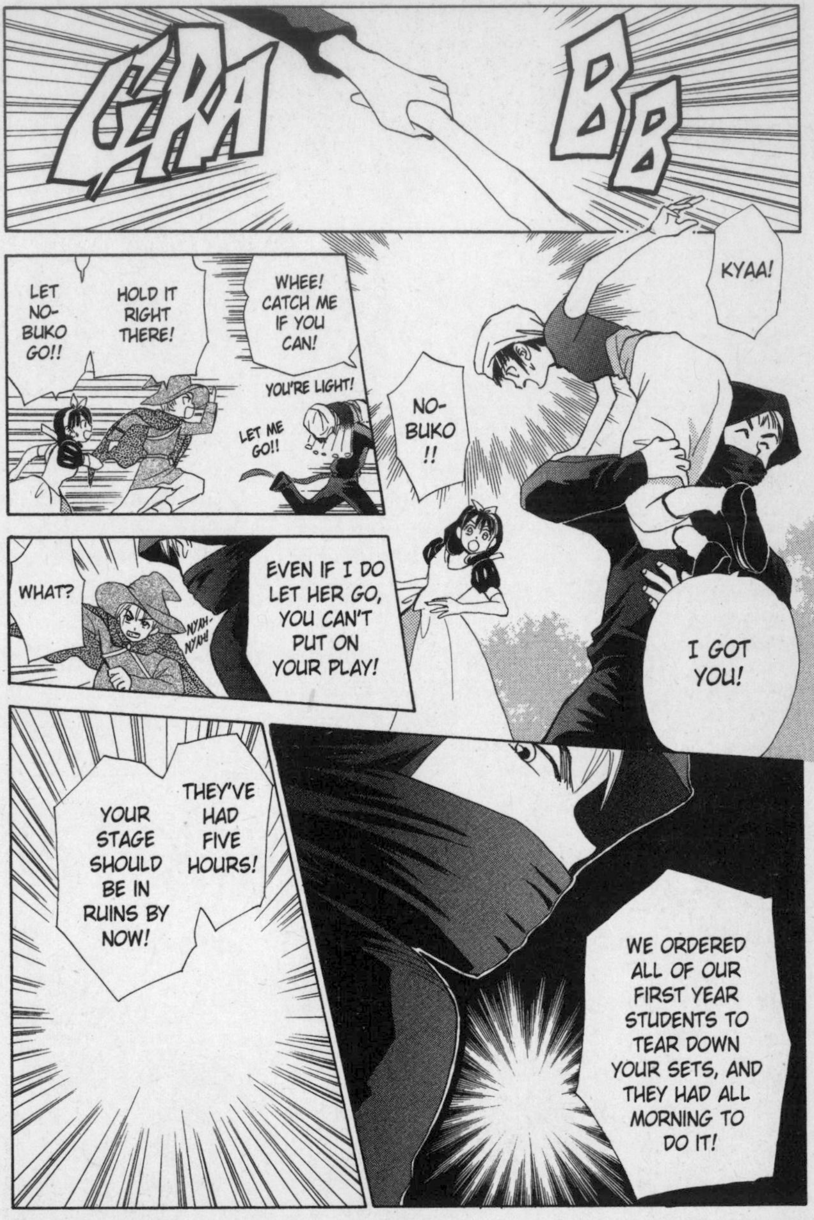
GRABB
KYAA!
NO-BUKO!!
I GOT YOU!
WHEE! CATCH ME IF YOU CAN!
YOU'RE LIGHT!
LET ME GO!!
HOLD IT RIGHT THERE!
LET NO-BUKO GO!!
EVEN IF I DO LET HER GO, YOU CAN'T PUT ON YOUR PLAY!
NYAH-NYAH
WHAT?
WE ORDERED ALL OF OUR FIRST YEAR STUDENTS TO TEAR DOWN YOUR SETS, AND THEY HAD ALL MORNING TO DO IT!
THEY'VE HAD FIVE HOURS!
YOUR STAGE SHOULD BE IN RUINS BY NOW!

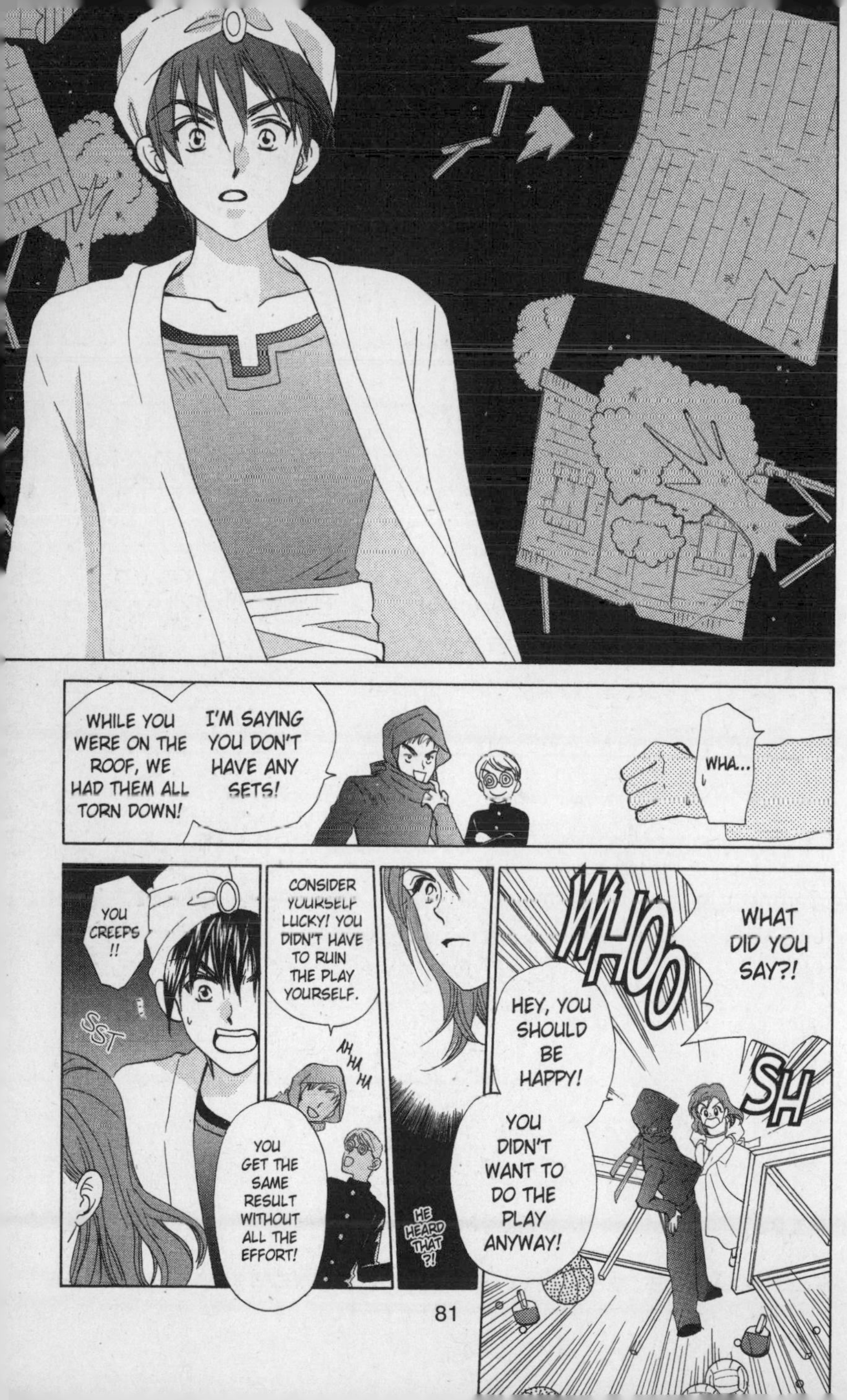
WHA...
I'M SAYING YOU DON'T HAVE ANY SETS!
WHILE YOU WERE ON THE ROOF, WE HAD THEM ALL TORN DOWN!
WHOO
WHAT DID YOU SAY?!
HEY, YOU SHOULD BE HAPPY!
SH
YOU DIDN'T WANT TO DO THE PLAY ANYWAY!
HE HEARD THAT?!
CONSIDER YOURSELF LUCKY! YOU DIDN'T HAVE TO RUIN THE PLAY YOURSELF.
AH HA HA
YOU GET THE SAME RESULT WITHOUT ALL THE EFFORT!
YOU CREEPS!!
SST

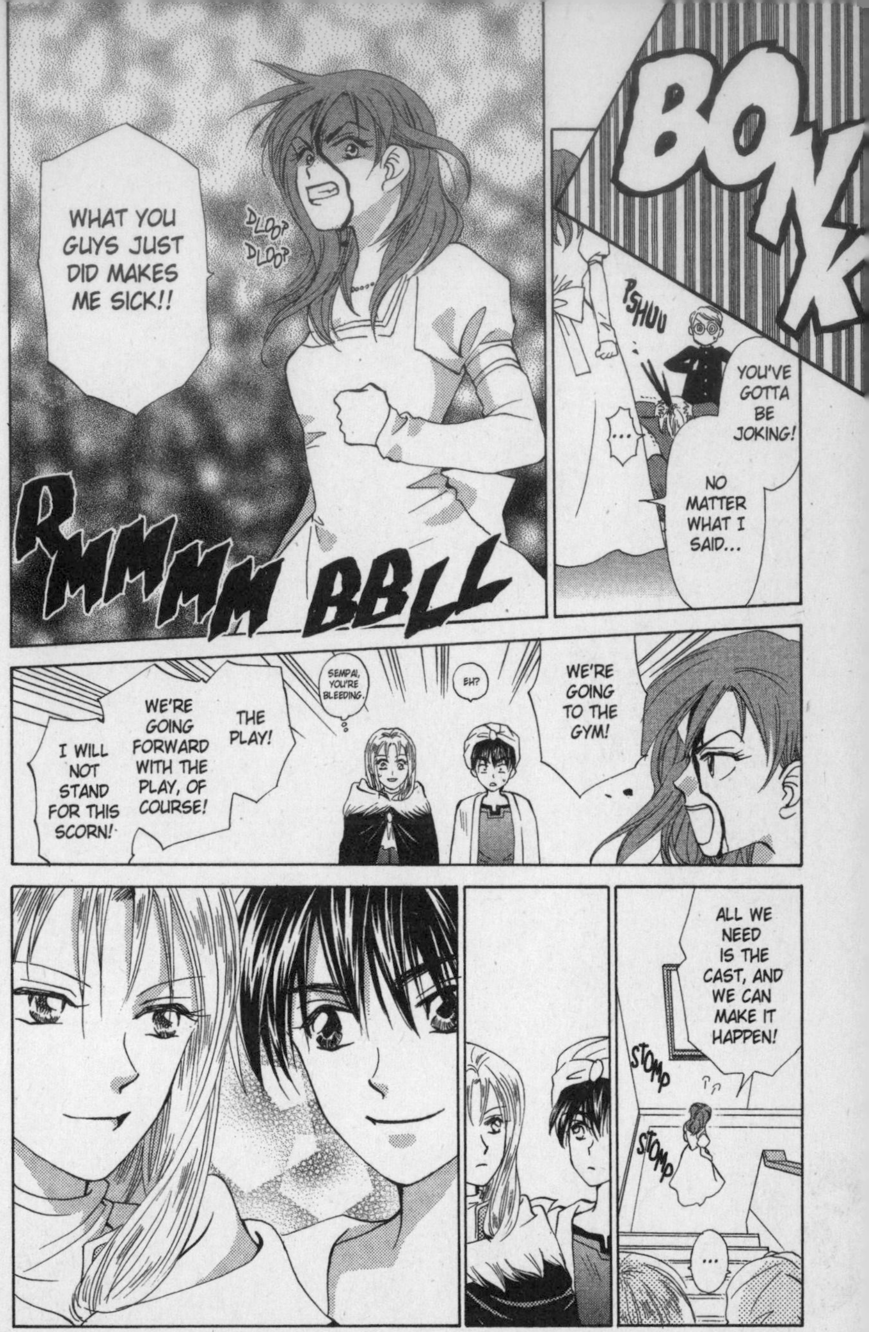
BOK
YOU'VE GOTTA BE JOKING!
PSHUU
NO MATTER WHAT I SAID...
...
WHAT YOU GUYS JUST DID MAKES ME SICK!!
DLOOP DLOOP
RMMMM BBLL
WE'RE GOING TO THE GYM!
EH?
SEMPAI, YOU'RE BLEEDING.
THE PLAY!
WE'RE GOING FORWARD WITH THE PLAY, OF COURSE!
I WILL NOT STAND FOR THIS SCORN!
ALL WE NEED IS THE CAST, AND WE CAN MAKE IT HAPPEN!
STOMP
STOMP
...

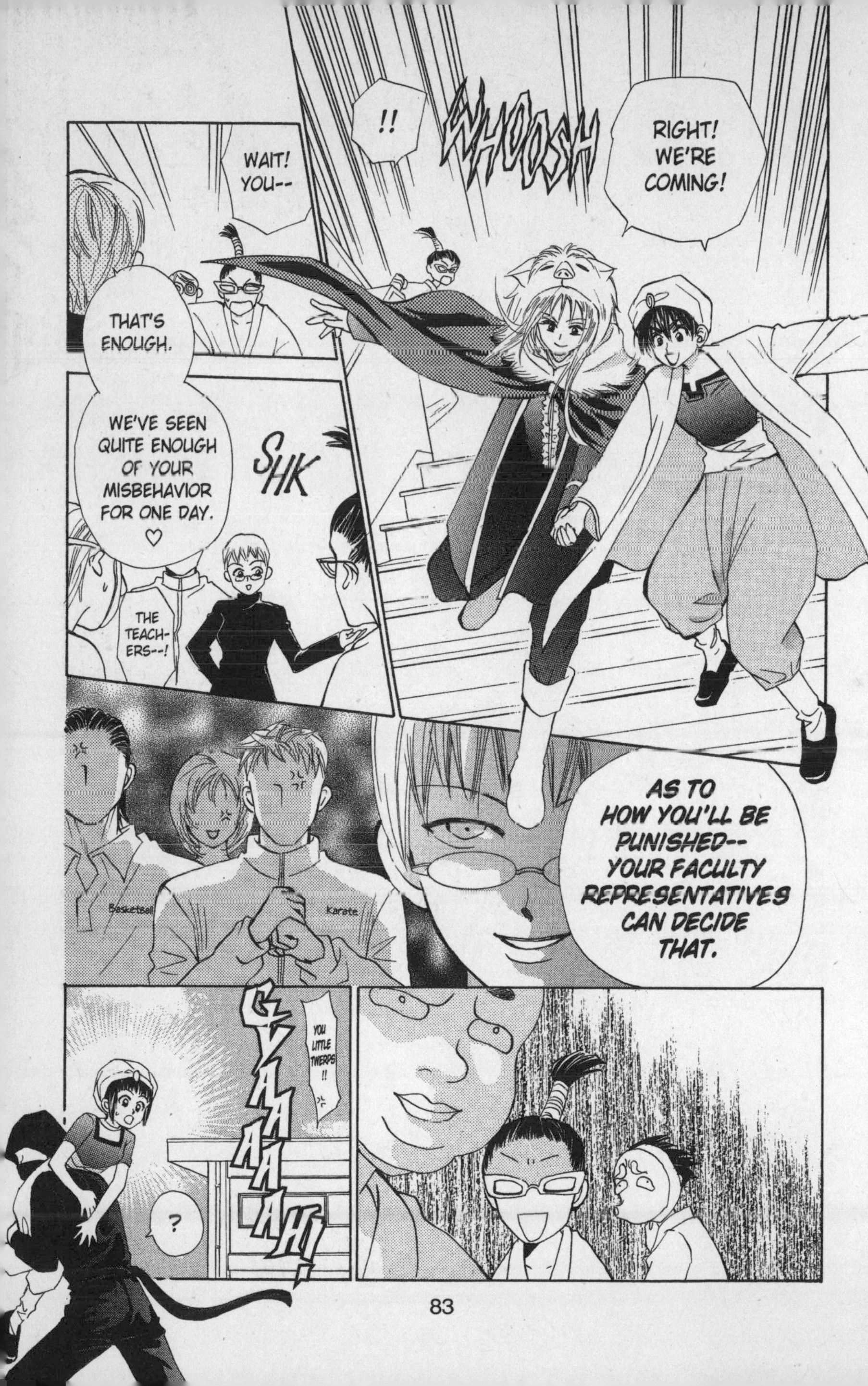
RIGHT! WE'RE COMING!
WHOOSH
!!
WAIT! YOU--
THAT'S ENOUGH.
WE'VE SEEN QUITE ENOUGH OF YOUR MISBEHAVIOR FOR ONE DAY. ♡
SHK
THE TEACHERS--!
AS TO HOW YOU'LL BE PUNISHED-- YOUR FACULTY REPRESENTATIVES CAN DECIDE THAT.
Karate
Basketball
GYAAAAAH!
YOU LITTLE TWERPS!!
?

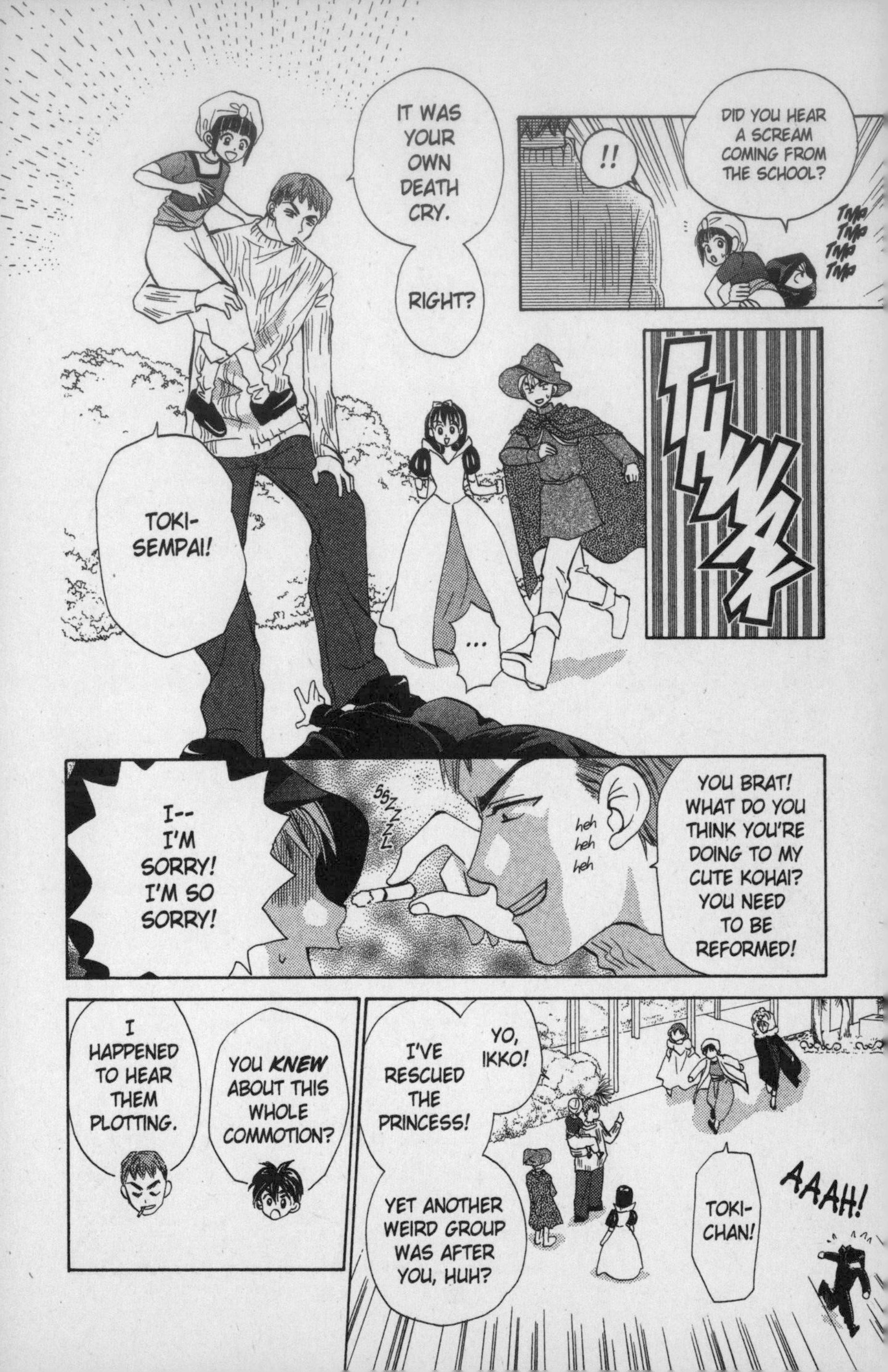

DID YOU HEAR A SCREAM COMING FROM THE SCHOOL?
!!
TMP TMP TMP TMP
THWK
IT WAS YOUR OWN DEATH CRY.
RIGHT?
TOKI-SEMPAI!
...
YOU BRAT! WHAT DO YOU THINK YOU'RE DOING TO MY CUTE KOHAI? YOU NEED TO BE REFORMED!
heh heh heh
SSZZZL
I-- I'M SORRY! I'M SO SORRY!
AAAH!
TOKI-CHAN!
YO, IKKO!
I'VE RESCUED THE PRINCESS!
YET ANOTHER WEIRD GROUP WAS AFTER YOU, HUH?
YOU *KNEW* ABOUT THIS WHOLE COMMOTION?
I HAPPENED TO HEAR THEM PLOTTING.

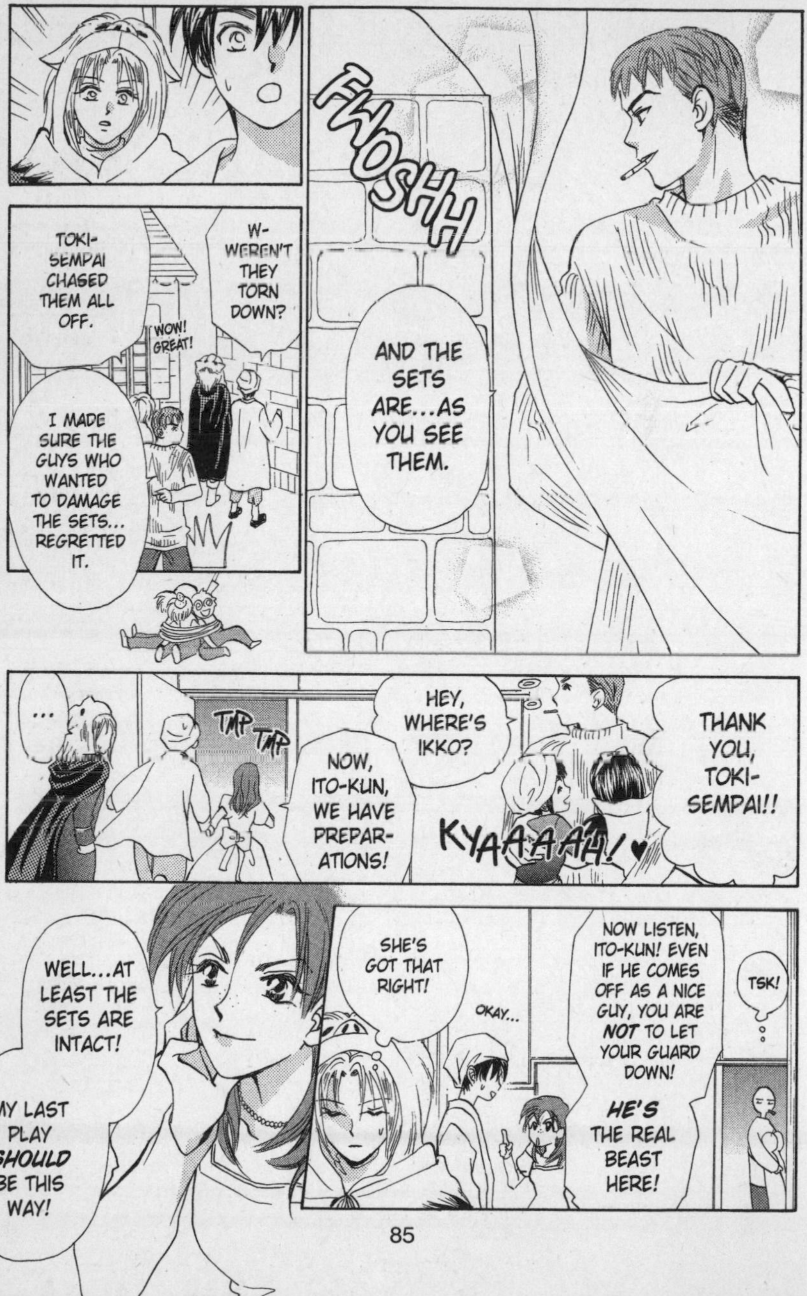
FWOSHH
AND THE SETS ARE...AS YOU SEE THEM.
W-WEREN'T THEY TORN DOWN?
TOKI-SEMPAI CHASED THEM ALL OFF.
WOW! GREAT!
I MADE SURE THE GUYS WHO WANTED TO DAMAGE THE SETS... REGRETTED IT.
THANK YOU, TOKI-SEMPAI!!
KYAAAAAH! ♥
HEY, WHERE'S IKKO?
NOW, ITO-KUN, WE HAVE PREPARATIONS!
TMP TMP
...
TSK!
NOW LISTEN, ITO-KUN! EVEN IF HE COMES OFF AS A NICE GUY, YOU ARE *NOT* TO LET YOUR GUARD DOWN!
HE'S THE REAL BEAST HERE!
OKAY...
SHE'S GOT THAT RIGHT!
WELL...AT LEAST THE SETS ARE INTACT!
MY LAST PLAY *SHOULD* BE THIS WAY!

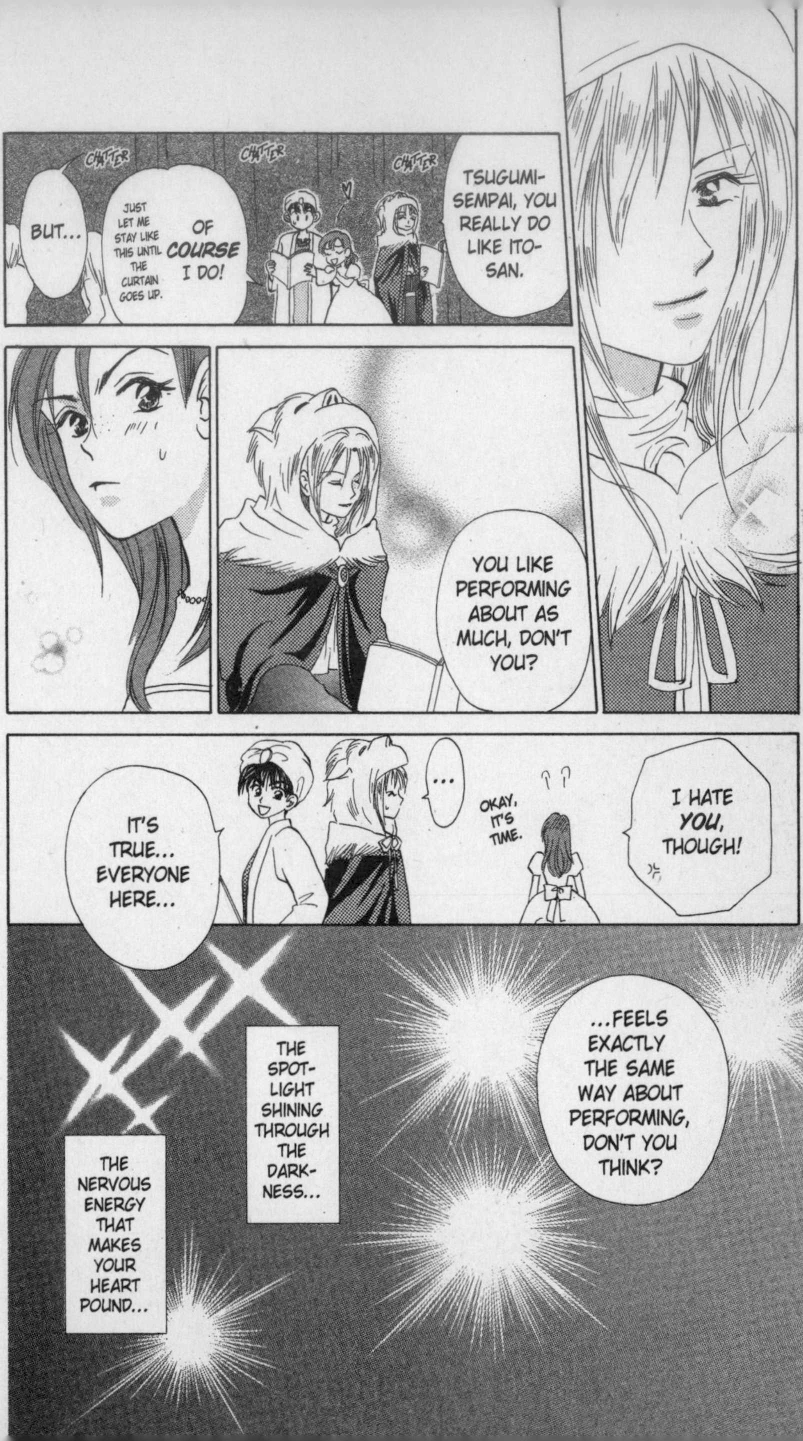
CHATTER
TSUGUMI-SEMPAI, YOU REALLY DO LIKE ITO-SAN.
CHATTER
OF COURSE I DO!
JUST LET ME STAY LIKE THIS UNTIL THE CURTAIN GOES UP.
CHATTER
BUT...
YOU LIKE PERFORMING ABOUT AS MUCH, DON'T YOU?
I HATE YOU, THOUGH!
OKAY, IT'S TIME.
...
IT'S TRUE... EVERYONE HERE...
...FEELS EXACTLY THE SAME WAY ABOUT PERFORMING, DON'T YOU THINK?
THE SPOTLIGHT SHINING THROUGH THE DARKNESS...
THE NERVOUS ENERGY THAT MAKES YOUR HEART POUND...

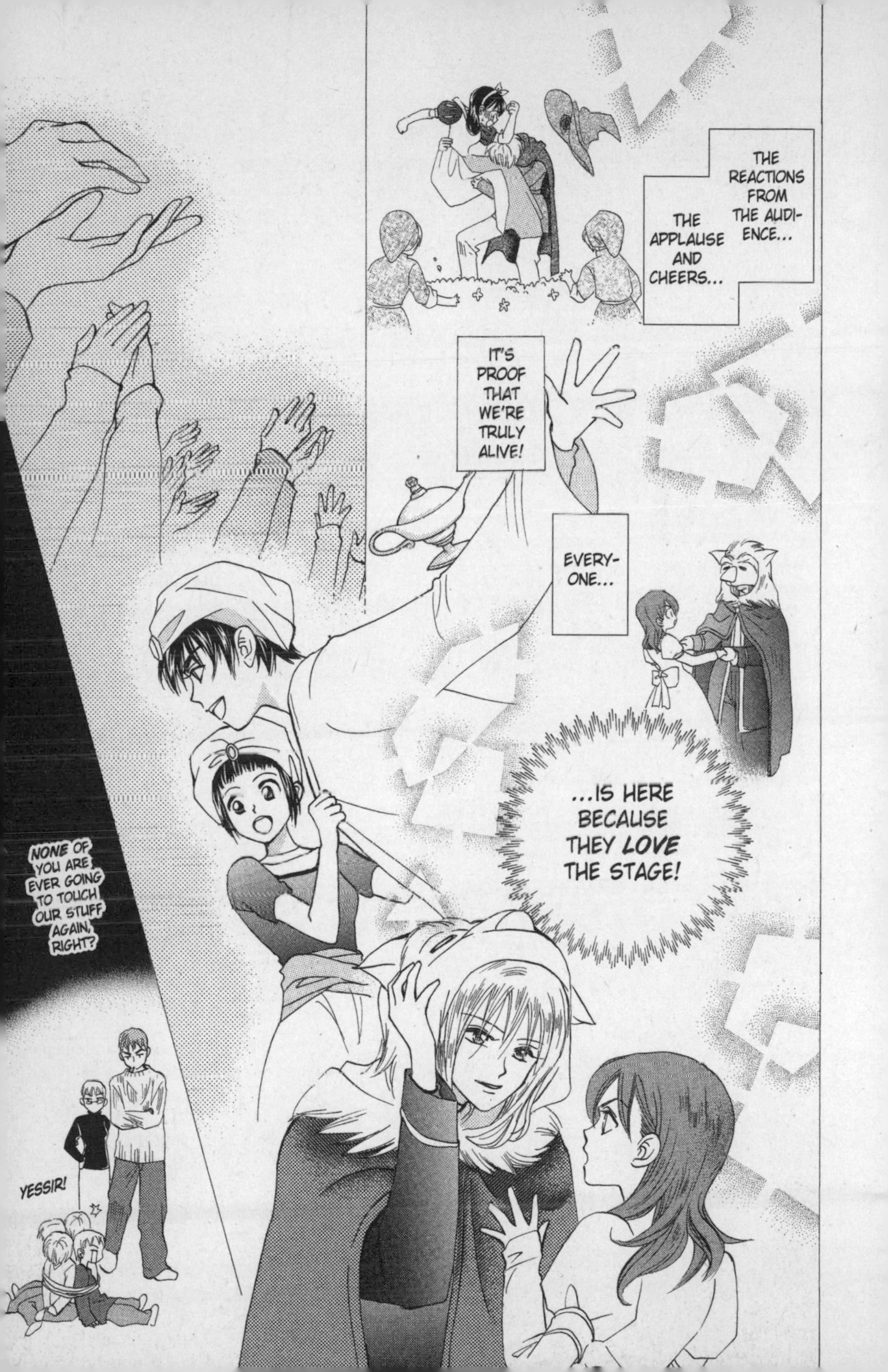
THE REACTIONS FROM THE AUDI- ENCE...
THE APPLAUSE AND CHEERS...
IT'S PROOF THAT WE'RE TRULY ALIVE!
EVERY- ONE...
...IS HERE BECAUSE THEY *LOVE* THE STAGE!
NONE OF YOU ARE EVER GOING TO TOUCH OUR STUFF AGAIN, RIGHT?
YESSIR!

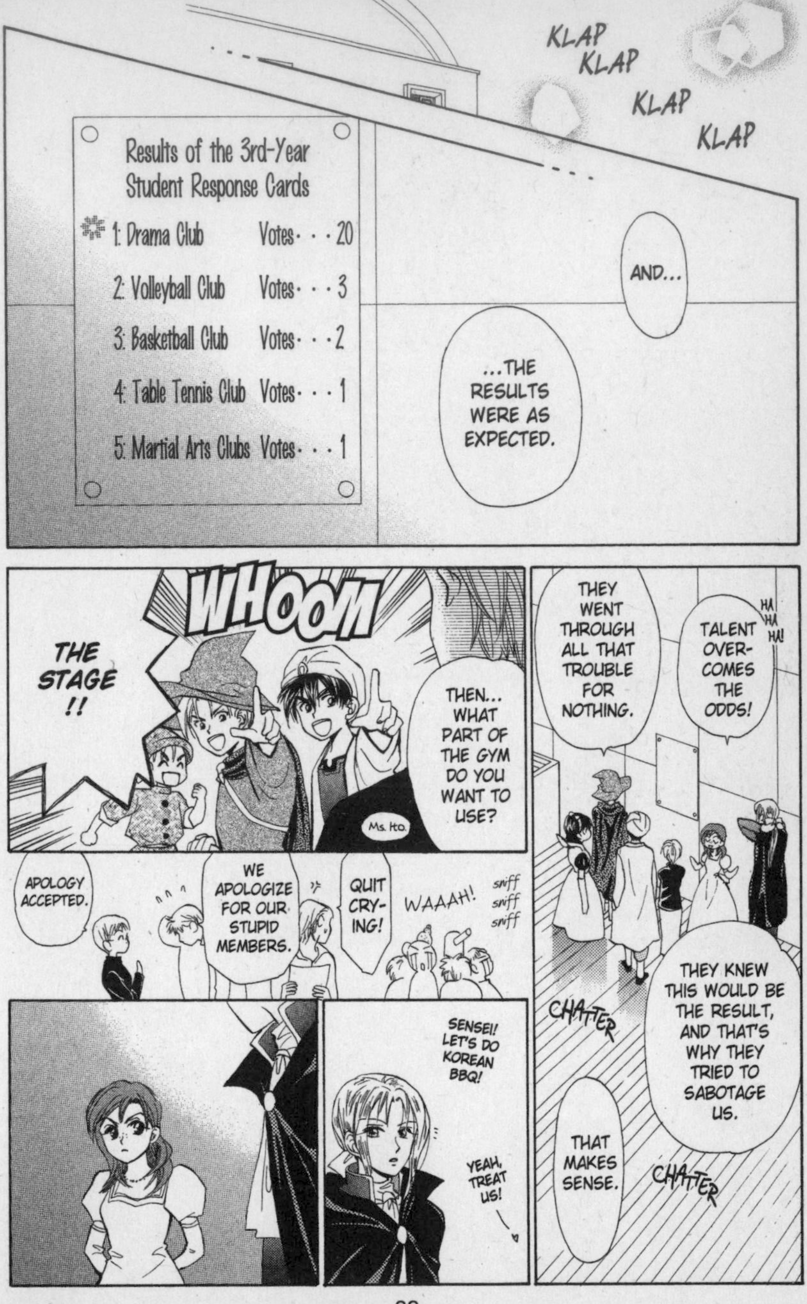
KLAP KLAP KLAP KLAP
AND...
...THE RESULTS WERE AS EXPECTED.
Results of the 3rd-Year Student Response Cards
1: Drama Club Votes・・・20
2: Volleyball Club Votes・・・3
3: Basketball Club Votes・・・2
4: Table Tennis Club Votes・・・1
5: Martial Arts Clubs Votes・・・1
HA HA HA!
TALENT OVERCOMES THE ODDS!
THEY WENT THROUGH ALL THAT TROUBLE FOR NOTHING.
THEY KNEW THIS WOULD BE THE RESULT, AND THAT'S WHY THEY TRIED TO SABOTAGE US.
THAT MAKES SENSE.
CHATTER
CHATTER
THEN... WHAT PART OF THE GYM DO YOU WANT TO USE?
Ms. Ito.
WHOOM
THE STAGE !!
sniff sniff sniff
WAAAH!
QUIT CRY-ING!
WE APOLOGIZE FOR OUR STUPID MEMBERS.
APOLOGY ACCEPTED.
SENSEI! LET'S DO KOREAN BBQ!
YEAH, TREAT US!

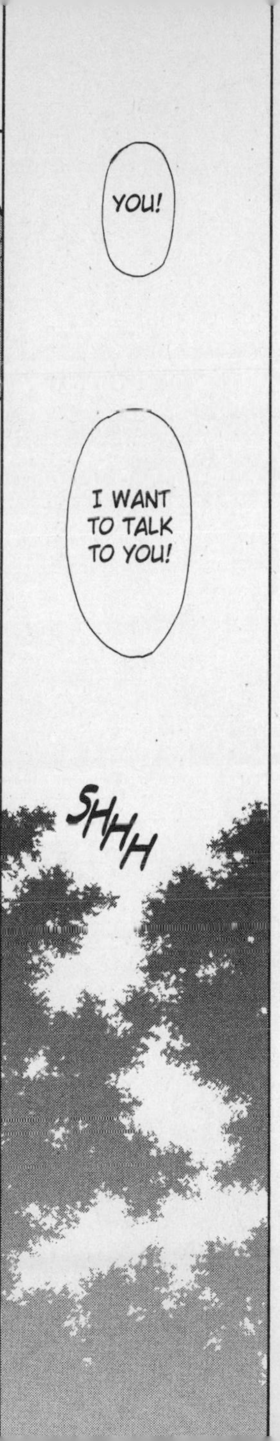
YOU!
I WANT TO TALK TO YOU!
SHHH

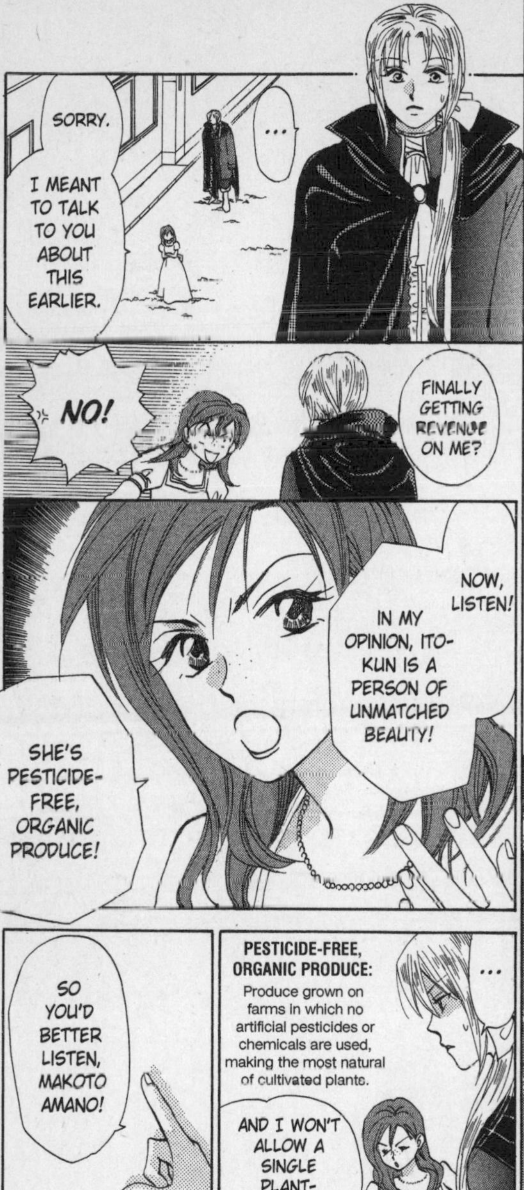
...
SORRY.
I MEANT TO TALK TO YOU ABOUT THIS EARLIER.
FINALLY GETTING REVENGE ON ME?
NO!
NOW, LISTEN!
IN MY OPINION, ITO-KUN IS A PERSON OF UNMATCHED BEAUTY!
SHE'S PESTICIDE-FREE, ORGANIC PRODUCE!
...
PESTICIDE-FREE, ORGANIC PRODUCE: Produce grown on farms in which no artificial pesticides or chemicals are used, making the most natural of cultivated plants.
AND I WON'T ALLOW A SINGLE PLANT-EATING BUG TO COME NEAR HER!
SO YOU'D BETTER LISTEN, MAKOTO AMANO!

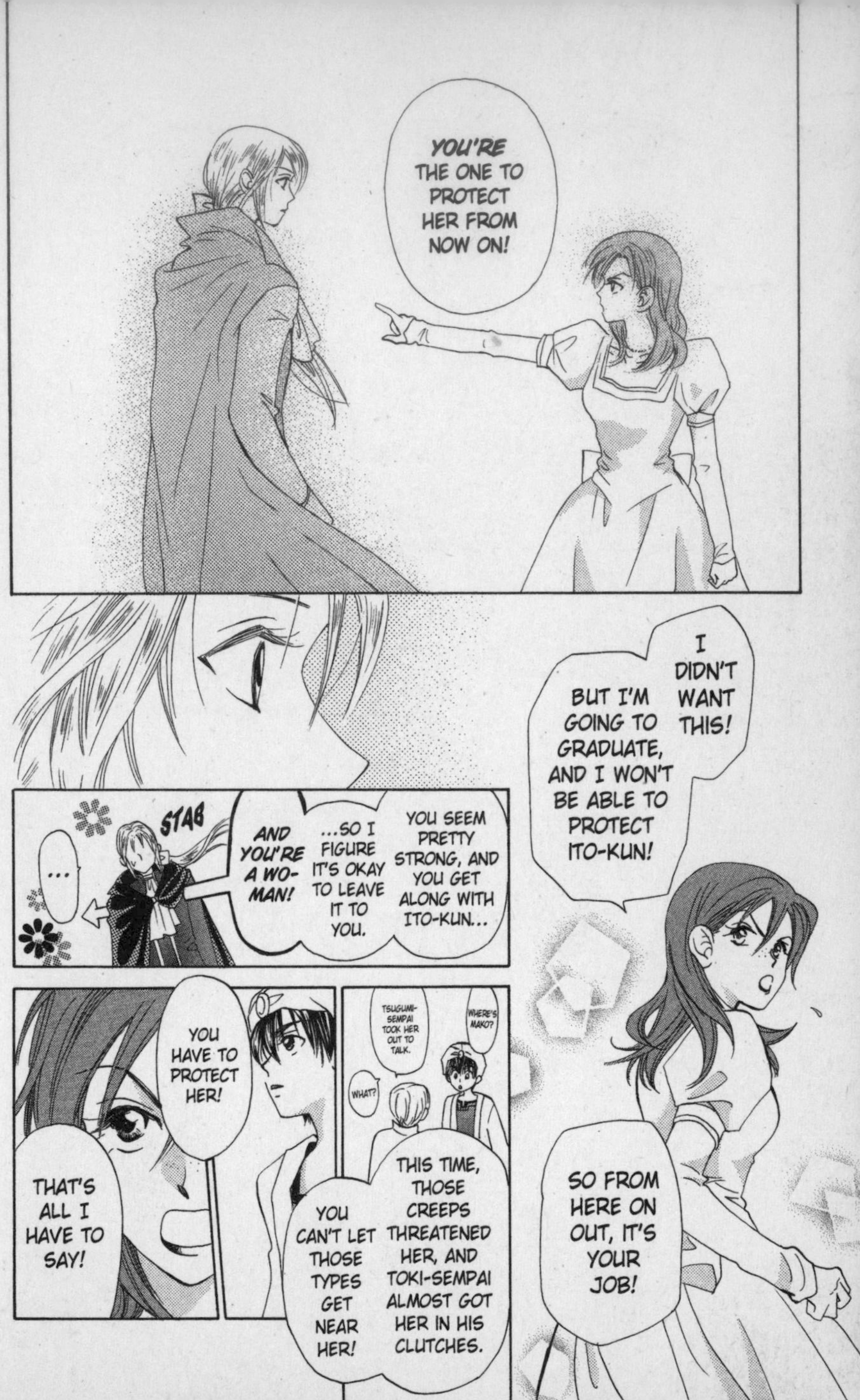
YOU'RE THE ONE TO PROTECT HER FROM NOW ON!
I DIDN'T WANT THIS!
BUT I'M GOING TO GRADUATE, AND I WON'T BE ABLE TO PROTECT ITO-KUN!
YOU SEEM PRETTY STRONG, AND YOU GET ALONG WITH ITO-KUN...
...SO I FIGURE IT'S OKAY TO LEAVE IT TO YOU.
AND YOU'RE A WO-MAN!
STAB
...
SO FROM HERE ON OUT, IT'S YOUR JOB!
WHERE'S MAKO?
TSUGUMI-SEMPAI TOOK HER OUT TO TALK.
WHAT?
THIS TIME, THOSE CREEPS THREATENED HER, AND TOKI-SEMPAI ALMOST GOT HER IN HIS CLUTCHES.
YOU CAN'T LET THOSE TYPES GET NEAR HER!
YOU HAVE TO PROTECT HER!
THAT'S ALL I HAVE TO SAY!

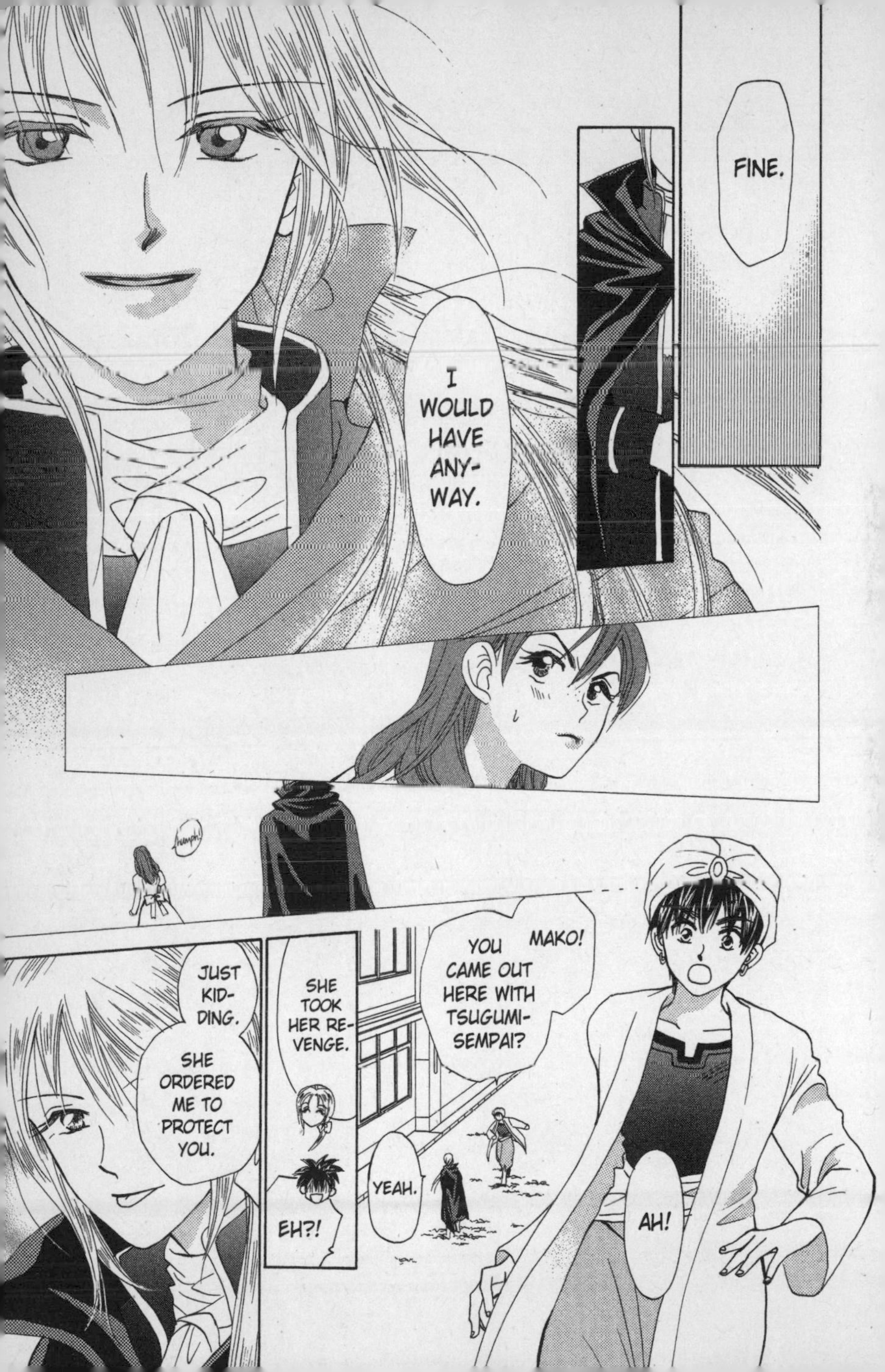
FINE.
I WOULD HAVE ANY-WAY.
humph!
MAKO!
YOU CAME OUT HERE WITH TSUGUMI-SEMPAI?
AH!
SHE TOOK HER RE-VENGE.
YEAH.
EH?!
JUST KID-DING.
SHE ORDERED ME TO PROTECT YOU.

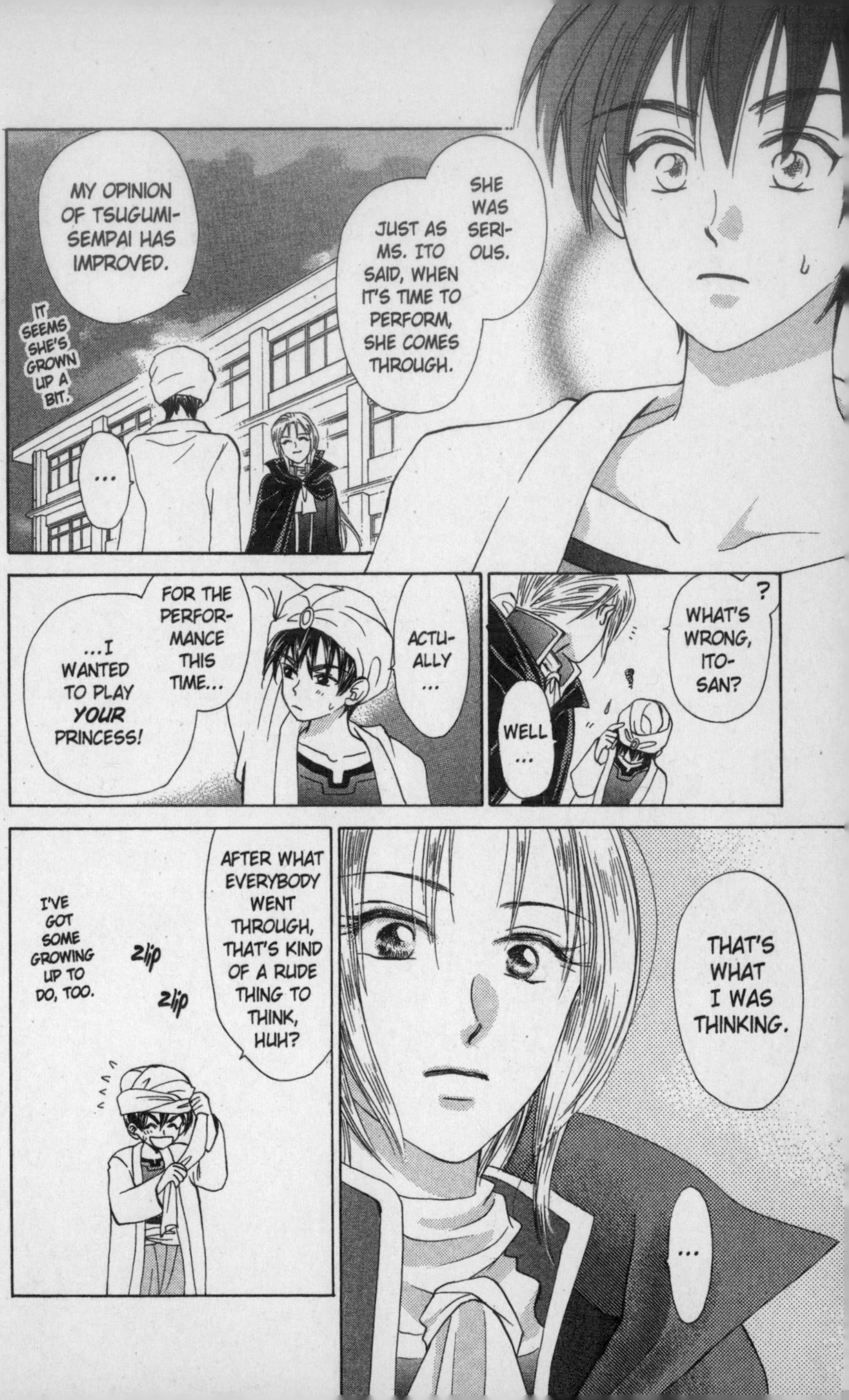
SHE WAS SERIOUS.
JUST AS MS. ITO SAID, WHEN IT'S TIME TO PERFORM, SHE COMES THROUGH.
MY OPINION OF TSUGUMI-SEMPAI HAS IMPROVED.
IT SEEMS SHE'S GROWN UP A BIT.
...
?
WHAT'S WRONG, ITO-SAN?
WELL...
ACTUALLY...
FOR THE PERFORMANCE THIS TIME...
...I WANTED TO PLAY ***YOUR*** PRINCESS!
THAT'S WHAT I WAS THINKING.
...
AFTER WHAT EVERYBODY WENT THROUGH, THAT'S KIND OF A RUDE THING TO THINK, HUH?
ZLIP
ZLIP
I'VE GOT SOME GROWING UP TO DO, TOO.

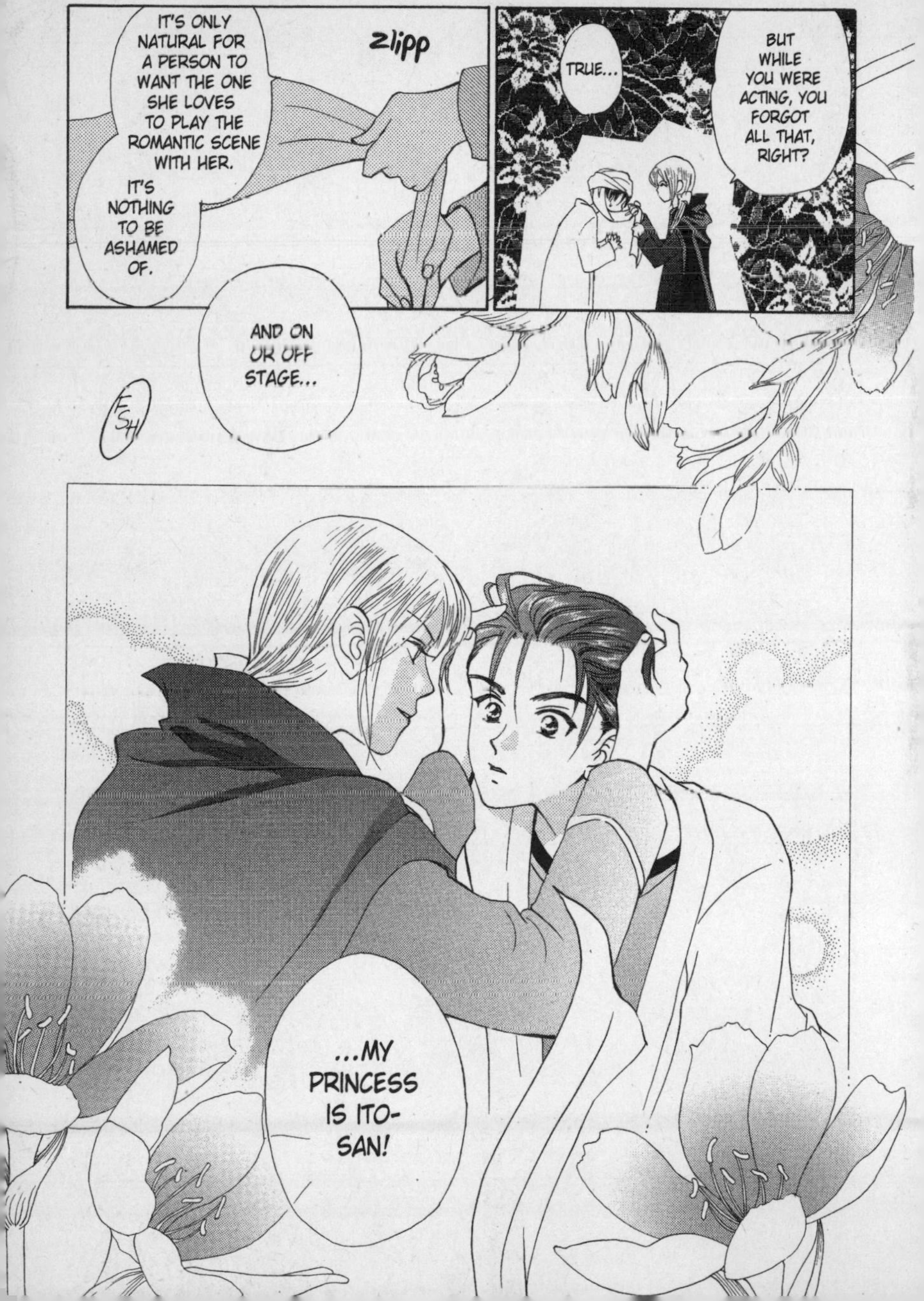
TRUE...
BUT WHILE YOU WERE ACTING, YOU FORGOT ALL THAT, RIGHT?
IT'S ONLY NATURAL FOR A PERSON TO WANT THE ONE SHE LOVES TO PLAY THE ROMANTIC SCENE WITH HER.
zlipp
IT'S NOTHING TO BE ASHAMED OF.
AND ON OR OFF STAGE...
FSH
...MY PRINCESS IS ITO-SAN!

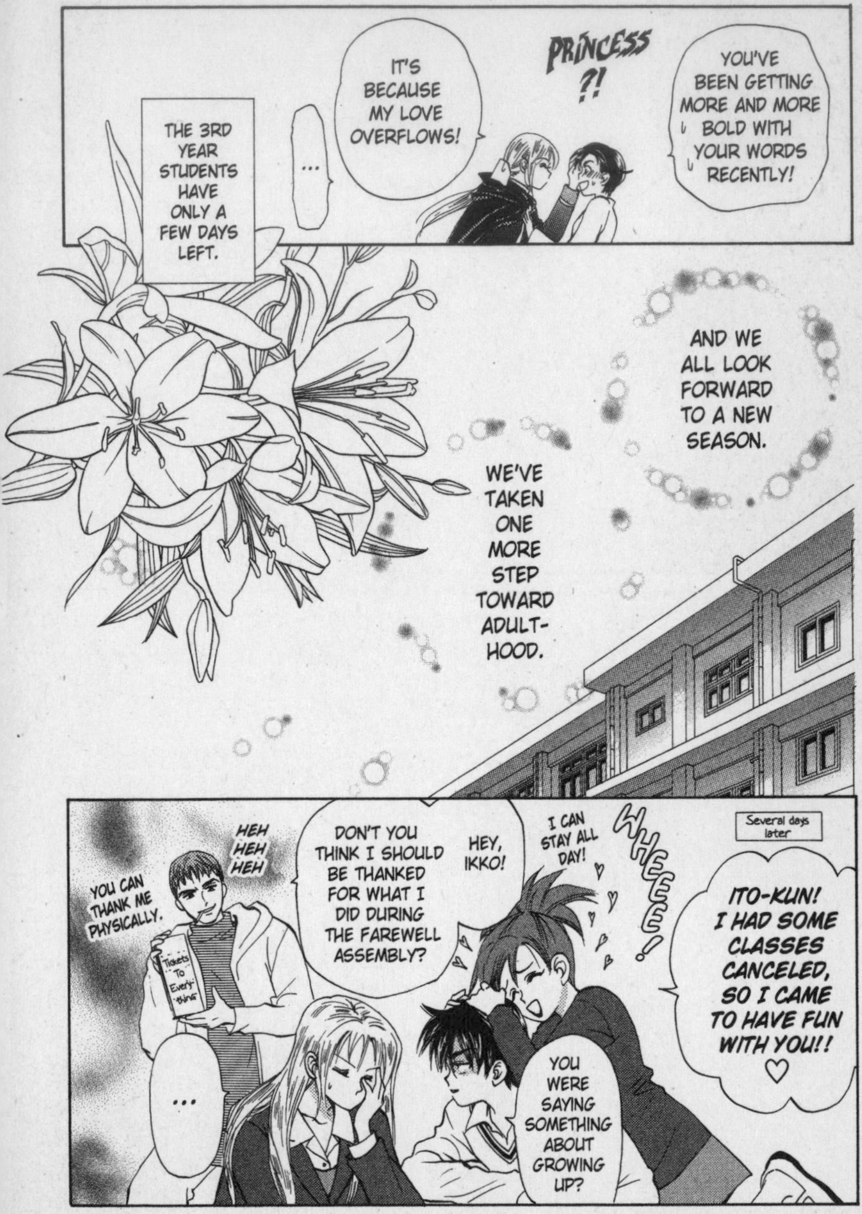
YOU'VE BEEN GETTING MORE AND MORE BOLD WITH YOUR WORDS RECENTLY!
PRINCESS ?!
IT'S BECAUSE MY LOVE OVERFLOWS!
...
THE 3RD YEAR STUDENTS HAVE ONLY A FEW DAYS LEFT.
AND WE ALL LOOK FORWARD TO A NEW SEASON.
WE'VE TAKEN ONE MORE STEP TOWARD ADULT-HOOD.
Several days later
ITO-KUN! I HAD SOME CLASSES CANCELED, SO I CAME TO HAVE FUN WITH YOU!! ♡
WHEEE!
I CAN STAY ALL DAY!
HEY, IKKO!
DON'T YOU THINK I SHOULD BE THANKED FOR WHAT I DID DURING THE FAREWELL ASSEMBLY?
HEH HEH HEH
YOU CAN THANK ME PHYSICALLY.
Tickets To Every-thing
YOU WERE SAYING SOMETHING ABOUT GROWING UP?
...

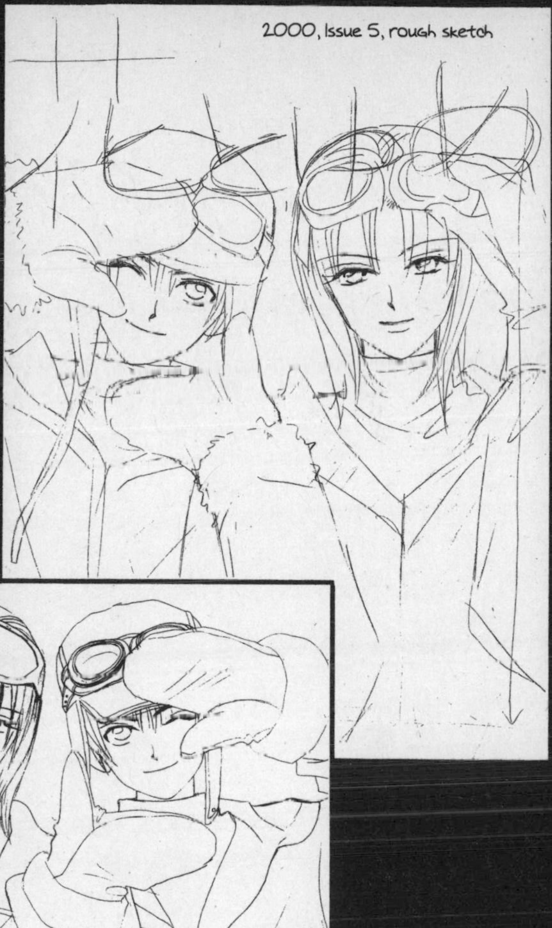
2000, Issue 5, rough sketch

↓PENCILS

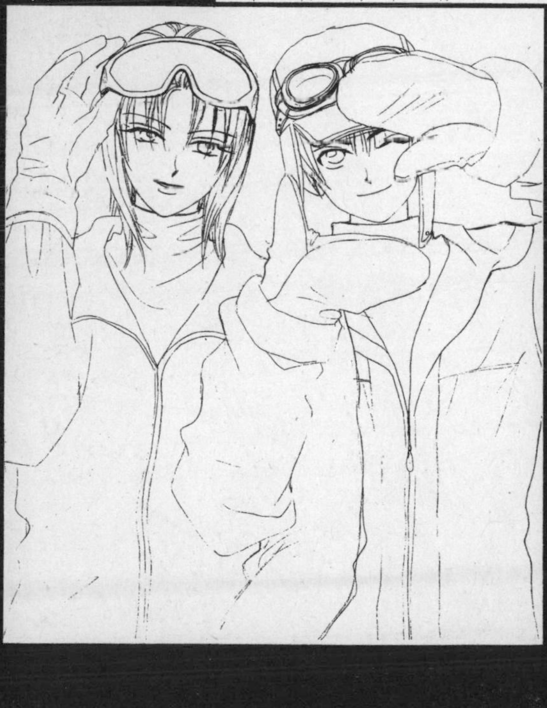

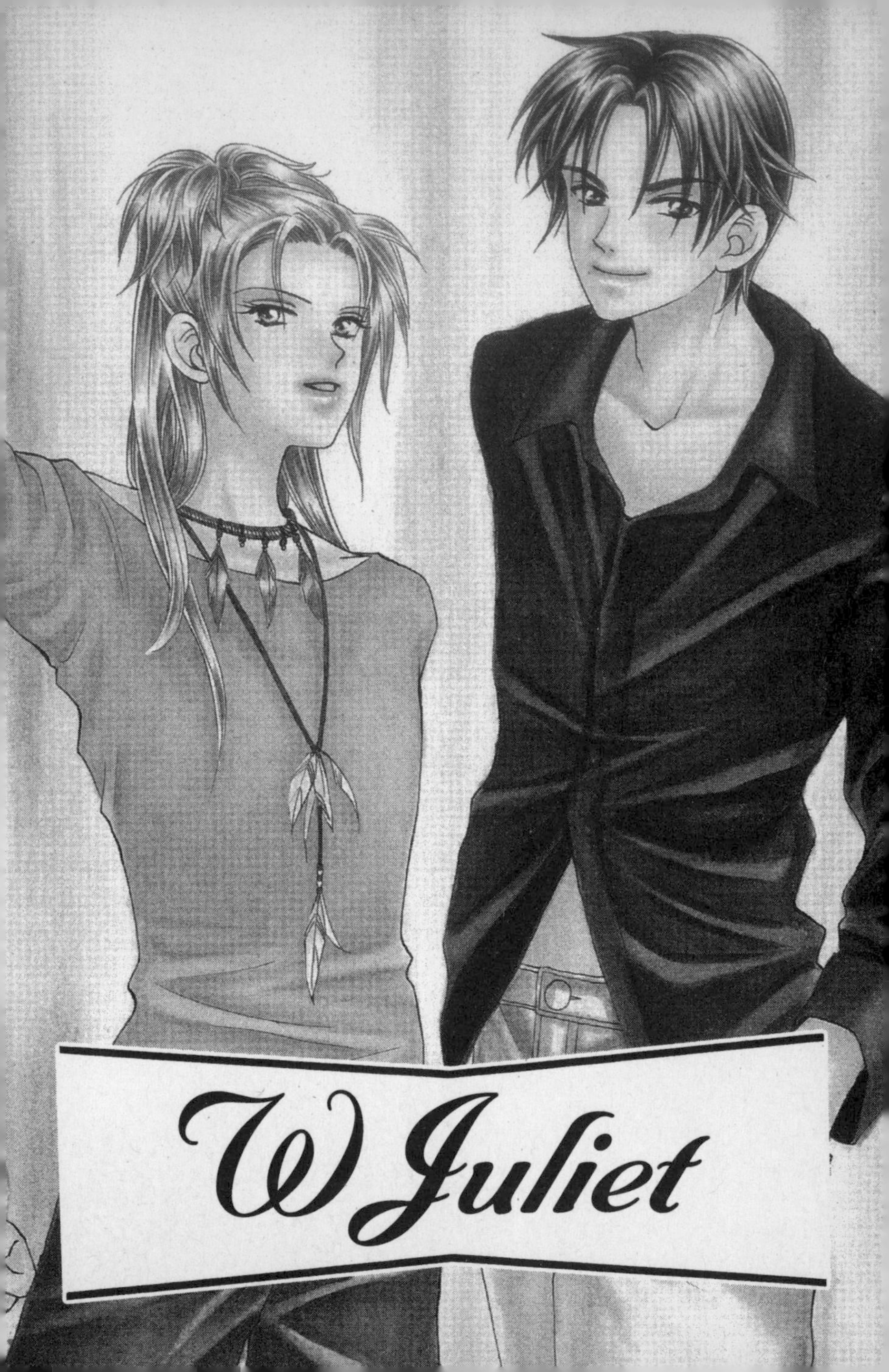
W Juliet

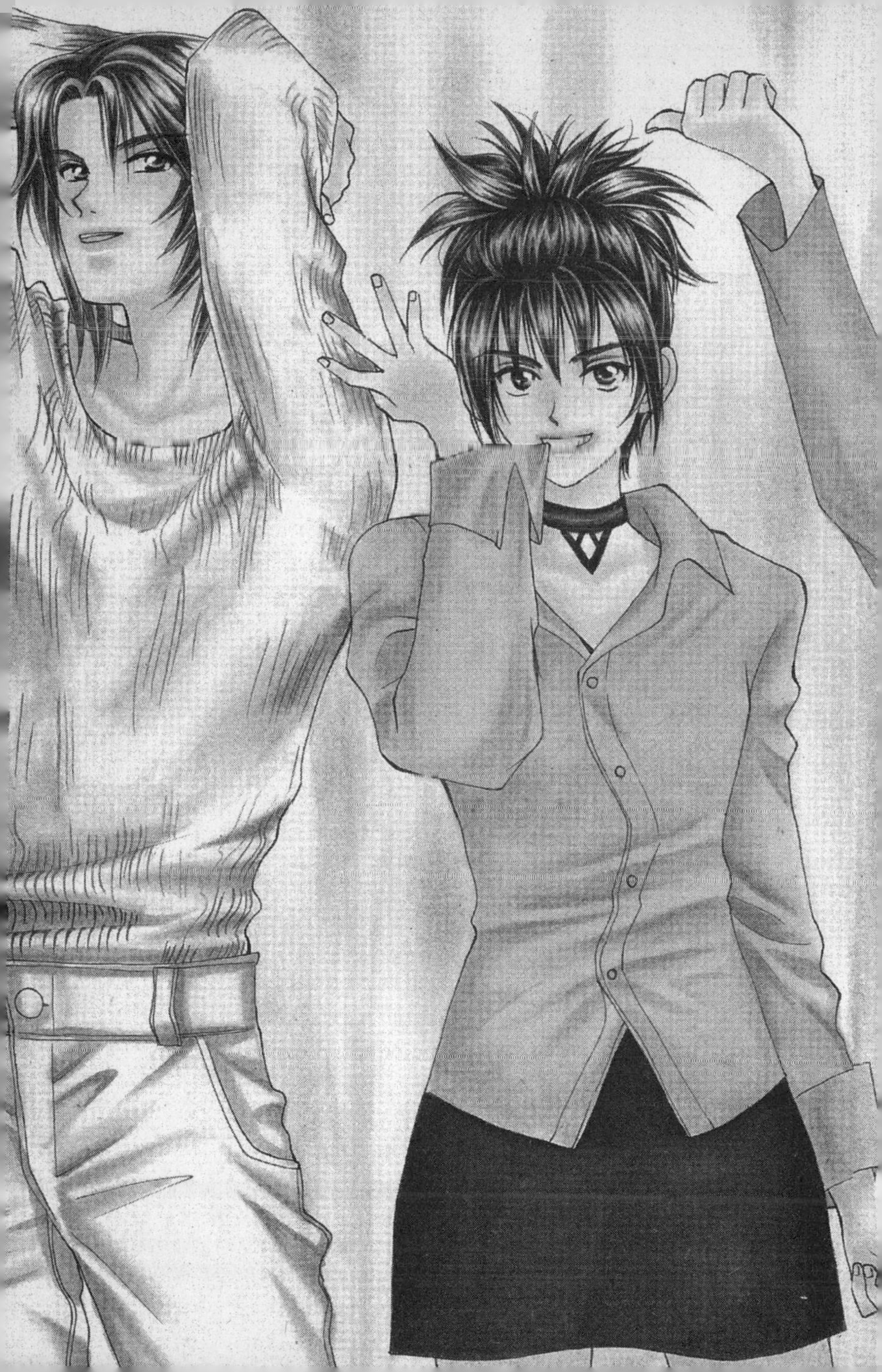

ROUGH. (PENCIL SKETCH 1) B5

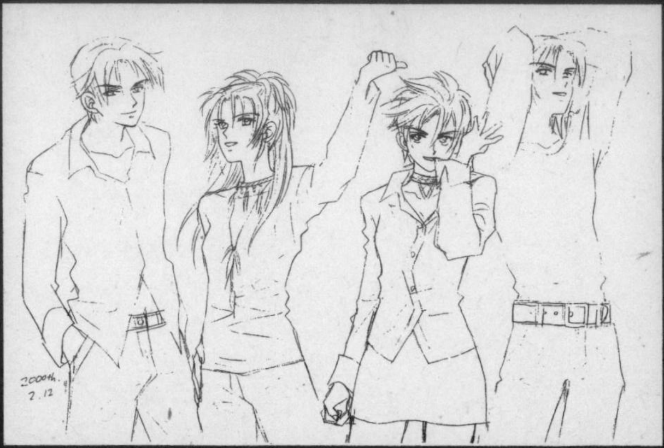
2000th.
2.12

PENCIL SKETCH 2 (ON TRACING PAPER) SPLASH-PAGE SIZE.

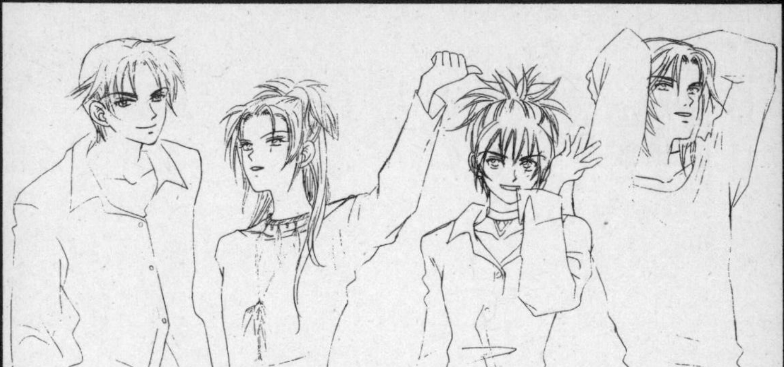

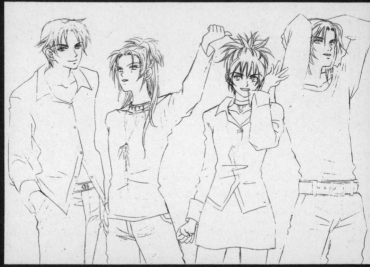

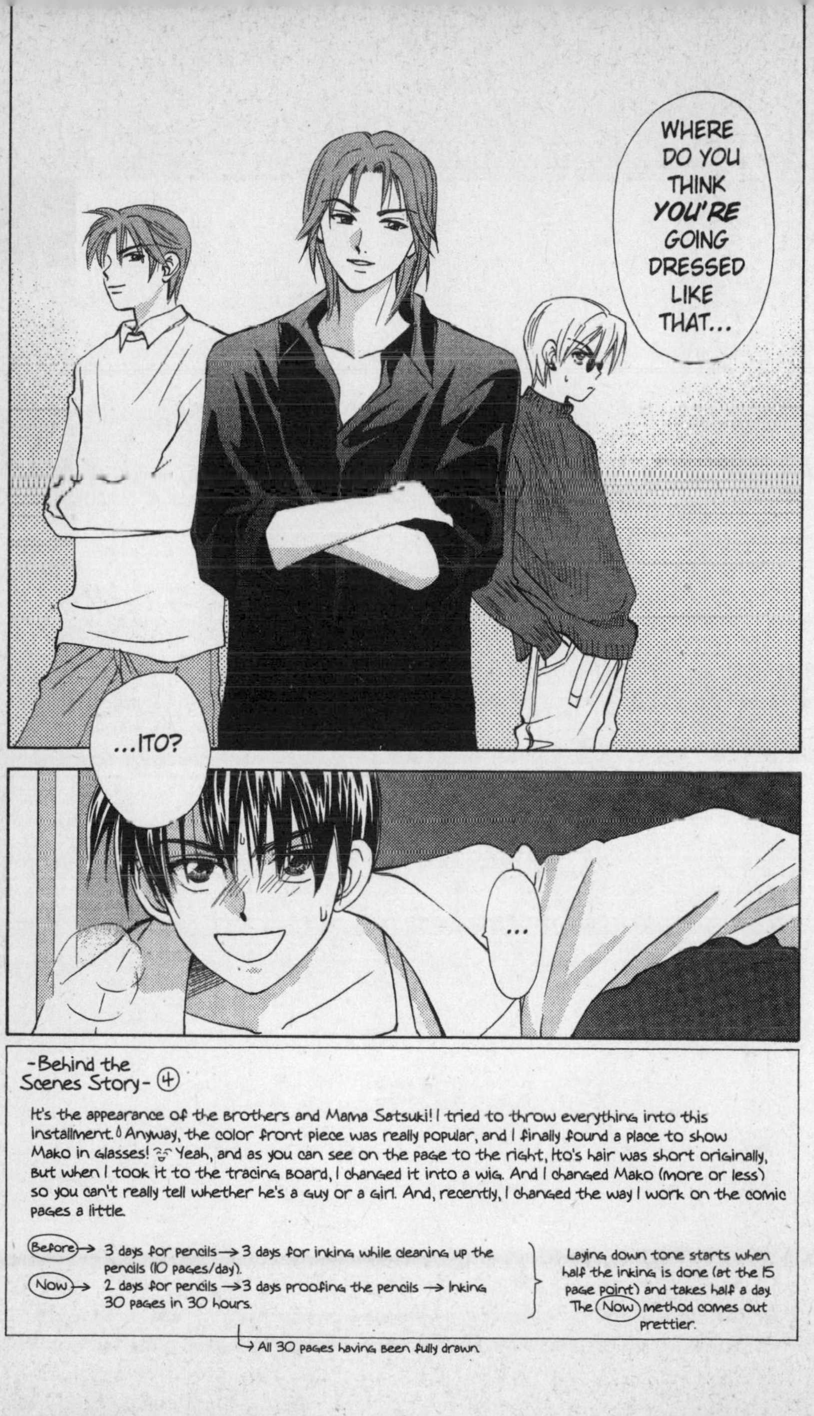
WHERE DO YOU THINK *YOU'RE* GOING DRESSED LIKE THAT...
...ITO?
...

-Behind the Scenes Story- ④

It's the appearance of the brothers and Mama Satsuki! I tried to throw everything into this installment. Anyway, the color front piece was really popular, and I finally found a place to show Mako in glasses! Yeah, and as you can see on the page to the right, Ito's hair was short originally, but when I took it to the tracing board, I changed it into a wig. And I changed Mako (more or less) so you can't really tell whether he's a guy or a girl. And, recently, I changed the way I work on the comic pages a little.

Before → 3 days for pencils → 3 days for inking while cleaning up the pencils (10 pages/day).
Now → 2 days for pencils → 3 days proofing the pencils → Inking 30 pages in 30 hours.

↳ All 30 pages having been fully drawn.

} Laying down tone starts when half the inking is done (at the 15 page point) and takes half a day. The Now method comes out prettier.

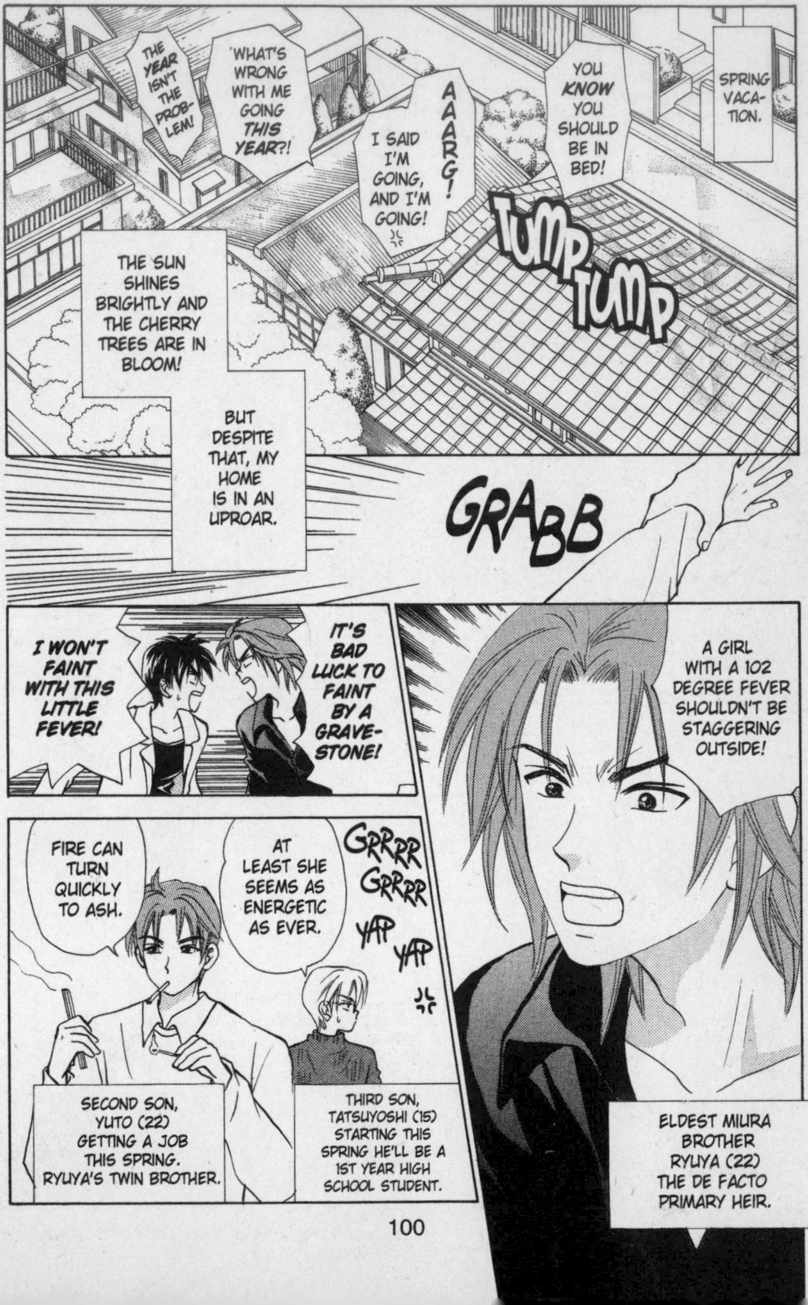
SPRING VACATION.
YOU KNOW YOU SHOULD BE IN BED!
AAAARG!
I SAID I'M GOING, AND I'M GOING!
WHAT'S WRONG WITH ME GOING THIS YEAR?!
THE YEAR ISN'T THE PROBLEM!
TUMP TUMP
THE SUN SHINES BRIGHTLY AND THE CHERRY TREES ARE IN BLOOM!
BUT DESPITE THAT, MY HOME IS IN AN UPROAR.
GRABB
A GIRL WITH A 102 DEGREE FEVER SHOULDN'T BE STAGGERING OUTSIDE!
ELDEST MIURA BROTHER RYUYA (22) THE DE FACTO PRIMARY HEIR.
IT'S BAD LUCK TO FAINT BY A GRAVESTONE!
I WON'T FAINT WITH THIS LITTLE FEVER!
GRRRR GRRRR
YAP YAP
AT LEAST SHE SEEMS AS ENERGETIC AS EVER.
FIRE CAN TURN QUICKLY TO ASH.
THIRD SON, TATSUYOSHI (15) STARTING THIS SPRING HE'LL BE A 1ST YEAR HIGH SCHOOL STUDENT.
SECOND SON, YUTO (22) GETTING A JOB THIS SPRING. RYUYA'S TWIN BROTHER.

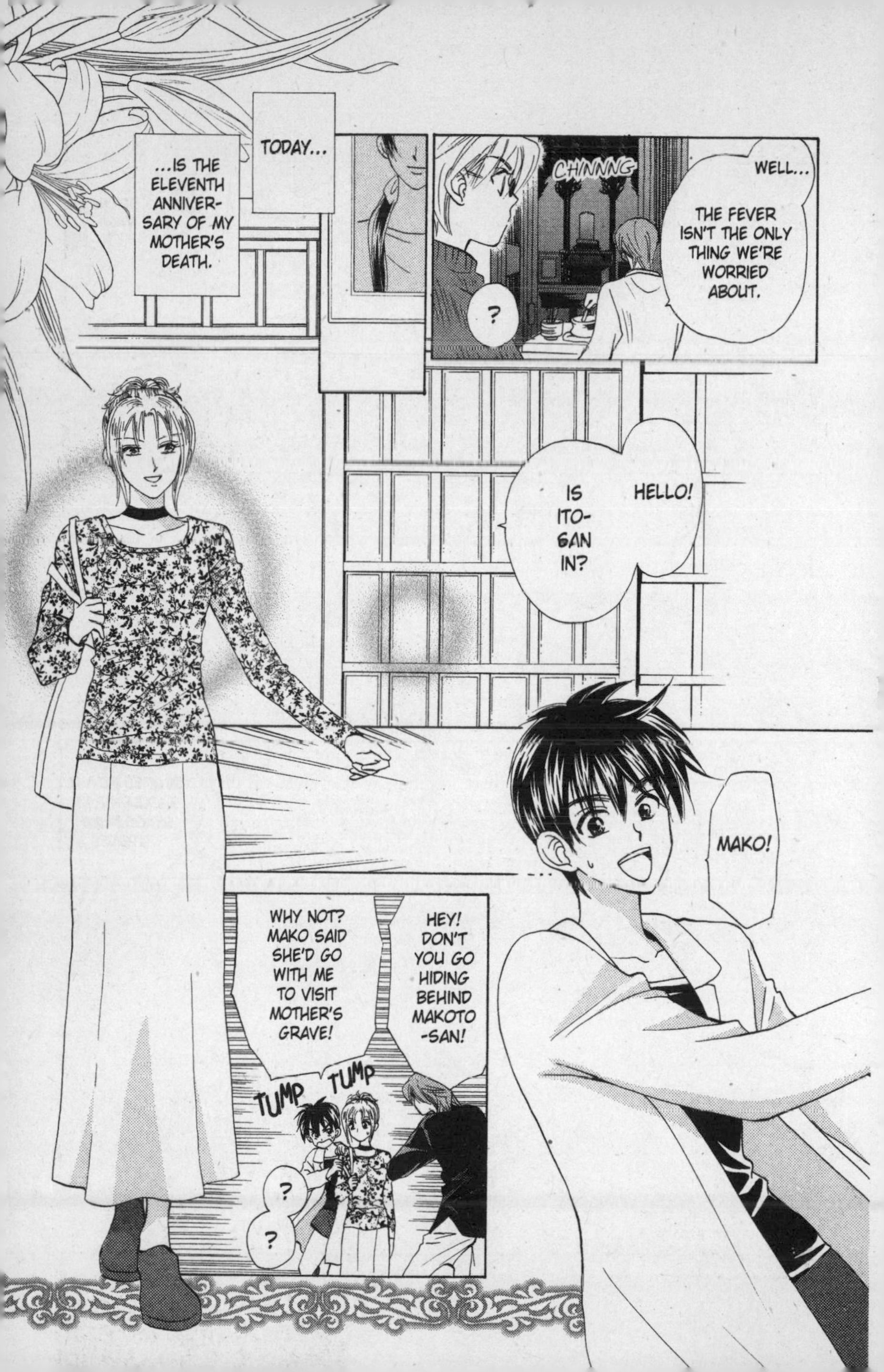
CHNNNG
WELL...
THE FEVER ISN'T THE ONLY THING WE'RE WORRIED ABOUT.
?
TODAY...
...IS THE ELEVENTH ANNIVERSARY OF MY MOTHER'S DEATH.
HELLO!
IS ITO-SAN IN?
MAKO!
HEY! DON'T YOU GO HIDING BEHIND MAKOTO-SAN!
WHY NOT? MAKO SAID SHE'D GO WITH ME TO VISIT MOTHER'S GRAVE!
TUMP
TUMP
?
?

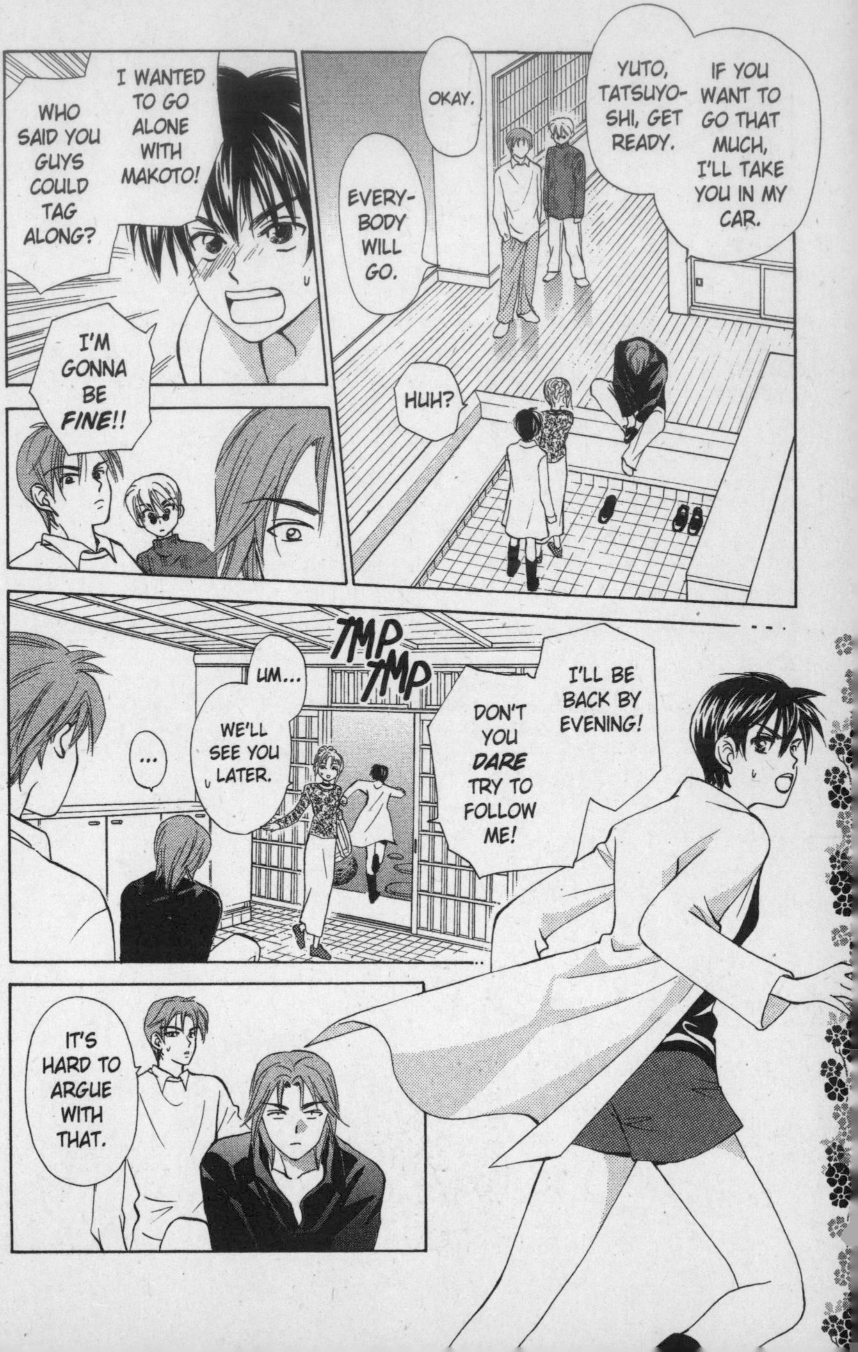
IF YOU WANT TO GO THAT MUCH, I'LL TAKE YOU IN MY CAR.
YUTO, TATSUYOSHI, GET READY.
OKAY.
EVERYBODY WILL GO.
HUH?
I WANTED TO GO ALONE WITH MAKOTO!
WHO SAID YOU GUYS COULD TAG ALONG?
I'M GONNA BE FINE!!
I'LL BE BACK BY EVENING!
DON'T YOU DARE TRY TO FOLLOW ME!
TMP TMP
UM...
WE'LL SEE YOU LATER.
...
IT'S HARD TO ARGUE WITH THAT.

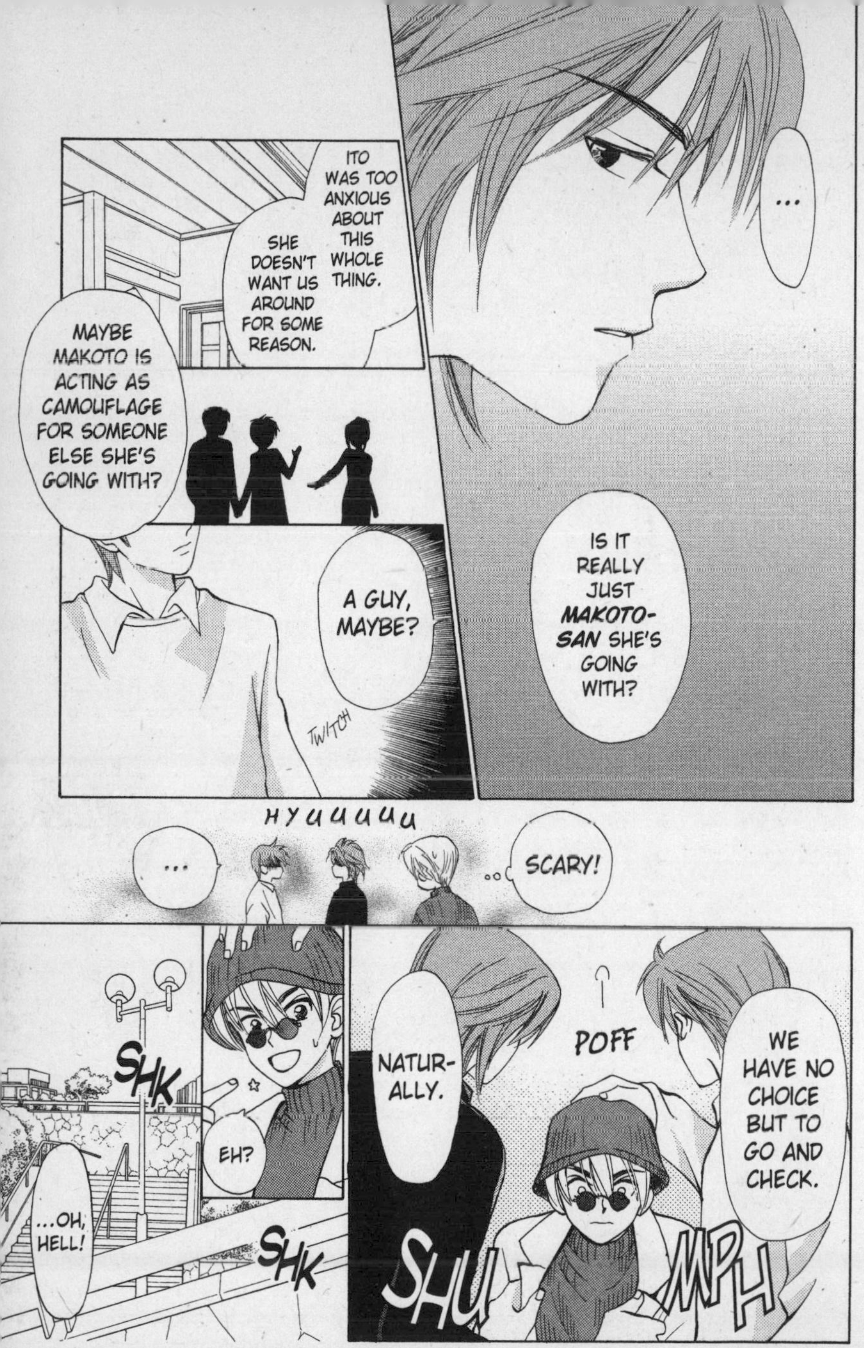
...
IS IT REALLY JUST MAKOTO-SAN SHE'S GOING WITH?
ITO WAS TOO ANXIOUS ABOUT THIS WHOLE THING.
SHE DOESN'T WANT US AROUND FOR SOME REASON.
MAYBE MAKOTO IS ACTING AS CAMOUFLAGE FOR SOMEONE ELSE SHE'S GOING WITH?
A GUY, MAYBE?
TWITCH
HYUUUUUU
SCARY!
...
WE HAVE NO CHOICE BUT TO GO AND CHECK.
POFF
MPH
NATUR-ALLY.
SHU
EH?
SHK
...OH, HELL!
SHK

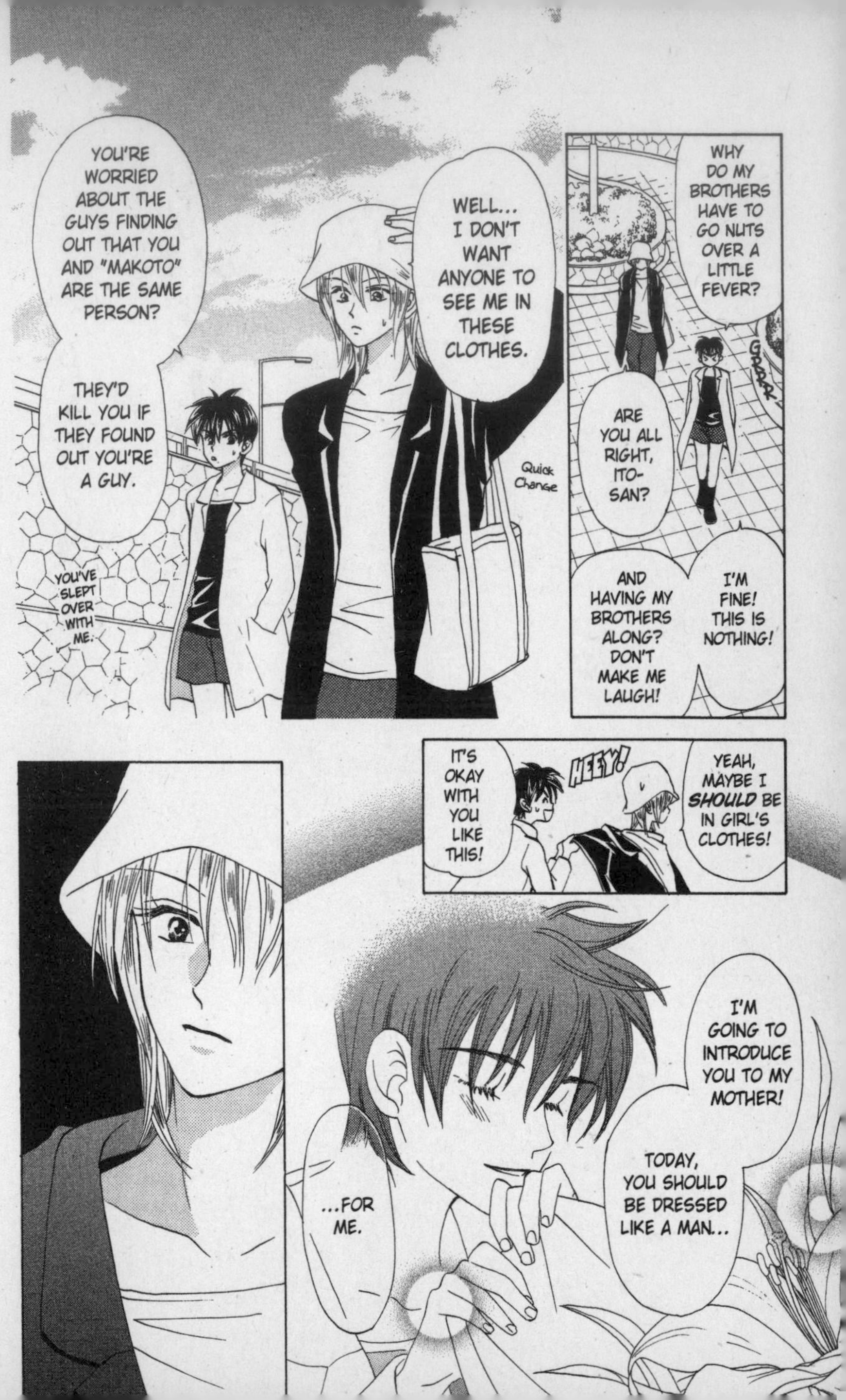
WHY DO MY BROTHERS HAVE TO GO NUTS OVER A LITTLE FEVER?
ARE YOU ALL RIGHT, ITO-SAN?
I'M FINE! THIS IS NOTHING!
AND HAVING MY BROTHERS ALONG? DON'T MAKE ME LAUGH!
WELL... I DON'T WANT ANYONE TO SEE ME IN THESE CLOTHES.
YOU'RE WORRIED ABOUT THE GUYS FINDING OUT THAT YOU AND "MAKOTO" ARE THE SAME PERSON?
Quick Change
THEY'D KILL YOU IF THEY FOUND OUT YOU'RE A GUY.
YOU'VE SLEPT OVER WITH ME.
YEAH, MAYBE I SHOULD BE IN GIRL'S CLOTHES!
HEEY!
IT'S OKAY WITH YOU LIKE THIS!
I'M GOING TO INTRODUCE YOU TO MY MOTHER!
TODAY, YOU SHOULD BE DRESSED LIKE A MAN...
...FOR ME.

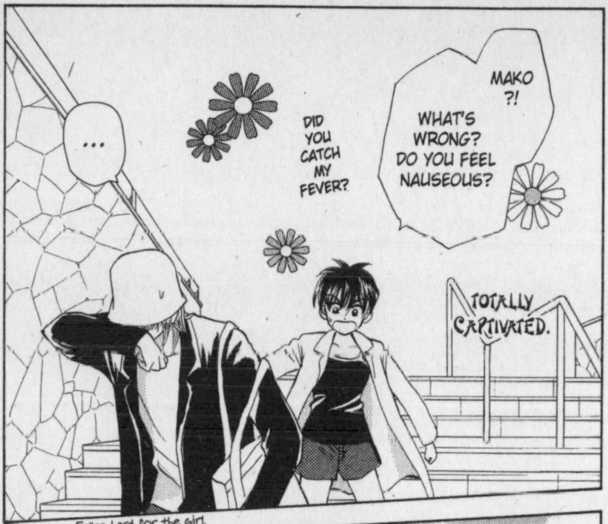
MAKO ?!
WHAT'S WRONG? DO YOU FEEL NAUSEOUS?
DID YOU CATCH MY FEVER?
TOTALLY CAPTIVATED.
...
Fallen hard for the Girl.

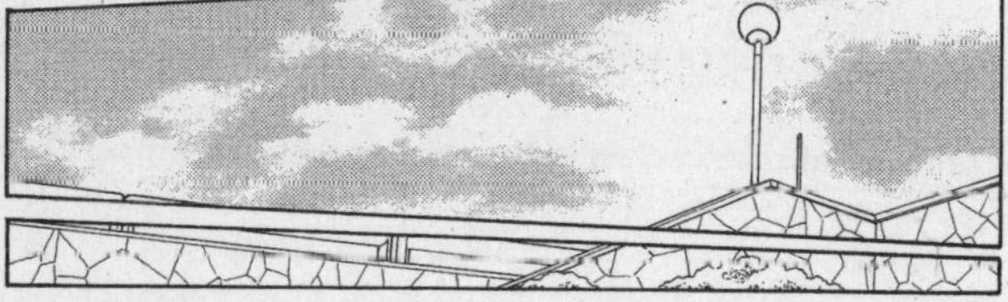

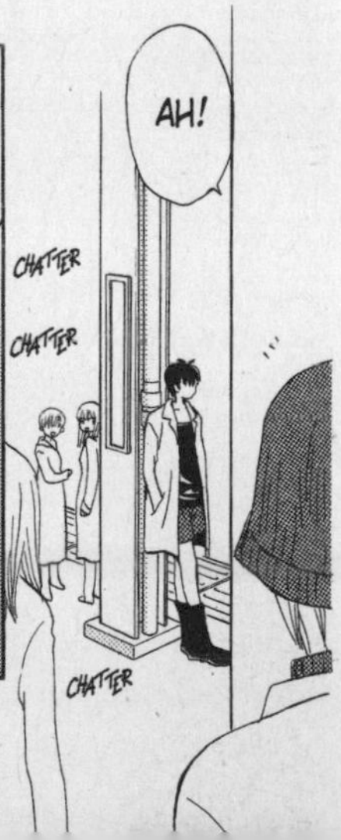
AH!
CHATTER
CHATTER
CHATTER

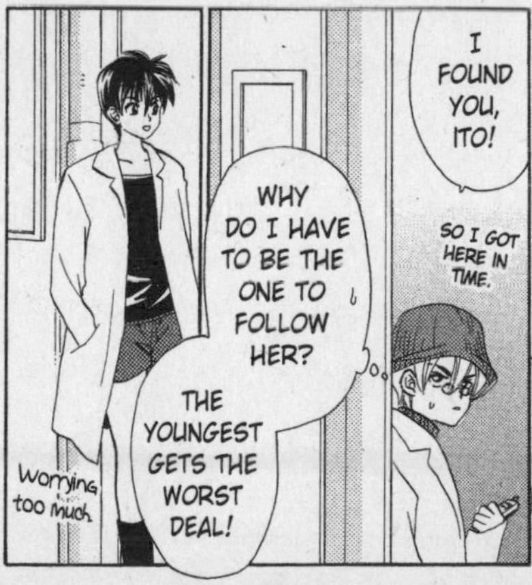
I FOUND YOU, ITO!
SO I GOT HERE IN TIME.
WHY DO I HAVE TO BE THE ONE TO FOLLOW HER?
THE YOUNGEST GETS THE WORST DEAL!
Worrying too much

- What clubs did you join in High School?

Ⓔ I was in Track & Field, but as a manager, not a runner! ♪ They still made me run, though...

- When did you make your debut?

Ⓔ See the end of the book

- The phantom third installment, "Summer Trip Story"... Will it ever get printed again, or is it really just a figment of everyone's imagination?

Ⓔ I don't think it's a figment of our imagination, but I don't know when it'll be reprinted in the graphic novels! (What goes into the graphic novels is decided by the Hakusensha editors.) I think! I hope and pray it'll be included in a graphic novel soon! My drawing style is changing so fast it's frightening! But this is one area where I'd be happy if you were to wait with some patience. I get that question a lot!! I'm sorry to make you wait...

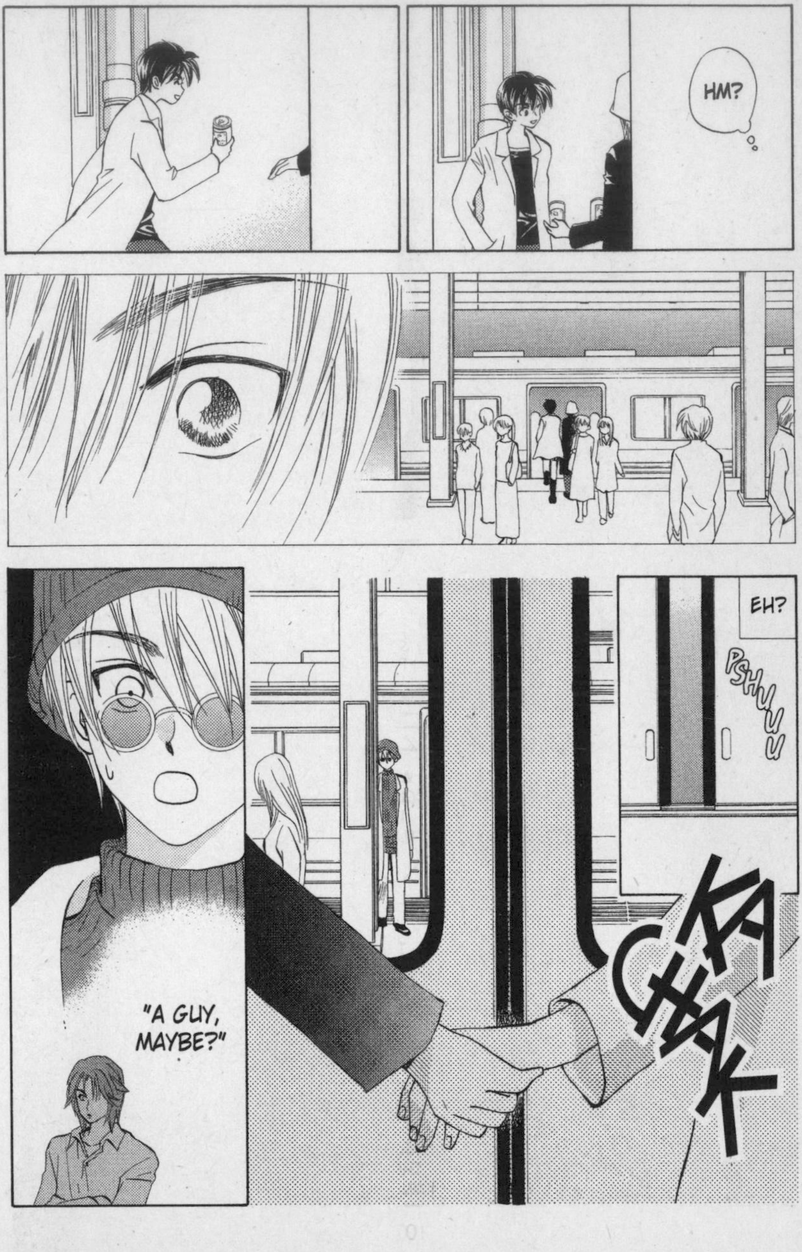
HM?
EH?
PSHUUU
KACHAK
"A GUY, MAYBE?"

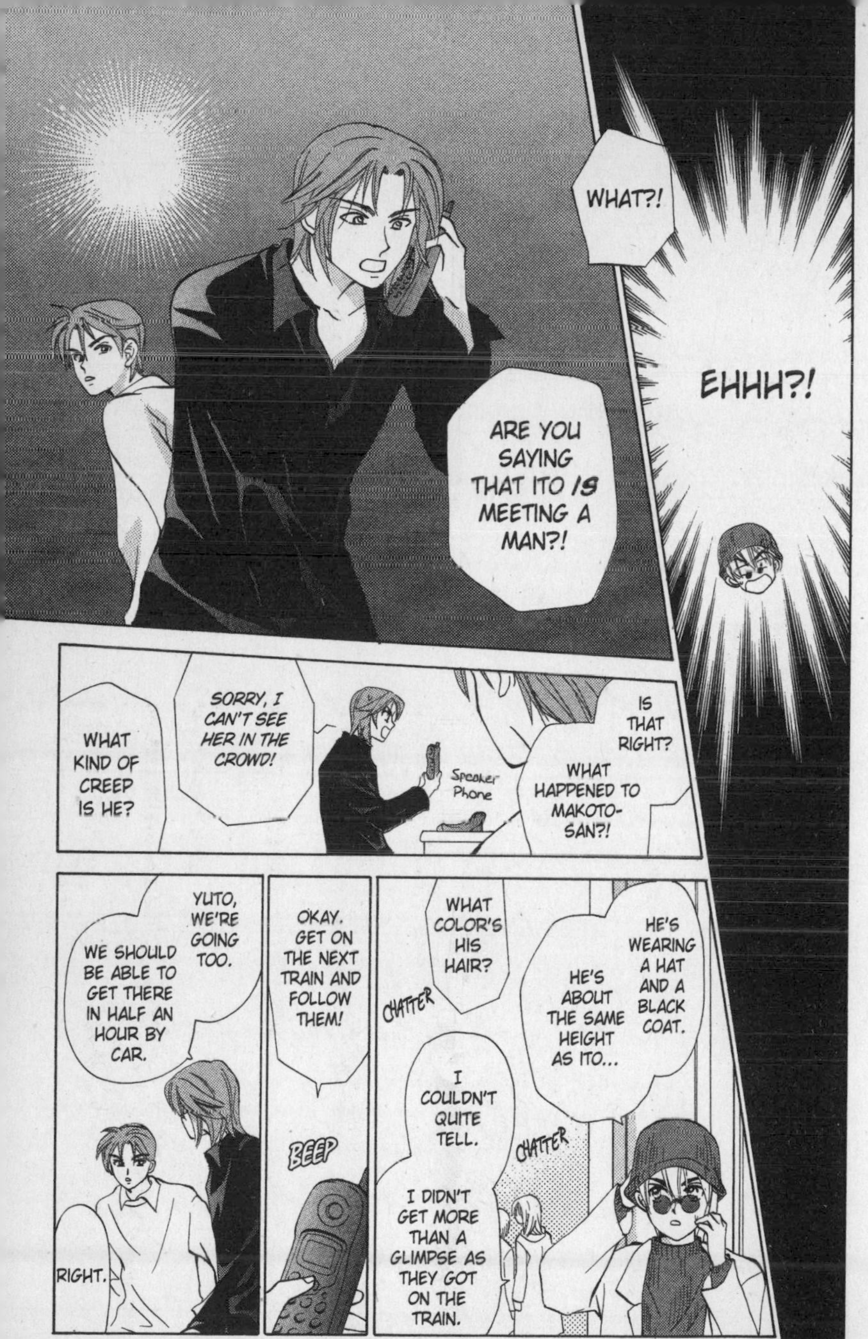
WHAT?!
EHHH?!
ARE YOU SAYING THAT ITO *IS* MEETING A MAN?!
IS THAT RIGHT?
WHAT HAPPENED TO MAKOTO-SAN?!
Speaker Phone
SORRY, I CAN'T SEE HER IN THE CROWD!
WHAT KIND OF CREEP IS HE?
HE'S WEARING A HAT AND A BLACK COAT.
HE'S ABOUT THE SAME HEIGHT AS ITO...
CHATTER
WHAT COLOR'S HIS HAIR?
CHATTER
I COULDN'T QUITE TELL.
I DIDN'T GET MORE THAN A GLIMPSE AS THEY GOT ON THE TRAIN.
OKAY. GET ON THE NEXT TRAIN AND FOLLOW THEM!
BEEP
YUTO, WE'RE GOING TOO.
WE SHOULD BE ABLE TO GET THERE IN HALF AN HOUR BY CAR.
RIGHT.

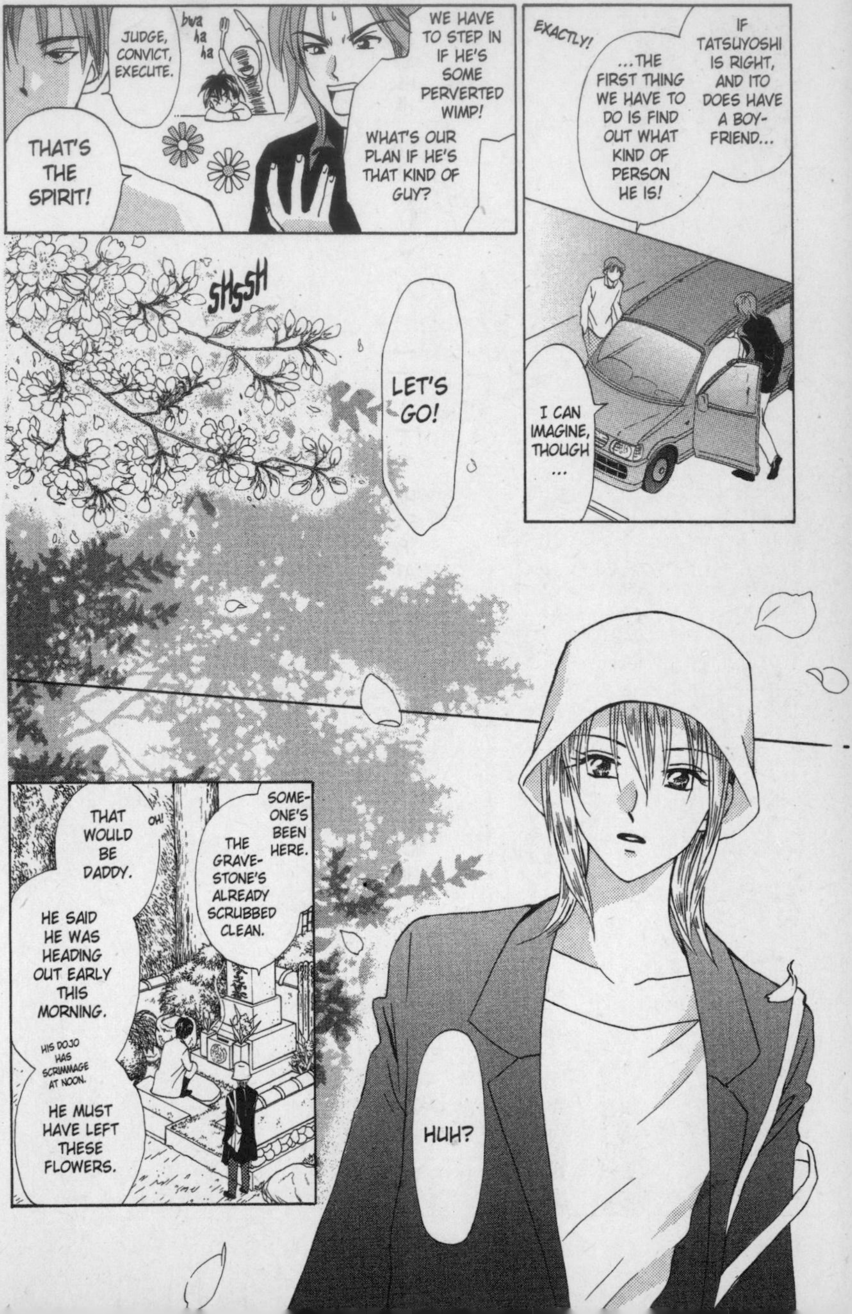
IF TATSUYOSHI IS RIGHT, AND ITO DOES HAVE A BOY-FRIEND...
...THE FIRST THING WE HAVE TO DO IS FIND OUT WHAT KIND OF PERSON HE IS!
EXACTLY!
WE HAVE TO STEP IN IF HE'S SOME PERVERTED WIMP!
WHAT'S OUR PLAN IF HE'S THAT KIND OF GUY?
bwa ha ha
JUDGE, CONVICT, EXECUTE.
THAT'S THE SPIRIT!
I CAN IMAGINE, THOUGH...
LET'S GO!
SHSSH
HUH?
SOME-ONE'S BEEN HERE.
THE GRAVE-STONE'S ALREADY SCRUBBED CLEAN.
OH!
THAT WOULD BE DADDY.
HE SAID HE WAS HEADING OUT EARLY THIS MORNING.
HIS DOJO HAS SCRIMMAGE AT NOON.
HE MUST HAVE LEFT THESE FLOWERS.

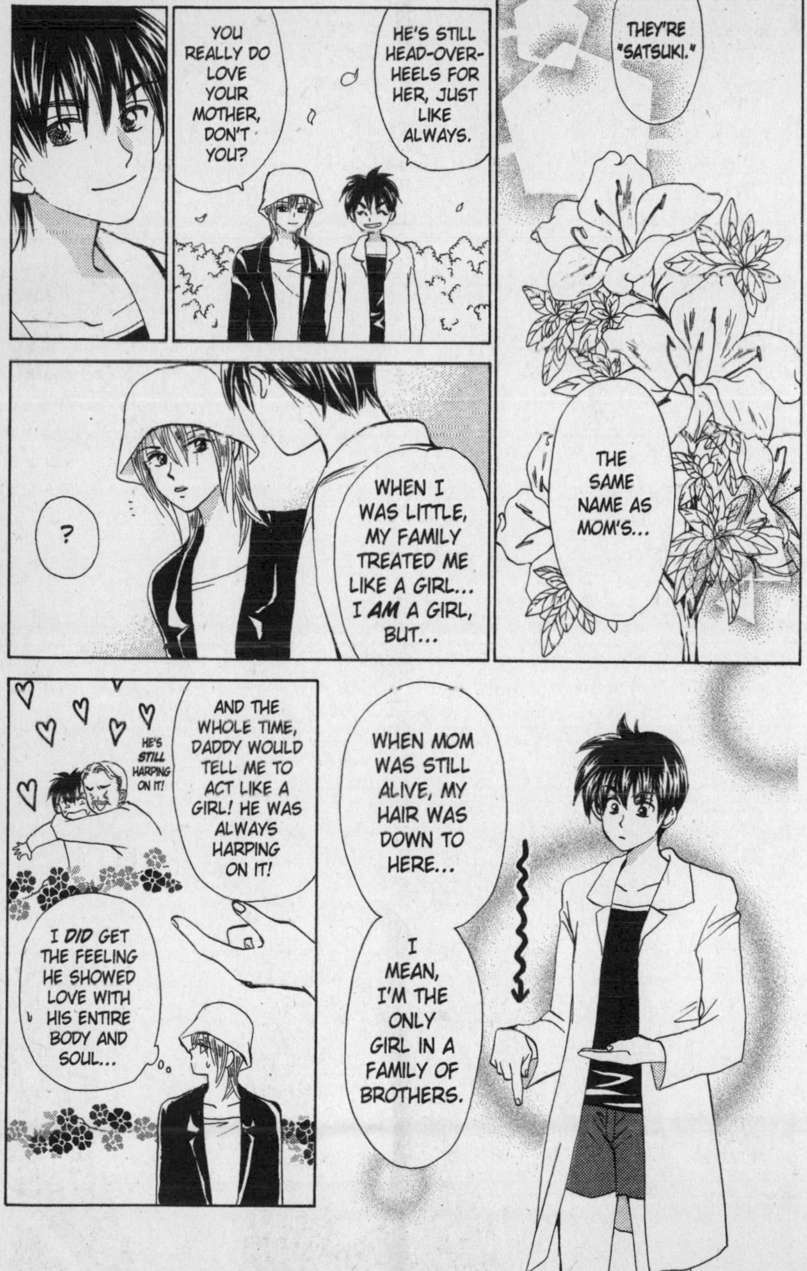
THEY'RE "SATSUKI."
THE SAME NAME AS MOM'S...
HE'S STILL HEAD-OVER-HEELS FOR HER, JUST LIKE ALWAYS.
YOU REALLY DO LOVE YOUR MOTHER, DON'T YOU?
WHEN I WAS LITTLE, MY FAMILY TREATED ME LIKE A GIRL... I *AM* A GIRL, BUT...
?
WHEN MOM WAS STILL ALIVE, MY HAIR WAS DOWN TO HERE...
I MEAN, I'M THE ONLY GIRL IN A FAMILY OF BROTHERS.
AND THE WHOLE TIME, DADDY WOULD TELL ME TO ACT LIKE A GIRL! HE WAS ALWAYS HARPING ON IT!
HE'S *STILL* HARPING ON IT!
I *DID* GET THE FEELING HE SHOWED LOVE WITH HIS ENTIRE BODY AND SOUL...

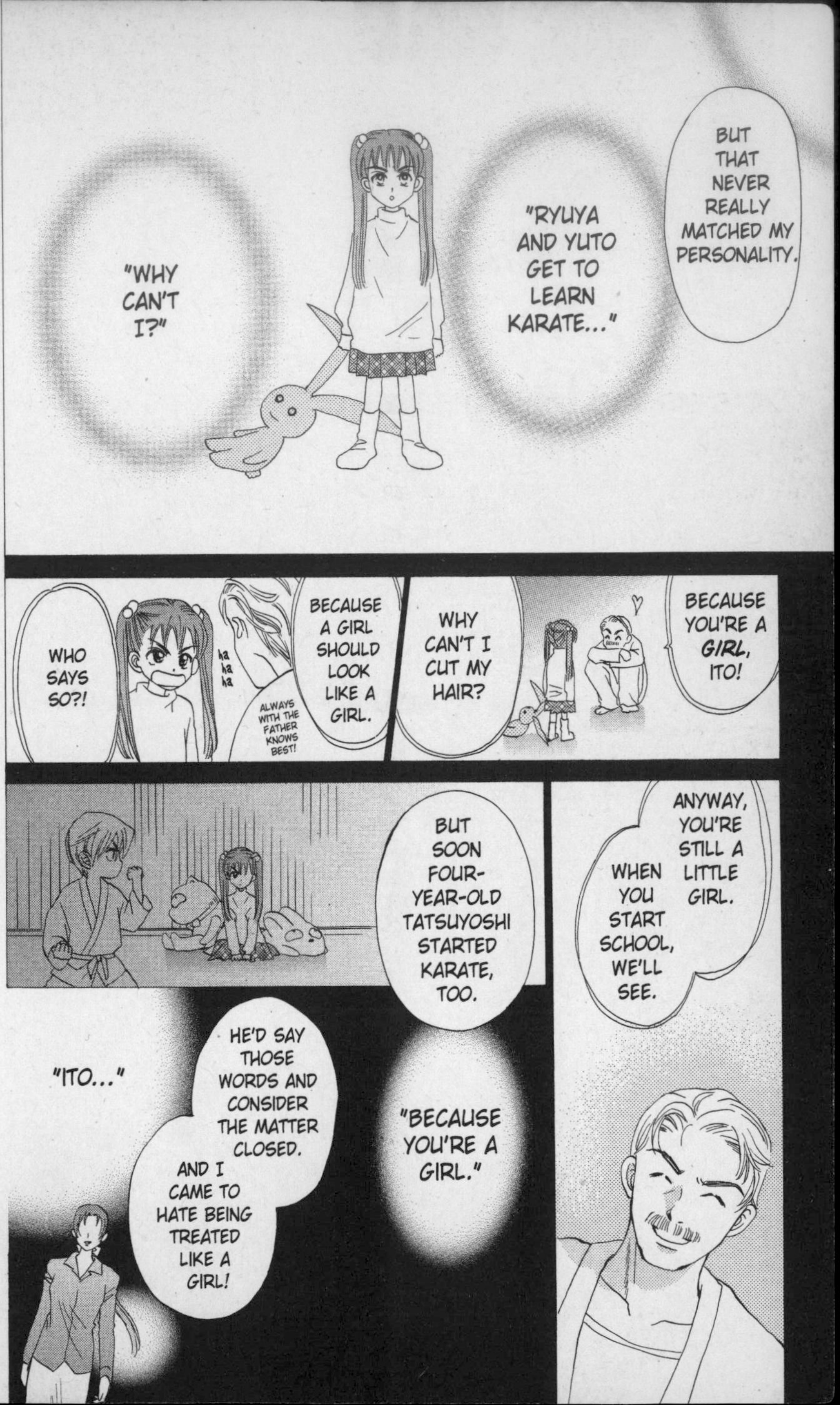
BUT THAT NEVER REALLY MATCHED MY PERSONALITY.
"RYUYA AND YUTO GET TO LEARN KARATE..."
"WHY CAN'T I?"
BECAUSE YOU'RE A *GIRL*, ITO!
WHY CAN'T I CUT MY HAIR?
BECAUSE A GIRL SHOULD LOOK LIKE A GIRL.
ha ha ha
ALWAYS WITH THE FATHER KNOWS BEST!
WHO SAYS SO?!
ANYWAY, YOU'RE STILL A LITTLE GIRL.
WHEN YOU START SCHOOL, WE'LL SEE.
BUT SOON FOUR-YEAR-OLD TATSUYOSHI STARTED KARATE, TOO.
"ITO..."
"BECAUSE YOU'RE A GIRL."
HE'D SAY THOSE WORDS AND CONSIDER THE MATTER CLOSED.
AND I CAME TO HATE BEING TREATED LIKE A GIRL!

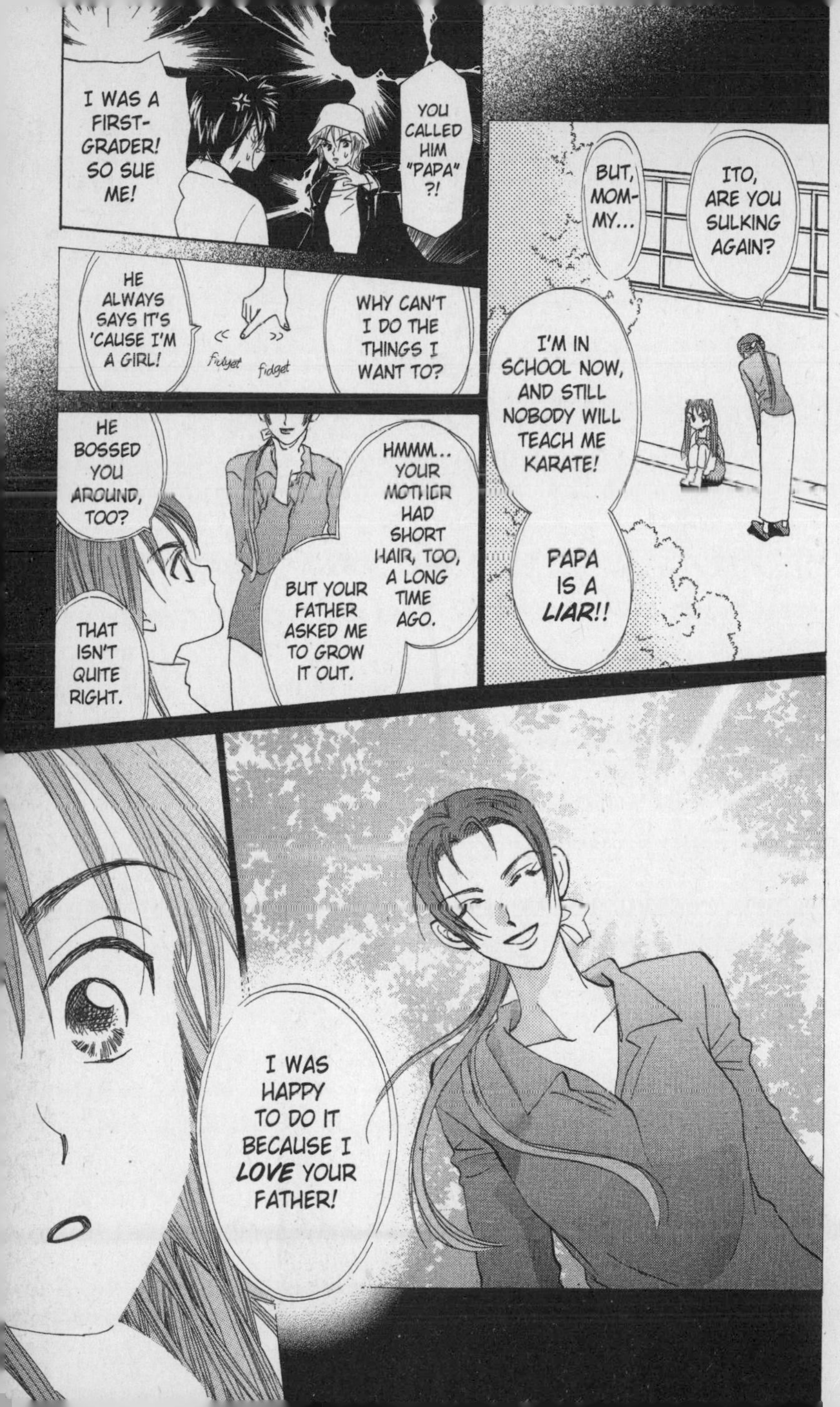
ITO, ARE YOU SULKING AGAIN?
BUT, MOM-MY...
I'M IN SCHOOL NOW, AND STILL NOBODY WILL TEACH ME KARATE!
PAPA IS A ***LIAR!!***
YOU CALLED HIM "PAPA" ?!
I WAS A FIRST-GRADER! SO SUE ME!
WHY CAN'T I DO THE THINGS I WANT TO?
HE ALWAYS SAYS IT'S 'CAUSE I'M A GIRL!
fidget fidget
HMMM... YOUR MOTHER HAD SHORT HAIR, TOO, A LONG TIME AGO.
BUT YOUR FATHER ASKED ME TO GROW IT OUT.
HE BOSSED YOU AROUND, TOO?
THAT ISN'T QUITE RIGHT.
I WAS HAPPY TO DO IT BECAUSE I ***LOVE*** YOUR FATHER!

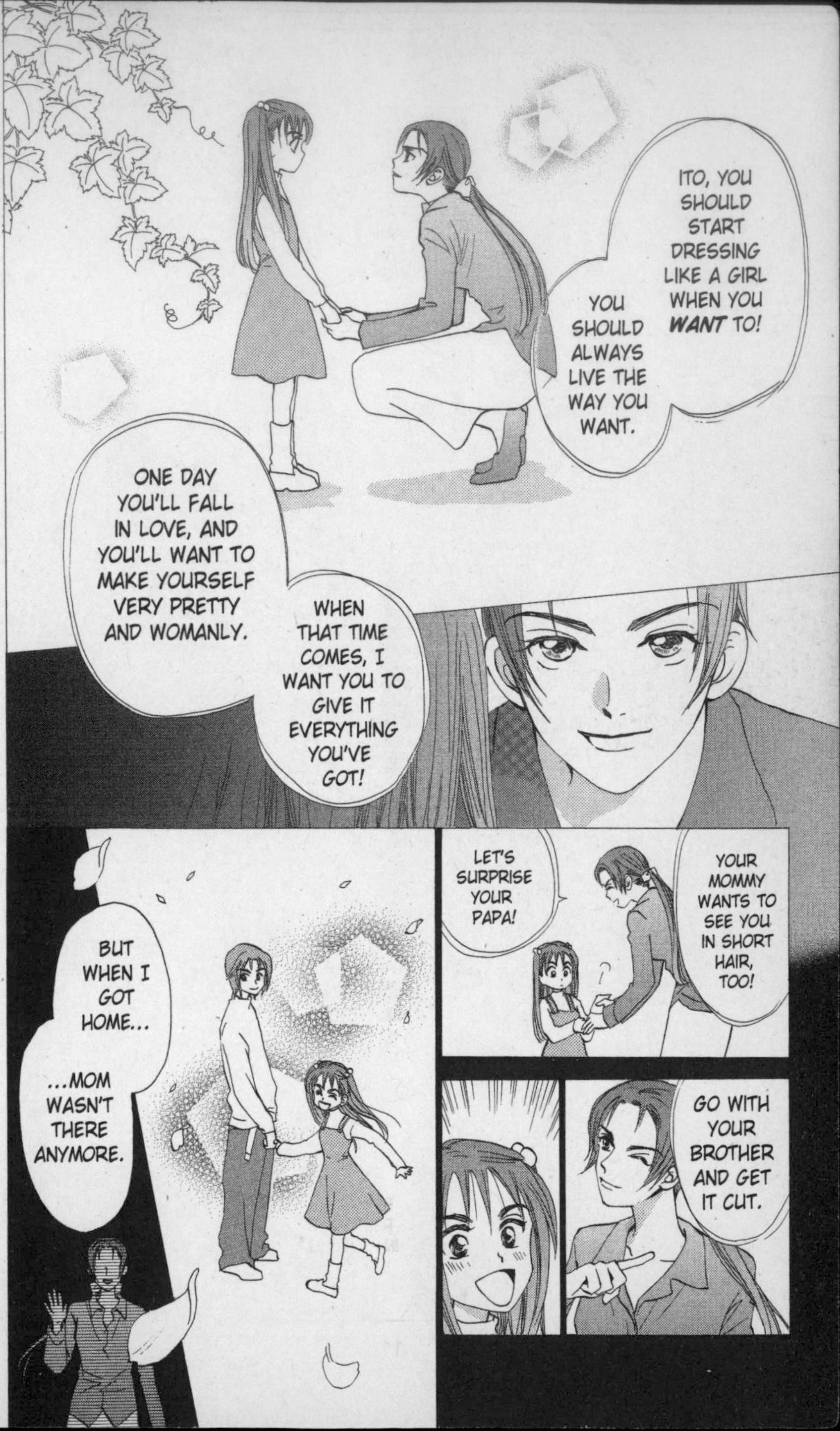
ITO, YOU SHOULD START DRESSING LIKE A GIRL WHEN YOU ***WANT*** TO!
YOU SHOULD ALWAYS LIVE THE WAY YOU WANT.
ONE DAY YOU'LL FALL IN LOVE, AND YOU'LL WANT TO MAKE YOURSELF VERY PRETTY AND WOMANLY.
WHEN THAT TIME COMES, I WANT YOU TO GIVE IT EVERYTHING YOU'VE GOT!
YOUR MOMMY WANTS TO SEE YOU IN SHORT HAIR, TOO!
LET'S SURPRISE YOUR PAPA!
GO WITH YOUR BROTHER AND GET IT CUT.
BUT WHEN I GOT HOME...
...MOM WASN'T THERE ANYMORE.

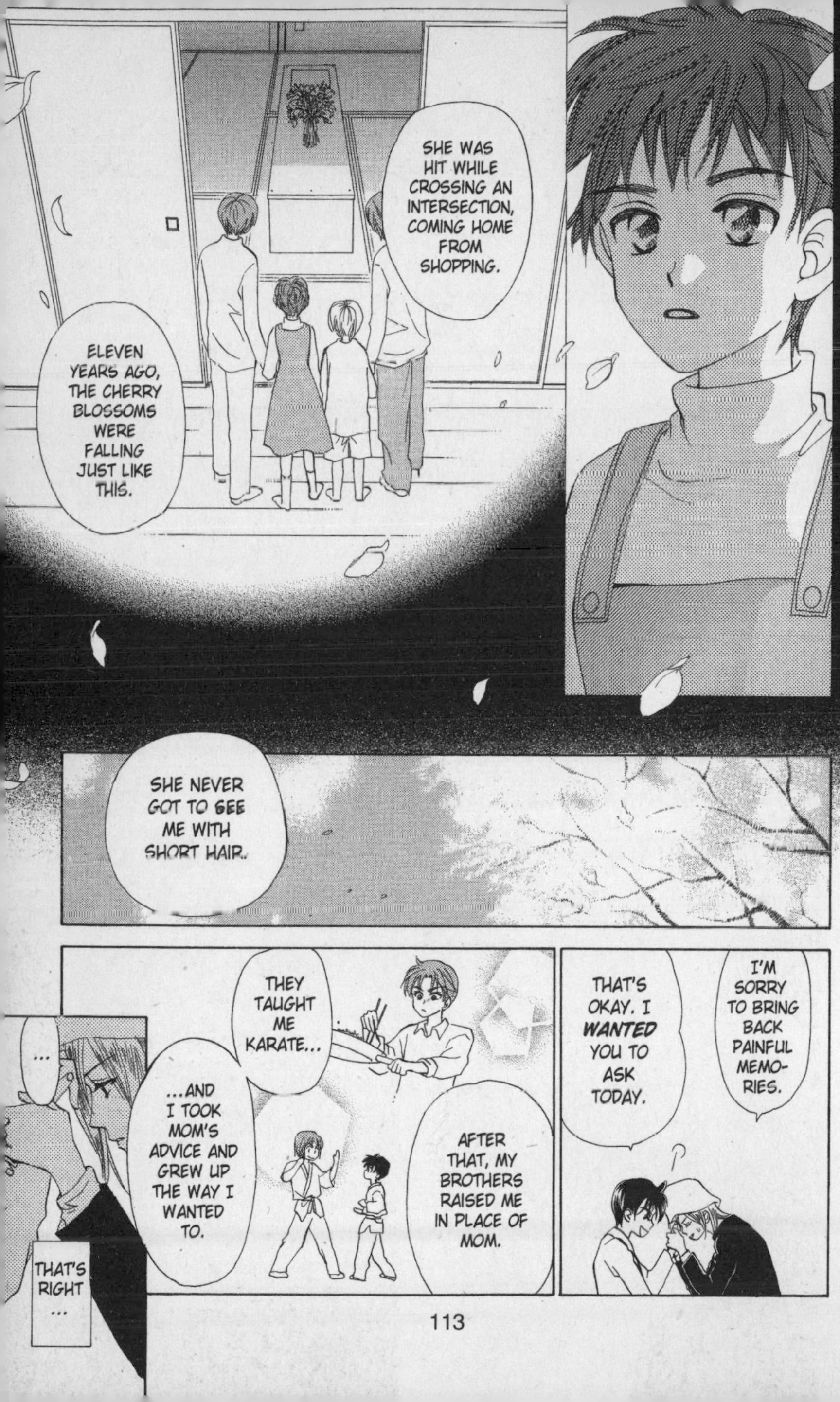
SHE WAS HIT WHILE CROSSING AN INTERSECTION, COMING HOME FROM SHOPPING.
ELEVEN YEARS AGO, THE CHERRY BLOSSOMS WERE FALLING JUST LIKE THIS.
SHE NEVER GOT TO SEE ME WITH SHORT HAIR.
I'M SORRY TO BRING BACK PAINFUL MEMO-RIES.
THAT'S OKAY. I **WANTED** YOU TO ASK TODAY.
AFTER THAT, MY BROTHERS RAISED ME IN PLACE OF MOM.
THEY TAUGHT ME KARATE...
...AND I TOOK MOM'S ADVICE AND GREW UP THE WAY I WANTED TO.
...
THAT'S RIGHT ...

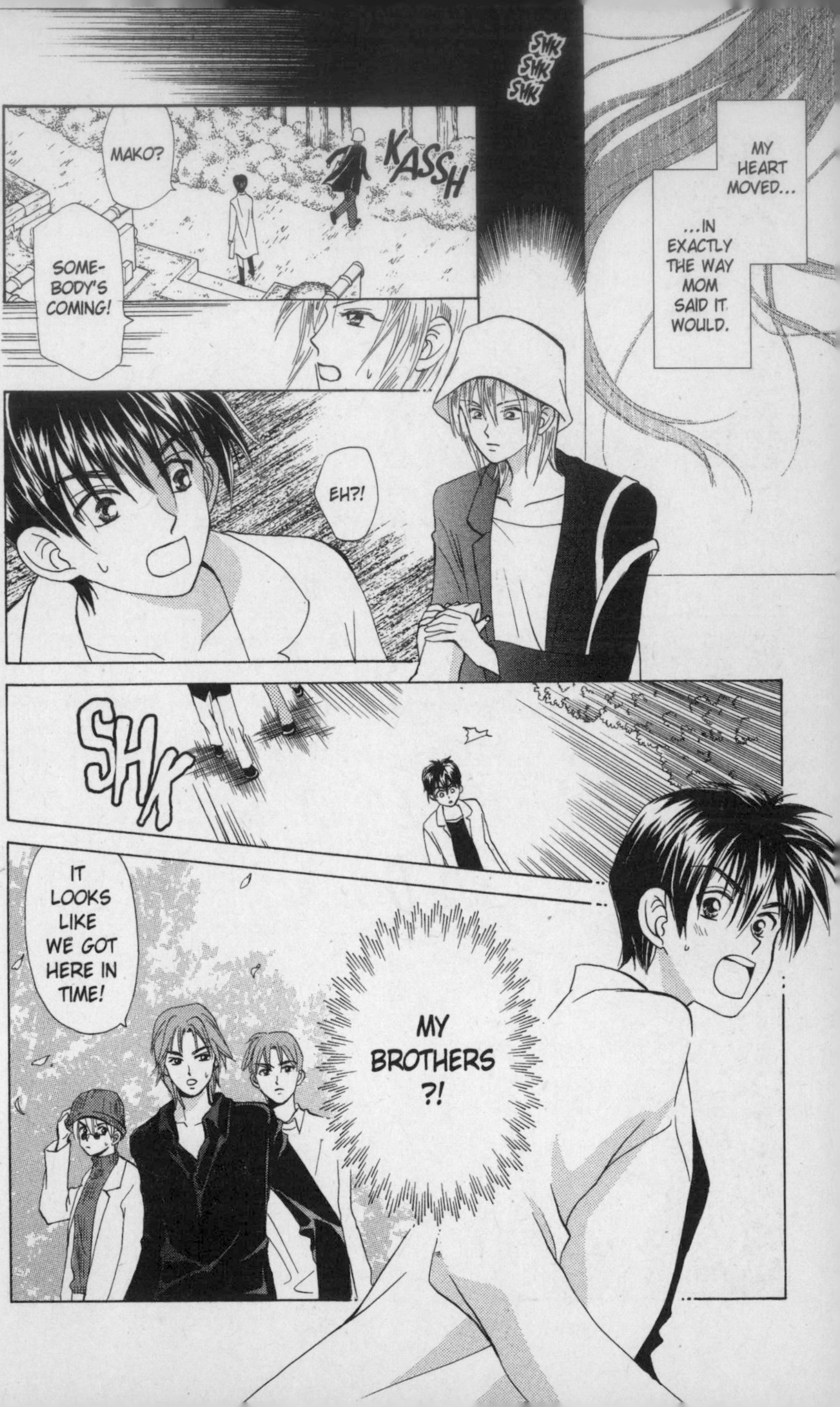

SWK SWK SWK
MY HEART MOVED...
...IN EXACTLY THE WAY MOM SAID IT WOULD.
KASSH
MAKO?
SOME-BODY'S COMING!
EH?!
SHK
IT LOOKS LIKE WE GOT HERE IN TIME!
MY BROTHERS ?!

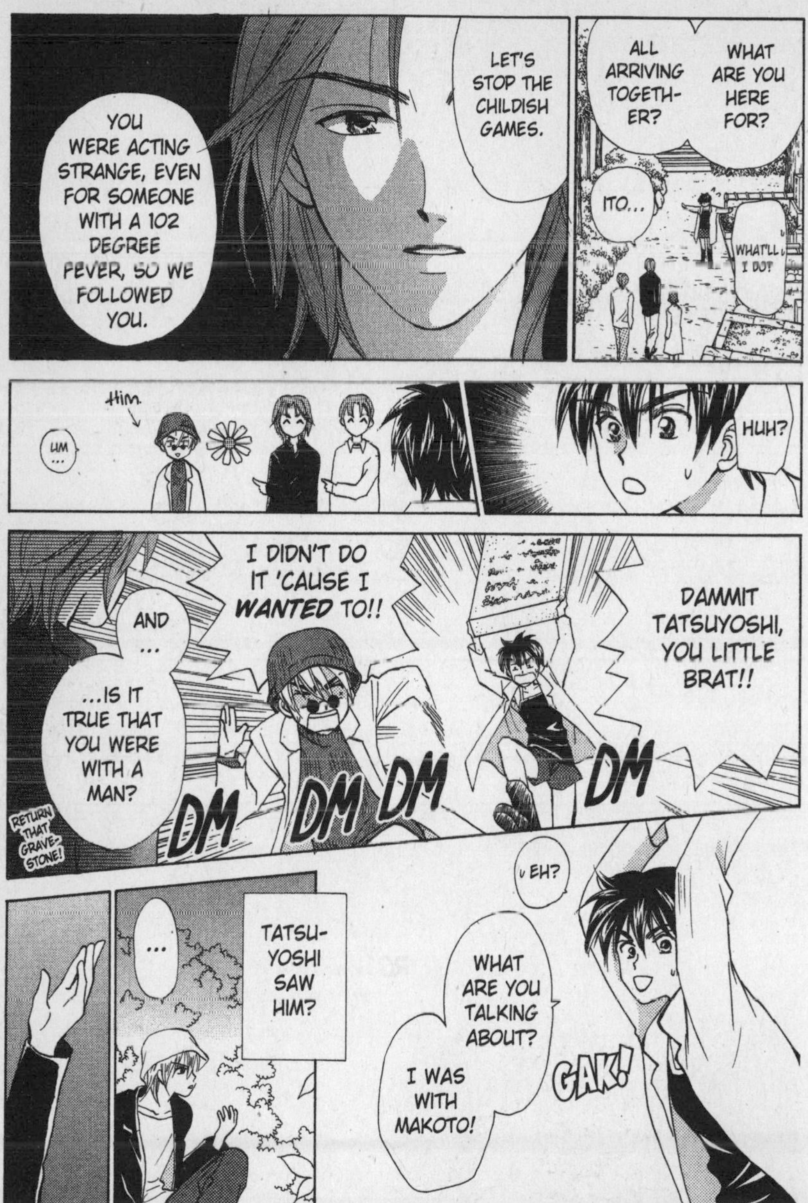
WHAT ARE YOU HERE FOR?
ALL ARRIVING TOGETH-ER?
ITO...
WHAT'LL I DO?
LET'S STOP THE CHILDISH GAMES.
YOU WERE ACTING STRANGE, EVEN FOR SOMEONE WITH A 102 DEGREE FEVER, SO WE FOLLOWED YOU.
HUH?
Him.
UM ...
DAMMIT TATSUYOSHI, YOU LITTLE BRAT!!
I DIDN'T DO IT 'CAUSE I WANTED TO!!
AND ...
...IS IT TRUE THAT YOU WERE WITH A MAN?
DM
DM DM
DM
RETURN THAT GRAVE-STONE!
EH?
WHAT ARE YOU TALKING ABOUT?
I WAS WITH MAKOTO!
GAK!
TATSU-YOSHI SAW HIM?
...

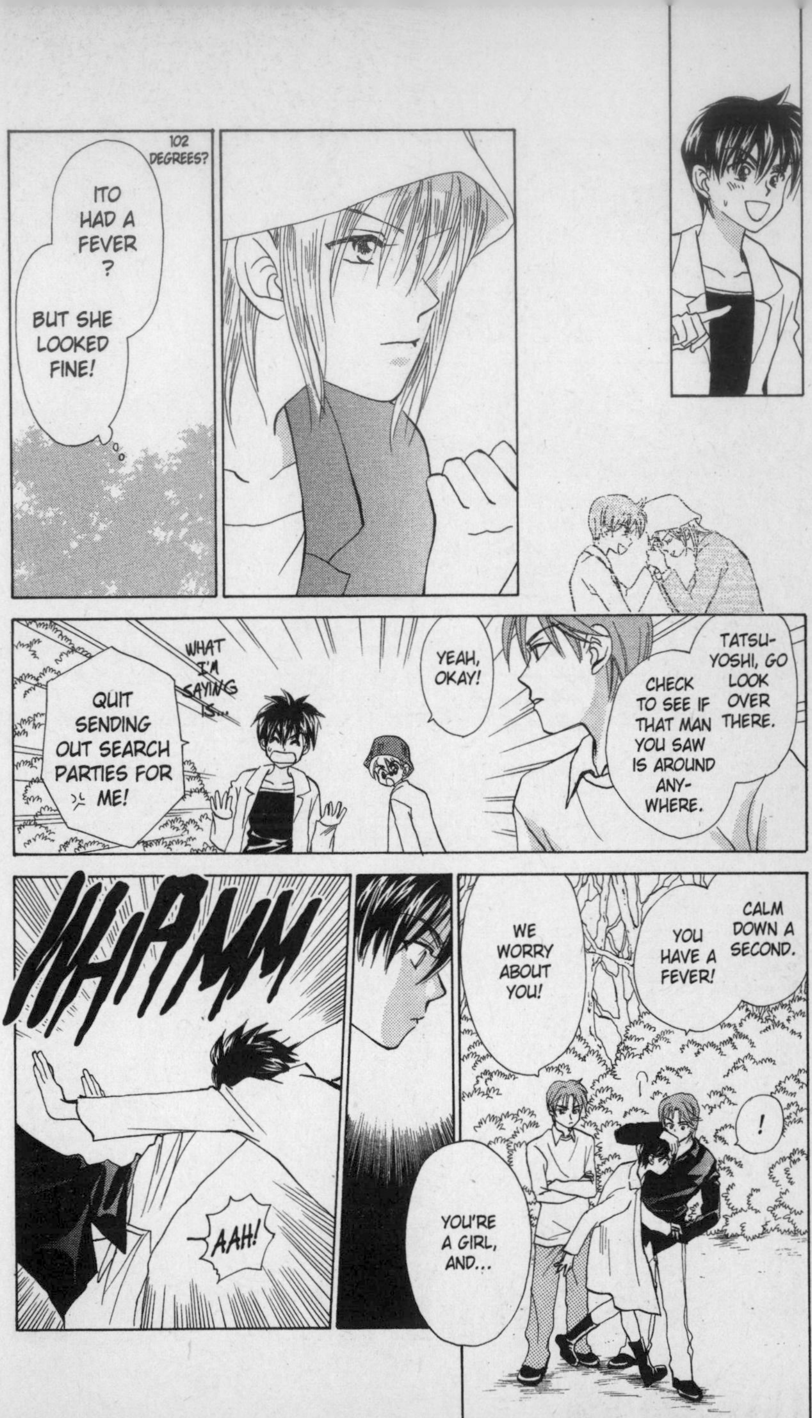
102 DEGREES?
ITO HAD A FEVER ?
BUT SHE LOOKED FINE!
TATSU-YOSHI, GO LOOK OVER THERE.
CHECK TO SEE IF THAT MAN YOU SAW IS AROUND ANY-WHERE.
YEAH, OKAY!
WHAT I'M SAYING IS...
QUIT SENDING OUT SEARCH PARTIES FOR ME!
CALM DOWN A SECOND.
YOU HAVE A FEVER!
WE WORRY ABOUT YOU!
!
YOU'RE A GIRL, AND...
WHAMM
AAH!

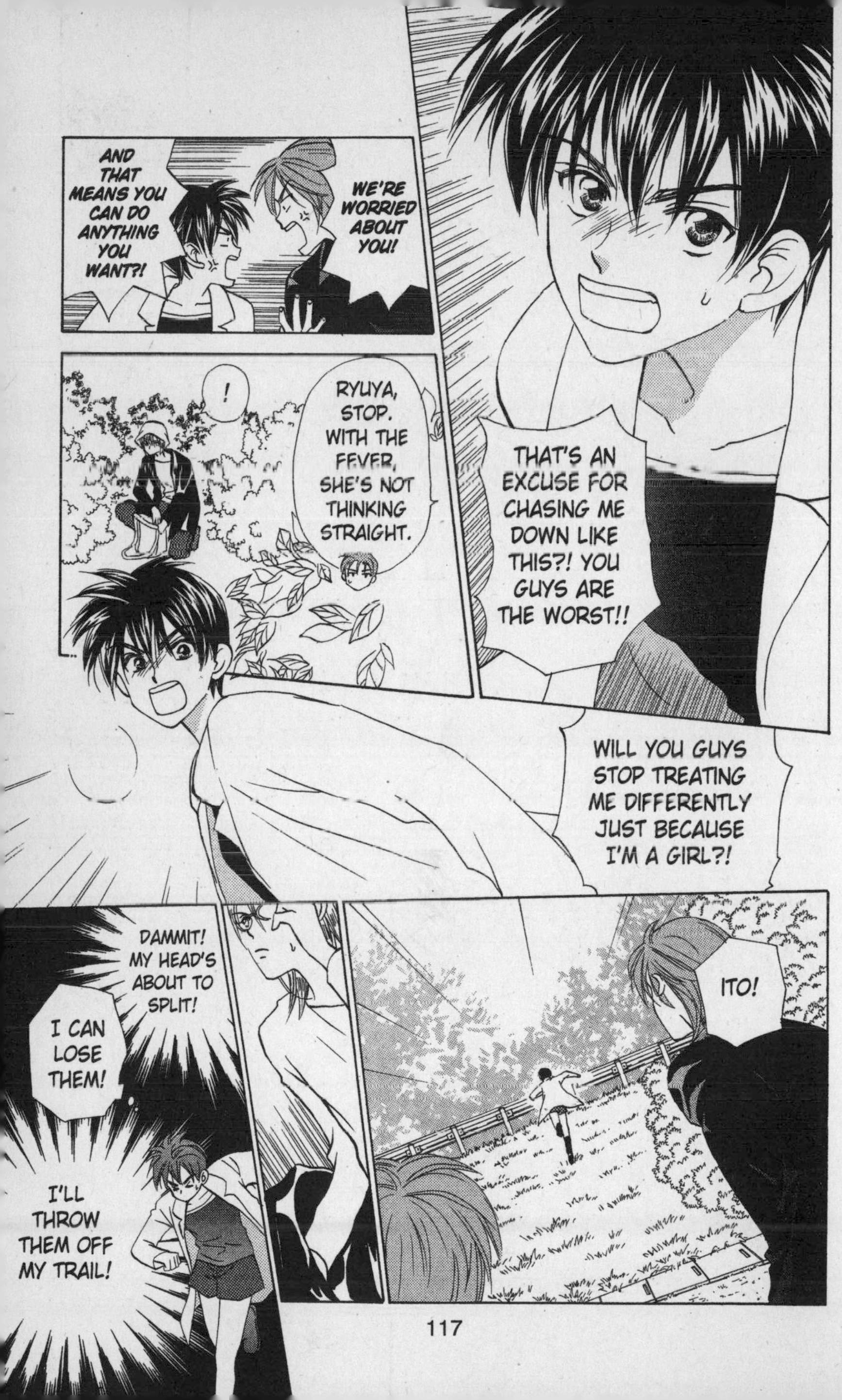
THAT'S AN EXCUSE FOR CHASING ME DOWN LIKE THIS?! YOU GUYS ARE THE WORST!!
WE'RE WORRIED ABOUT YOU!
AND THAT MEANS YOU CAN DO ANYTHING YOU WANT?!
RYUYA, STOP. WITH THE FEVER, SHE'S NOT THINKING STRAIGHT.
!
WILL YOU GUYS STOP TREATING ME DIFFERENTLY JUST BECAUSE I'M A GIRL?!
ITO!
DAMMIT! MY HEAD'S ABOUT TO SPLIT!
I CAN LOSE THEM!
I'LL THROW THEM OFF MY TRAIL!

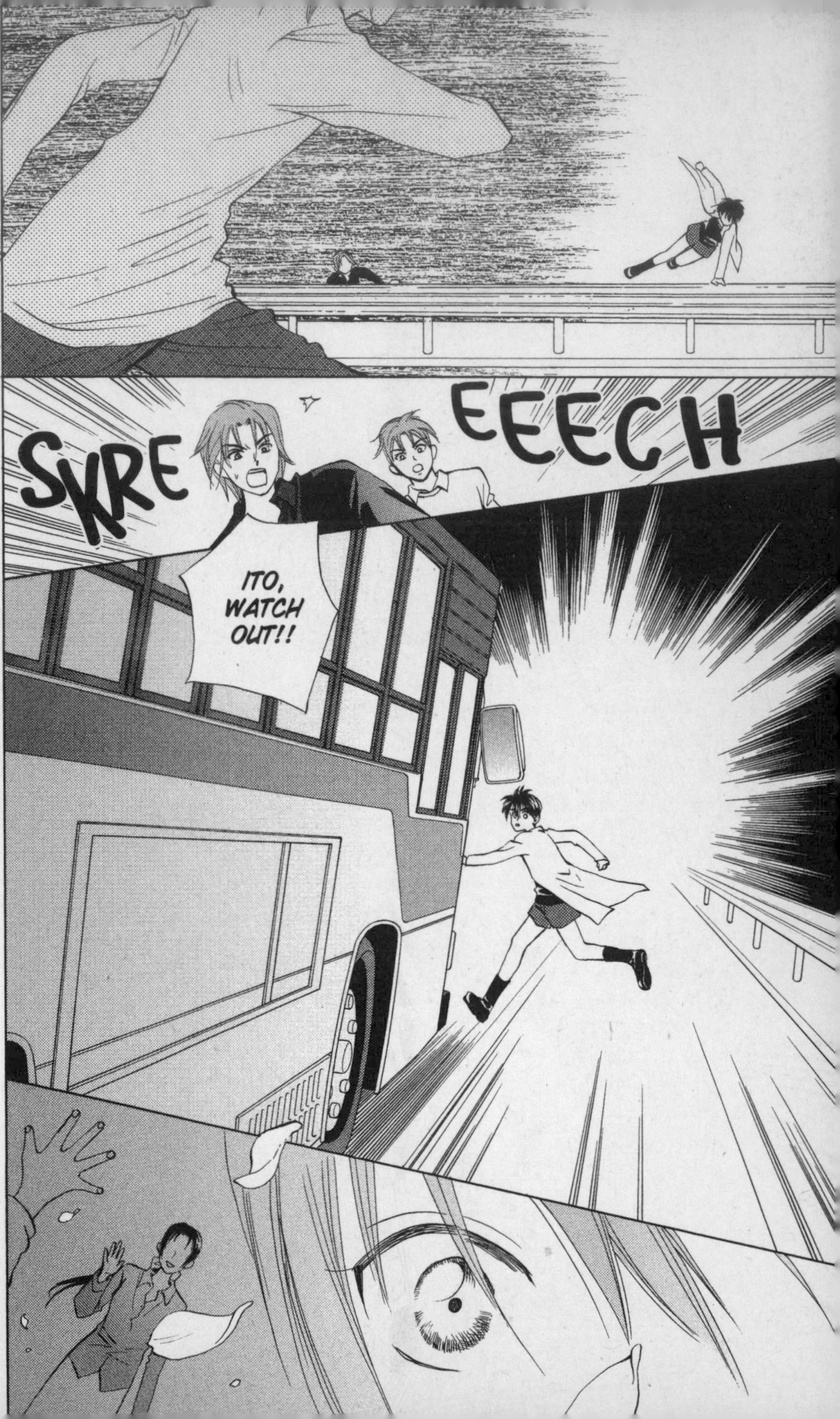
SKRE EEECH
ITO, WATCH OUT!!

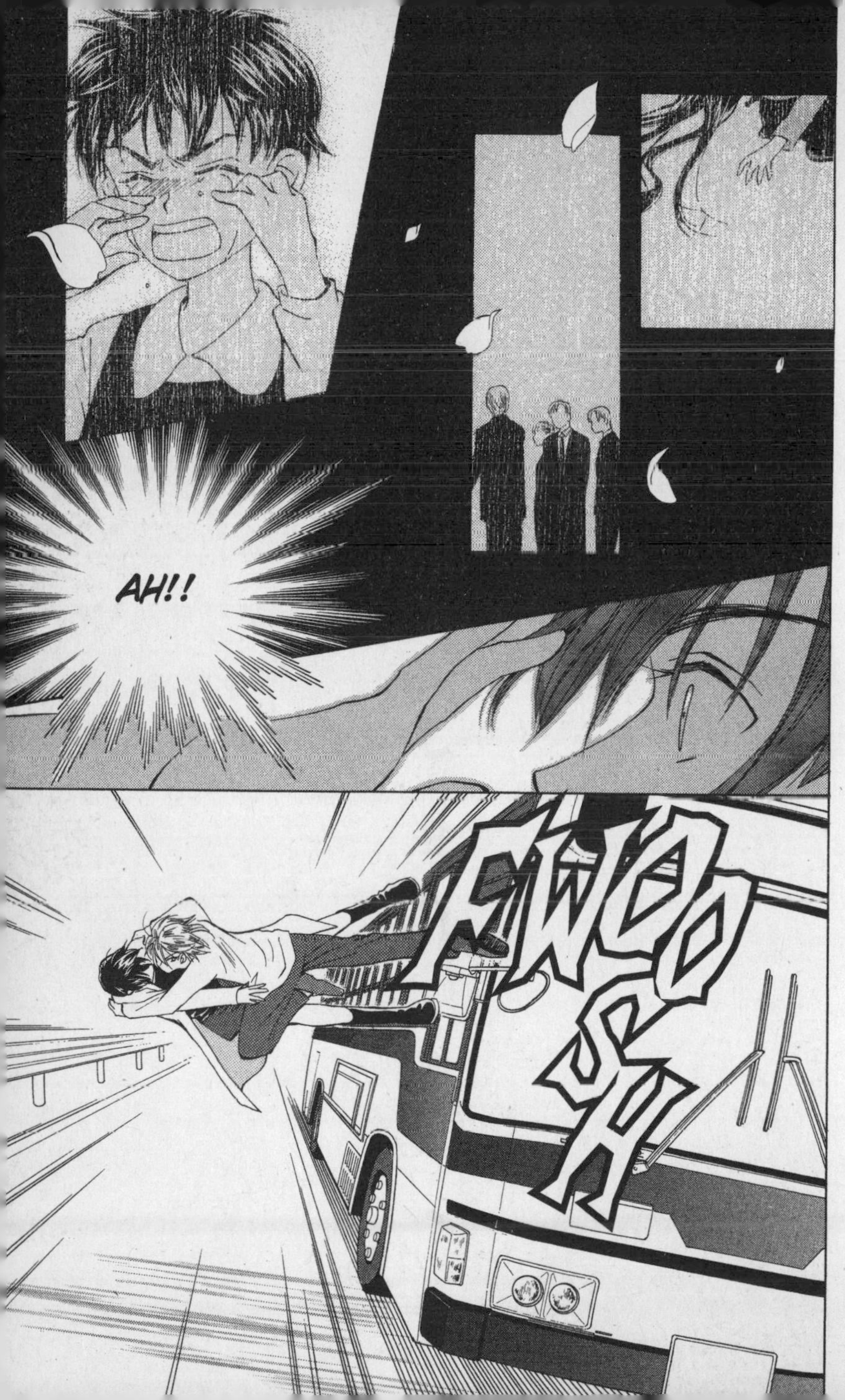
AH!!
FWOOSH

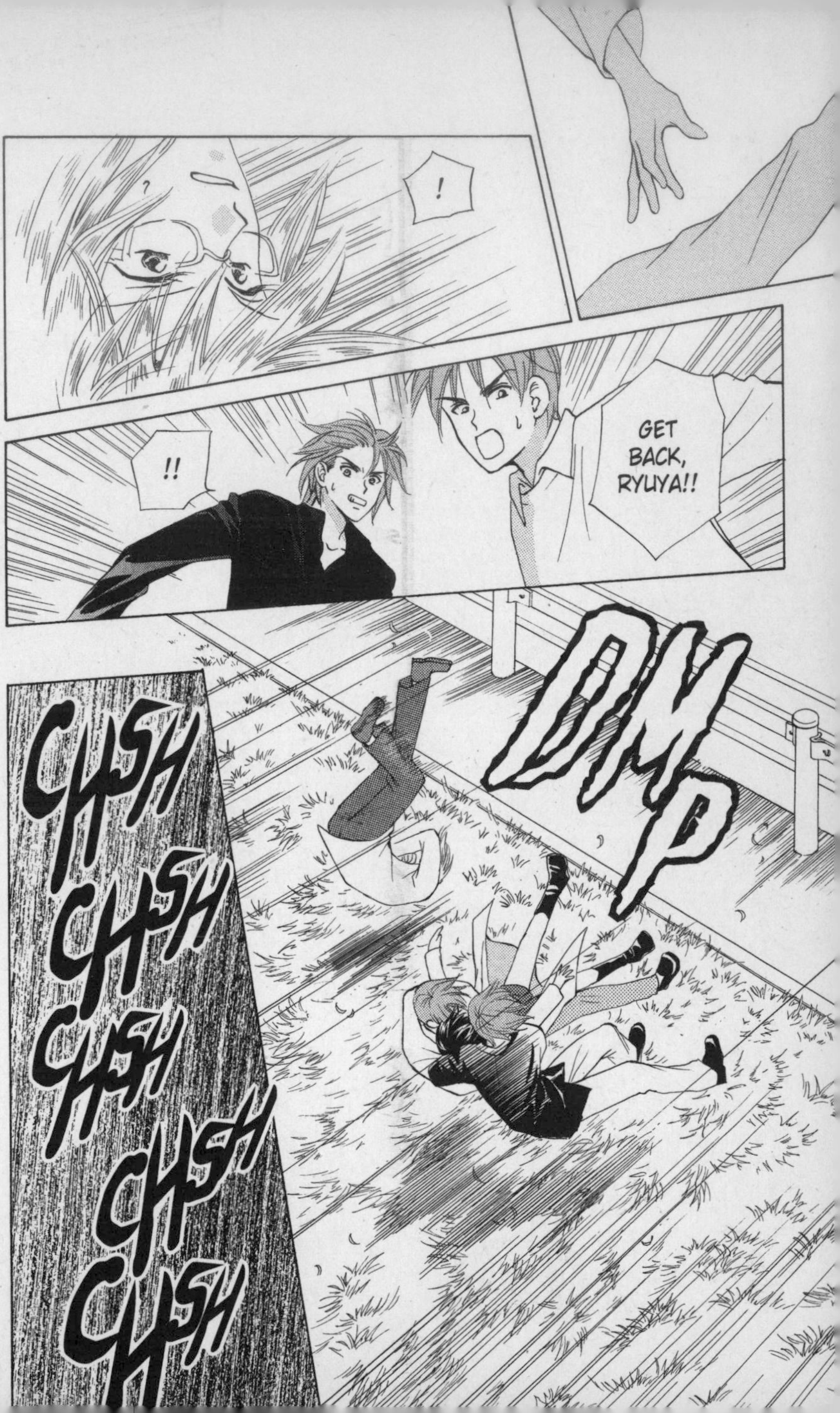
!
GET BACK, RYUYA!!
!!
DMP
CHSH CHSH CHSH CHSH CHSH

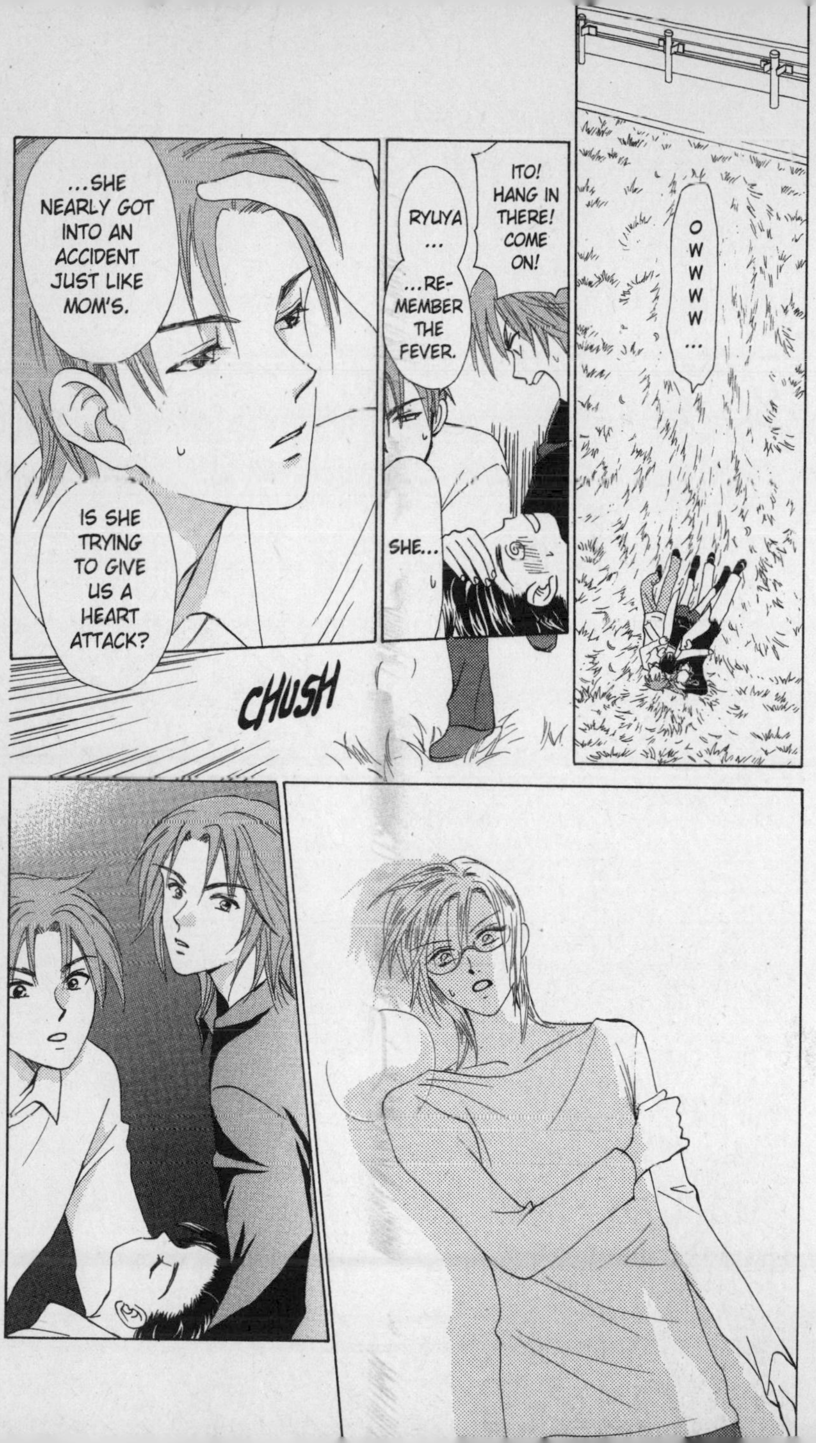
OWWWW...
ITO! HANG IN THERE! COME ON!
RYUYA...
...REMEMBER THE FEVER.
SHE...
...SHE NEARLY GOT INTO AN ACCIDENT JUST LIKE MOM'S.
IS SHE TRYING TO GIVE US A HEART ATTACK?
CHUSH

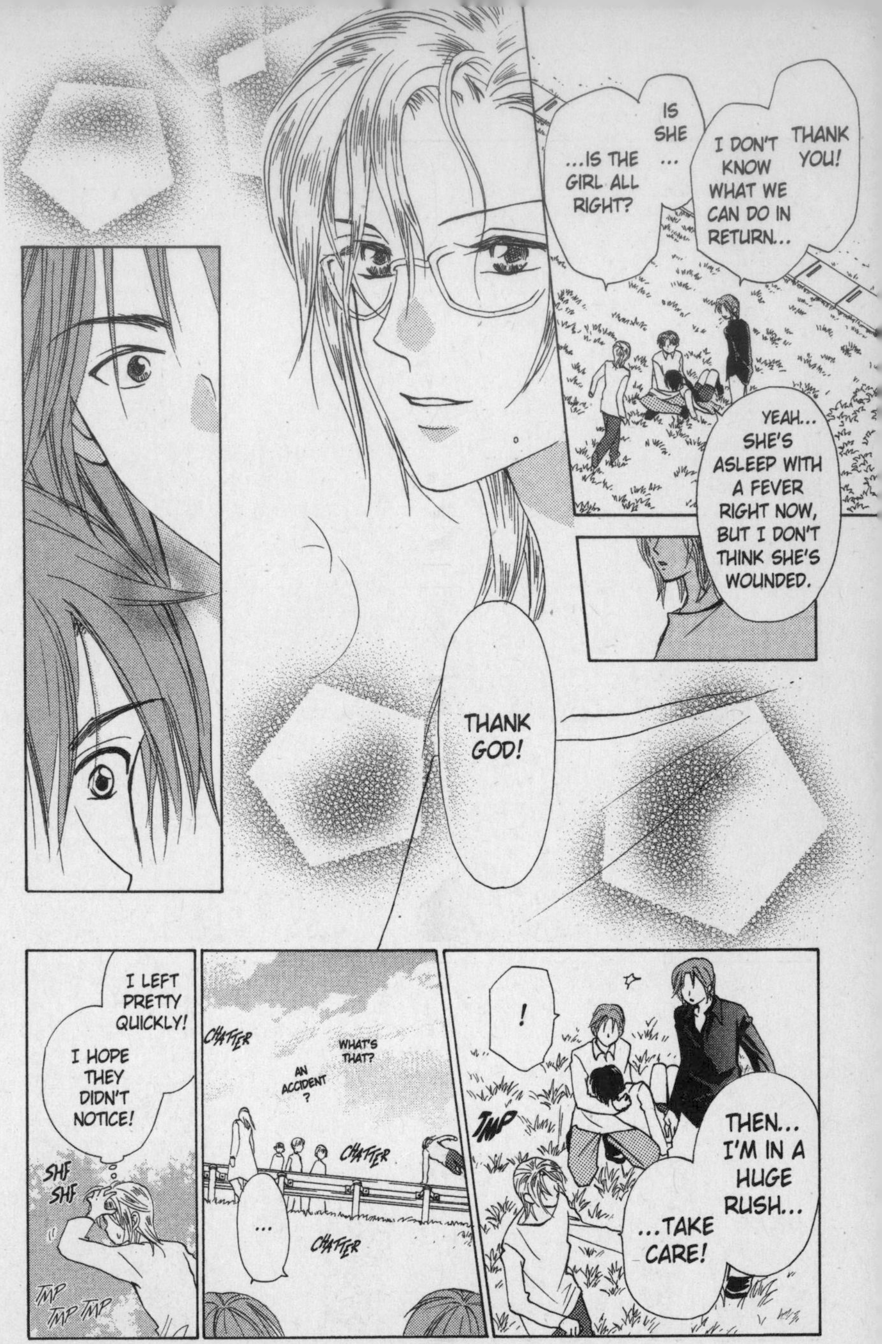
THANK YOU!
I DON'T KNOW WHAT WE CAN DO IN RETURN...
IS SHE ...
...IS THE GIRL ALL RIGHT?
YEAH... SHE'S ASLEEP WITH A FEVER RIGHT NOW, BUT I DON'T THINK SHE'S WOUNDED.
THANK GOD!
!
THEN... I'M IN A HUGE RUSH...
...TAKE CARE!
TMP
WHAT'S THAT?
AN ACCIDENT?
CHATTER
CHATTER
CHATTER
...
I LEFT PRETTY QUICKLY!
I HOPE THEY DIDN'T NOTICE!
SHF SHF
TMP TMP TMP

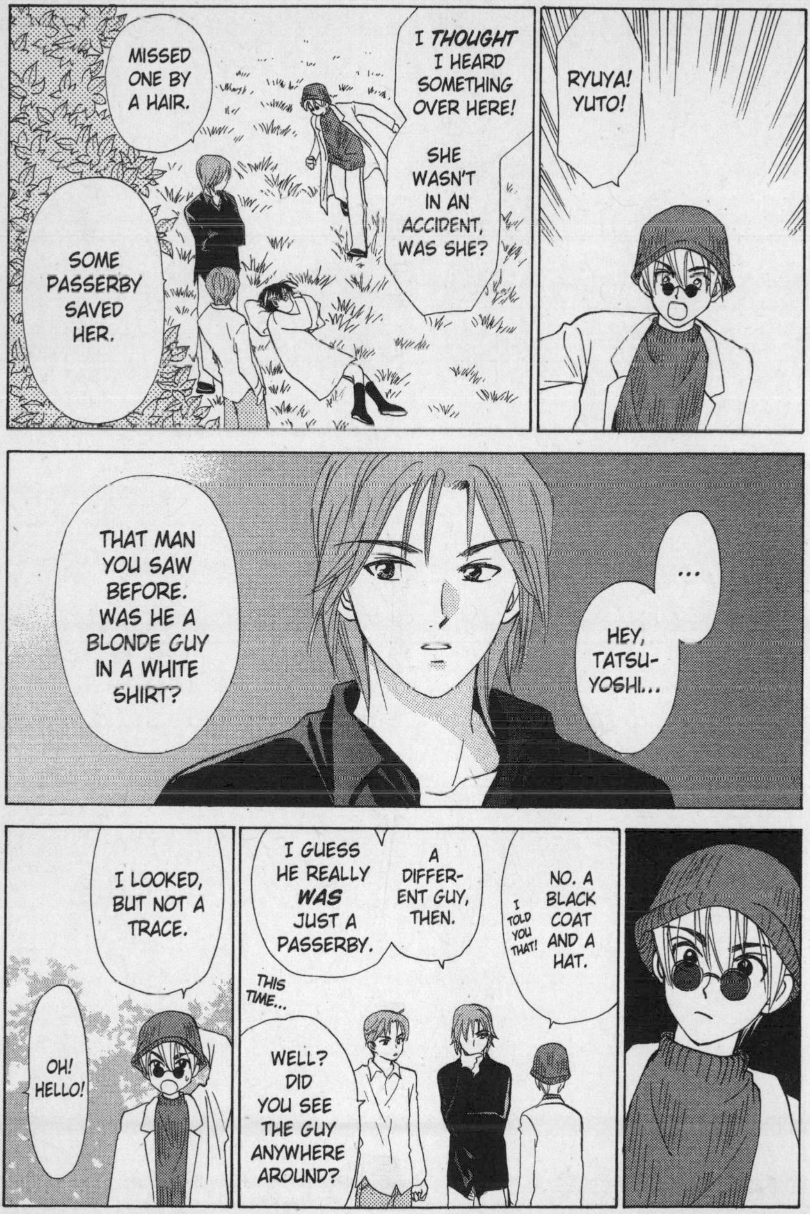
RYUYA! YUTO!
I *THOUGHT* I HEARD SOMETHING OVER HERE!
SHE WASN'T IN AN ACCIDENT, WAS SHE?
MISSED ONE BY A HAIR.
SOME PASSERBY SAVED HER.
...
HEY, TATSU-YOSHI...
THAT MAN YOU SAW BEFORE. WAS HE A BLONDE GUY IN A WHITE SHIRT?
NO. A BLACK COAT AND A HAT.
I TOLD YOU THAT!
A DIFFER-ENT GUY, THEN.
I GUESS HE REALLY *WAS* JUST A PASSERBY.
THIS TIME...
WELL? DID YOU SEE THE GUY ANYWHERE AROUND?
I LOOKED, BUT NOT A TRACE.
OH! HELLO!

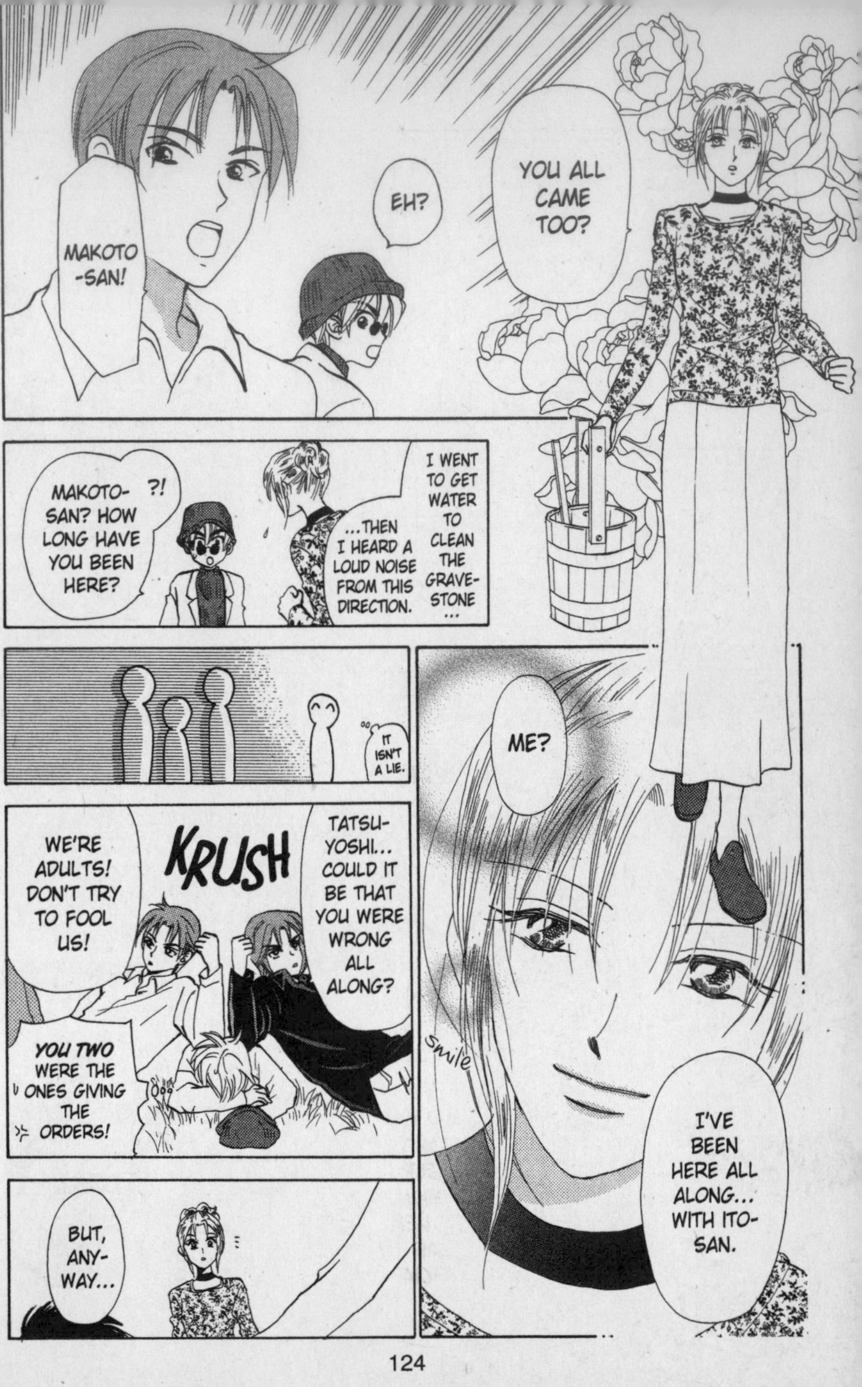
YOU ALL CAME TOO?
EH?
MAKOTO-SAN!
I WENT TO GET WATER TO CLEAN THE GRAVESTONE...
...THEN I HEARD A LOUD NOISE FROM THIS DIRECTION.
?!
MAKOTO-SAN? HOW LONG HAVE YOU BEEN HERE?
ME?
smile
I'VE BEEN HERE ALL ALONG... WITH ITO-SAN.
IT ISN'T A LIE.
TATSUYOSHI... COULD IT BE THAT YOU WERE WRONG ALL ALONG?
KRUSH
WE'RE ADULTS! DON'T TRY TO FOOL US!
YOU TWO WERE THE ONES GIVING THE ORDERS!
BUT, ANYWAY...

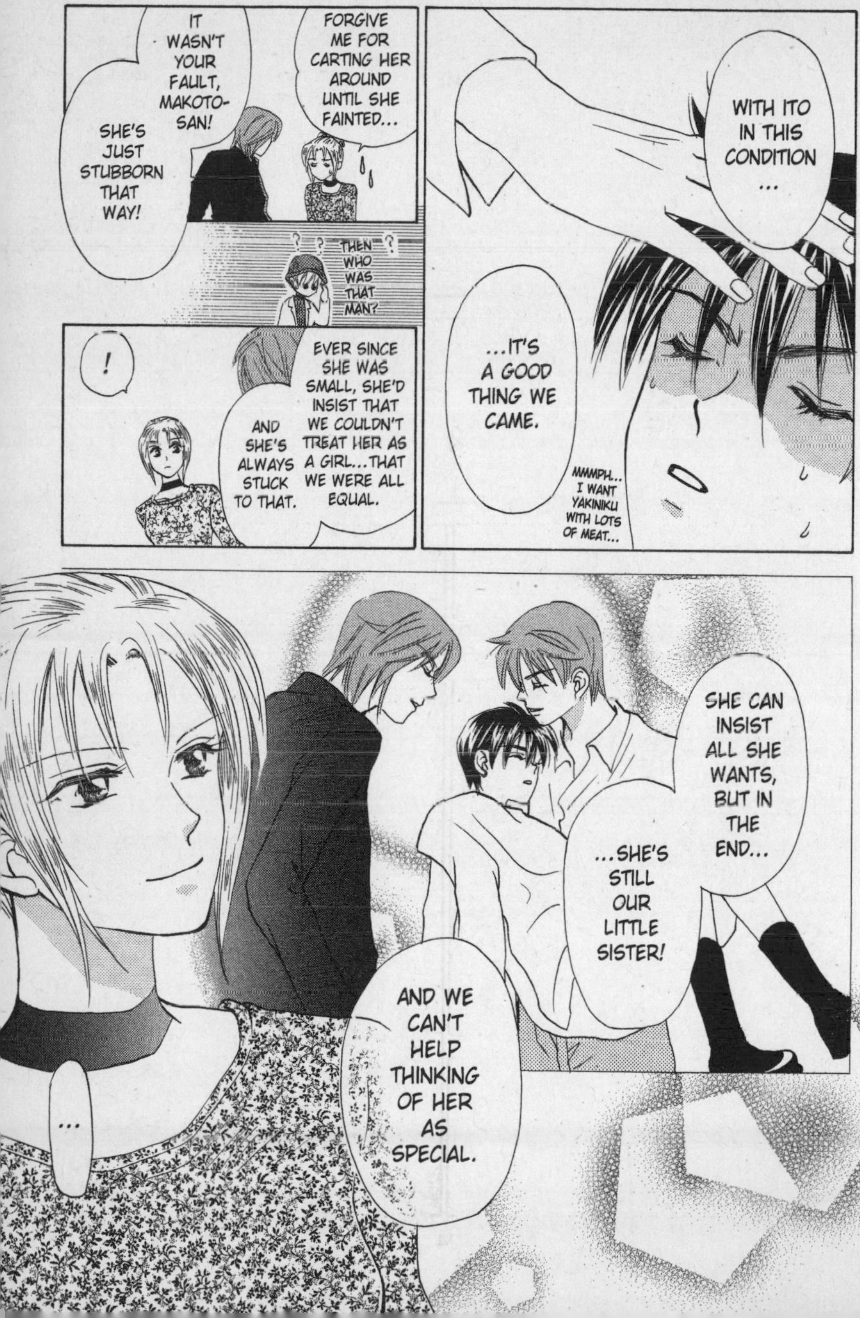
WITH ITO IN THIS CONDITION ...
...IT'S A GOOD THING WE CAME.
MMMPH... I WANT YAKINIKU WITH LOTS OF MEAT...
FORGIVE ME FOR CARTING HER AROUND UNTIL SHE FAINTED...
IT WASN'T YOUR FAULT, MAKOTO-SAN!
SHE'S JUST STUBBORN THAT WAY!
THEN WHO WAS THAT MAN?
EVER SINCE SHE WAS SMALL, SHE'D INSIST THAT WE COULDN'T TREAT HER AS A GIRL...THAT WE WERE ALL EQUAL.
AND SHE'S ALWAYS STUCK TO THAT.
!
SHE CAN INSIST ALL SHE WANTS, BUT IN THE END...
...SHE'S STILL OUR LITTLE SISTER!
AND WE CAN'T HELP THINKING OF HER AS SPECIAL.
...

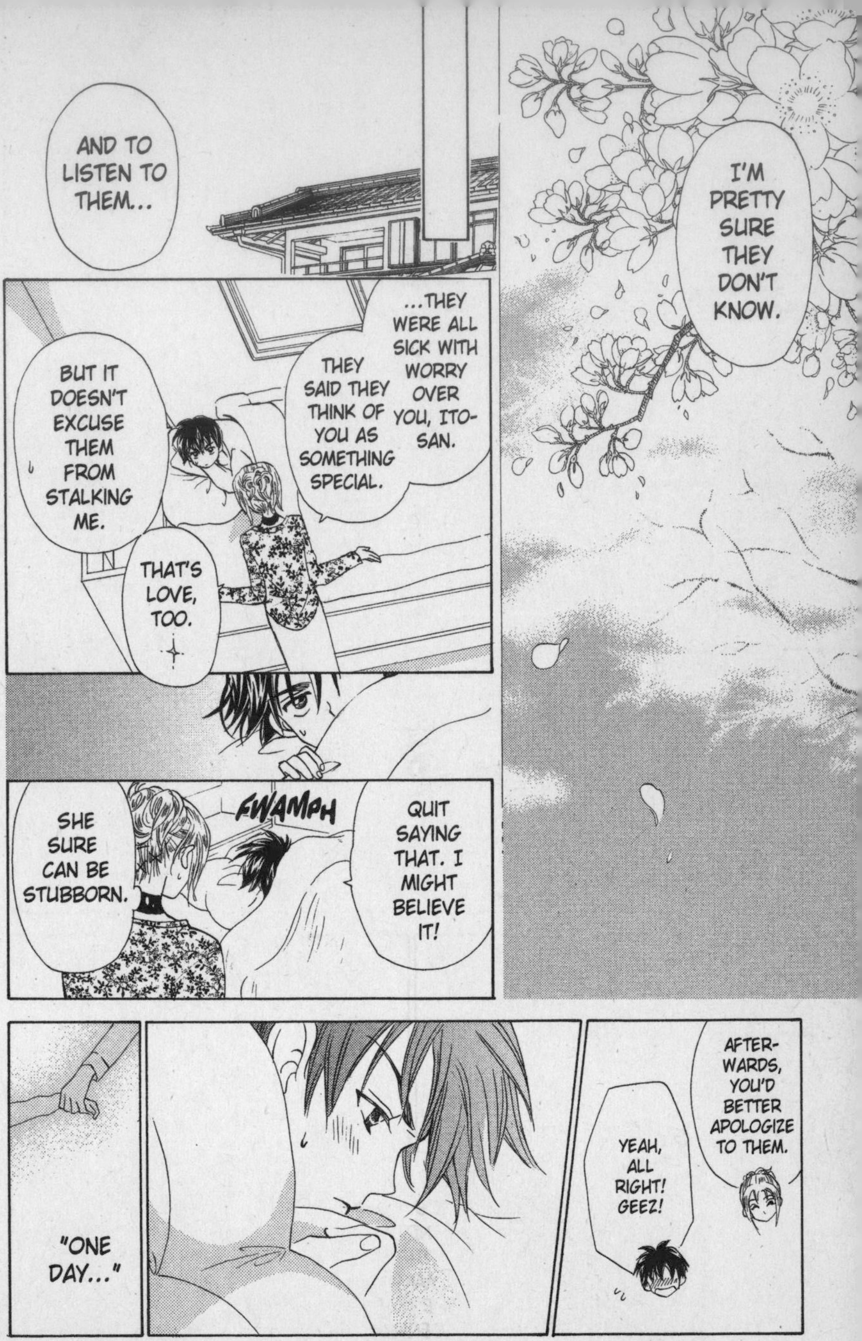
I'M PRETTY SURE THEY DON'T KNOW.
AND TO LISTEN TO THEM...
...THEY WERE ALL SICK WITH WORRY OVER YOU, ITO-SAN.
THEY SAID THEY THINK OF YOU AS SOMETHING SPECIAL.
BUT IT DOESN'T EXCUSE THEM FROM STALKING ME.
THAT'S LOVE, TOO.
QUIT SAYING THAT. I MIGHT BELIEVE IT!
FWAMPH
SHE SURE CAN BE STUBBORN.
AFTER-WARDS, YOU'D BETTER APOLOGIZE TO THEM.
YEAH, ALL RIGHT! GEEZ!
"ONE DAY..."

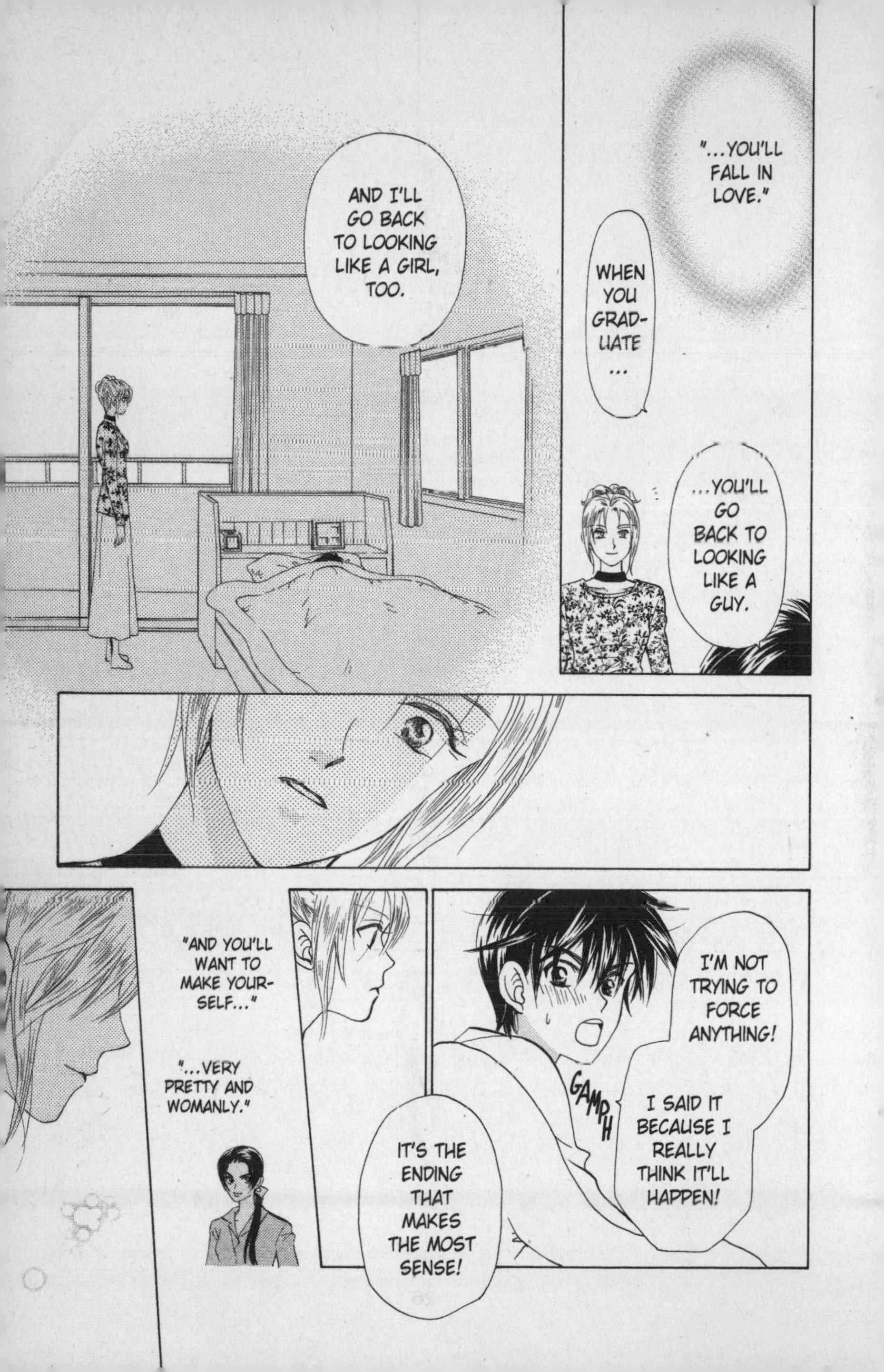
"...YOU'LL FALL IN LOVE."
WHEN YOU GRAD-UATE...
...YOU'LL GO BACK TO LOOKING LIKE A GUY.
AND I'LL GO BACK TO LOOKING LIKE A GIRL, TOO.
I'M NOT TRYING TO FORCE ANYTHING!
GAMPH
I SAID IT BECAUSE I REALLY THINK IT'LL HAPPEN!
IT'S THE ENDING THAT MAKES THE MOST SENSE!
"AND YOU'LL WANT TO MAKE YOUR-SELF..."
"...VERY PRETTY AND WOMANLY."

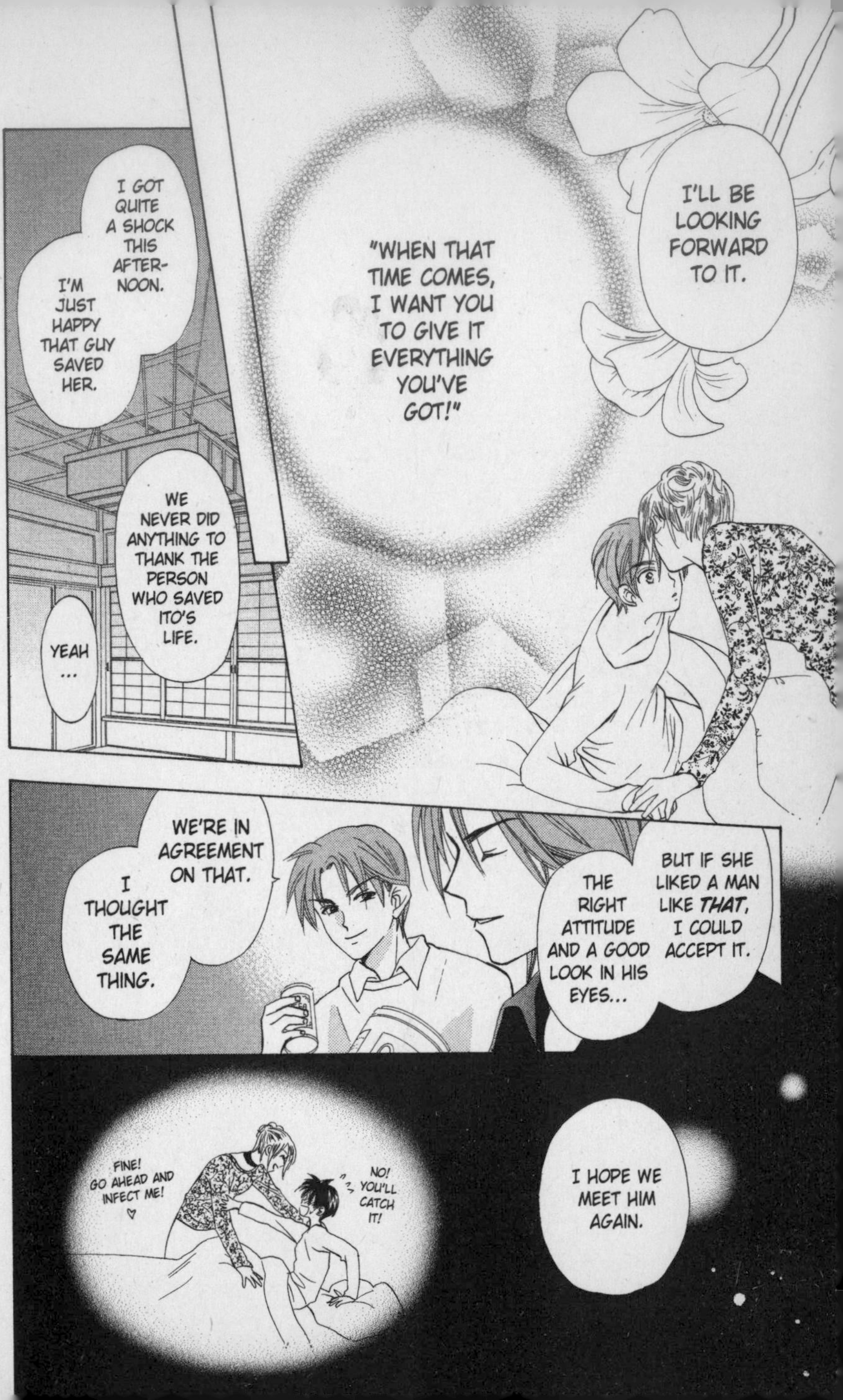
I'LL BE LOOKING FORWARD TO IT.
"WHEN THAT TIME COMES, I WANT YOU TO GIVE IT EVERYTHING YOU'VE GOT!"
I GOT QUITE A SHOCK THIS AFTER-NOON.
I'M JUST HAPPY THAT GUY SAVED HER.
WE NEVER DID ANYTHING TO THANK THE PERSON WHO SAVED ITO'S LIFE.
YEAH...
BUT IF SHE LIKED A MAN LIKE *THAT*, I COULD ACCEPT IT.
THE RIGHT ATTITUDE AND A GOOD LOOK IN HIS EYES...
WE'RE IN AGREEMENT ON THAT.
I THOUGHT THE SAME THING.
I HOPE WE MEET HIM AGAIN.
NO! YOU'LL CATCH IT!
FINE! GO AHEAD AND INFECT ME! ♡

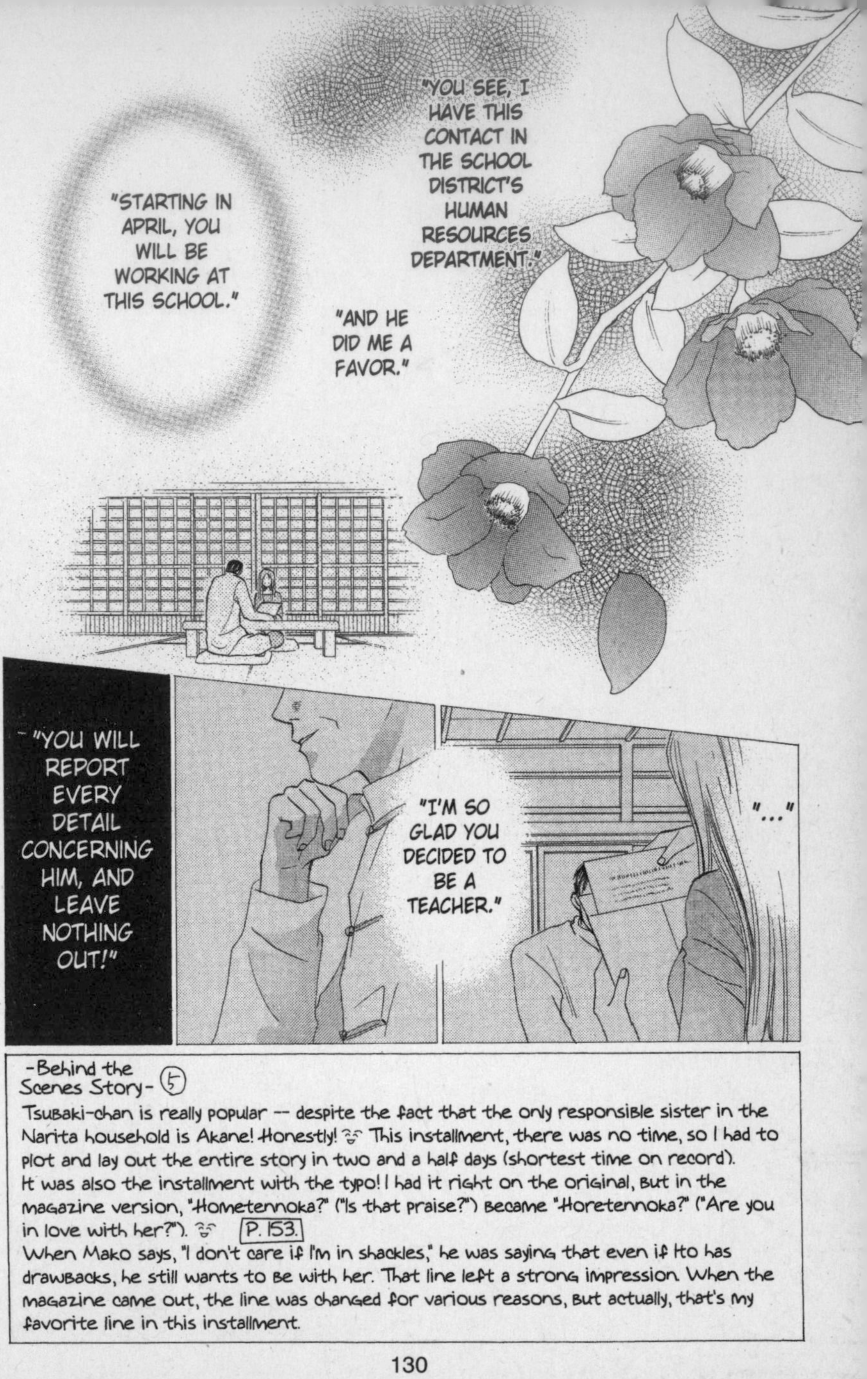
"YOU SEE, I HAVE THIS CONTACT IN THE SCHOOL DISTRICT'S HUMAN RESOURCES DEPARTMENT."
"STARTING IN APRIL, YOU WILL BE WORKING AT THIS SCHOOL."
"AND HE DID ME A FAVOR."
"..."
"I'M SO GLAD YOU DECIDED TO BE A TEACHER."
-"YOU WILL REPORT EVERY DETAIL CONCERNING HIM, AND LEAVE NOTHING OUT!"

-Behind the Scenes Story- ⑤

Tsubaki-chan is really popular -- despite the fact that the only responsible sister in the Narita household is Akane! Honestly! This installment, there was no time, so I had to plot and lay out the entire story in two and a half days (shortest time on record).
It was also the installment with the typo! I had it right on the original, but in the magazine version, "Hometennoka?" ("Is that praise?") became "Horetennoka?" ("Are you in love with her?"). P. 153.
When Mako says, "I don't care if I'm in shackles," he was saying that even if Ito has drawbacks, he still wants to be with her. That line left a strong impression. When the magazine came out, the line was changed for various reasons, but actually, that's my favorite line in this installment.

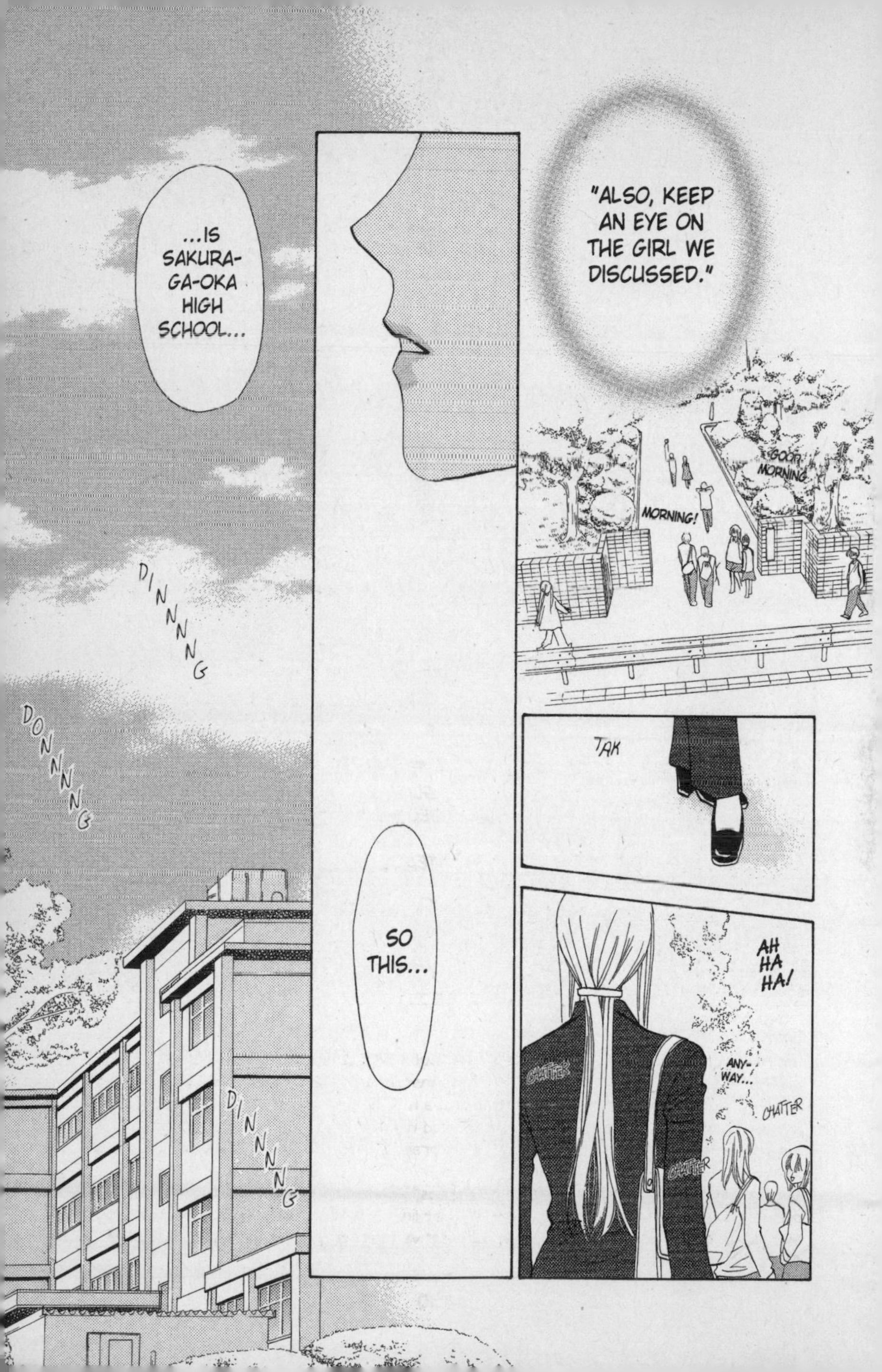
"ALSO, KEEP AN EYE ON THE GIRL WE DISCUSSED."
GOOD MORNING
MORNING!
TAK
AH HA HA!
ANY-WAY...
CHATTER
CHATTER
CHATTER
SO THIS...
...IS SAKURA-GA-OKA HIGH SCHOOL...
DINNNNG
DONNNNG
DINNNNG

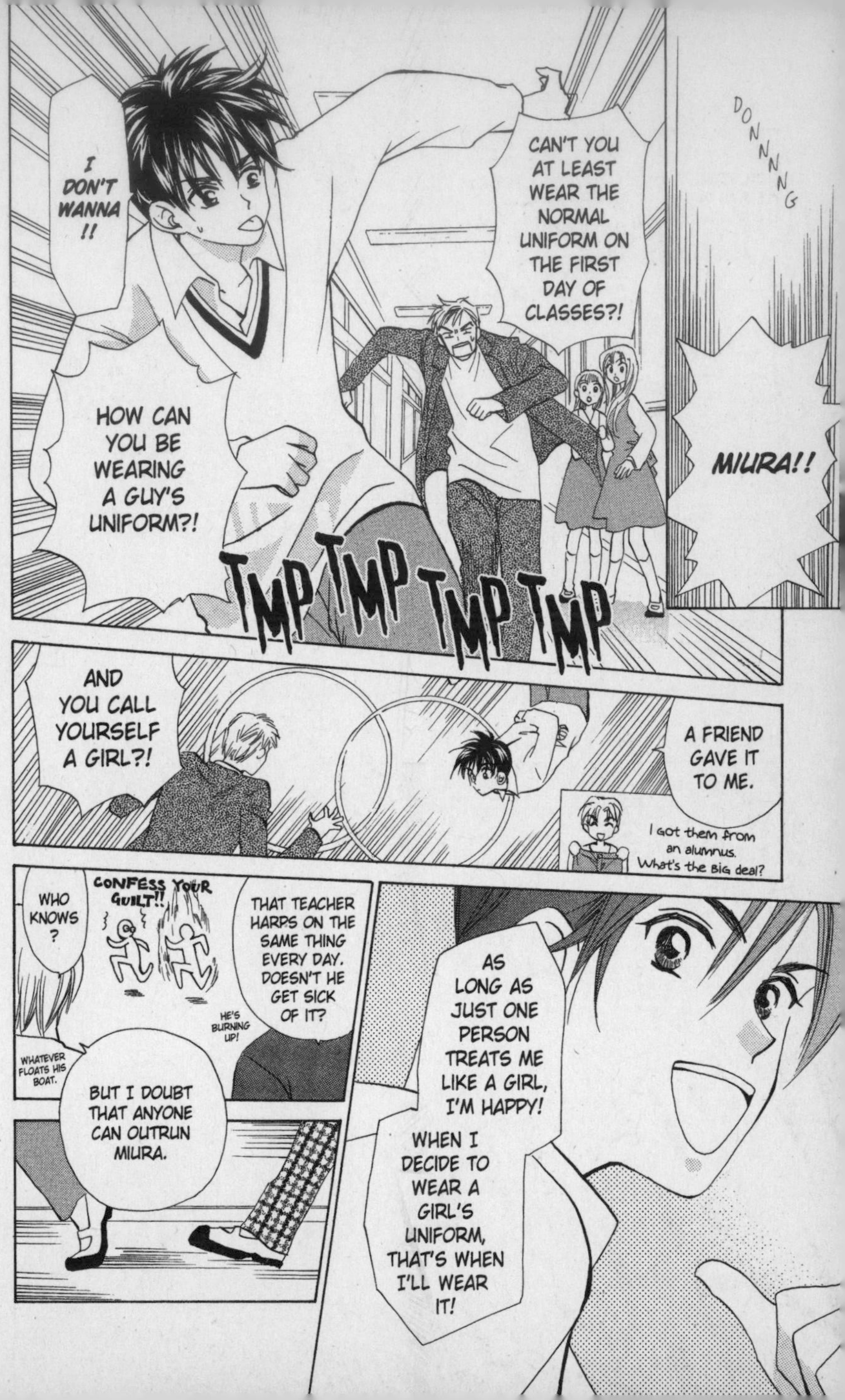
DONNNNG
MIURA!!
CAN'T YOU AT LEAST WEAR THE NORMAL UNIFORM ON THE FIRST DAY OF CLASSES?!
I DON'T WANNA!!
HOW CAN YOU BE WEARING A GUY'S UNIFORM?!
TMP TMP TMP TMP
A FRIEND GAVE IT TO ME.
I got them from an alumnus. What's the big deal?
AND YOU CALL YOURSELF A GIRL?!
AS LONG AS JUST ONE PERSON TREATS ME LIKE A GIRL, I'M HAPPY!
WHEN I DECIDE TO WEAR A GIRL'S UNIFORM, THAT'S WHEN I'LL WEAR IT!
THAT TEACHER HARPS ON THE SAME THING EVERY DAY. DOESN'T HE GET SICK OF IT?
HE'S BURNING UP!
CONFESS YOUR GUILT!!
WHO KNOWS?
WHATEVER FLOATS HIS BOAT.
BUT I DOUBT THAT ANYONE CAN OUTRUN MIURA.

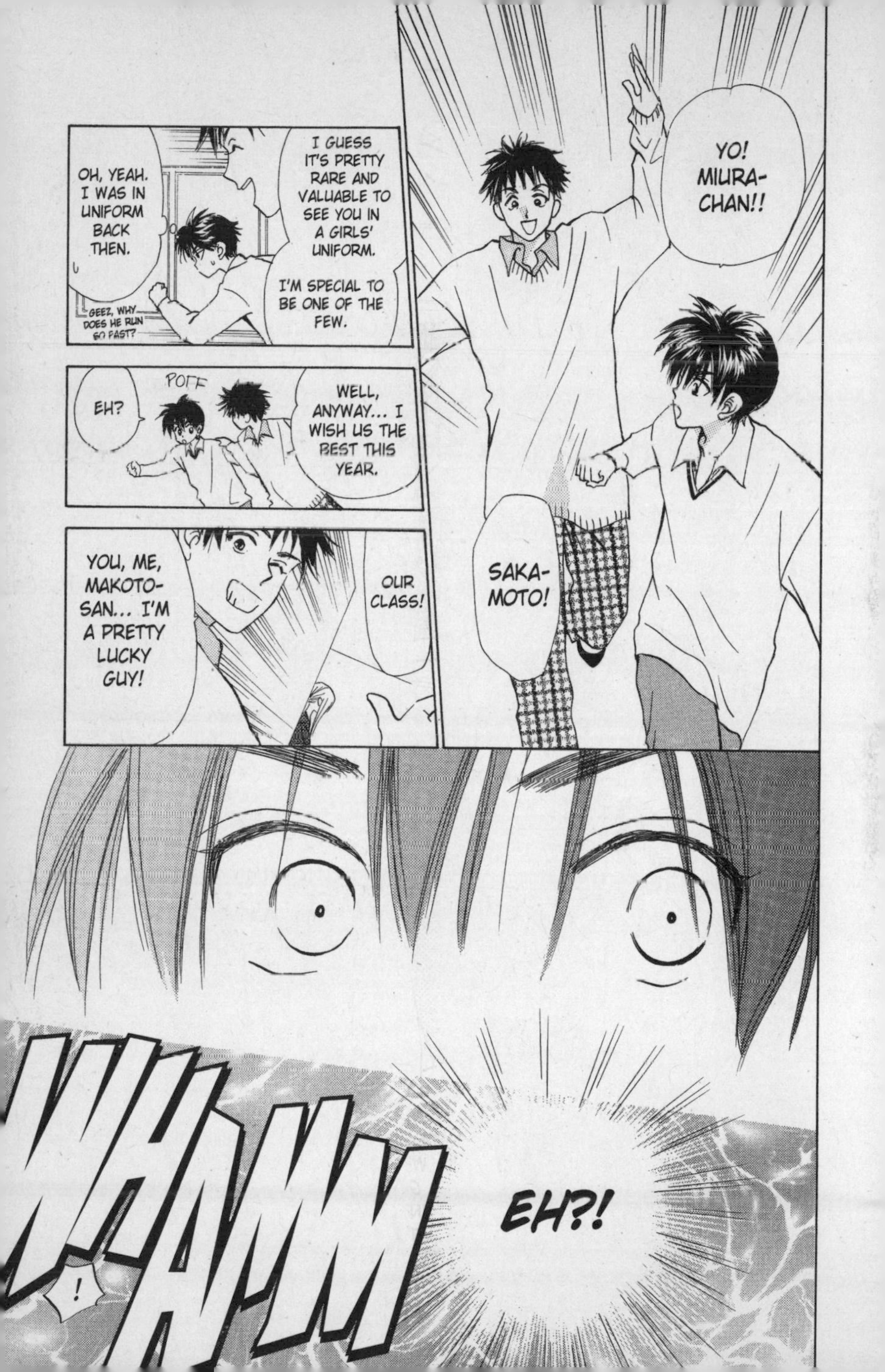
YO! MIURA-CHAN!!
SAKA-MOTO!
I GUESS IT'S PRETTY RARE AND VALUABLE TO SEE YOU IN A GIRLS' UNIFORM.
I'M SPECIAL TO BE ONE OF THE FEW.
OH, YEAH. I WAS IN UNIFORM BACK THEN.
GEEZ, WHY DOES HE RUN SO FAST?
WELL, ANYWAY... I WISH US THE BEST THIS YEAR.
POFF
EH?
OUR CLASS!
YOU, ME, MAKOTO-SAN... I'M A PRETTY LUCKY GUY!
EH?!
WHAMM
!

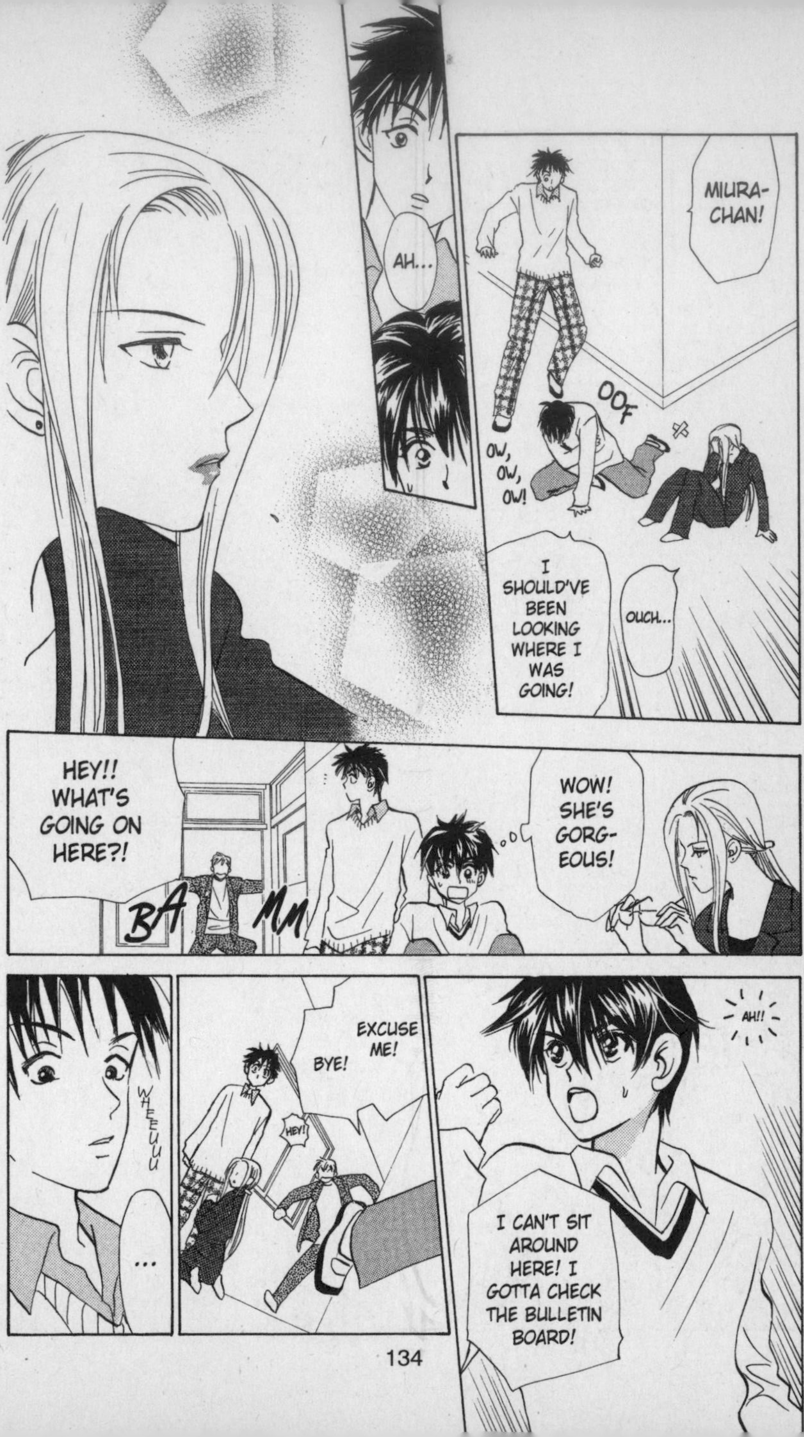
MIURA-CHAN!
OOF
OW, OW, OW!
OUCH...
I SHOULD'VE BEEN LOOKING WHERE I WAS GOING!
AH...
WOW! SHE'S GORGEOUS!
BAMM
HEY!! WHAT'S GOING ON HERE?!
AH!!
I CAN'T SIT AROUND HERE! I GOTTA CHECK THE BULLETIN BOARD!
EXCUSE ME!
BYE!
HEY!
WHEEUUU
...

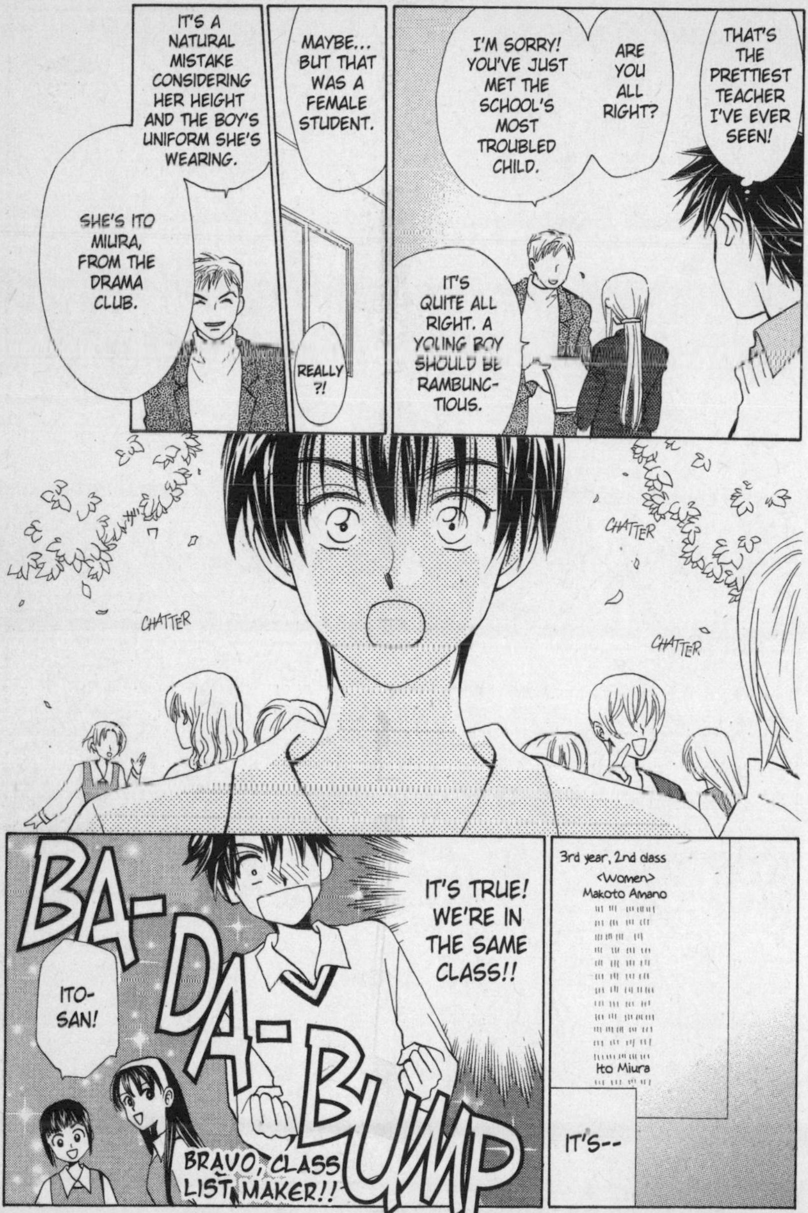
THAT'S THE PRETTIEST TEACHER I'VE EVER SEEN!
ARE YOU ALL RIGHT?
I'M SORRY! YOU'VE JUST MET THE SCHOOL'S MOST TROUBLED CHILD.
IT'S QUITE ALL RIGHT. A YOUNG BOY SHOULD BE RAMBUNCTIOUS.
MAYBE... BUT THAT WAS A FEMALE STUDENT.
REALLY ?!
IT'S A NATURAL MISTAKE CONSIDERING HER HEIGHT AND THE BOY'S UNIFORM SHE'S WEARING.
SHE'S ITO MIURA, FROM THE DRAMA CLUB.
CHATTER
CHATTER
CHATTER
3rd year, 2nd class
<Women>
Makoto Amano
Ito Miura
IT'S--
IT'S TRUE! WE'RE IN THE SAME CLASS!!
BA-DA-BUMP
ITO-SAN!
BRAVO, CLASS LIST MAKER!!

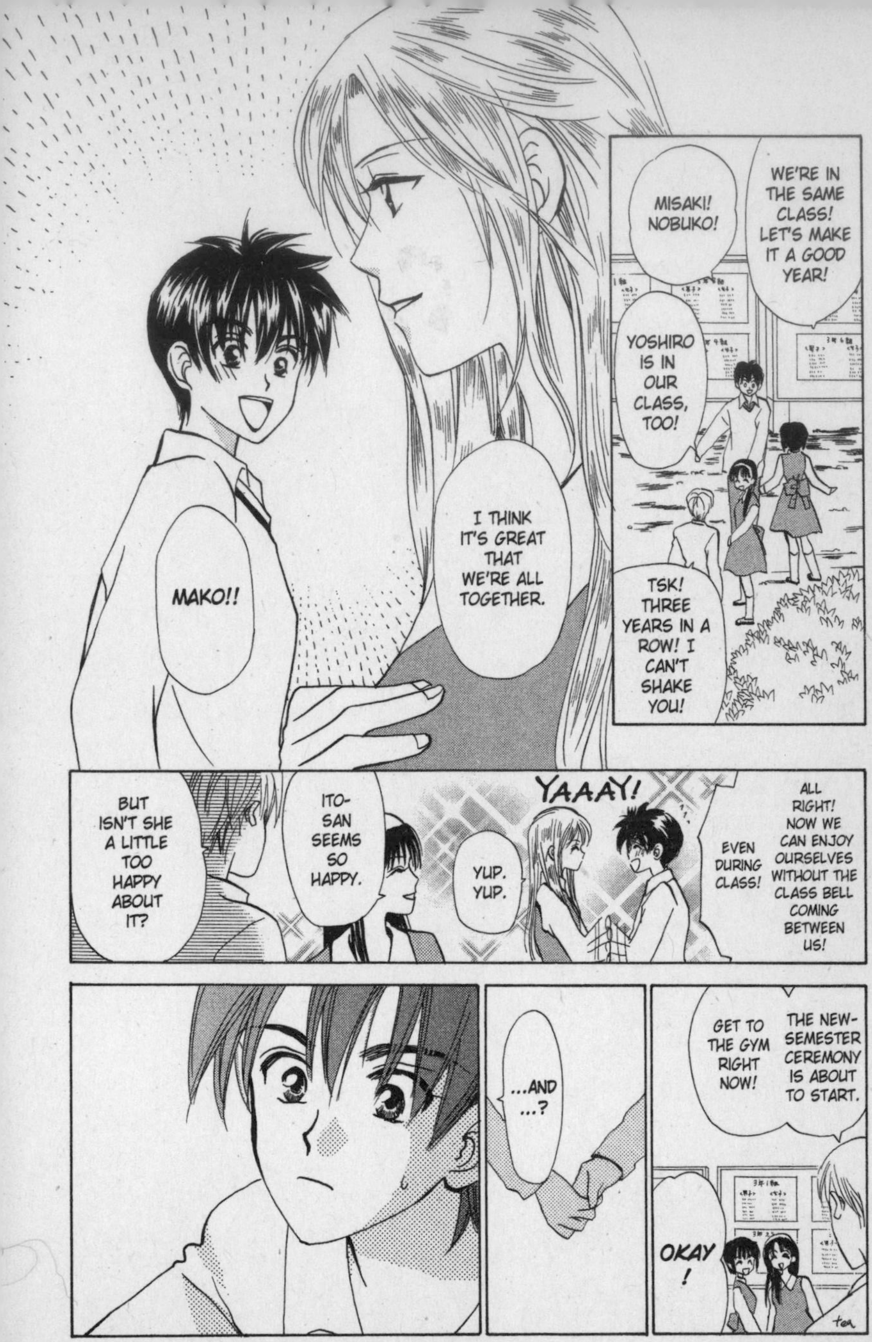
WE'RE IN THE SAME CLASS! LET'S MAKE IT A GOOD YEAR!
MISAKI! NOBUKO!
YOSHIRO IS IN OUR CLASS, TOO!
TSK! THREE YEARS IN A ROW! I CAN'T SHAKE YOU!
I THINK IT'S GREAT THAT WE'RE ALL TOGETHER.
MAKO!!
ALL RIGHT! NOW WE CAN ENJOY OURSELVES WITHOUT THE CLASS BELL COMING BETWEEN US!
EVEN DURING CLASS!
YAAAY!
YUP. YUP.
ITO-SAN SEEMS SO HAPPY.
BUT ISN'T SHE A LITTLE TOO HAPPY ABOUT IT?
THE NEW-SEMESTER CEREMONY IS ABOUT TO START.
GET TO THE GYM RIGHT NOW!
OKAY!
...AND ...?

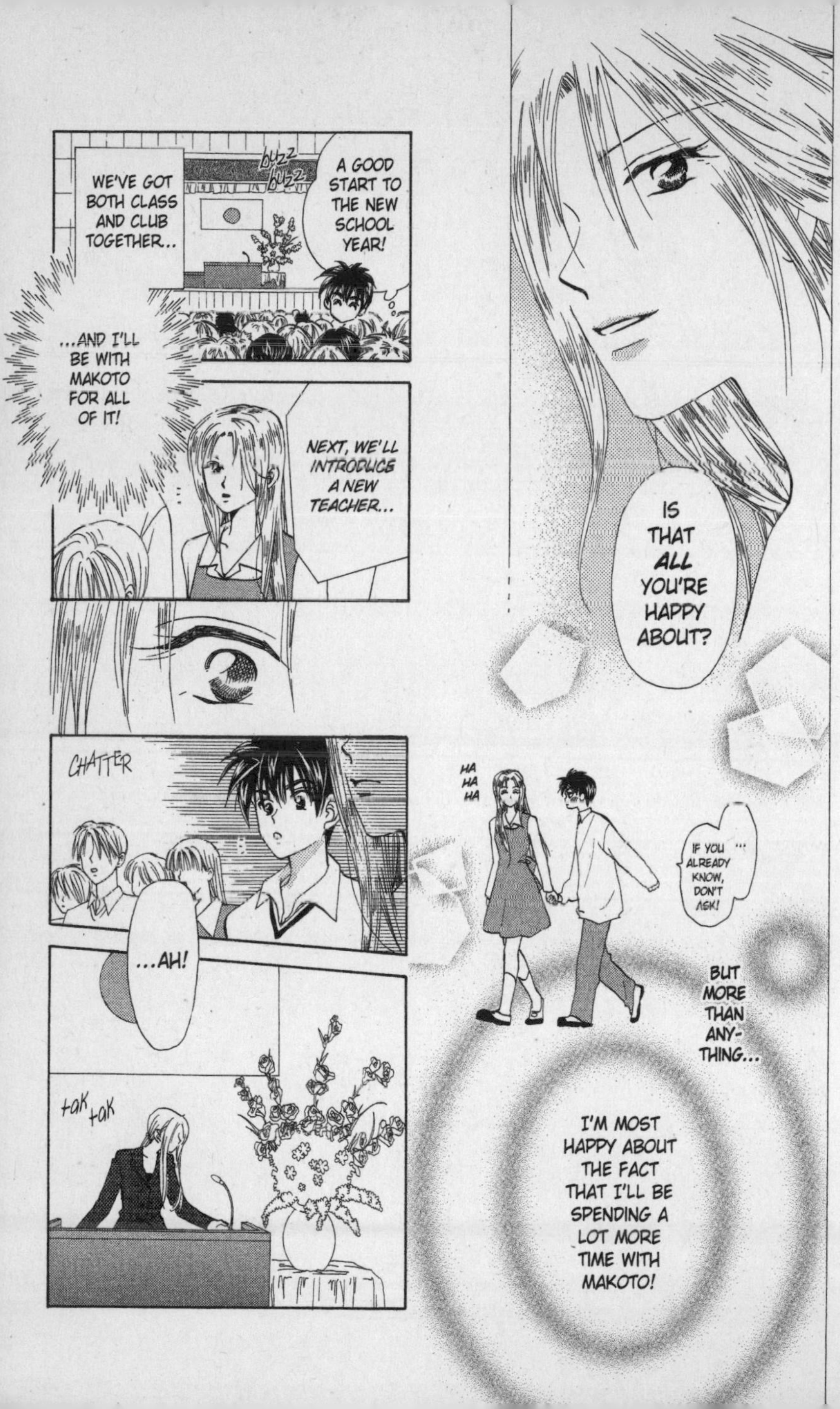
IS THAT ALL YOU'RE HAPPY ABOUT?
HA HA HA
IF YOU ALREADY KNOW, DON'T ASK!
BUT MORE THAN ANY-THING...
I'M MOST HAPPY ABOUT THE FACT THAT I'LL BE SPENDING A LOT MORE TIME WITH MAKOTO!
A GOOD START TO THE NEW SCHOOL YEAR!
buzz buzz
WE'VE GOT BOTH CLASS AND CLUB TOGETHER...
...AND I'LL BE WITH MAKOTO FOR ALL OF IT!
NEXT, WE'LL INTRODUCE A NEW TEACHER...
CHATTER
...AH!
tak tak

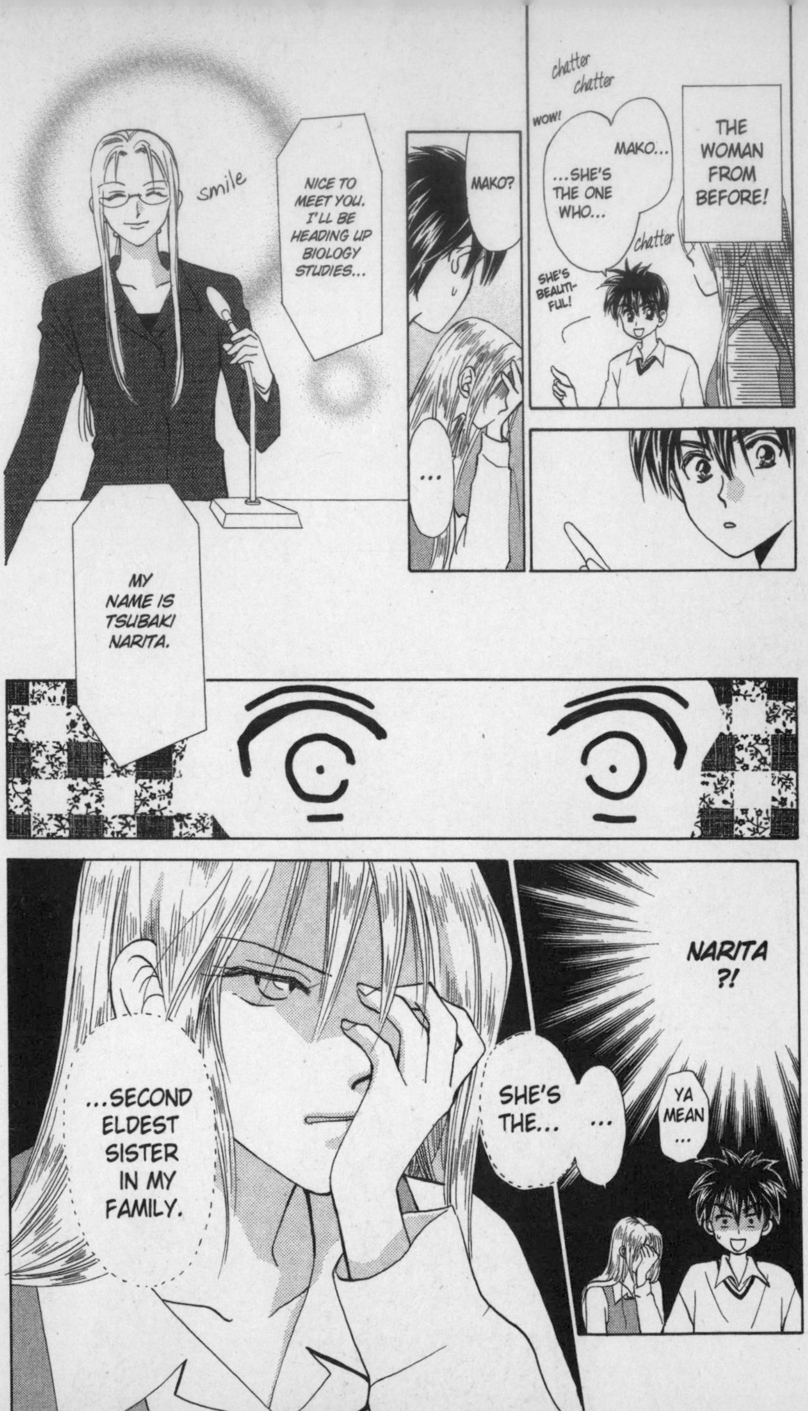
THE WOMAN FROM BEFORE!
chatter chatter
WOW!
MAKO... ...SHE'S THE ONE WHO...
chatter
SHE'S BEAUTI-FUL!
MAKO?
...
smile
NICE TO MEET YOU. I'LL BE HEADING UP BIOLOGY STUDIES...
MY NAME IS TSUBAKI NARITA.
NARITA ?!
YA MEAN ...
SHE'S THE... ...
...SECOND ELDEST SISTER IN MY FAMILY.

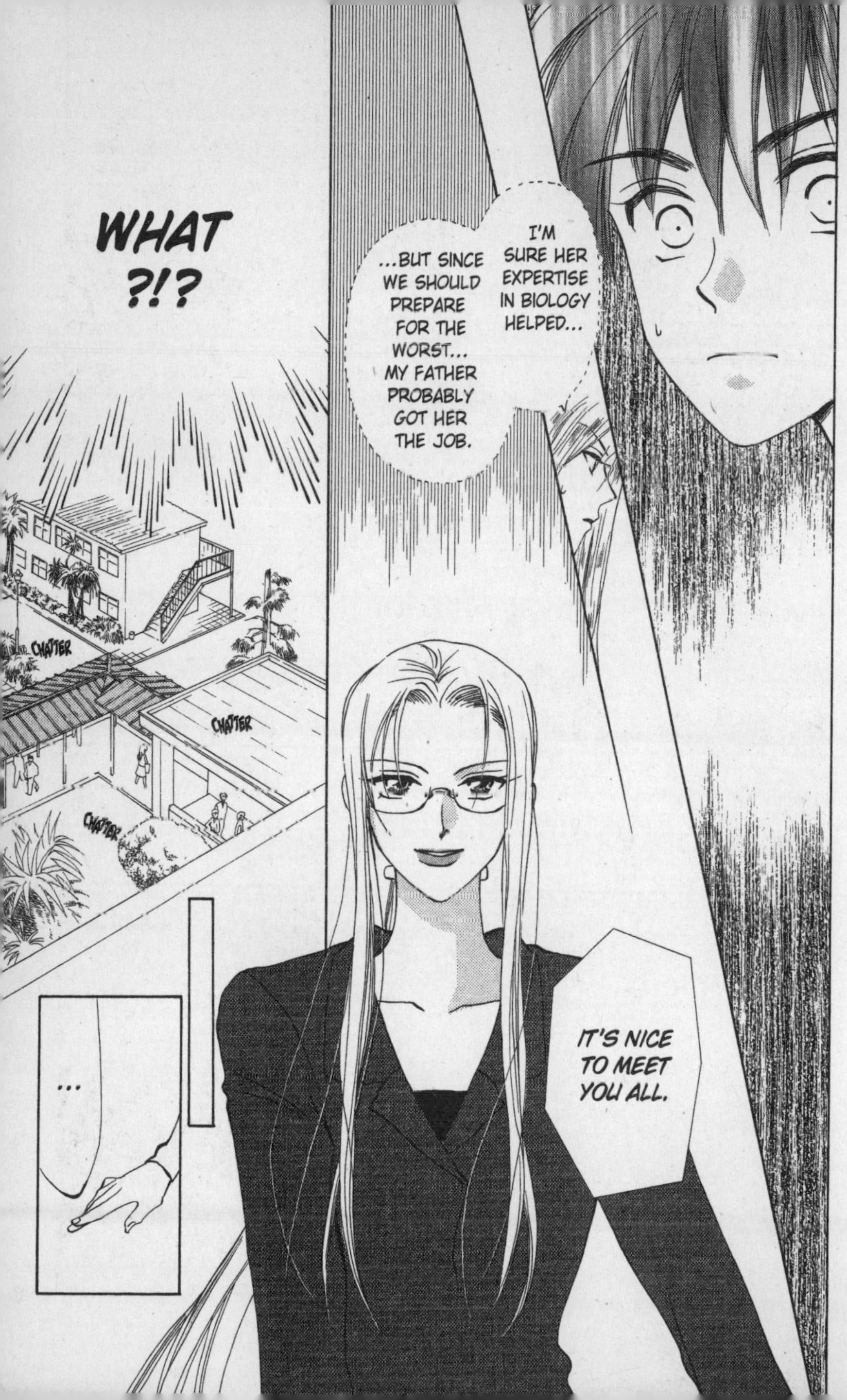
I'M SURE HER EXPERTISE IN BIOLOGY HELPED...
...BUT SINCE WE SHOULD PREPARE FOR THE WORST... MY FATHER PROBABLY GOT HER THE JOB.
IT'S NICE TO MEET YOU ALL.
WHAT ?!?
CHATTER
CHATTER
CHATTER
...

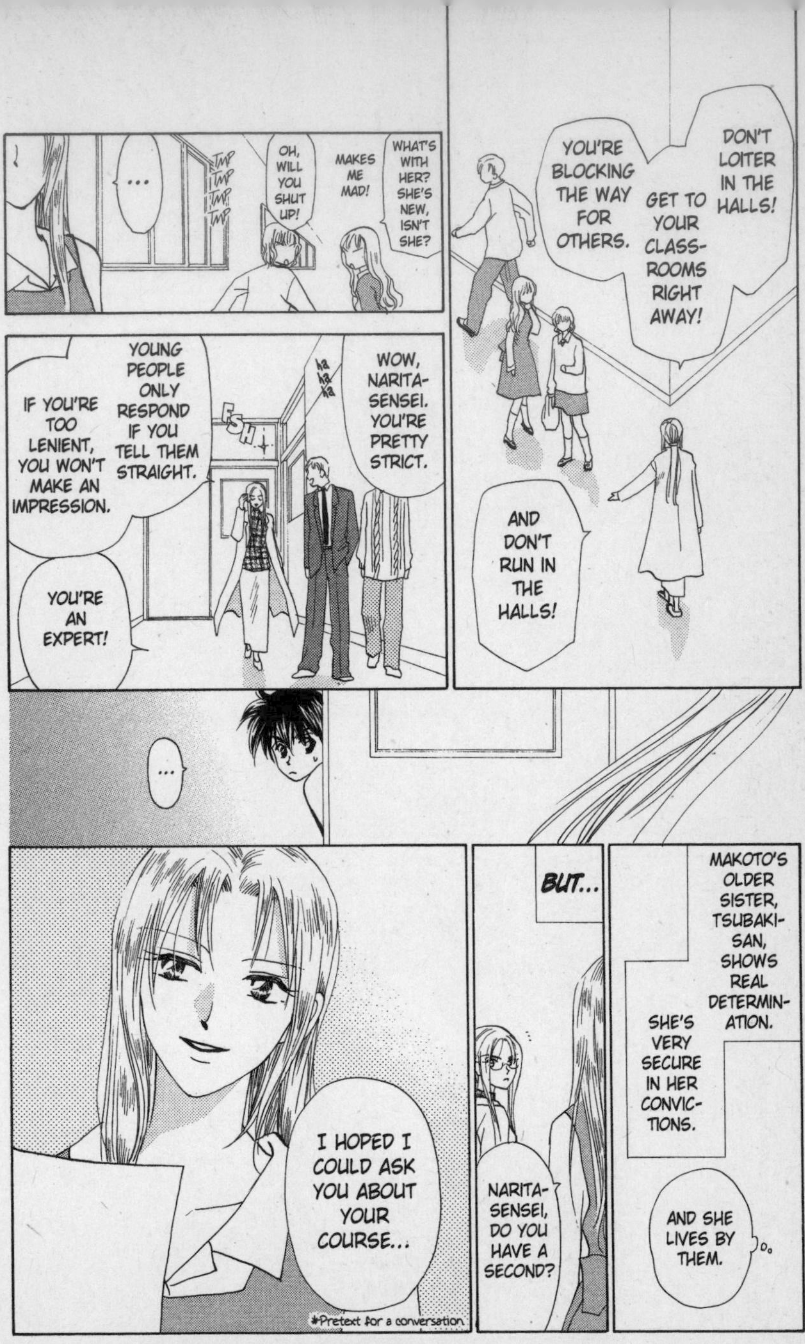
DON'T LOITER IN THE HALLS!
GET TO YOUR CLASSROOMS RIGHT AWAY!
YOU'RE BLOCKING THE WAY FOR OTHERS.
AND DON'T RUN IN THE HALLS!
WHAT'S WITH HER? SHE'S NEW, ISN'T SHE?
MAKES ME MAD!
OH, WILL YOU SHUT UP!
TMP TMP TMP TMP
...
WOW, NARITA-SENSEI. YOU'RE PRETTY STRICT.
ha ha ha
FSH
YOUNG PEOPLE ONLY RESPOND IF YOU TELL THEM STRAIGHT.
IF YOU'RE TOO LENIENT, YOU WON'T MAKE AN IMPRESSION.
YOU'RE AN EXPERT!
...
MAKOTO'S OLDER SISTER, TSUBAKI-SAN, SHOWS REAL DETERMINATION.
SHE'S VERY SECURE IN HER CONVICTIONS.
AND SHE LIVES BY THEM.
BUT...
NARITA-SENSEI, DO YOU HAVE A SECOND?
I HOPED I COULD ASK YOU ABOUT YOUR COURSE...
*Pretext for a conversation.

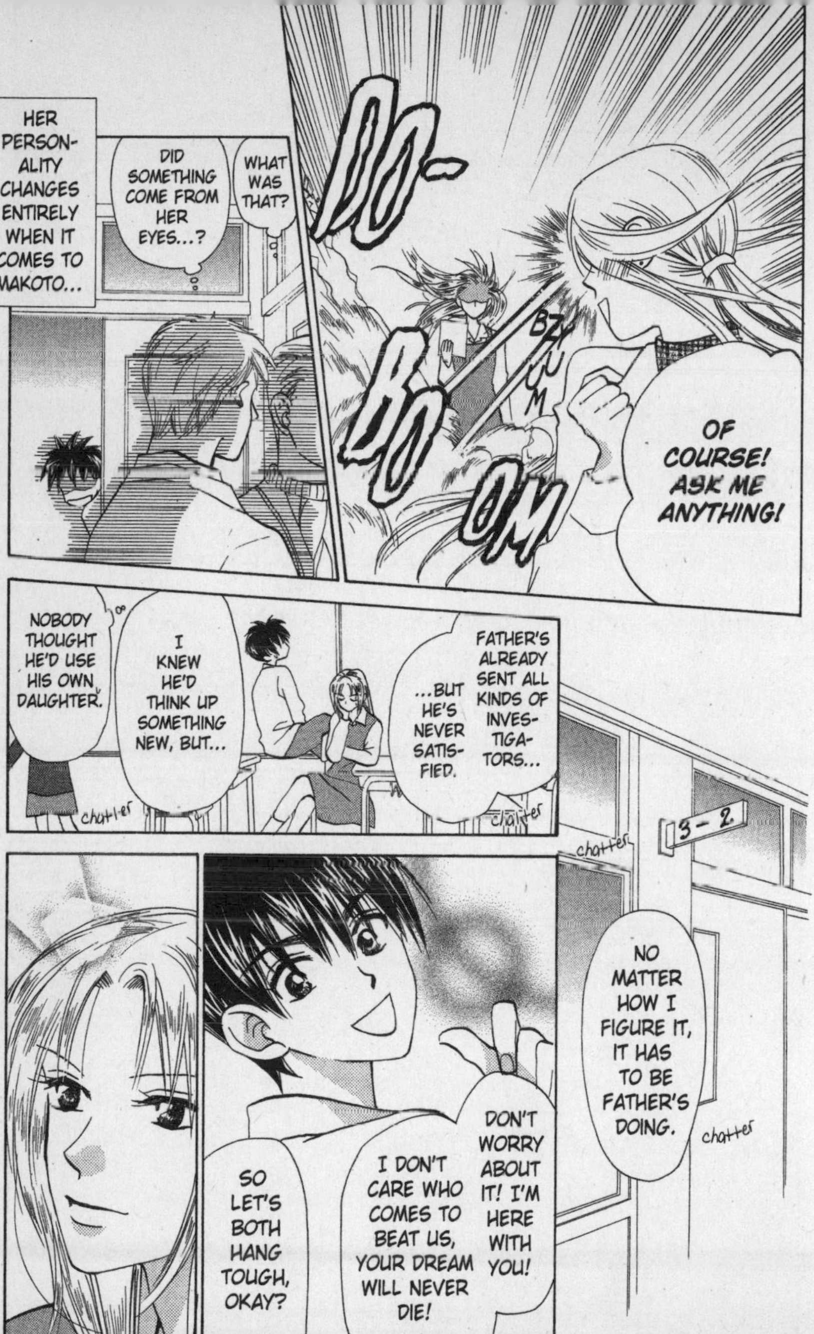
DO-BOOM
BZZUUM
OF COURSE! ASK ME ANYTHING!
WHAT WAS THAT?
DID SOMETHING COME FROM HER EYES...?
HER PERSONALITY CHANGES ENTIRELY WHEN IT COMES TO MAKOTO...
3-2
chatter
NO MATTER HOW I FIGURE IT, IT HAS TO BE FATHER'S DOING.
chatter
FATHER'S ALREADY SENT ALL KINDS OF INVESTIGATORS...
...BUT HE'S NEVER SATISFIED.
chatter
I KNEW HE'D THINK UP SOMETHING NEW, BUT...
NOBODY THOUGHT HE'D USE HIS OWN DAUGHTER.
chatter
DON'T WORRY ABOUT IT! I'M HERE WITH YOU!
I DON'T CARE WHO COMES TO BEAT US, YOUR DREAM WILL NEVER DIE!
SO LET'S BOTH HANG TOUGH, OKAY?

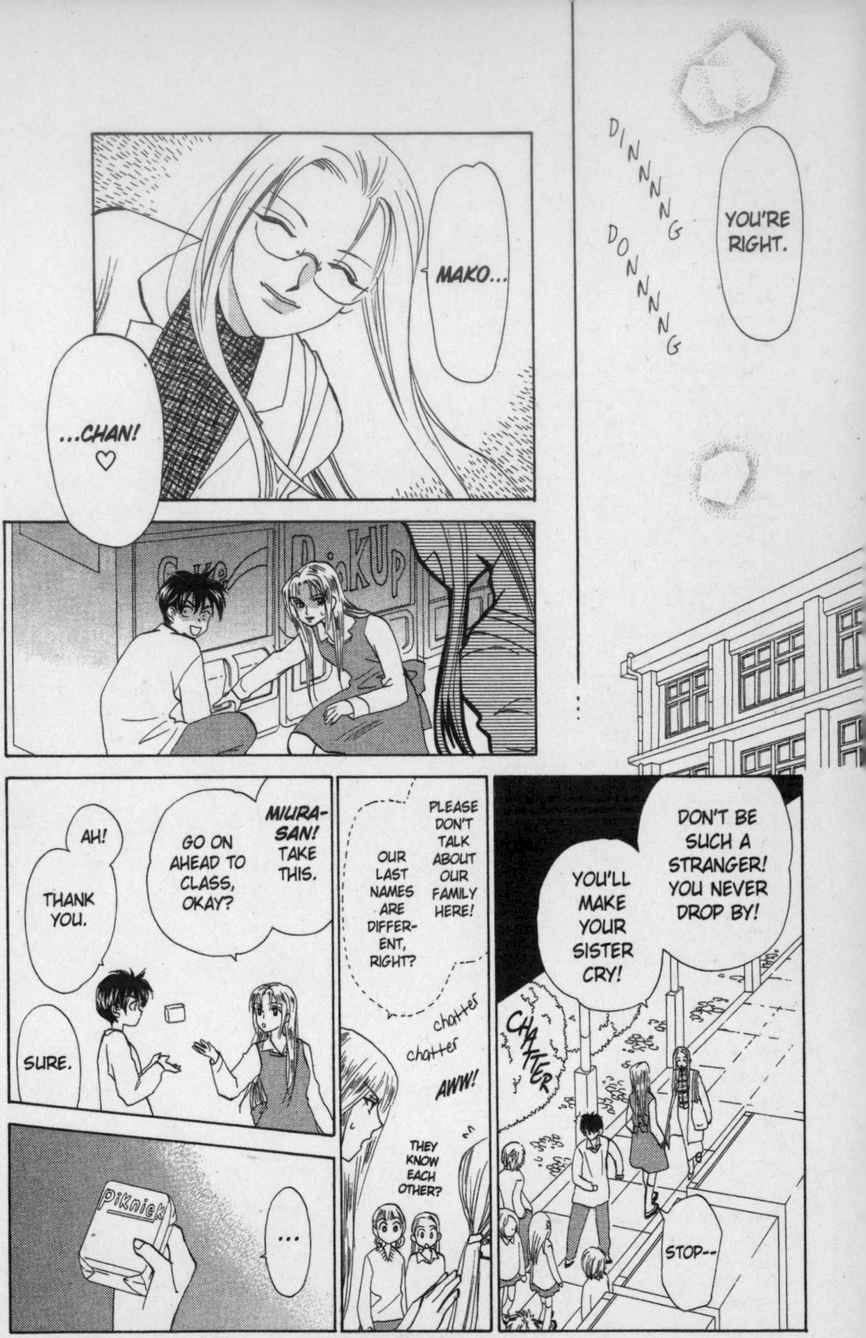
DINNNNG DONNNNG
YOU'RE RIGHT.
...
MAKO...
...CHAN! ♡
DON'T BE SUCH A STRANGER! YOU NEVER DROP BY!
YOU'LL MAKE YOUR SISTER CRY!
CHATTER
STOP--
PLEASE DON'T TALK ABOUT OUR FAMILY HERE!
OUR LAST NAMES ARE DIFFER-ENT, RIGHT?
chatter
chatter
AWW!
THEY KNOW EACH OTHER?
MIURA-SAN! TAKE THIS.
GO ON AHEAD TO CLASS, OKAY?
AH!
THANK YOU.
SURE.
pikniek
...

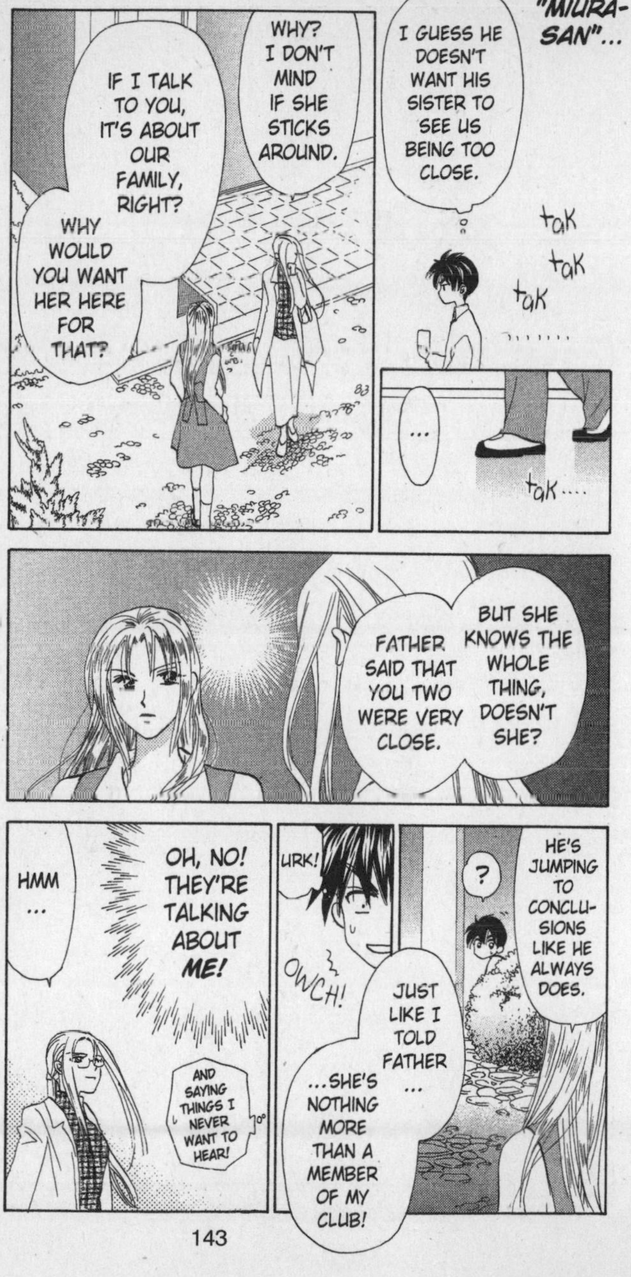
"MIURA-SAN"...
I GUESS HE DOESN'T WANT HIS SISTER TO SEE US BEING TOO CLOSE.
tak
tak
tak
......
...
tak....
WHY? I DON'T MIND IF SHE STICKS AROUND.
IF I TALK TO YOU, IT'S ABOUT OUR FAMILY, RIGHT?
WHY WOULD YOU WANT HER HERE FOR THAT?
BUT SHE KNOWS THE WHOLE THING, DOESN'T SHE?
FATHER SAID THAT YOU TWO WERE VERY CLOSE.
HE'S JUMPING TO CONCLUSIONS LIKE HE ALWAYS DOES.
?
JUST LIKE I TOLD FATHER...
...SHE'S NOTHING MORE THAN A MEMBER OF MY CLUB!
URK!
OWCH!
OH, NO! THEY'RE TALKING ABOUT ME!
HMM...
AND SAYING THINGS I NEVER WANT TO HEAR!

- Is your real name Emura?

Ⓔ No. ◊ It's a pen name that has absolutely no connection to my real name. Unfortunately, I won't be revealing my real name. ◊

- When Ito-san says, "If we put some distance between ourselves," is she trying to break up with Makoto?

Ⓔ "If we put some distance between ourselves," means Ito thinks they should put some distance between themselves. She is not trying to break up. Ito would never try to do that!

- Please send me an autographed sketch!

Ⓔ I'm sorry, but I can't. In fact, there seems to be a taboo against it.

I'd get found out!

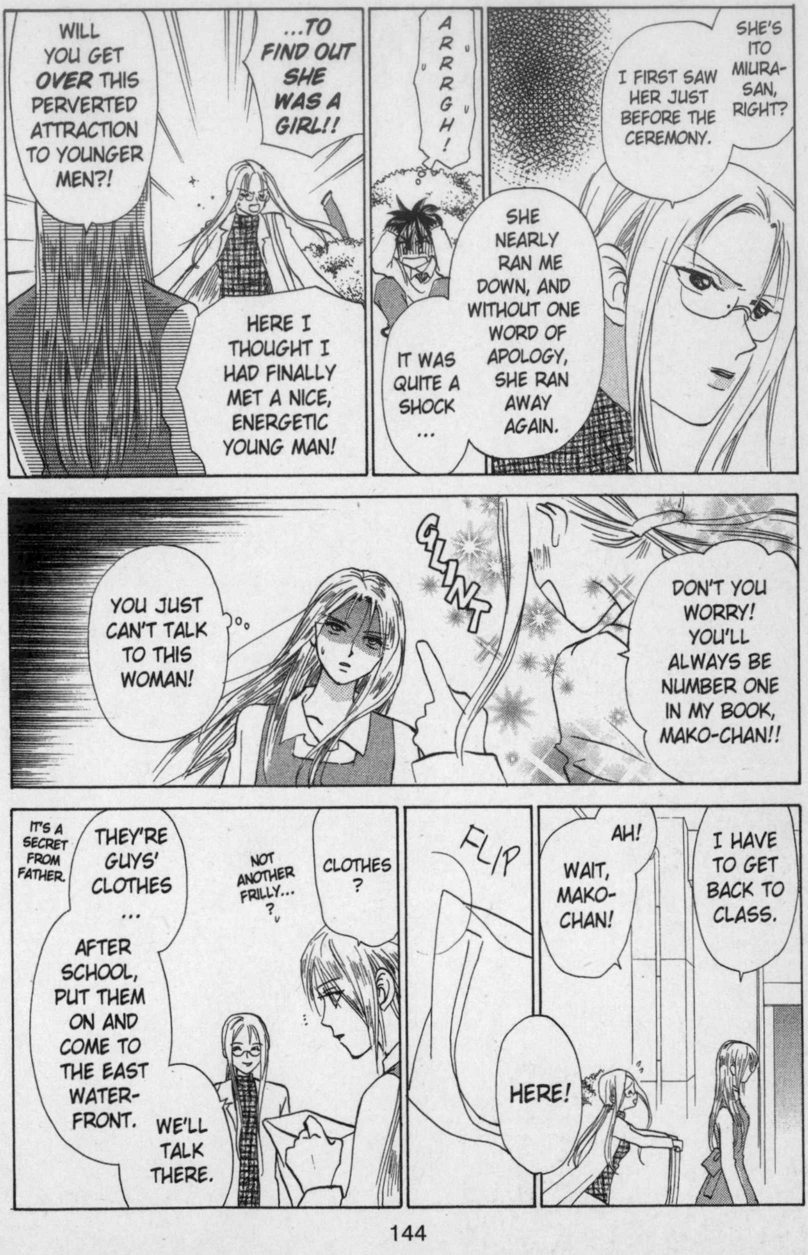
SHE'S ITO MIURA-SAN, RIGHT?
I FIRST SAW HER JUST BEFORE THE CEREMONY.
SHE NEARLY RAN ME DOWN, AND WITHOUT ONE WORD OF APOLOGY, SHE RAN AWAY AGAIN.
ARRRGH!
IT WAS QUITE A SHOCK ...
...TO FIND OUT SHE WAS A GIRL!!
HERE I THOUGHT I HAD FINALLY MET A NICE, ENERGETIC YOUNG MAN!
WILL YOU GET OVER THIS PERVERTED ATTRACTION TO YOUNGER MEN?!
DON'T YOU WORRY! YOU'LL ALWAYS BE NUMBER ONE IN MY BOOK, MAKO-CHAN!!
GLINT
YOU JUST CAN'T TALK TO THIS WOMAN!
I HAVE TO GET BACK TO CLASS.
AH!
WAIT, MAKO-CHAN!
HERE!
FLIP
CLOTHES ?
NOT ANOTHER FRILLY... ?
THEY'RE GUYS' CLOTHES ...
IT'S A SECRET FROM FATHER.
AFTER SCHOOL, PUT THEM ON AND COME TO THE EAST WATER-FRONT.
WE'LL TALK THERE.

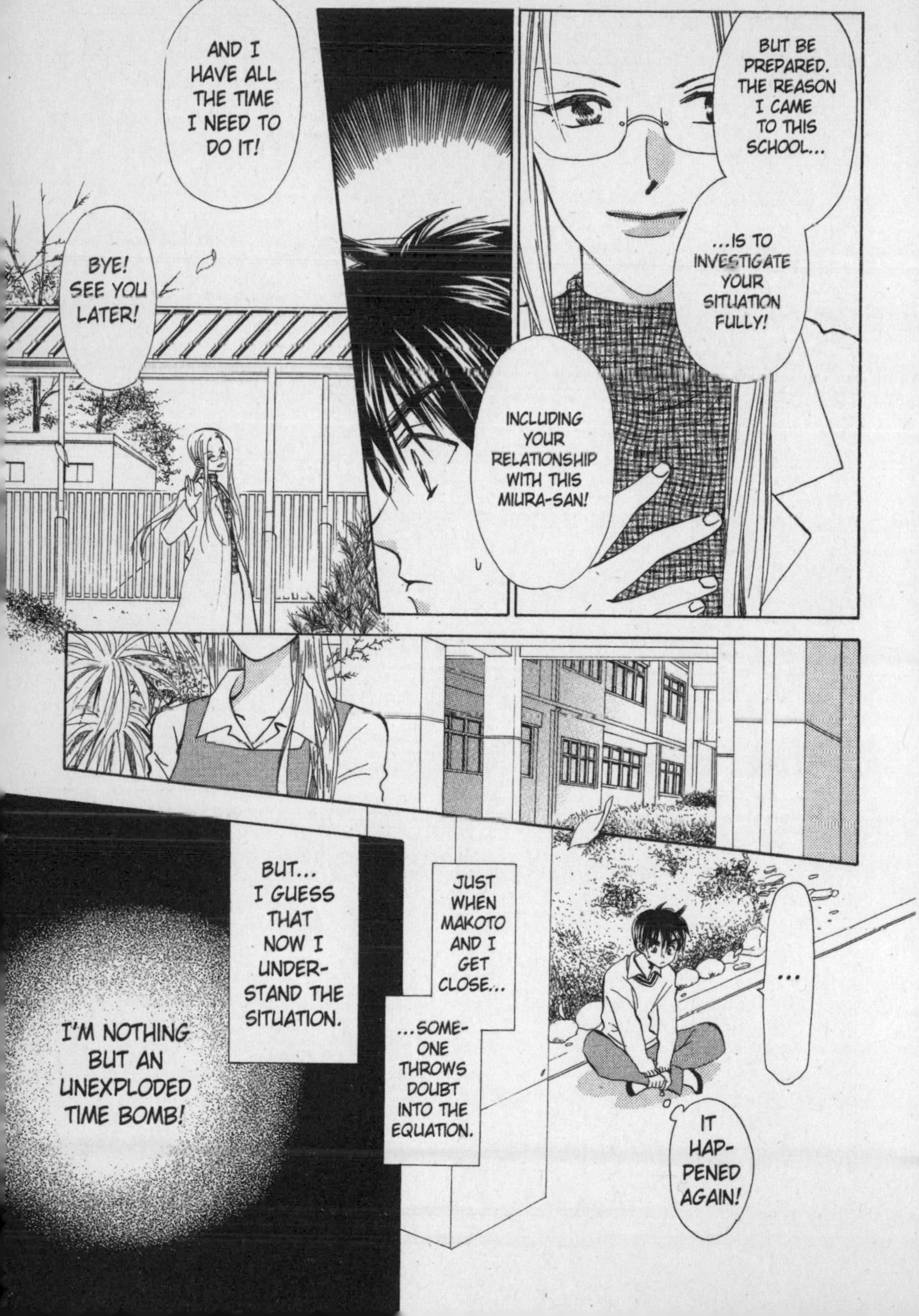
BUT BE PREPARED. THE REASON I CAME TO THIS SCHOOL...
...IS TO INVESTIGATE YOUR SITUATION FULLY!
INCLUDING YOUR RELATIONSHIP WITH THIS MIURA-SAN!
AND I HAVE ALL THE TIME I NEED TO DO IT!
BYE! SEE YOU LATER!
...
IT HAP-PENED AGAIN!
JUST WHEN MAKOTO AND I GET CLOSE...
...SOME-ONE THROWS DOUBT INTO THE EQUATION.
BUT... I GUESS THAT NOW I UNDER-STAND THE SITUATION.
I'M NOTHING BUT AN UNEXPLODED TIME BOMB!

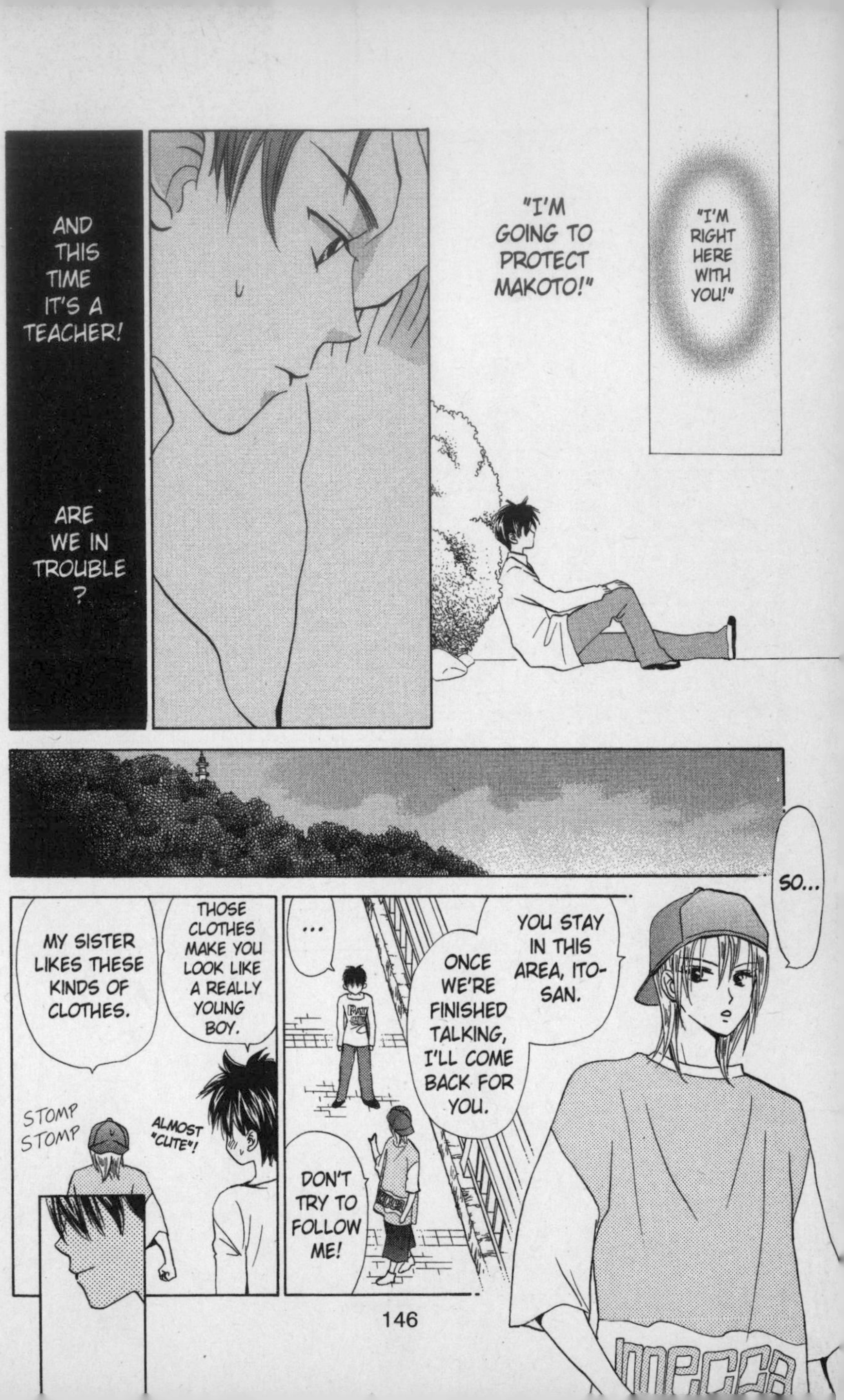
"I'M RIGHT HERE WITH YOU!"
"I'M GOING TO PROTECT MAKOTO!"
AND THIS TIME IT'S A TEACHER!
ARE WE IN TROUBLE ?
SO...
YOU STAY IN THIS AREA, ITO-SAN.
ONCE WE'RE FINISHED TALKING, I'LL COME BACK FOR YOU.
...
DON'T TRY TO FOLLOW ME!
THOSE CLOTHES MAKE YOU LOOK LIKE A REALLY YOUNG BOY.
MY SISTER LIKES THESE KINDS OF CLOTHES.
ALMOST "CUTE"!
STOMP STOMP

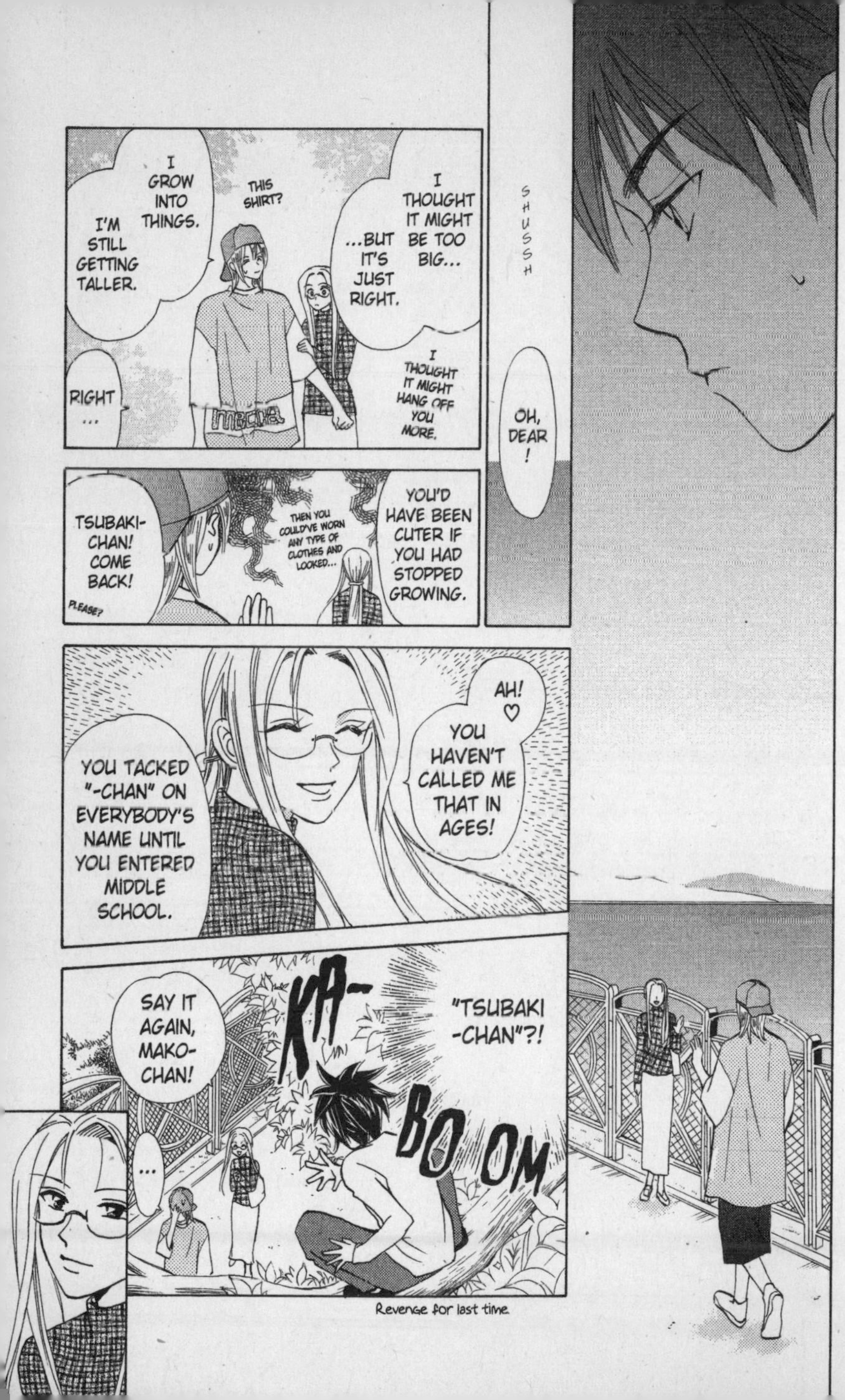
SHUSSH
OH, DEAR!
I THOUGHT IT MIGHT BE TOO BIG...
...BUT IT'S JUST RIGHT.
I THOUGHT IT MIGHT HANG OFF YOU MORE.
THIS SHIRT?
I GROW INTO THINGS.
I'M STILL GETTING TALLER.
RIGHT...
YOU'D HAVE BEEN CUTER IF YOU HAD STOPPED GROWING.
THEN YOU COULD'VE WORN ANY TYPE OF CLOTHES AND LOOKED...
TSUBAKI-CHAN! COME BACK!
PLEASE?
AH! ♡ YOU HAVEN'T CALLED ME THAT IN AGES!
YOU TACKED "-CHAN" ON EVERYBODY'S NAME UNTIL YOU ENTERED MIDDLE SCHOOL.
"TSUBAKI-CHAN"?!
KA-BOOM
SAY IT AGAIN, MAKO-CHAN!
...
Revenge for last time.

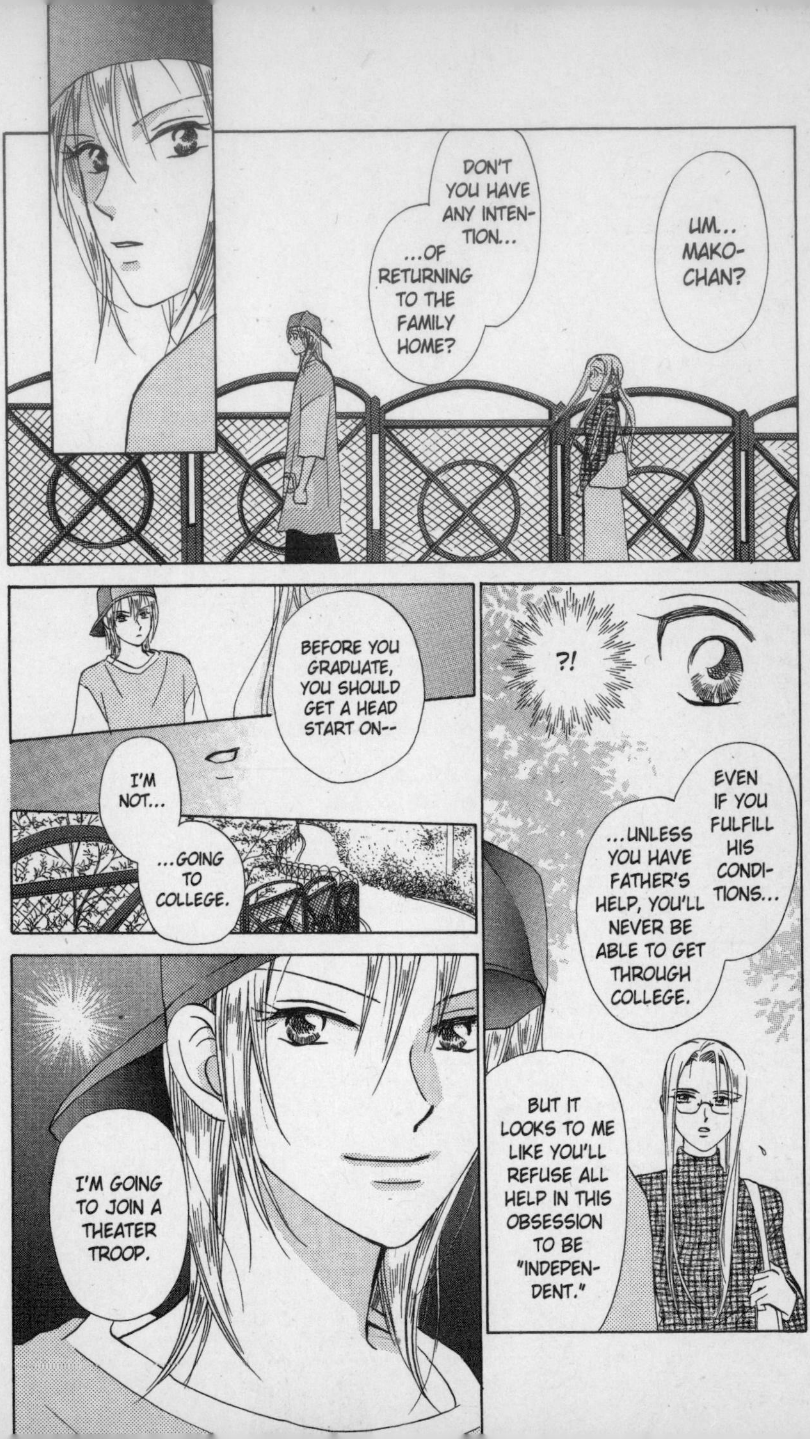
UM... MAKO-CHAN?
DON'T YOU HAVE ANY INTENTION... ...OF RETURNING TO THE FAMILY HOME?
?!
EVEN IF YOU FULFILL HIS CONDITIONS...
...UNLESS YOU HAVE FATHER'S HELP, YOU'LL NEVER BE ABLE TO GET THROUGH COLLEGE.
BUT IT LOOKS TO ME LIKE YOU'LL REFUSE ALL HELP IN THIS OBSESSION TO BE "INDEPENDENT."
BEFORE YOU GRADUATE, YOU SHOULD GET A HEAD START ON--
I'M NOT...
...GOING TO COLLEGE.
I'M GOING TO JOIN A THEATER TROOP.

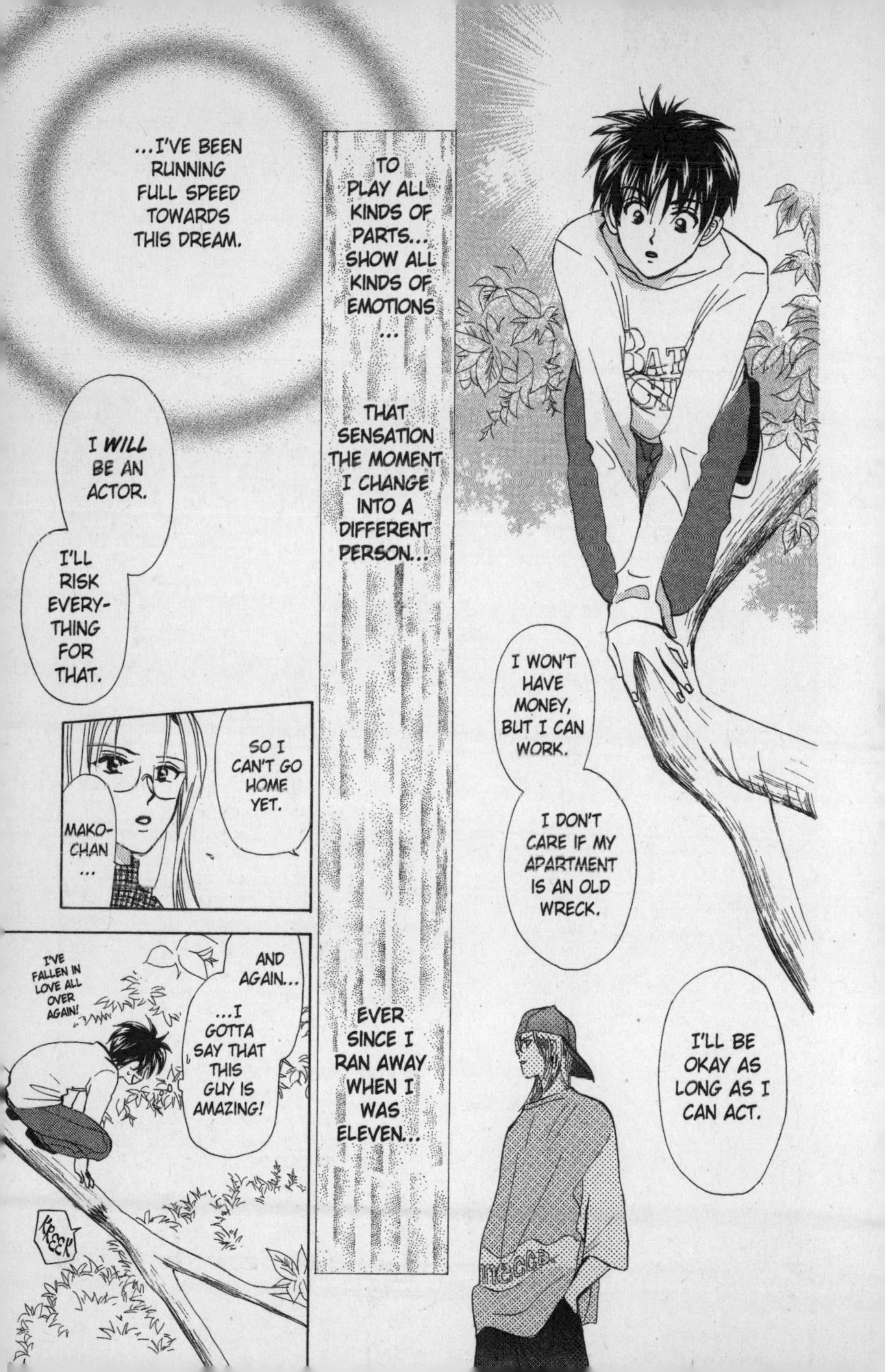
I WON'T HAVE MONEY, BUT I CAN WORK.
I DON'T CARE IF MY APARTMENT IS AN OLD WRECK.
I'LL BE OKAY AS LONG AS I CAN ACT.
TO PLAY ALL KINDS OF PARTS... SHOW ALL KINDS OF EMOTIONS ...
THAT SENSATION THE MOMENT I CHANGE INTO A DIFFERENT PERSON...
EVER SINCE I RAN AWAY WHEN I WAS ELEVEN...
...I'VE BEEN RUNNING FULL SPEED TOWARDS THIS DREAM.
I *WILL* BE AN ACTOR.
I'LL RISK EVERY-THING FOR THAT.
SO I CAN'T GO HOME YET.
MAKO-CHAN ...
AND AGAIN...
...I GOTTA SAY THAT THIS GUY IS AMAZING!
I'VE FALLEN IN LOVE ALL OVER AGAIN!
KREEK

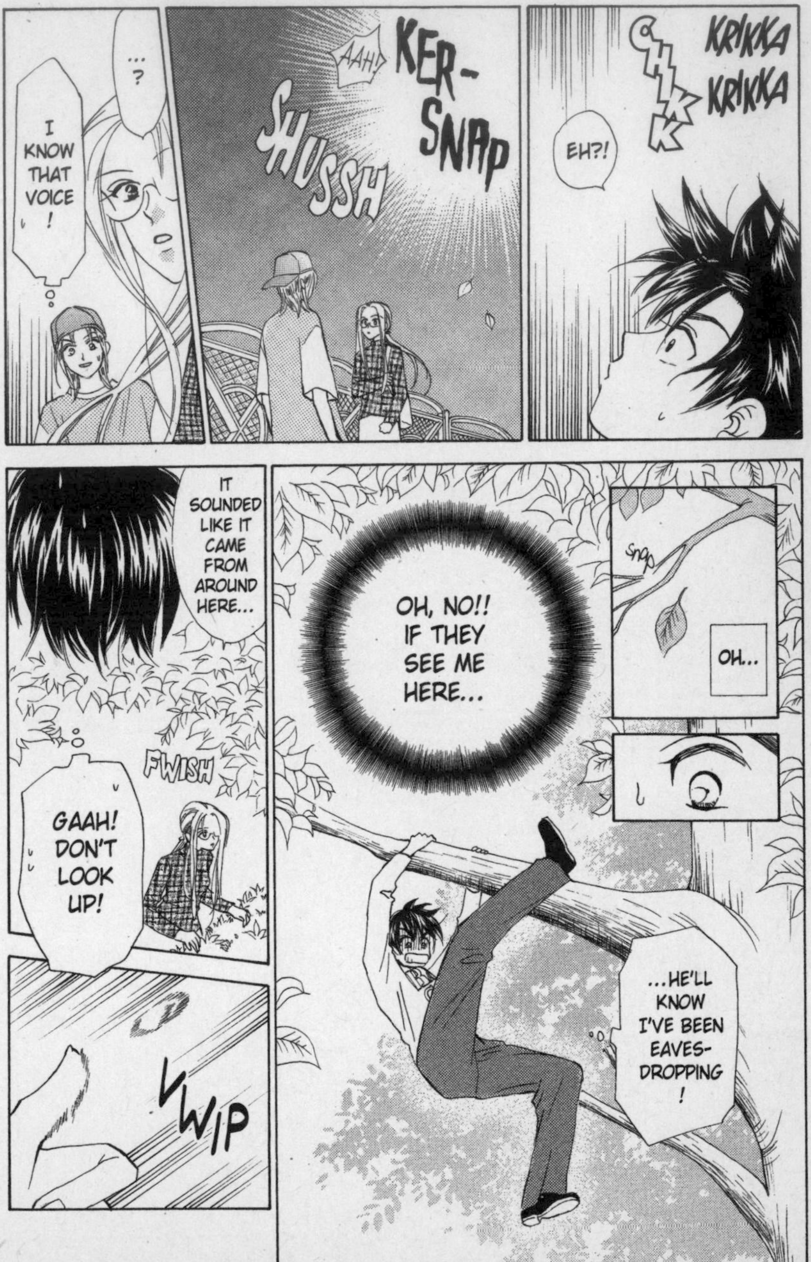
KRIKKA KRIKKA
CHIKK
EH?!
AAH!
KER-SNAP
SHUSSH
...?
I KNOW THAT VOICE!
snap
OH...
OH, NO!! IF THEY SEE ME HERE...
...HE'LL KNOW I'VE BEEN EAVES-DROPPING!
IT SOUNDED LIKE IT CAME FROM AROUND HERE...
FWISH
GAAH! DON'T LOOK UP!
VWIP

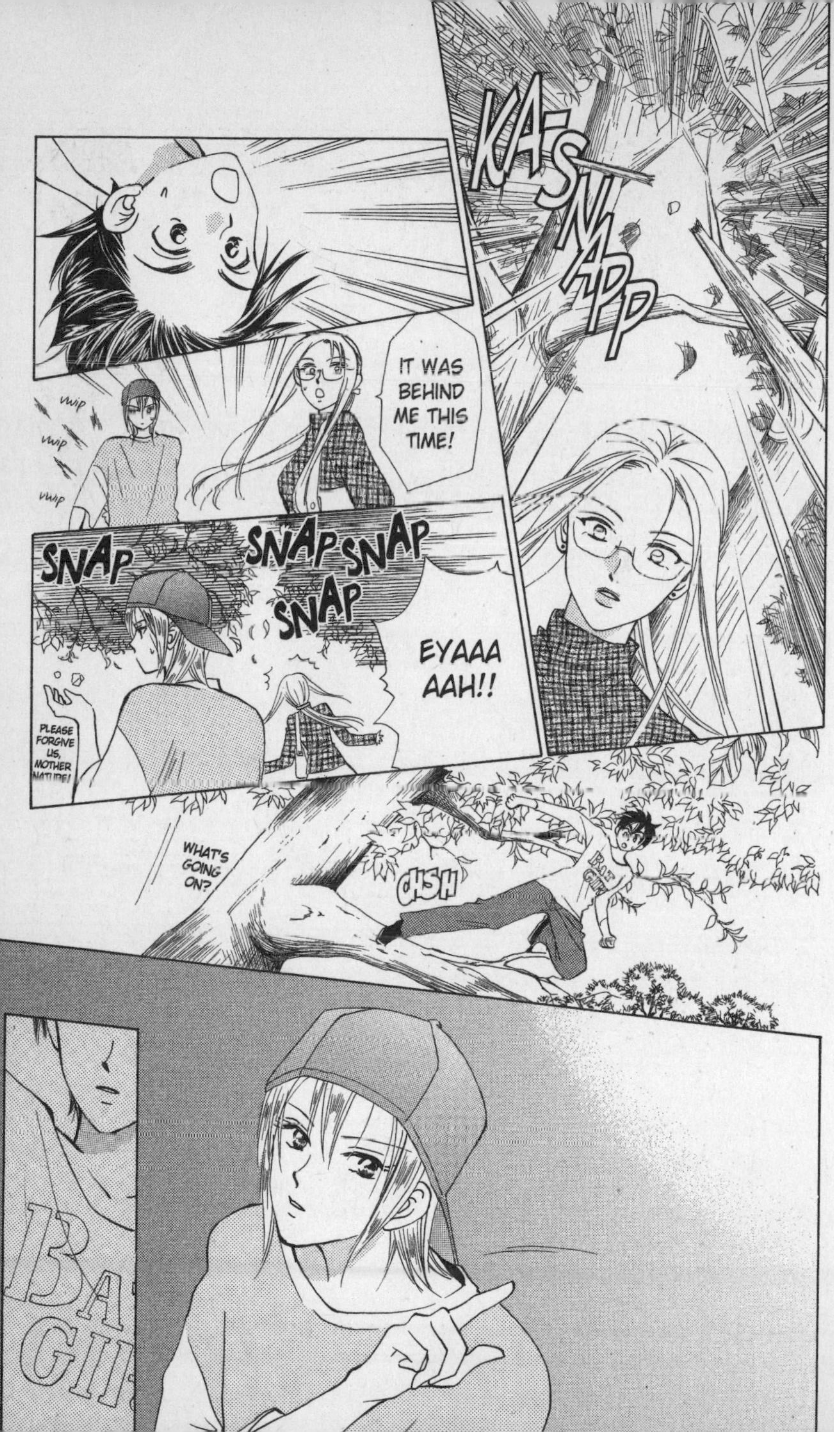
KA-SNAPP
IT WAS BEHIND ME THIS TIME!
vwip
vwip
vwip
SNAP SNAP
EYAAA AAH!!
SNAP
SNAP
PLEASE FORGIVE US, MOTHER NATURE!
CHSH
WHAT'S GOING ON?

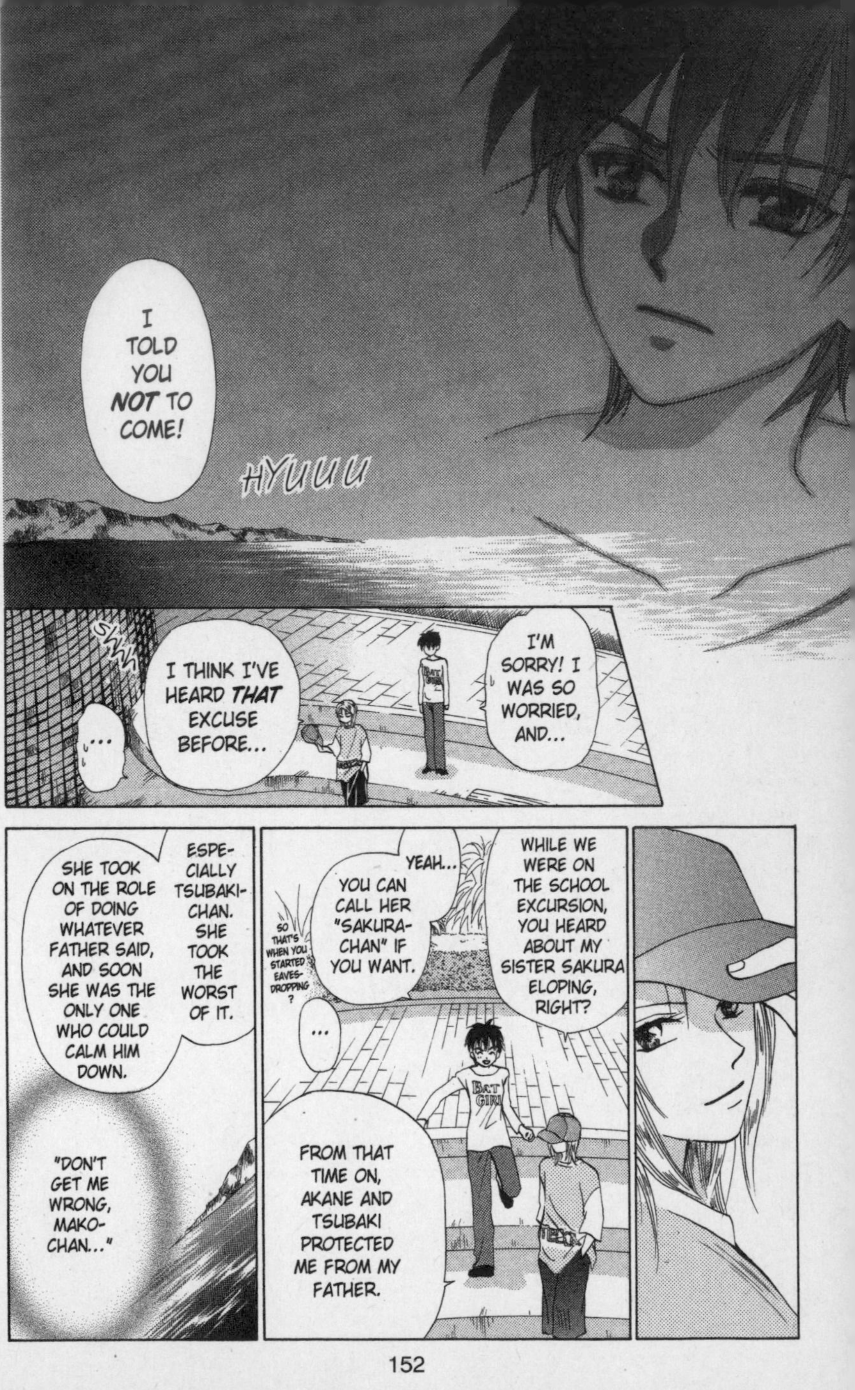
I TOLD YOU **NOT** TO COME!
HYUUU
I'M SORRY! I WAS SO WORRIED, AND...
I THINK I'VE HEARD **THAT** EXCUSE BEFORE...
...
WHILE WE WERE ON THE SCHOOL EXCURSION, YOU HEARD ABOUT MY SISTER SAKURA ELOPING, RIGHT?
YEAH...
YOU CAN CALL HER "SAKURA-CHAN" IF YOU WANT.
SO THAT'S WHEN YOU STARTED EAVES-DROPPING?
...
FROM THAT TIME ON, AKANE AND TSUBAKI PROTECTED ME FROM MY FATHER.
ESPE-CIALLY TSUBAKI-CHAN. SHE TOOK THE WORST OF IT.
SHE TOOK ON THE ROLE OF DOING WHATEVER FATHER SAID, AND SOON SHE WAS THE ONLY ONE WHO COULD CALM HIM DOWN.
"DON'T GET ME WRONG, MAKO-CHAN..."

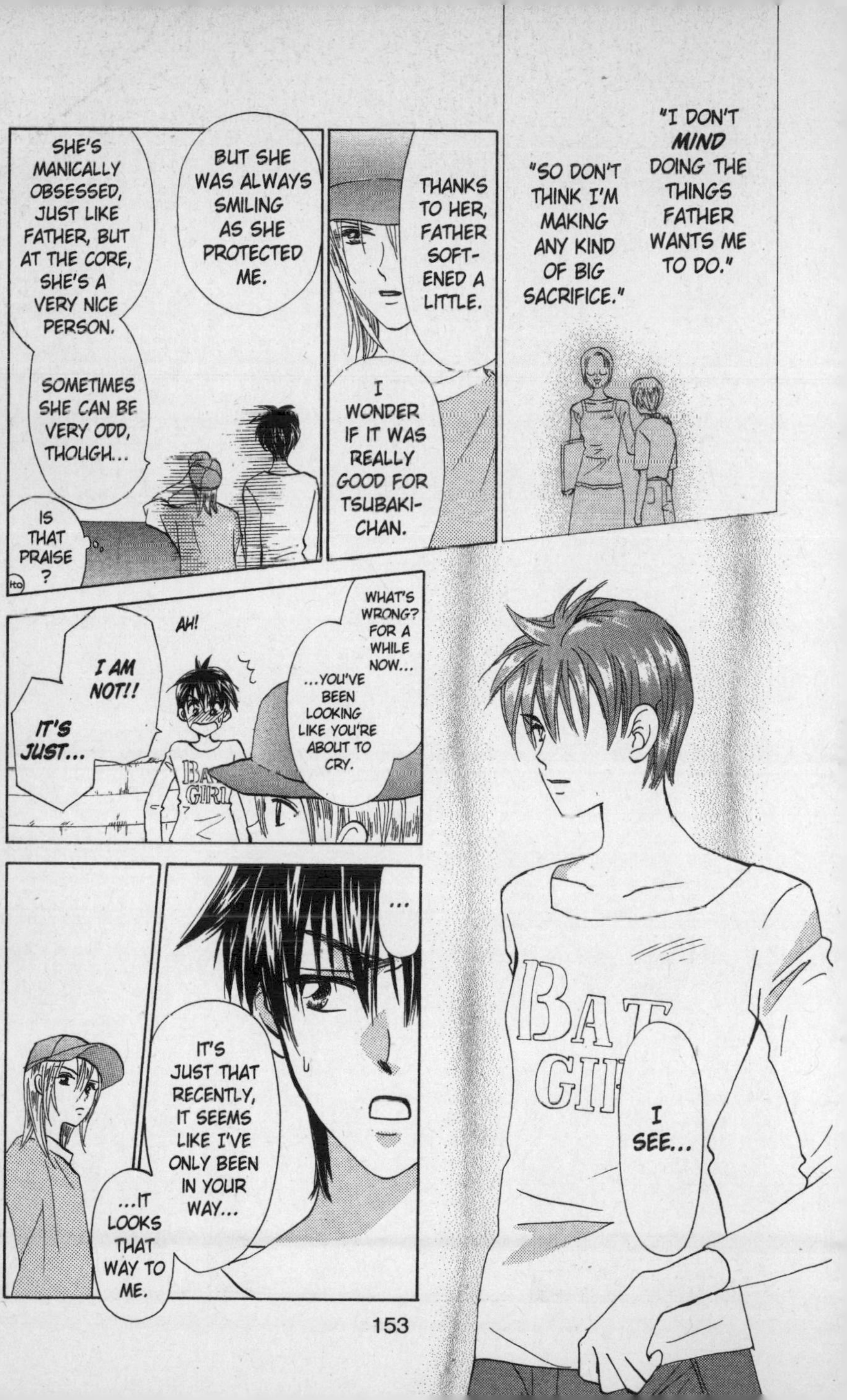
"I DON'T MIND DOING THE THINGS FATHER WANTS ME TO DO."
"SO DON'T THINK I'M MAKING ANY KIND OF BIG SACRIFICE."
THANKS TO HER, FATHER SOFT- ENED A LITTLE.
I WONDER IF IT WAS REALLY GOOD FOR TSUBAKI- CHAN.
BUT SHE WAS ALWAYS SMILING AS SHE PROTECTED ME.
SHE'S MANICALLY OBSESSED, JUST LIKE FATHER, BUT AT THE CORE, SHE'S A VERY NICE PERSON.
SOMETIMES SHE CAN BE VERY ODD, THOUGH...
IS THAT PRAISE ?
I SEE...
WHAT'S WRONG? FOR A WHILE NOW...
...YOU'VE BEEN LOOKING LIKE YOU'RE ABOUT TO CRY.
AH!
I AM NOT!!
IT'S JUST...
...
IT'S JUST THAT RECENTLY, IT SEEMS LIKE I'VE ONLY BEEN IN YOUR WAY...
...IT LOOKS THAT WAY TO ME.

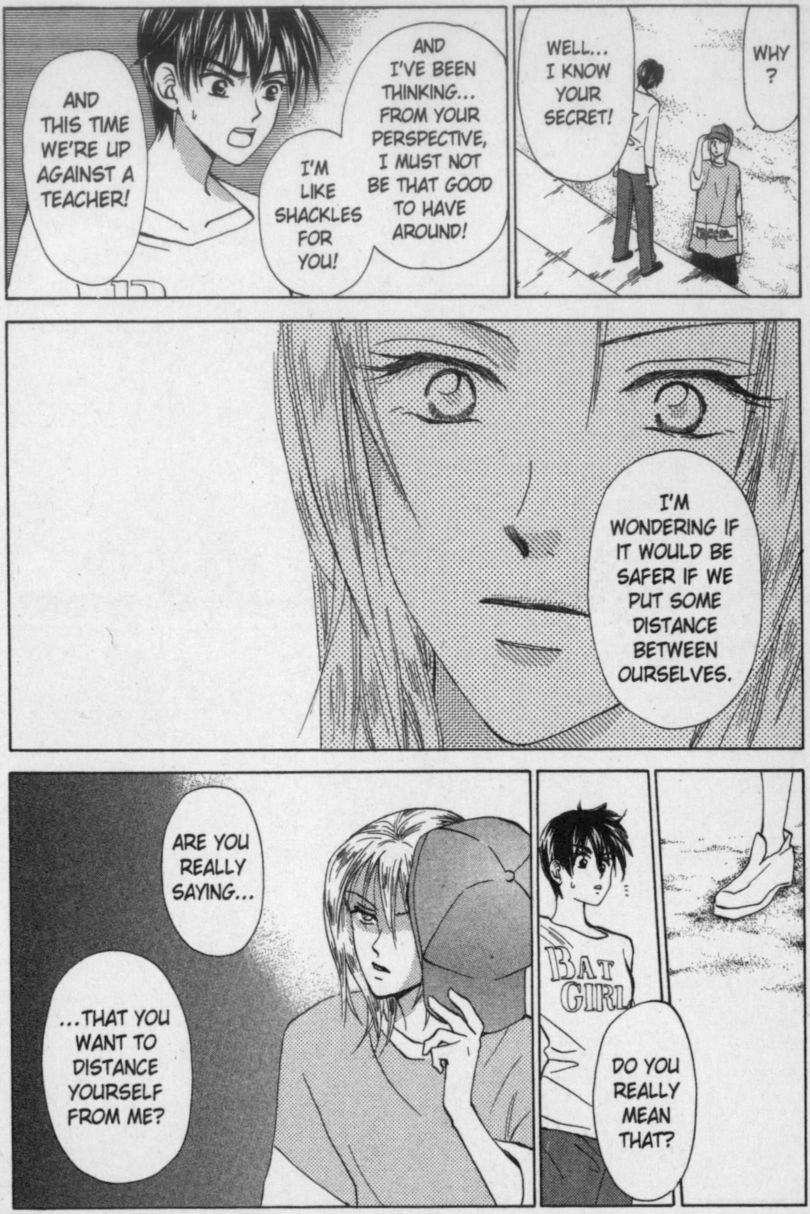
WHY ?
WELL... I KNOW YOUR SECRET!
AND I'VE BEEN THINKING... FROM YOUR PERSPECTIVE, I MUST NOT BE THAT GOOD TO HAVE AROUND!
I'M LIKE SHACKLES FOR YOU!
AND THIS TIME WE'RE UP AGAINST A TEACHER!
I'M WONDERING IF IT WOULD BE SAFER IF WE PUT SOME DISTANCE BETWEEN OURSELVES.
BAT GIRL
DO YOU REALLY MEAN THAT?
ARE YOU REALLY SAYING...
...THAT YOU WANT TO DISTANCE YOURSELF FROM ME?

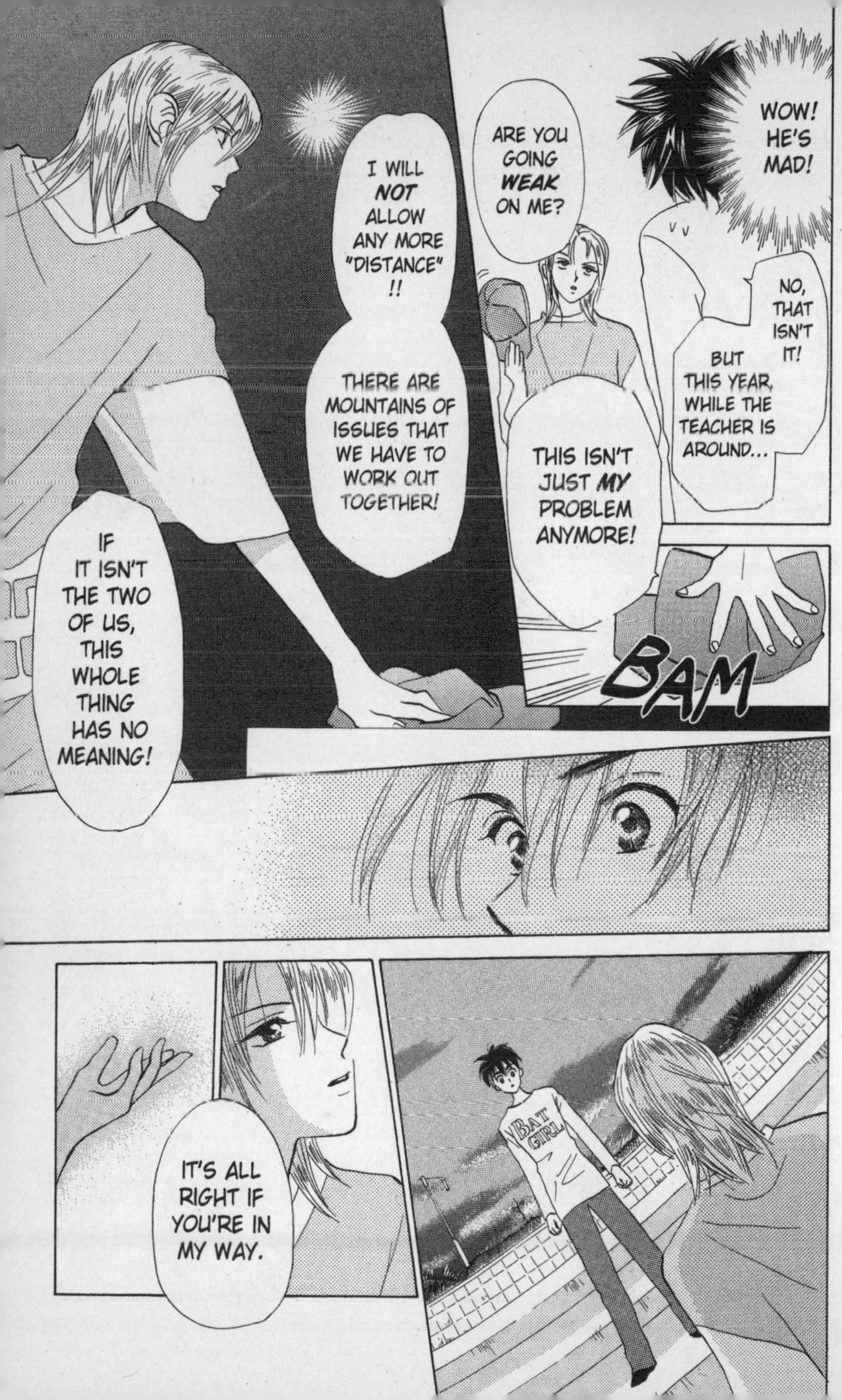
WOW! HE'S MAD!
ARE YOU GOING WEAK ON ME?
NO, THAT ISN'T IT!
BUT THIS YEAR, WHILE THE TEACHER IS AROUND...
BAM
THIS ISN'T JUST MY PROBLEM ANYMORE!
I WILL NOT ALLOW ANY MORE "DISTANCE" !!
THERE ARE MOUNTAINS OF ISSUES THAT WE HAVE TO WORK OUT TOGETHER!
IF IT ISN'T THE TWO OF US, THIS WHOLE THING HAS NO MEANING!
BAT GIRL
IT'S ALL RIGHT IF YOU'RE IN MY WAY.

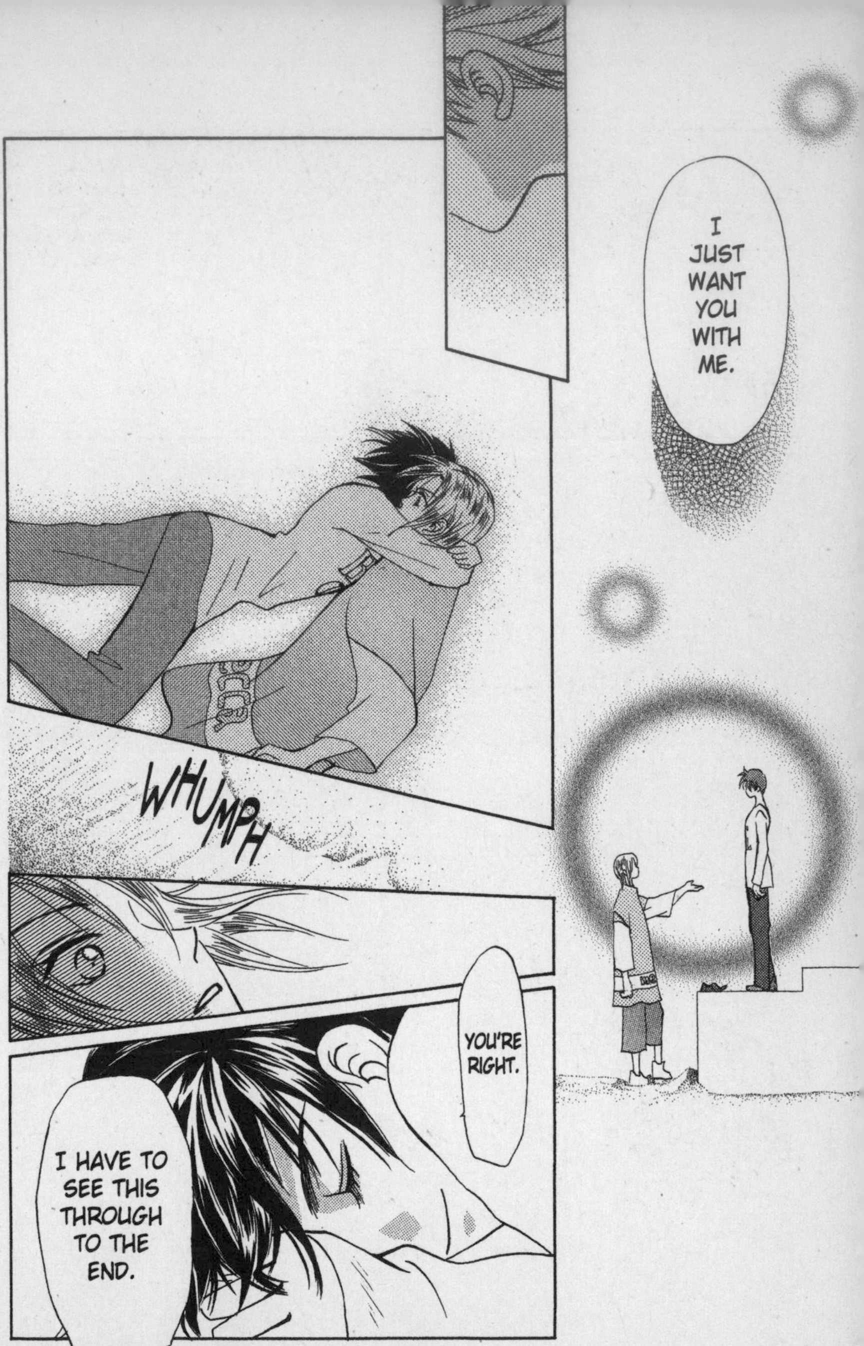
I JUST WANT YOU WITH ME.
WHUMPH
YOU'RE RIGHT.
I HAVE TO SEE THIS THROUGH TO THE END.

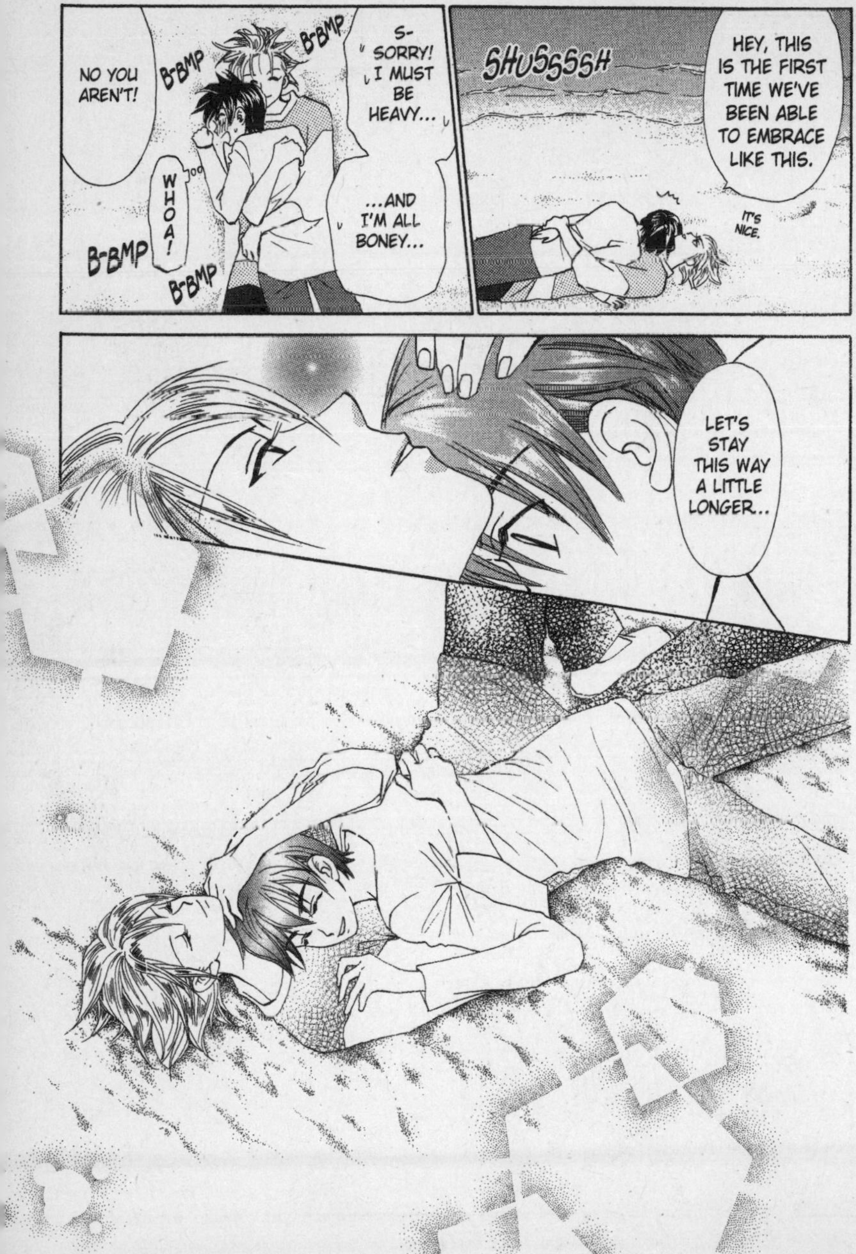
SHUSSSSH
HEY, THIS IS THE FIRST TIME WE'VE BEEN ABLE TO EMBRACE LIKE THIS.
IT'S NICE.
B-BMP
S- SORRY! I MUST BE HEAVY...
B-BMP
NO YOU AREN'T!
WHOA!
...AND I'M ALL BONEY...
B-BMP
B-BMP
LET'S STAY THIS WAY A LITTLE LONGER...

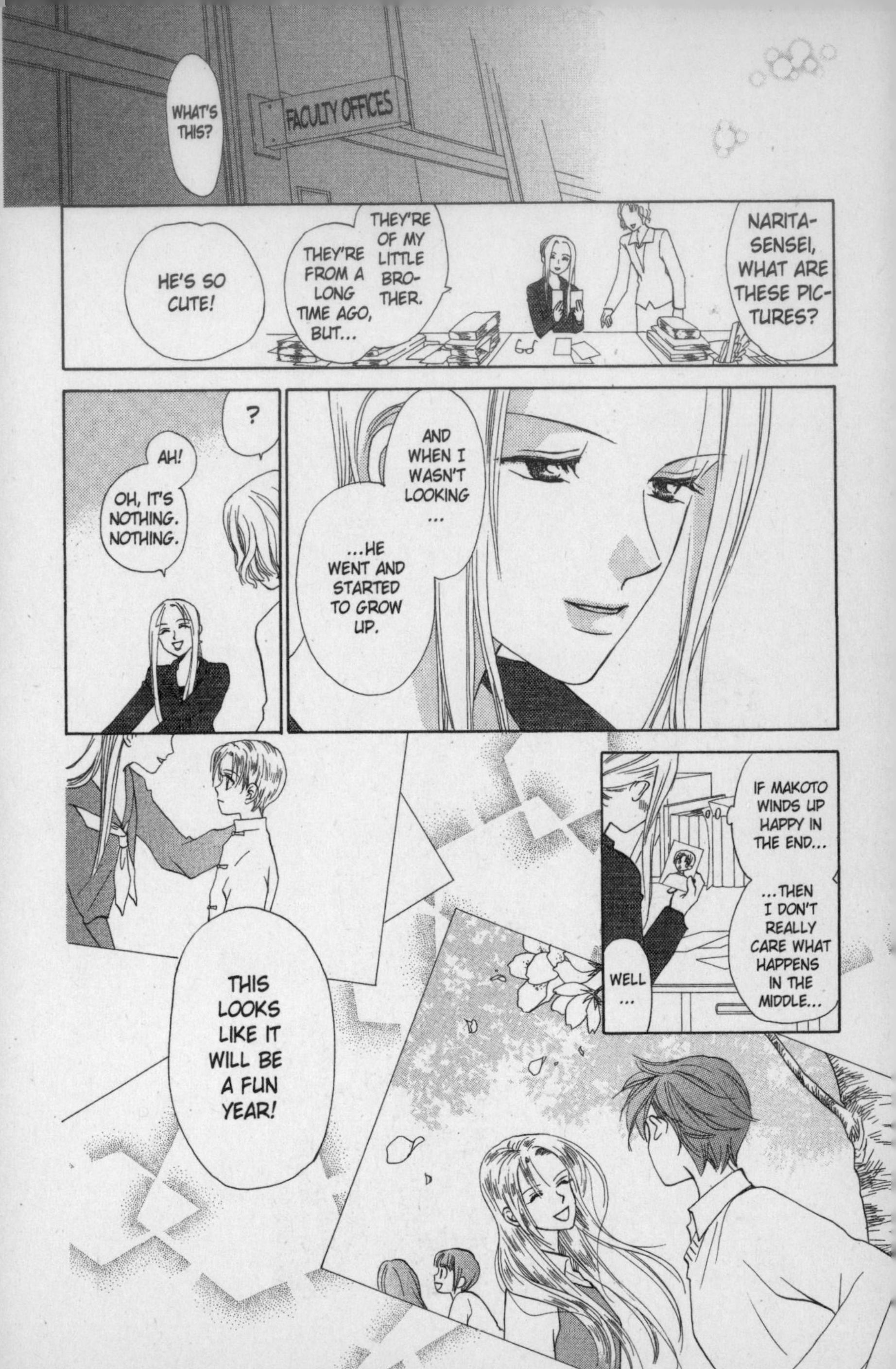
FACULTY OFFICES
WHAT'S THIS?
NARITA-SENSEI, WHAT ARE THESE PICTURES?
THEY'RE OF MY LITTLE BROTHER.
THEY'RE FROM A LONG TIME AGO, BUT...
HE'S SO CUTE!
AND WHEN I WASN'T LOOKING...
...HE WENT AND STARTED TO GROW UP.
?
AH!
OH, IT'S NOTHING. NOTHING.
IF MAKOTO WINDS UP HAPPY IN THE END...
...THEN I DON'T REALLY CARE WHAT HAPPENS IN THE MIDDLE...
WELL...
THIS LOOKS LIKE IT WILL BE A FUN YEAR!

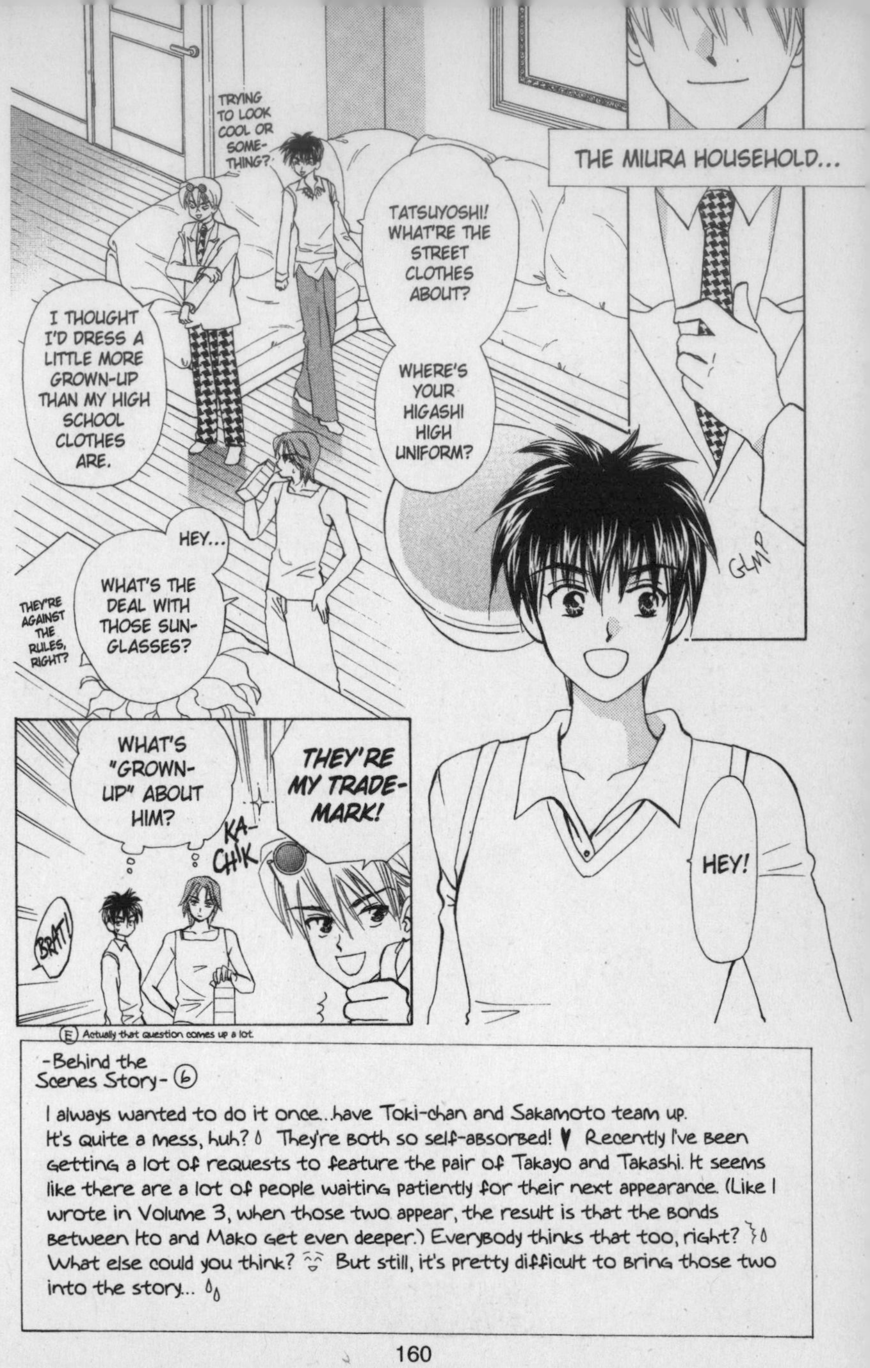
THE MIURA HOUSEHOLD...
GLMP
HEY!
TATSUYOSHI! WHAT'RE THE STREET CLOTHES ABOUT?
WHERE'S YOUR HIGASHI HIGH UNIFORM?
TRYING TO LOOK COOL OR SOME-THING?
I THOUGHT I'D DRESS A LITTLE MORE GROWN-UP THAN MY HIGH SCHOOL CLOTHES ARE.
HEY...
WHAT'S THE DEAL WITH THOSE SUN-GLASSES?
THEY'RE AGAINST THE RULES, RIGHT?
THEY'RE MY TRADE-MARK!
KA-CHIK
WHAT'S "GROWN-UP" ABOUT HIM?
BRAT!

Ⓔ Actually that question comes up a lot.

-Behind the Scenes Story- ⑥

I always wanted to do it once...have Toki-chan and Sakamoto team up. It's quite a mess, huh? They're both so self-absorbed! ♥ Recently I've been getting a lot of requests to feature the pair of Takayo and Takashi. It seems like there are a lot of people waiting patiently for their next appearance. (Like I wrote in Volume 3, when those two appear, the result is that the bonds between Ito and Mako get even deeper.) Everybody thinks that too, right? What else could you think? But still, it's pretty difficult to bring those two into the story...

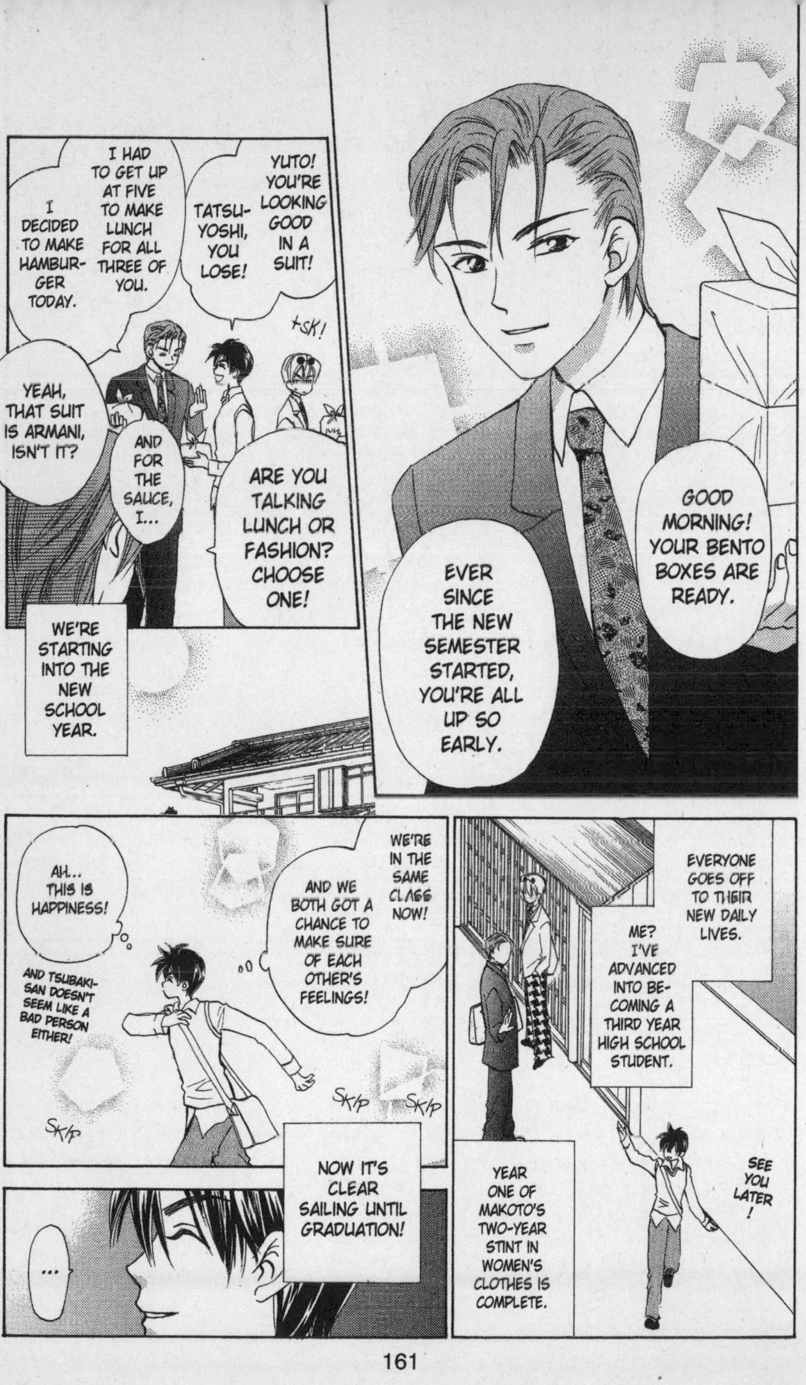
GOOD MORNING! YOUR BENTO BOXES ARE READY.
EVER SINCE THE NEW SEMESTER STARTED, YOU'RE ALL UP SO EARLY.
YUTO! YOU'RE LOOKING GOOD IN A SUIT!
TATSU-YOSHI, YOU LOSE!
I HAD TO GET UP AT FIVE TO MAKE LUNCH FOR ALL THREE OF YOU.
I DECIDED TO MAKE HAMBUR-GER TODAY.
TSK!
YEAH, THAT SUIT IS ARMANI, ISN'T IT?
AND FOR THE SAUCE, I...
ARE YOU TALKING LUNCH OR FASHION? CHOOSE ONE!
WE'RE STARTING INTO THE NEW SCHOOL YEAR.
EVERYONE GOES OFF TO THEIR NEW DAILY LIVES.
ME? I'VE ADVANCED INTO BE-COMING A THIRD YEAR HIGH SCHOOL STUDENT.
SEE YOU LATER!
YEAR ONE OF MAKOTO'S TWO-YEAR STINT IN WOMEN'S CLOTHES IS COMPLETE.
WE'RE IN THE SAME CLASS NOW!
AND WE BOTH GOT A CHANCE TO MAKE SURE OF EACH OTHER'S FEELINGS!
AH... THIS IS HAPPINESS!
AND TSUBAKI-SAN DOESN'T SEEM LIKE A BAD PERSON EITHER!
SKIP
SKIP
SKIP
NOW IT'S CLEAR SAILING UNTIL GRADUATION!
...

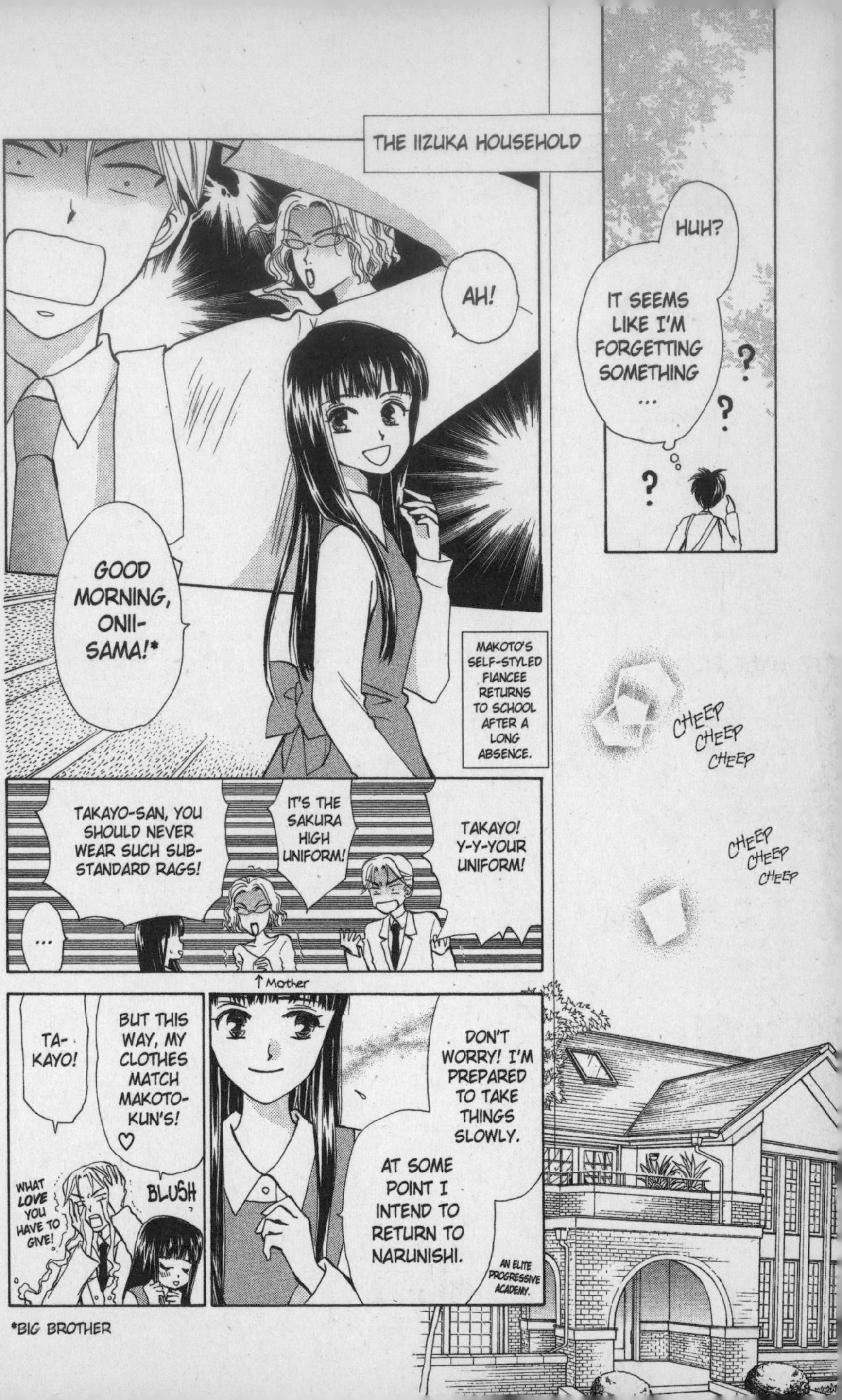
HUH?
IT SEEMS LIKE I'M FORGETTING SOMETHING ...
CHEEP CHEEP CHEEP
CHEEP CHEEP CHEEP
THE IIZUKA HOUSEHOLD
AH!
GOOD MORNING, ONII-SAMA!*
MAKOTO'S SELF-STYLED FIANCEE RETURNS TO SCHOOL AFTER A LONG ABSENCE.
TAKAYO! Y-Y-YOUR UNIFORM!
IT'S THE SAKURA HIGH UNIFORM!
TAKAYO-SAN, YOU SHOULD NEVER WEAR SUCH SUB-STANDARD RAGS!
...
↑Mother
DON'T WORRY! I'M PREPARED TO TAKE THINGS SLOWLY.
AT SOME POINT I INTEND TO RETURN TO NARUNISHI.
AN ELITE PROGRESSIVE ACADEMY.
TA-KAYO!
BUT THIS WAY, MY CLOTHES MATCH MAKOTO-KUN'S! ♡
BLUSH
WHAT LOVE YOU HAVE TO GIVE!

*BIG BROTHER

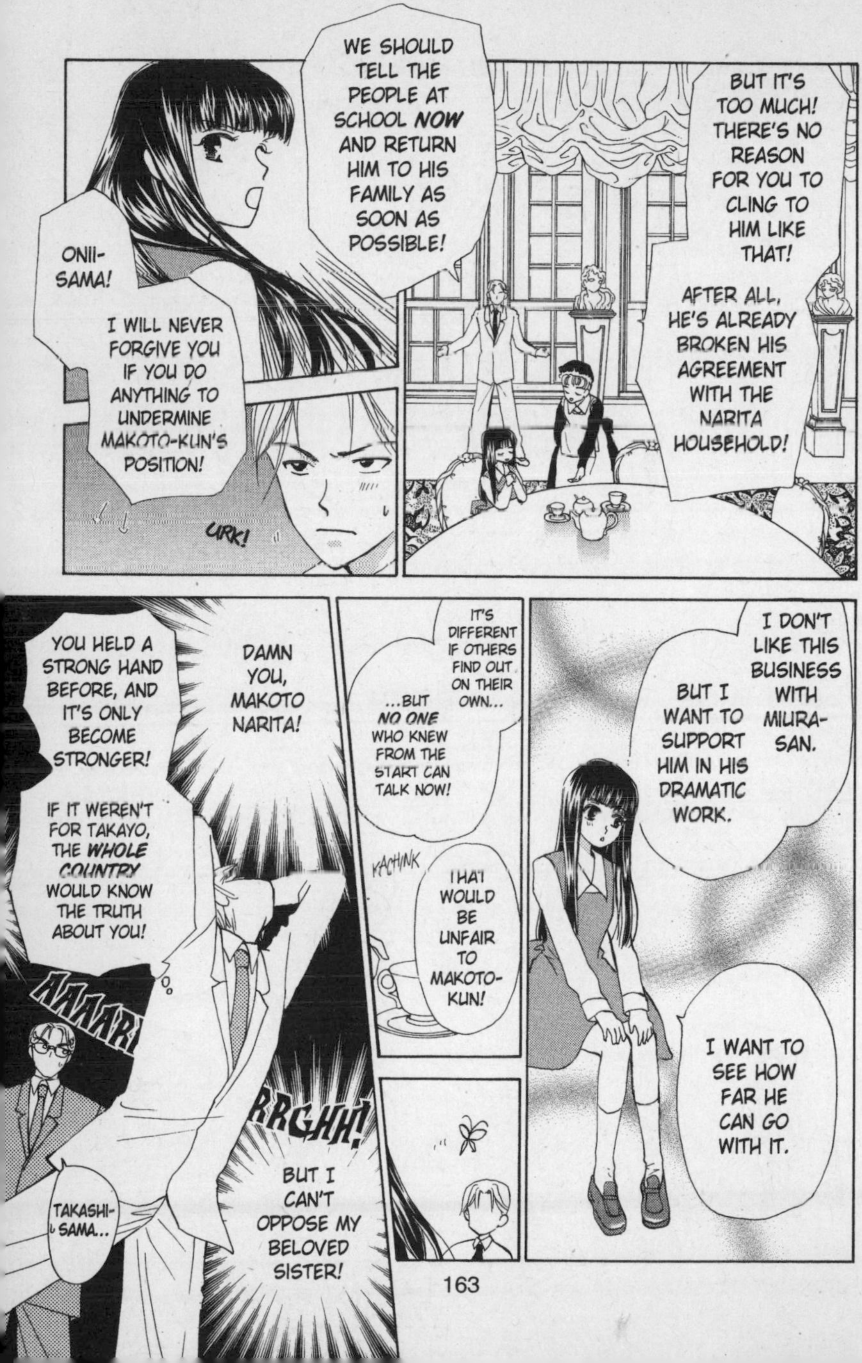
WE SHOULD TELL THE PEOPLE AT SCHOOL NOW AND RETURN HIM TO HIS FAMILY AS SOON AS POSSIBLE!
BUT IT'S TOO MUCH! THERE'S NO REASON FOR YOU TO CLING TO HIM LIKE THAT!
AFTER ALL, HE'S ALREADY BROKEN HIS AGREEMENT WITH THE NARITA HOUSEHOLD!
ONII-SAMA!
I WILL NEVER FORGIVE YOU IF YOU DO ANYTHING TO UNDERMINE MAKOTO-KUN'S POSITION!
URK!
I DON'T LIKE THIS BUSINESS WITH MIURA-SAN.
BUT I WANT TO SUPPORT HIM IN HIS DRAMATIC WORK.
I WANT TO SEE HOW FAR HE CAN GO WITH IT.
IT'S DIFFERENT IF OTHERS FIND OUT ON THEIR OWN...
...BUT NO ONE WHO KNEW FROM THE START CAN TALK NOW!
KACHINK
THAT WOULD BE UNFAIR TO MAKOTO-KUN!
DAMN YOU, MAKOTO NARITA!
YOU HELD A STRONG HAND BEFORE, AND IT'S ONLY BECOME STRONGER!
IF IT WEREN'T FOR TAKAYO, THE WHOLE COUNTRY WOULD KNOW THE TRUTH ABOUT YOU!
AAAARRRGHH!
BUT I CAN'T OPPOSE MY BELOVED SISTER!
TAKASHI-SAMA...

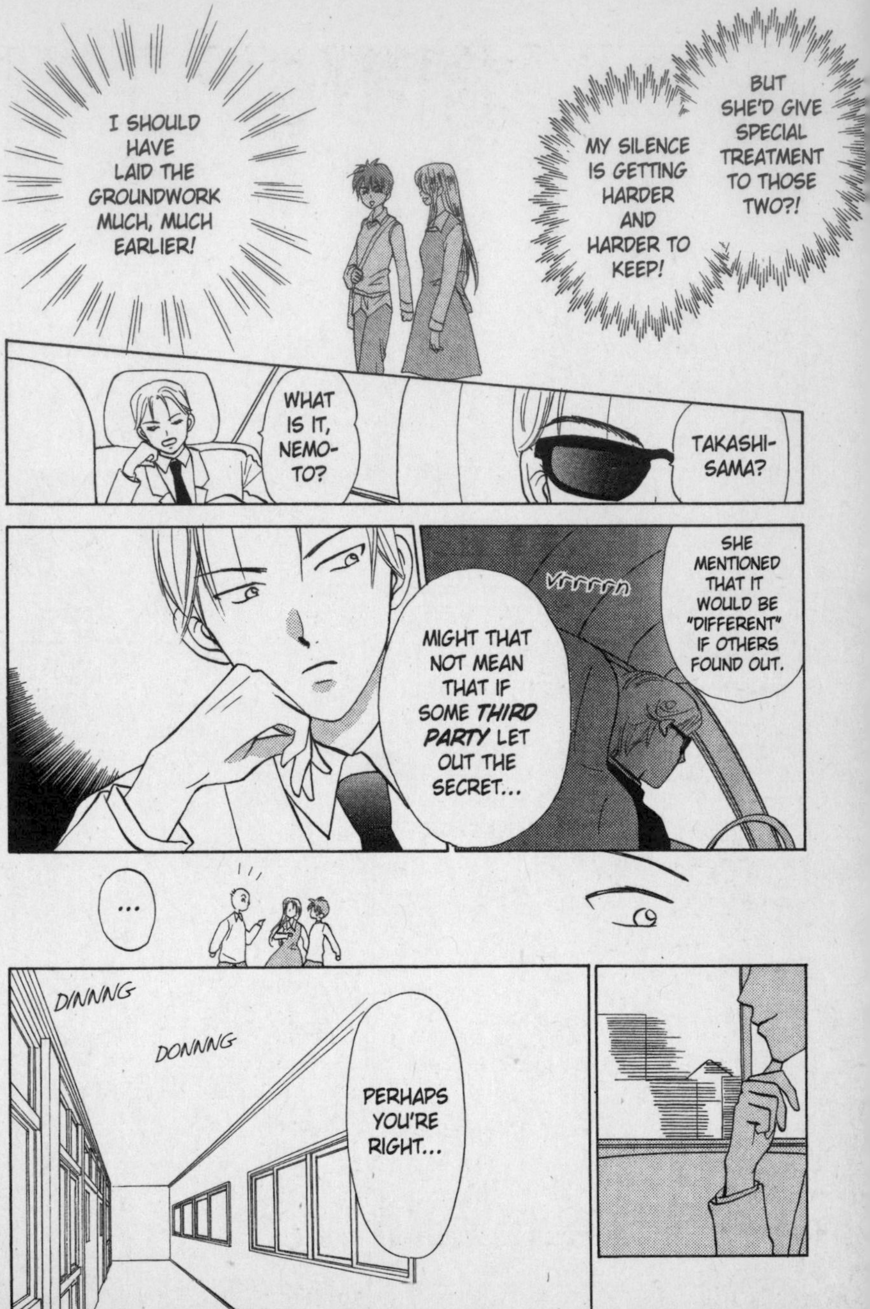
BUT SHE'D GIVE SPECIAL TREATMENT TO THOSE TWO?!
MY SILENCE IS GETTING HARDER AND HARDER TO KEEP!
I SHOULD HAVE LAID THE GROUNDWORK MUCH, MUCH EARLIER!
TAKASHI-SAMA?
WHAT IS IT, NEMOTO?
SHE MENTIONED THAT IT WOULD BE "DIFFERENT" IF OTHERS FOUND OUT.
Vrrrrrn
MIGHT THAT NOT MEAN THAT IF SOME THIRD PARTY LET OUT THE SECRET...
...
DINNNG
DONNNG
PERHAPS YOU'RE RIGHT...

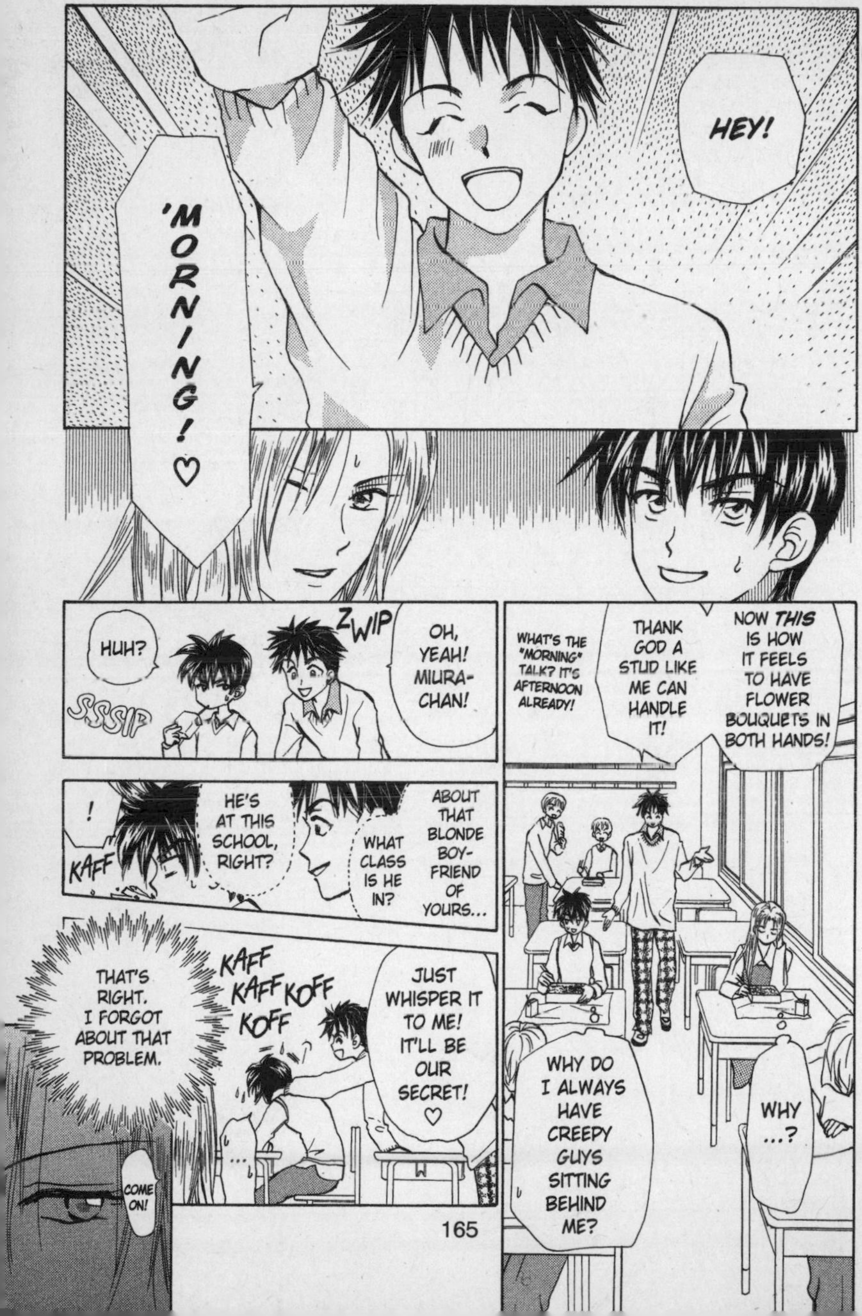
HEY!
'MORNING! ♡
NOW THIS IS HOW IT FEELS TO HAVE FLOWER BOUQUETS IN BOTH HANDS!
THANK GOD A STUD LIKE ME CAN HANDLE IT!
WHAT'S THE "MORNING" TALK? IT'S AFTERNOON ALREADY!
WHY ...?
WHY DO I ALWAYS HAVE CREEPY GUYS SITTING BEHIND ME?
OH, YEAH! MIURA-CHAN!
ZWIP
HUH?
SSSIP
ABOUT THAT BLONDE BOY-FRIEND OF YOURS...
WHAT CLASS IS HE IN?
HE'S AT THIS SCHOOL, RIGHT?
!
KAFF
JUST WHISPER IT TO ME! IT'LL BE OUR SECRET! ♡
KAFF KAFF KOFF KOFF
THAT'S RIGHT. I FORGOT ABOUT THAT PROBLEM.
...
COME ON!

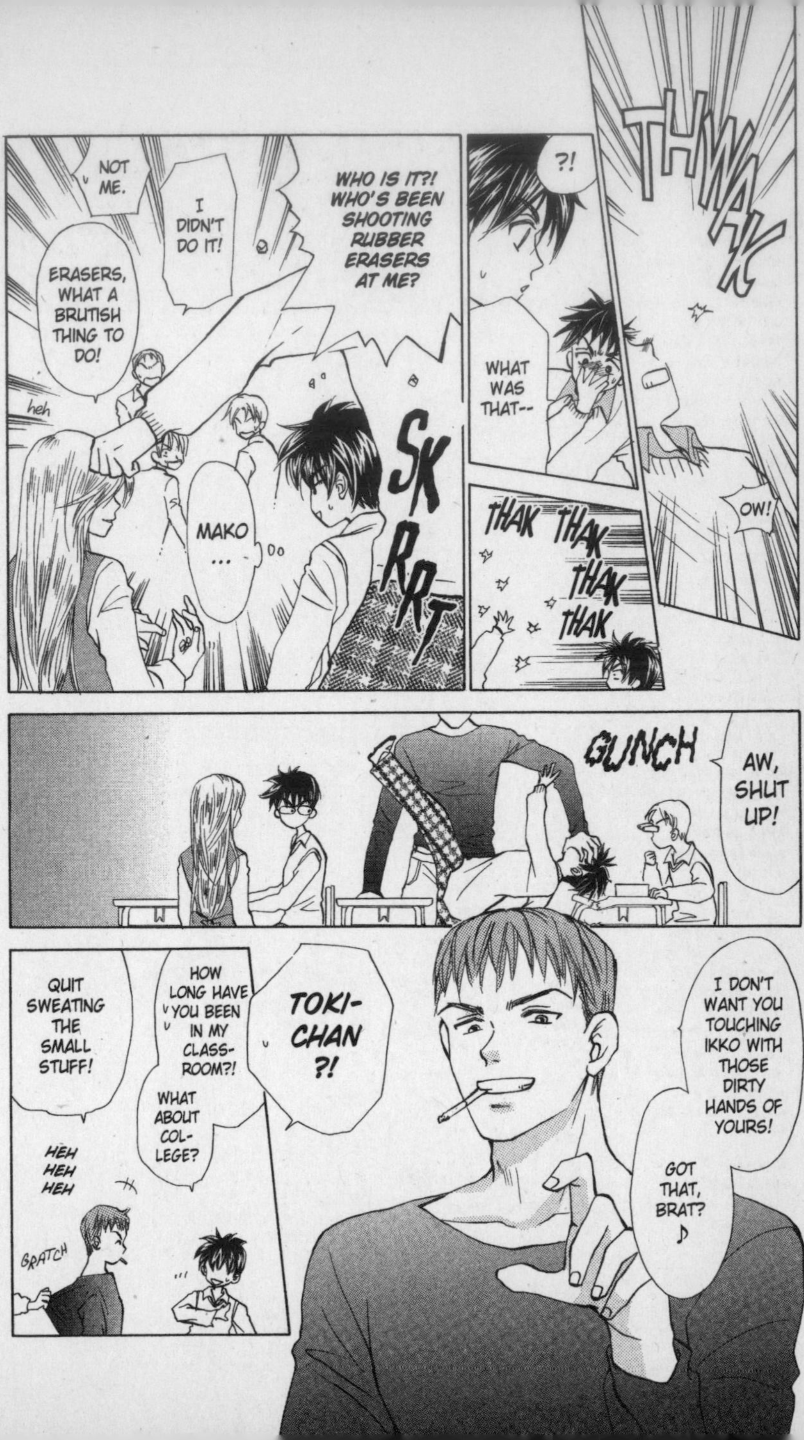
THWAK
OW!
?!
WHAT WAS THAT--
THAK THAK THAK THAK
WHO IS IT?! WHO'S BEEN SHOOTING RUBBER ERASERS AT ME?
SKRRT
I DIDN'T DO IT!
NOT ME.
ERASERS, WHAT A BRUTISH THING TO DO!
MAKO...
heh
GUNCH
AW, SHUT UP!
I DON'T WANT YOU TOUCHING IKKO WITH THOSE DIRTY HANDS OF YOURS!
GOT THAT, BRAT? ♪
TOKI-CHAN?!
HOW LONG HAVE YOU BEEN IN MY CLASSROOM?!
WHAT ABOUT COLLEGE?
QUIT SWEATING THE SMALL STUFF!
HEH HEH HEH
GRATCH

SO YOU'RE THE RUBBER ERASER FIEND, ARE YA?
HUH?
WHAT'S THIS GARBAGE YOU'RE SPOUTING?
DON'T PLAY DUMB YOU BIG APE!!
GRRR GROWL
WHAT'S WITH YOU, YOU LITTLE MONKEY ?!
NOW...
THERE'S ONE GOOD THING ABOUT SAKAMOTO...
...HE MAKES RUNNING FROM TOKI-SEMPAI EASIER.
I AGREE.
YES!
BUT THE BAD THING ABOUT BOTH IS THAT THEY'VE BOTH SEEN MAKOTO AS A MAN.
NEITHER OF THEM CAN FIGURE IT OUT THOUGH.
JUST MAKE SURE YOU DON'T APPEAR IN MEN'S CLOTHING!
WELL...
...WHEN I DO, YOU CAN BET...
...IT'LL BE FOR YOUR SAKE.

- How can I become a manga-ka?

Ⓔ Awwww... There it is! It's such a difficult question! It's different than just going out and finding a job! I've nothing against going to a specialty school and learning the manga ropes, but that won't turn you into a manga-ka. Even just once or twice, try entering your manga into one of the contests in the magazines.
The **Hana to Yume** line has:
- HMC
- Big Challenge
- Athena New Artists Award

Frankly, if you place high in these contests, the path to becoming a manga artist will open up for you even if you don't go to a specialty school. It happened for me just as I was graduating from high school. In any case, draw a lot of manga and submit your work to your favorite magazines! Also, you need to really **want** to draw manga! So go for it!

...and with that... I'm sorry I didn't draw much in these little page columns! And this is where I'll end.
See you all next time!

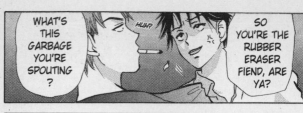

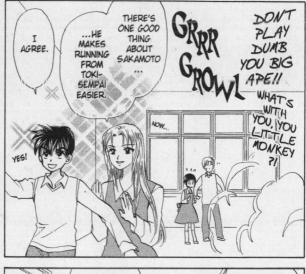

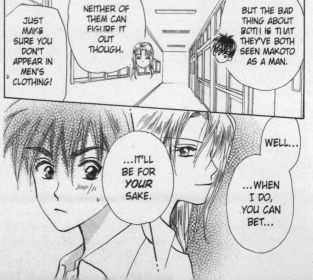

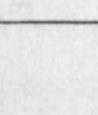

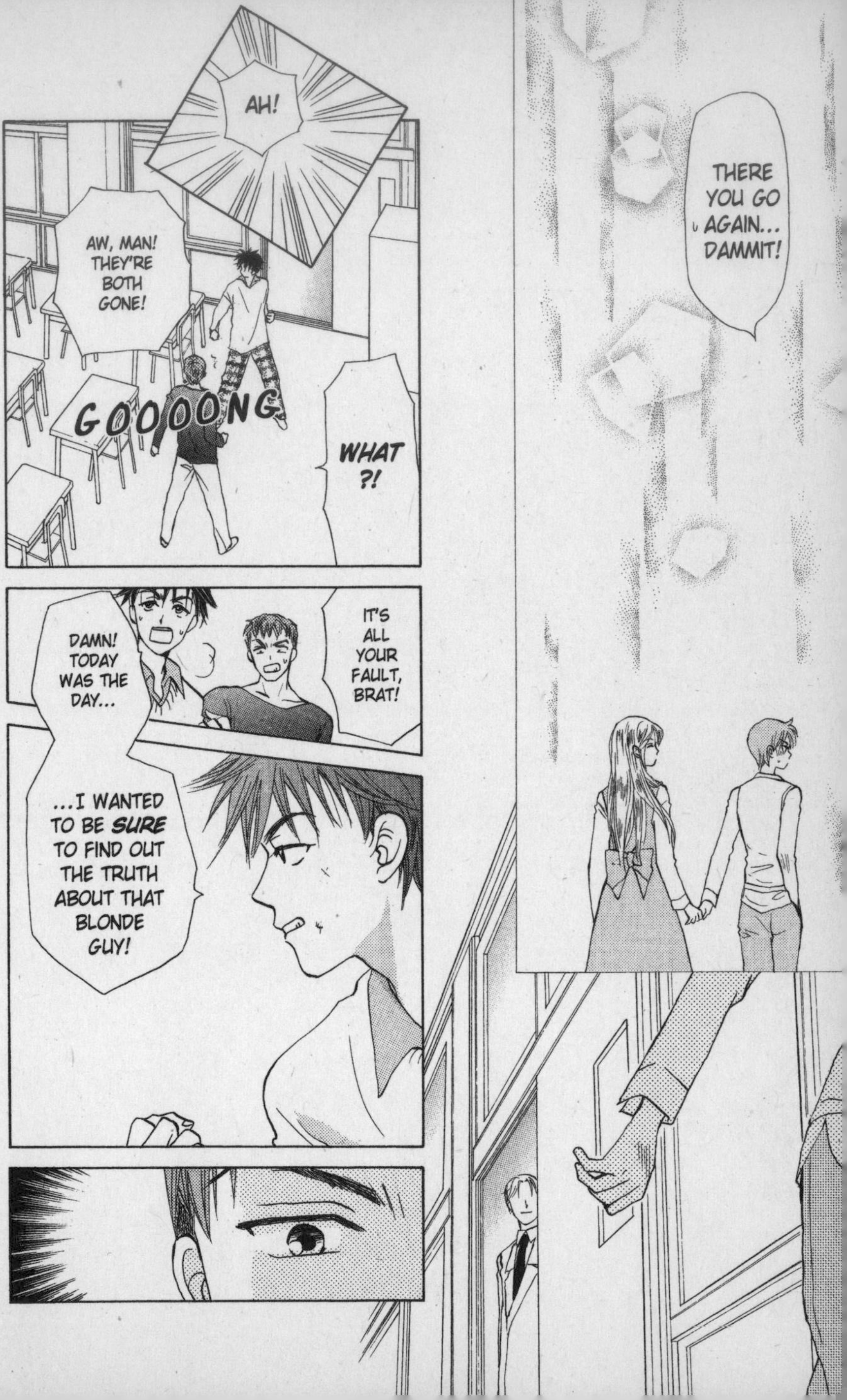
THERE YOU GO AGAIN... DAMMIT!
AH!
AW, MAN! THEY'RE BOTH GONE!
GOOOOONG
WHAT?!
IT'S ALL YOUR FAULT, BRAT!
DAMN! TODAY WAS THE DAY...
...I WANTED TO BE *SURE* TO FIND OUT THE TRUTH ABOUT THAT BLONDE GUY!

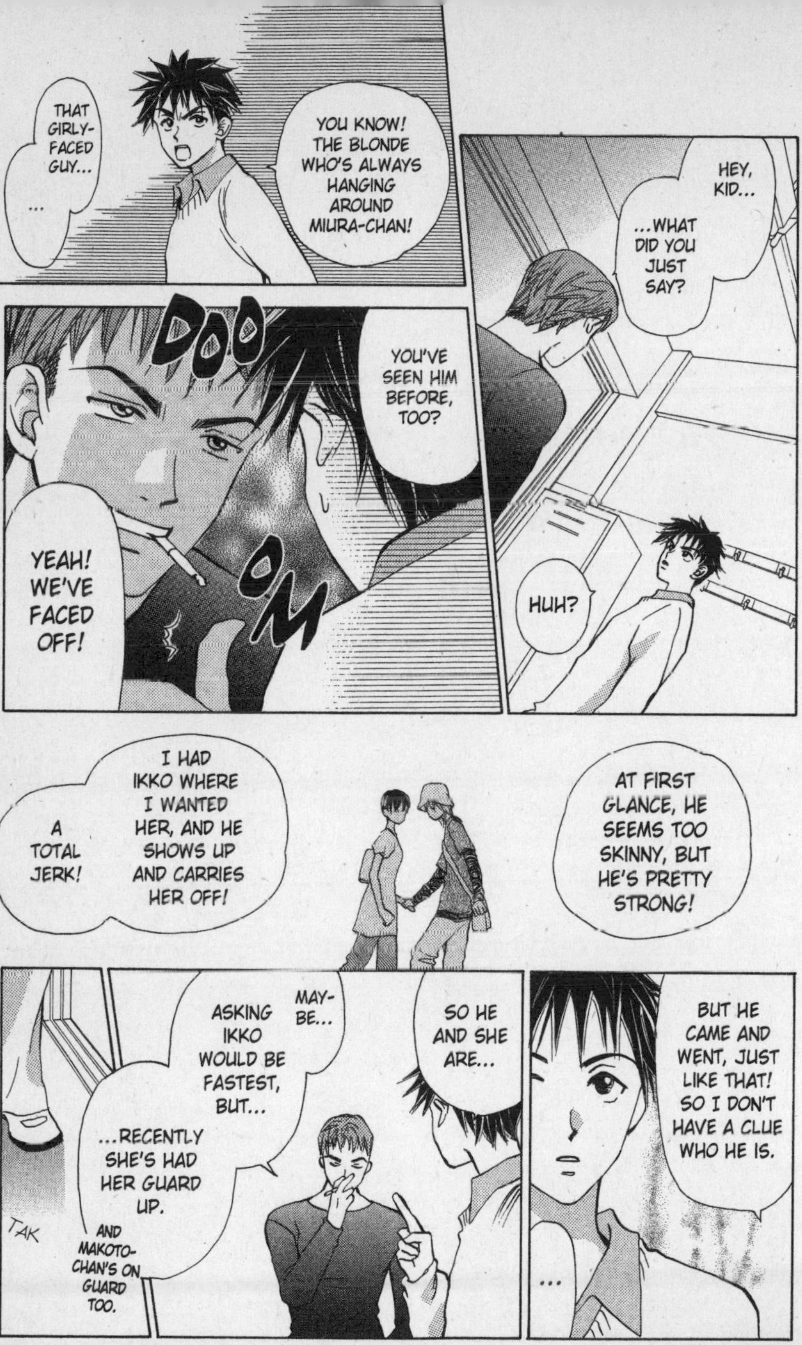
YOU KNOW! THE BLONDE WHO'S ALWAYS HANGING AROUND MIURA-CHAN!
THAT GIRLY-FACED GUY... ...
HEY, KID... ...WHAT DID YOU JUST SAY?
HUH?
DOOOM
YOU'VE SEEN HIM BEFORE, TOO?
YEAH! WE'VE FACED OFF!
AT FIRST GLANCE, HE SEEMS TOO SKINNY, BUT HE'S PRETTY STRONG!
I HAD IKKO WHERE I WANTED HER, AND HE SHOWS UP AND CARRIES HER OFF!
A TOTAL JERK!
BUT HE CAME AND WENT, JUST LIKE THAT! SO I DON'T HAVE A CLUE WHO HE IS.
...
SO HE AND SHE ARE...
MAY-BE...
ASKING IKKO WOULD BE FASTEST, BUT...
...RECENTLY SHE'S HAD HER GUARD UP.
AND MAKOTO-CHAN'S ON GUARD TOO.
TAK

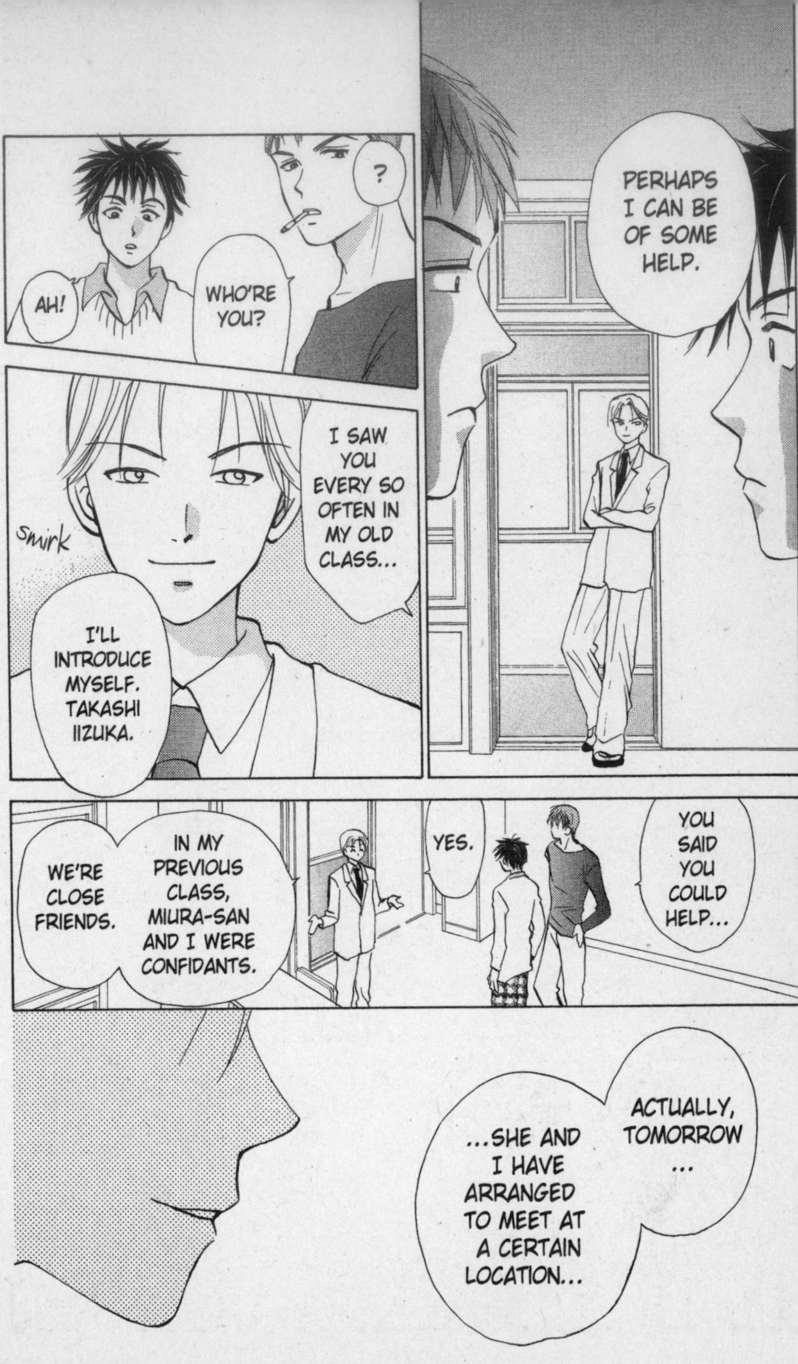
PERHAPS I CAN BE OF SOME HELP.
?
WHO'RE YOU?
AH!
I SAW YOU EVERY SO OFTEN IN MY OLD CLASS...
smirk
I'LL INTRODUCE MYSELF. TAKASHI IIZUKA.
YOU SAID YOU COULD HELP...
YES.
IN MY PREVIOUS CLASS, MIURA-SAN AND I WERE CONFIDANTS.
WE'RE CLOSE FRIENDS.
ACTUALLY, TOMORROW ...
...SHE AND I HAVE ARRANGED TO MEET AT A CERTAIN LOCATION...

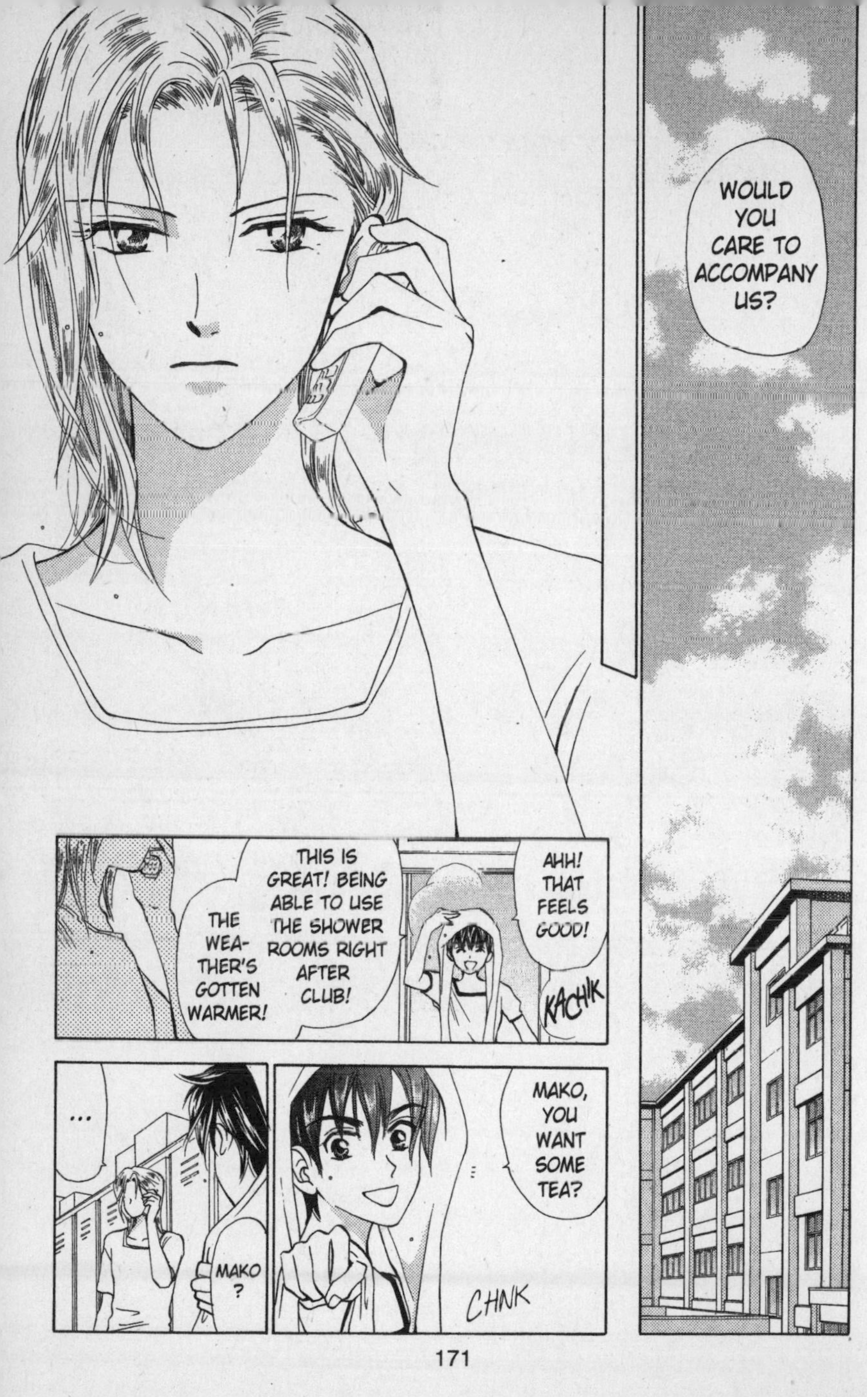
WOULD YOU CARE TO ACCOMPANY US?
AHH! THAT FEELS GOOD!
KACHIK
THIS IS GREAT! BEING ABLE TO USE THE SHOWER ROOMS RIGHT AFTER CLUB!
THE WEA-THER'S GOTTEN WARMER!
MAKO, YOU WANT SOME TEA?
CHNK
...
MAKO?

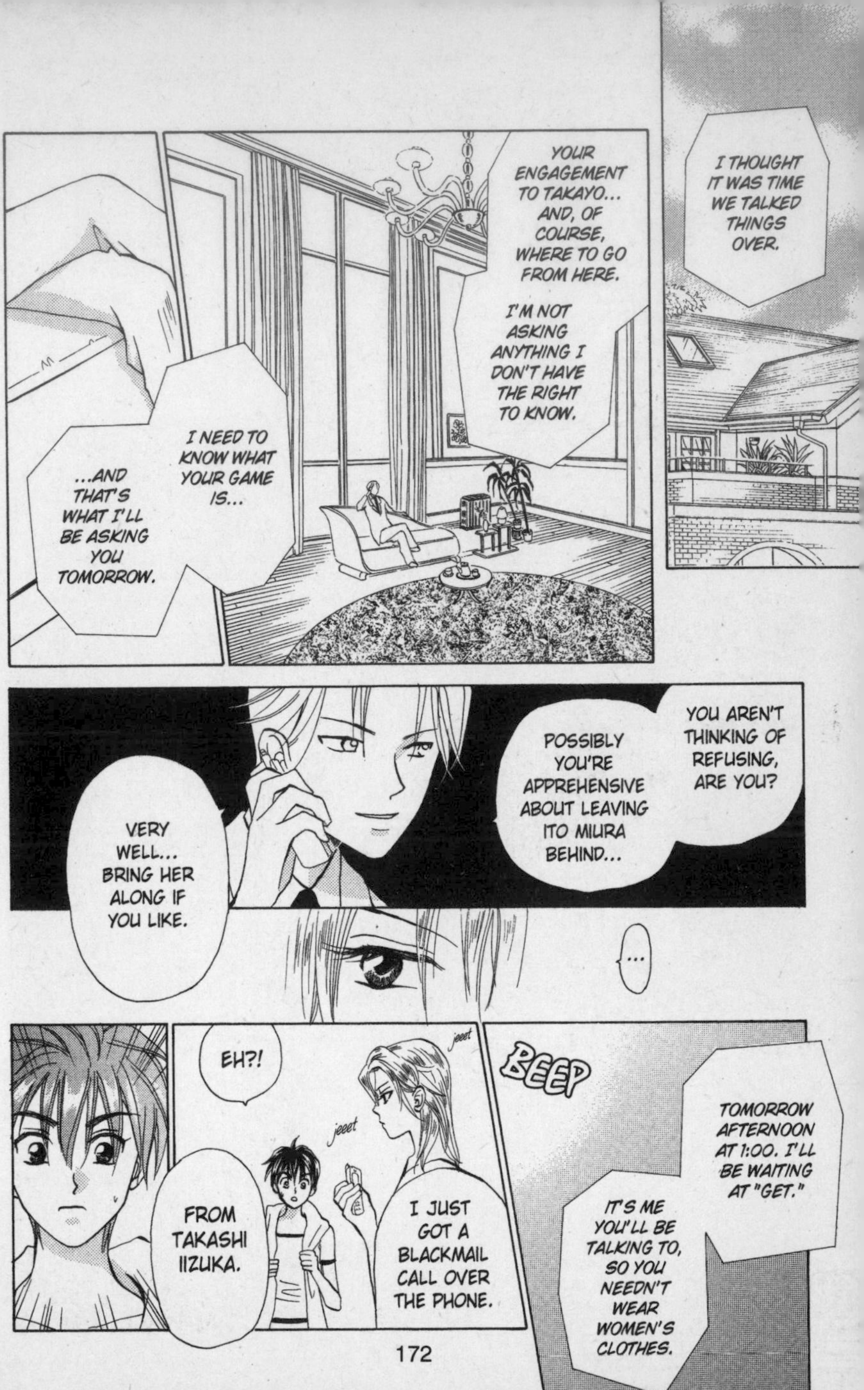
I THOUGHT IT WAS TIME WE TALKED THINGS OVER.
YOUR ENGAGEMENT TO TAKAYO... AND, OF COURSE, WHERE TO GO FROM HERE.
I'M NOT ASKING ANYTHING I DON'T HAVE THE RIGHT TO KNOW.
I NEED TO KNOW WHAT YOUR GAME IS...
...AND THAT'S WHAT I'LL BE ASKING YOU TOMORROW.
YOU AREN'T THINKING OF REFUSING, ARE YOU?
POSSIBLY YOU'RE APPREHENSIVE ABOUT LEAVING ITO MIURA BEHIND...
VERY WELL... BRING HER ALONG IF YOU LIKE.
...
BEEP
TOMORROW AFTERNOON AT 1:00. I'LL BE WAITING AT "GET."
IT'S ME YOU'LL BE TALKING TO, SO YOU NEEDN'T WEAR WOMEN'S CLOTHES.
jeeet
EH?!
jeeet
I JUST GOT A BLACKMAIL CALL OVER THE PHONE.
FROM TAKASHI IIZUKA.

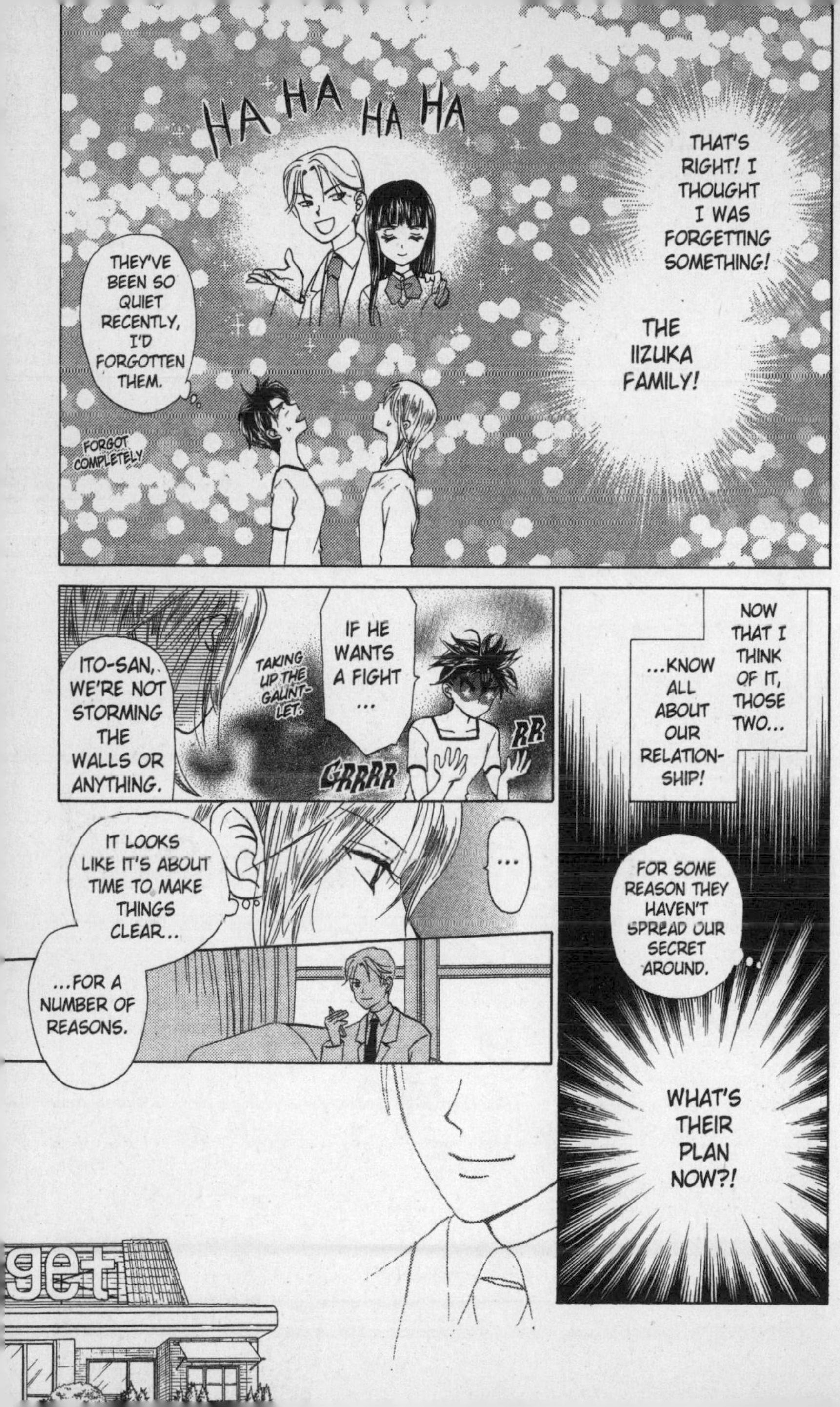
THAT'S RIGHT! I THOUGHT I WAS FORGETTING SOMETHING!
THE IIZUKA FAMILY!
HA HA HA HA
THEY'VE BEEN SO QUIET RECENTLY, I'D FORGOTTEN THEM.
FORGOT COMPLETELY
NOW THAT I THINK OF IT, THOSE TWO...
...KNOW ALL ABOUT OUR RELATIONSHIP!
FOR SOME REASON THEY HAVEN'T SPREAD OUR SECRET AROUND.
WHAT'S THEIR PLAN NOW?!
IF HE WANTS A FIGHT ...
TAKING UP THE GAUNT-LET.
RR
GRRRRR
ITO-SAN, WE'RE NOT STORMING THE WALLS OR ANYTHING.
...
IT LOOKS LIKE IT'S ABOUT TIME TO MAKE THINGS CLEAR...
...FOR A NUMBER OF REASONS.
get

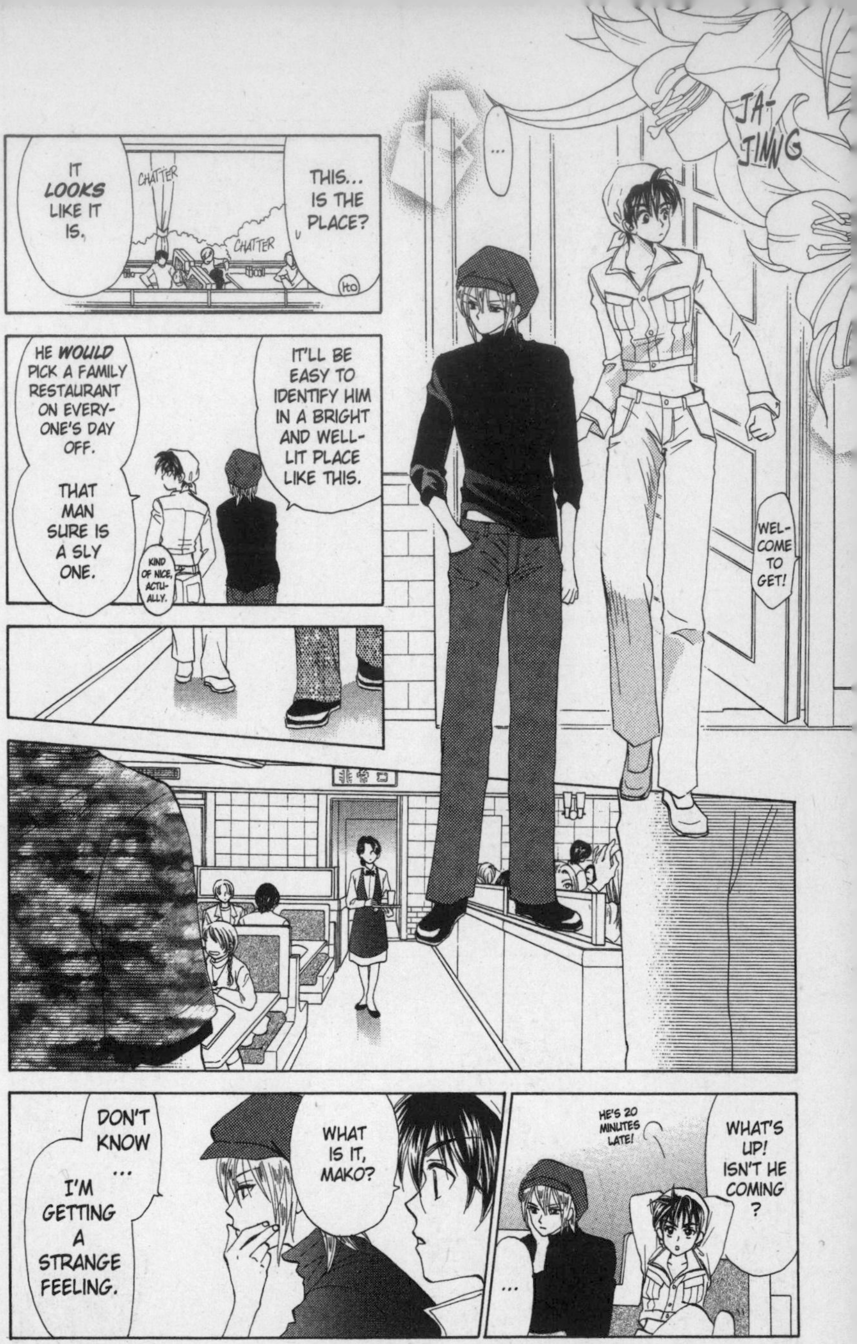
JA-JINNG
...
WEL-COME TO GET!
THIS... IS THE PLACE?
CHATTER
CHATTER
IT LOOKS LIKE IT IS.
IT'LL BE EASY TO IDENTIFY HIM IN A BRIGHT AND WELL-LIT PLACE LIKE THIS.
HE WOULD PICK A FAMILY RESTAURANT ON EVERY-ONE'S DAY OFF.
THAT MAN SURE IS A SLY ONE.
KIND OF NICE, ACTU-ALLY.
WHAT'S UP! ISN'T HE COMING?
HE'S 20 MINUTES LATE!
...
WHAT IS IT, MAKO?
DON'T KNOW ...
I'M GETTING A STRANGE FEELING.

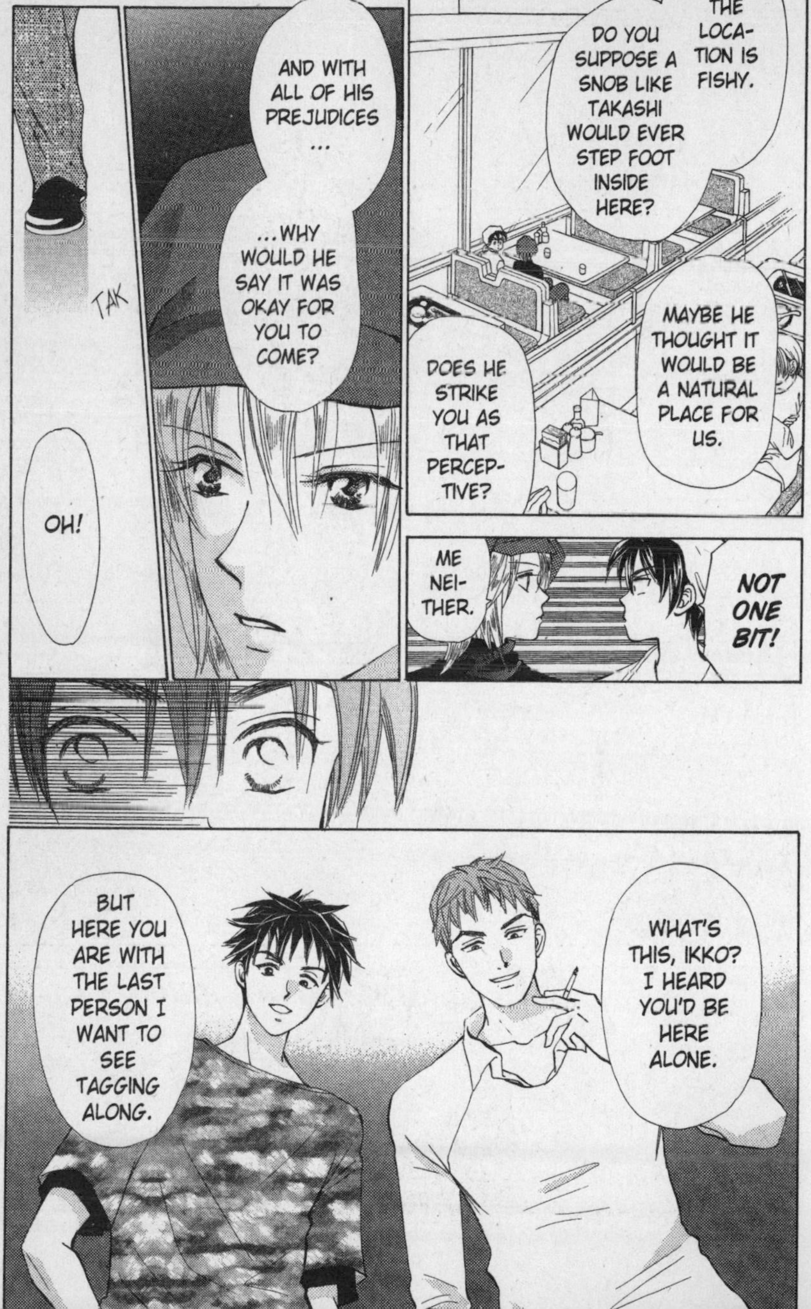
THE LOCATION IS FISHY.
DO YOU SUPPOSE A SNOB LIKE TAKASHI WOULD EVER STEP FOOT INSIDE HERE?
MAYBE HE THOUGHT IT WOULD BE A NATURAL PLACE FOR US.
DOES HE STRIKE YOU AS THAT PERCEPTIVE?
NOT ONE BIT!
ME NEITHER.
AND WITH ALL OF HIS PREJUDICES ...
...WHY WOULD HE SAY IT WAS OKAY FOR YOU TO COME?
TAK
OH!
WHAT'S THIS, IKKO? I HEARD YOU'D BE HERE ALONE.
BUT HERE YOU ARE WITH THE LAST PERSON I WANT TO SEE TAGGING ALONG.

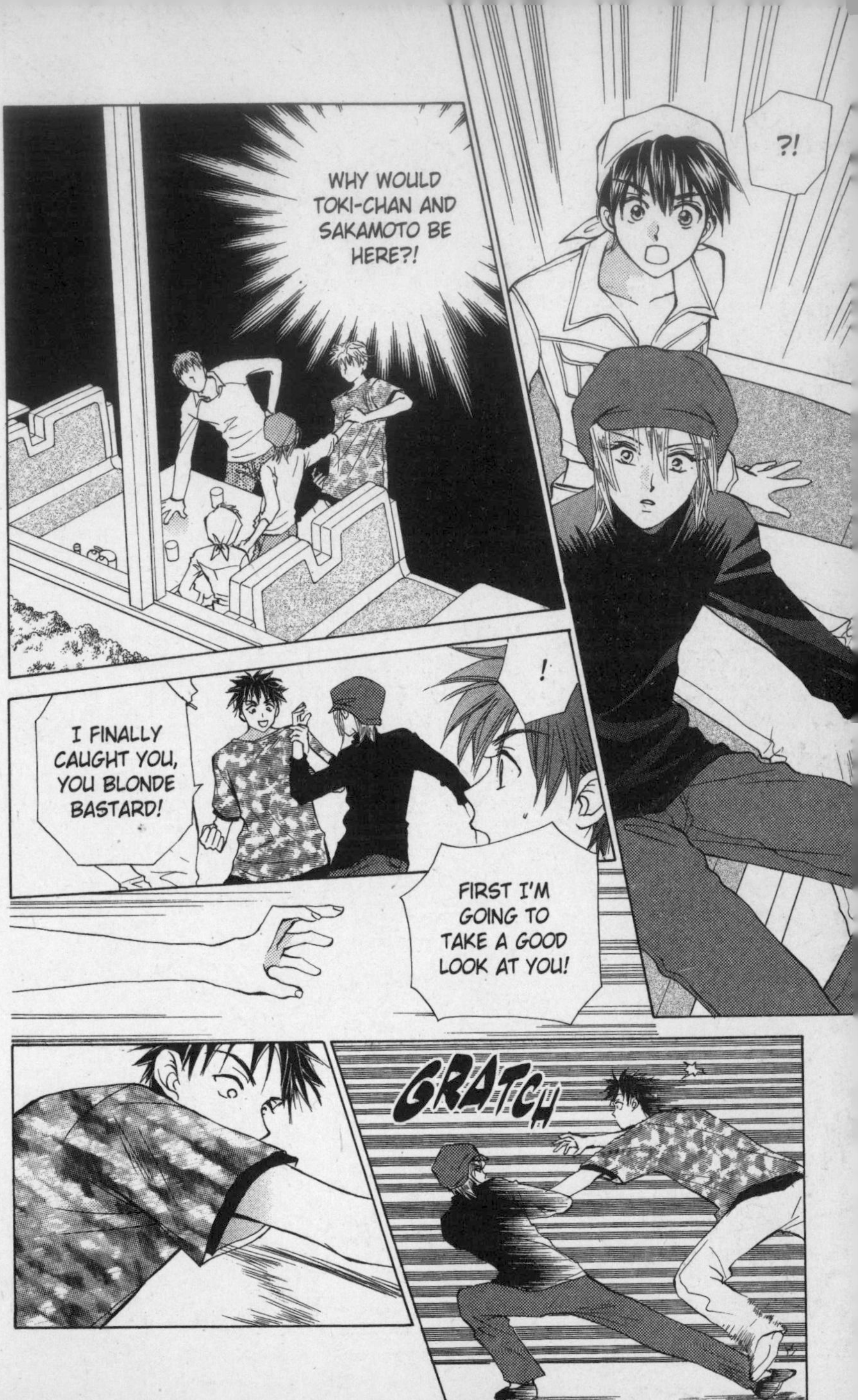
?!
WHY WOULD TOKI-CHAN AND SAKAMOTO BE HERE?!
!
I FINALLY CAUGHT YOU, YOU BLONDE BASTARD!
FIRST I'M GOING TO TAKE A GOOD LOOK AT YOU!
GRATCH

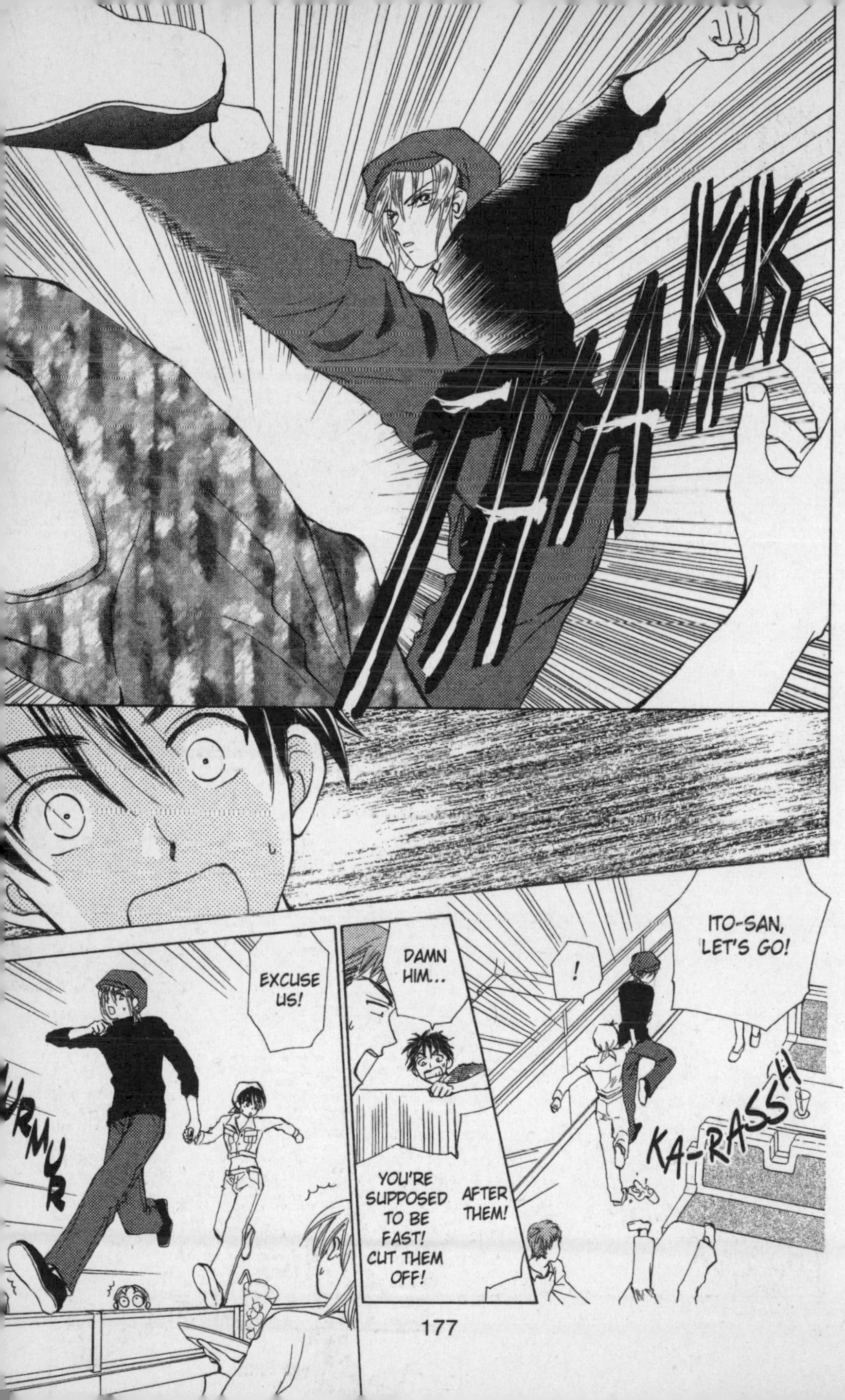
THWAKK
ITO-SAN, LET'S GO!
!
KA-RASSH
DAMN HIM...
AFTER THEM!
YOU'RE SUPPOSED TO BE FAST! CUT THEM OFF!
EXCUSE US!
URMUR

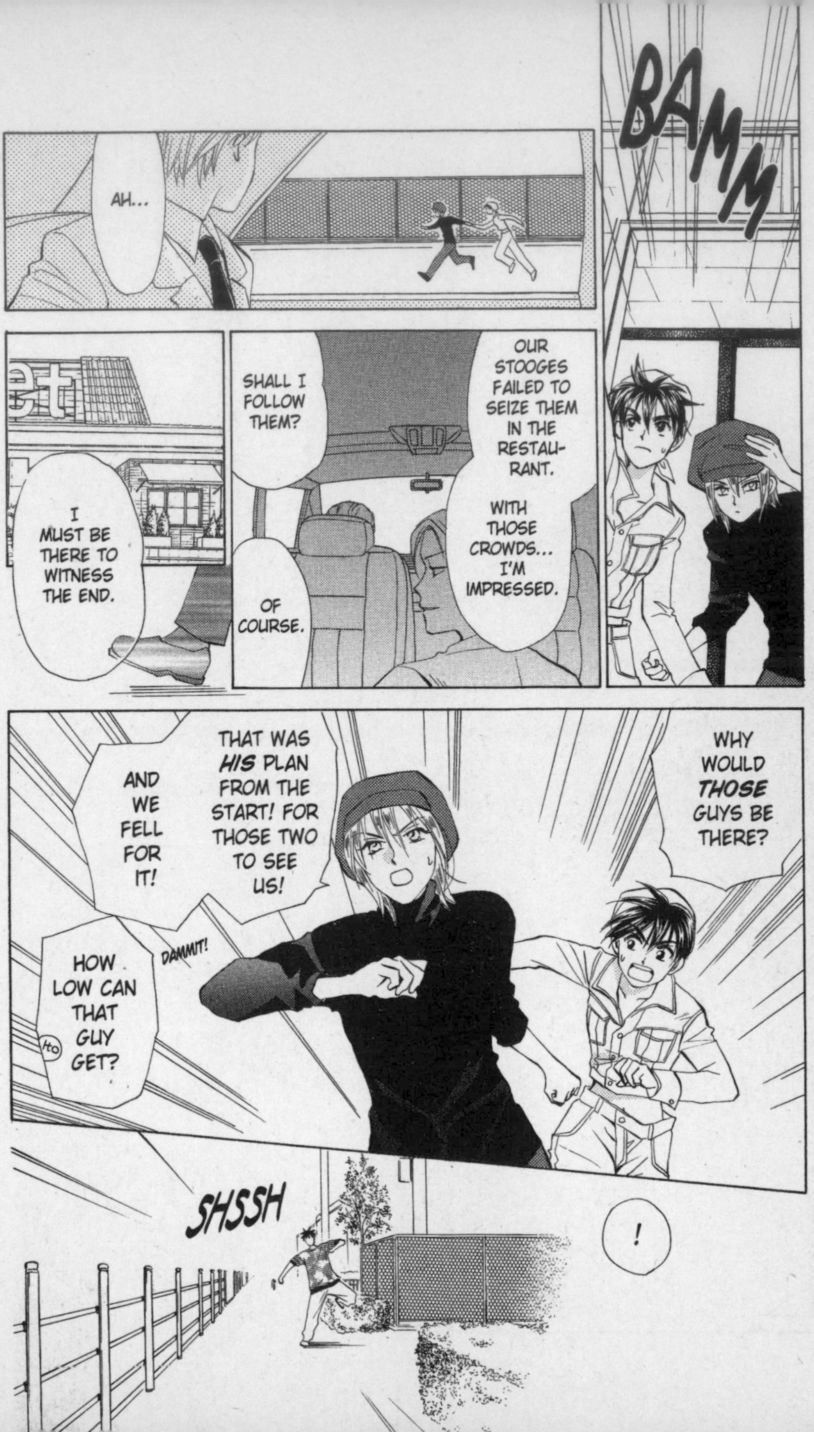
BAMM
AH...
OUR STOOGES FAILED TO SEIZE THEM IN THE RESTAURANT.
SHALL I FOLLOW THEM?
WITH THOSE CROWDS... I'M IMPRESSED.
OF COURSE.
I MUST BE THERE TO WITNESS THE END.
WHY WOULD THOSE GUYS BE THERE?
THAT WAS HIS PLAN FROM THE START! FOR THOSE TWO TO SEE US!
AND WE FELL FOR IT!
DAMMIT!
HOW LOW CAN THAT GUY GET?
Ito
!
SHSSH

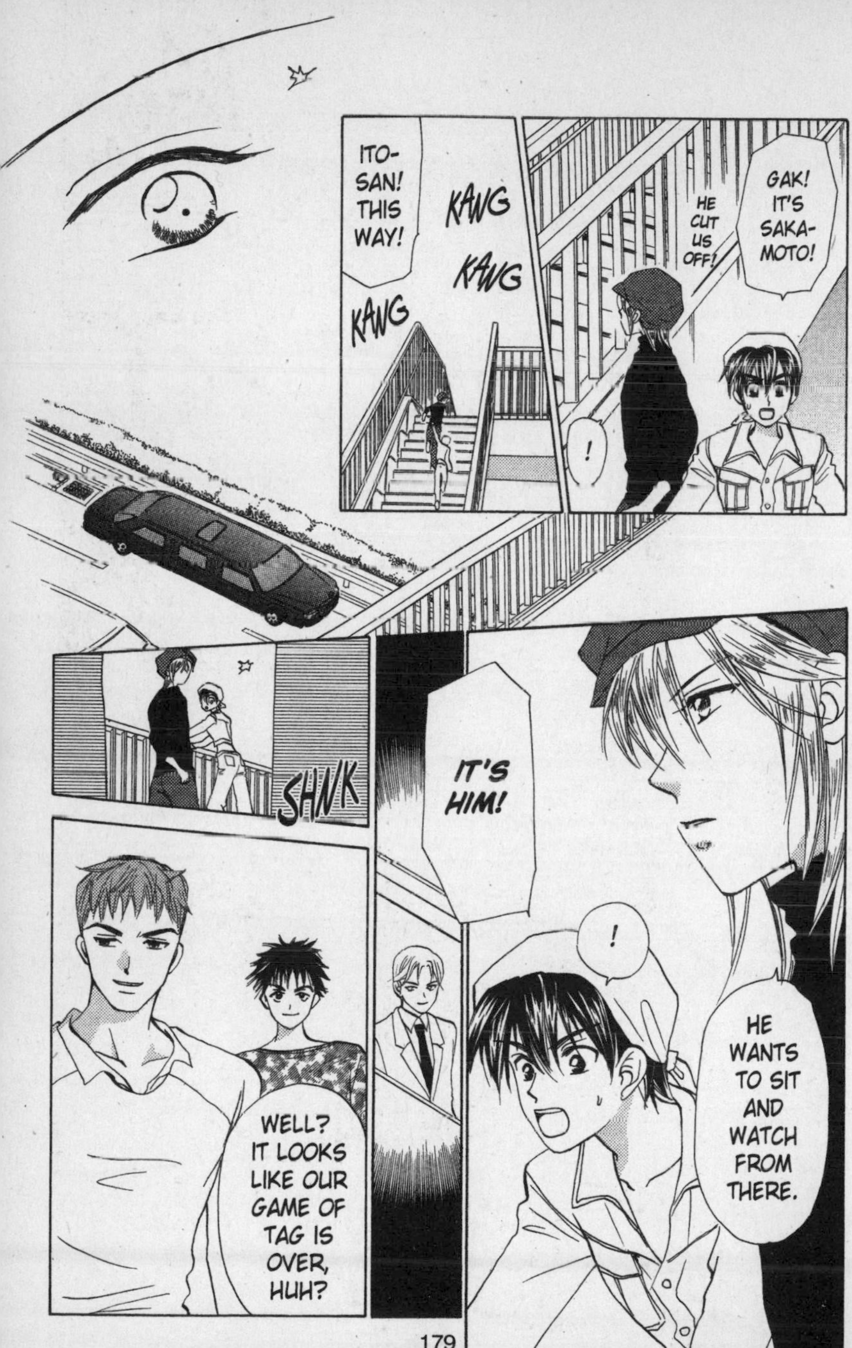
GAK! IT'S SAKA-MOTO!
HE CUT US OFF!
!
ITO-SAN! THIS WAY!
KANG
KANG
KANG
!
HE WANTS TO SIT AND WATCH FROM THERE.
IT'S HIM!
SHNK
WELL? IT LOOKS LIKE OUR GAME OF TAG IS OVER, HUH?

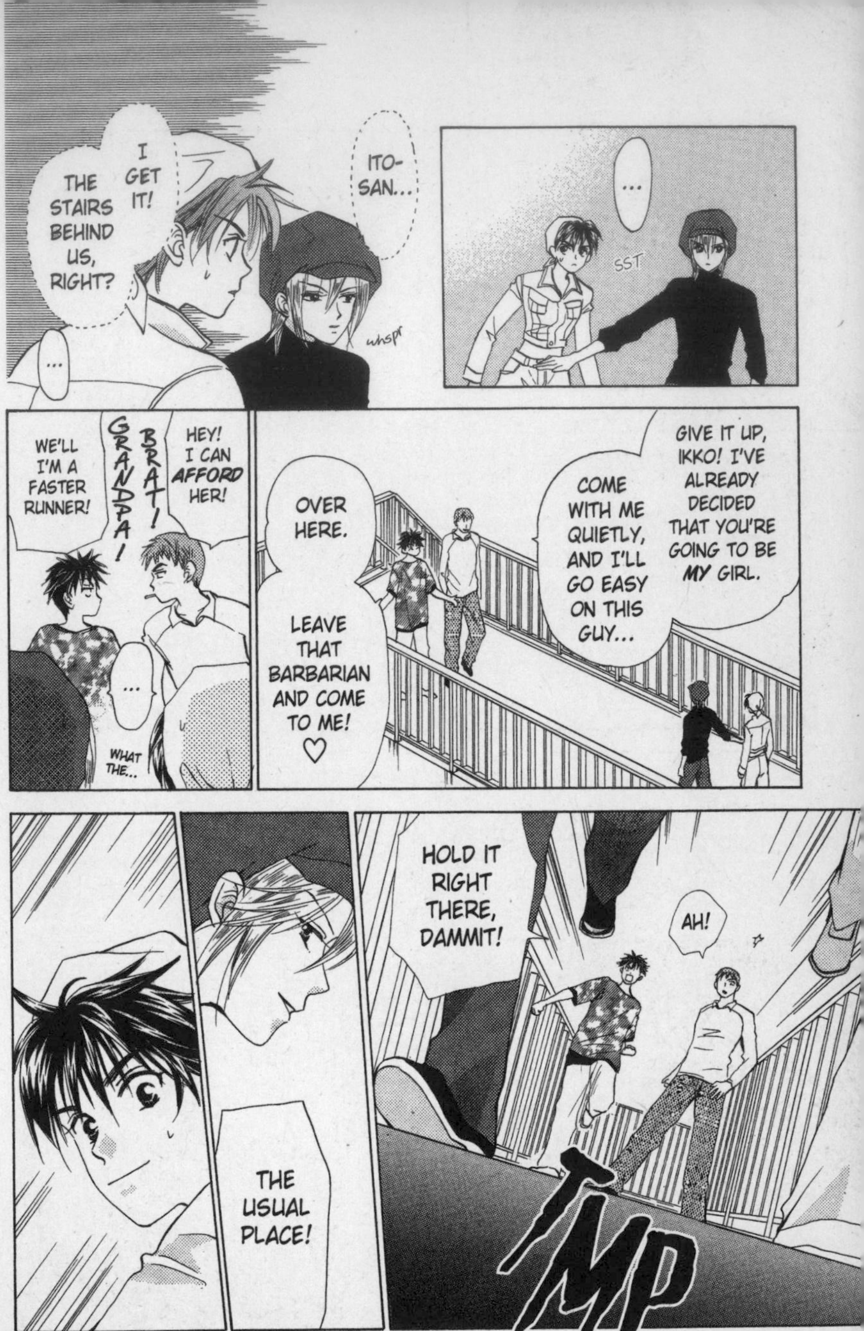
...
SST
ITO-SAN...
I GET IT!
THE STAIRS BEHIND US, RIGHT?
...
whspr
GIVE IT UP, IKKO! I'VE ALREADY DECIDED THAT YOU'RE GOING TO BE MY GIRL.
COME WITH ME QUIETLY, AND I'LL GO EASY ON THIS GUY...
OVER HERE.
LEAVE THAT BARBARIAN AND COME TO ME! ♡
HEY! I CAN AFFORD HER!
BRAT!
GRANDPA!
WE'LL I'M A FASTER RUNNER!
...
WHAT THE...
HOLD IT RIGHT THERE, DAMMIT!
AH!
TMP
THE USUAL PLACE!

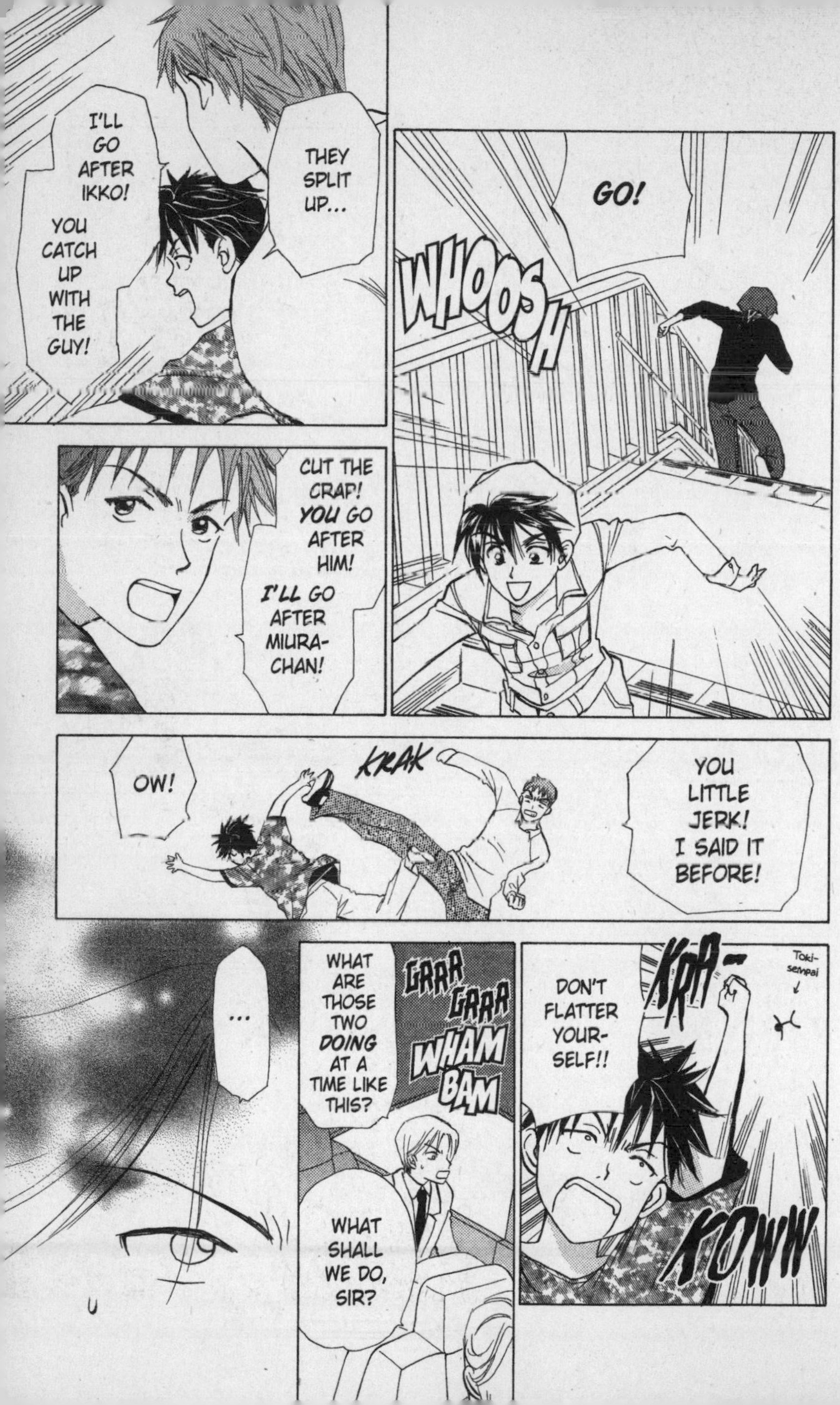
GO!
WHOOSH
THEY SPLIT UP...
I'LL GO AFTER IKKO!
YOU CATCH UP WITH THE GUY!
CUT THE CRAP! *YOU* GO AFTER HIM!
I'LL GO AFTER MIURA-CHAN!
YOU LITTLE JERK! I SAID IT BEFORE!
KRAK
OW!
KRA-
DON'T FLATTER YOURSELF!!
Toki-sempai
KOWW
GRAR GRAR
WHAM BAM
WHAT ARE THOSE TWO *DOING* AT A TIME LIKE THIS?
WHAT SHALL WE DO, SIR?
...

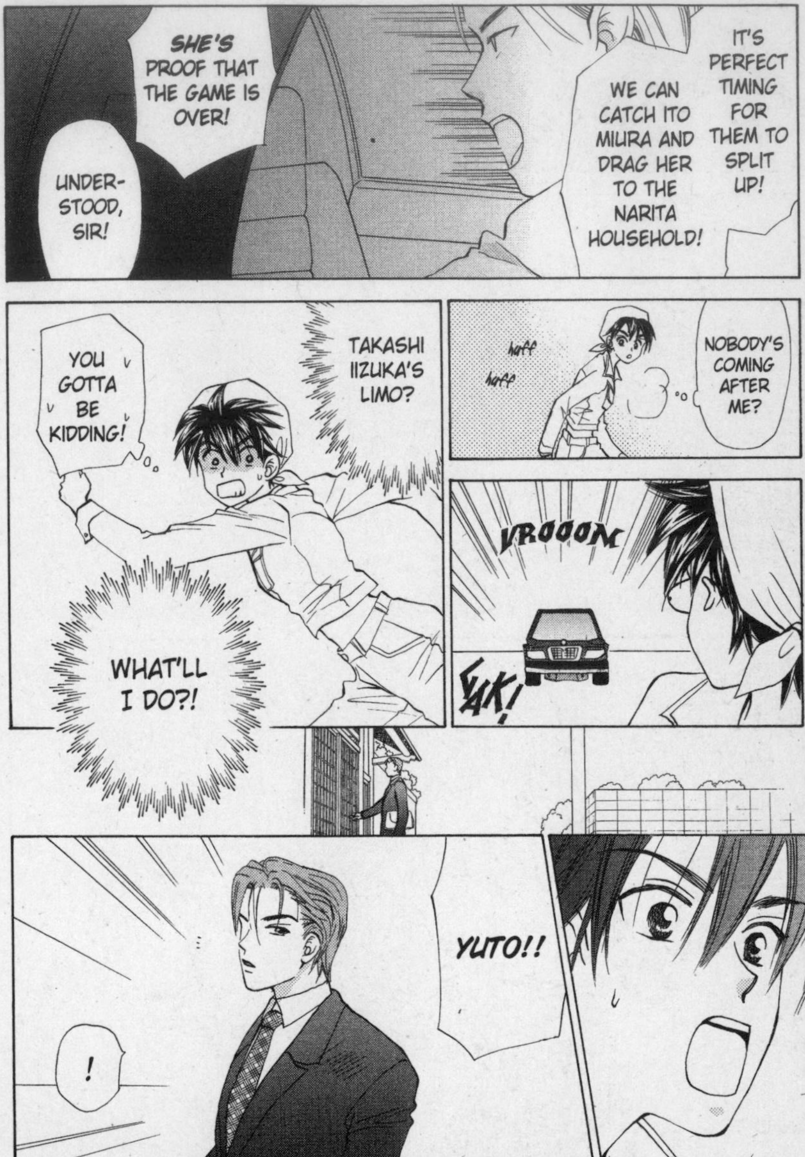
IT'S PERFECT TIMING FOR THEM TO SPLIT UP!
WE CAN CATCH ITO MIURA AND DRAG HER TO THE NARITA HOUSEHOLD!
SHE'S PROOF THAT THE GAME IS OVER!
UNDER-STOOD, SIR!
huff huff
NOBODY'S COMING AFTER ME?
VROOOM
TAKASHI IIZUKA'S LIMO?
YOU GOTTA BE KIDDING!
WHAT'LL I DO?!
YUTO!!
...
!

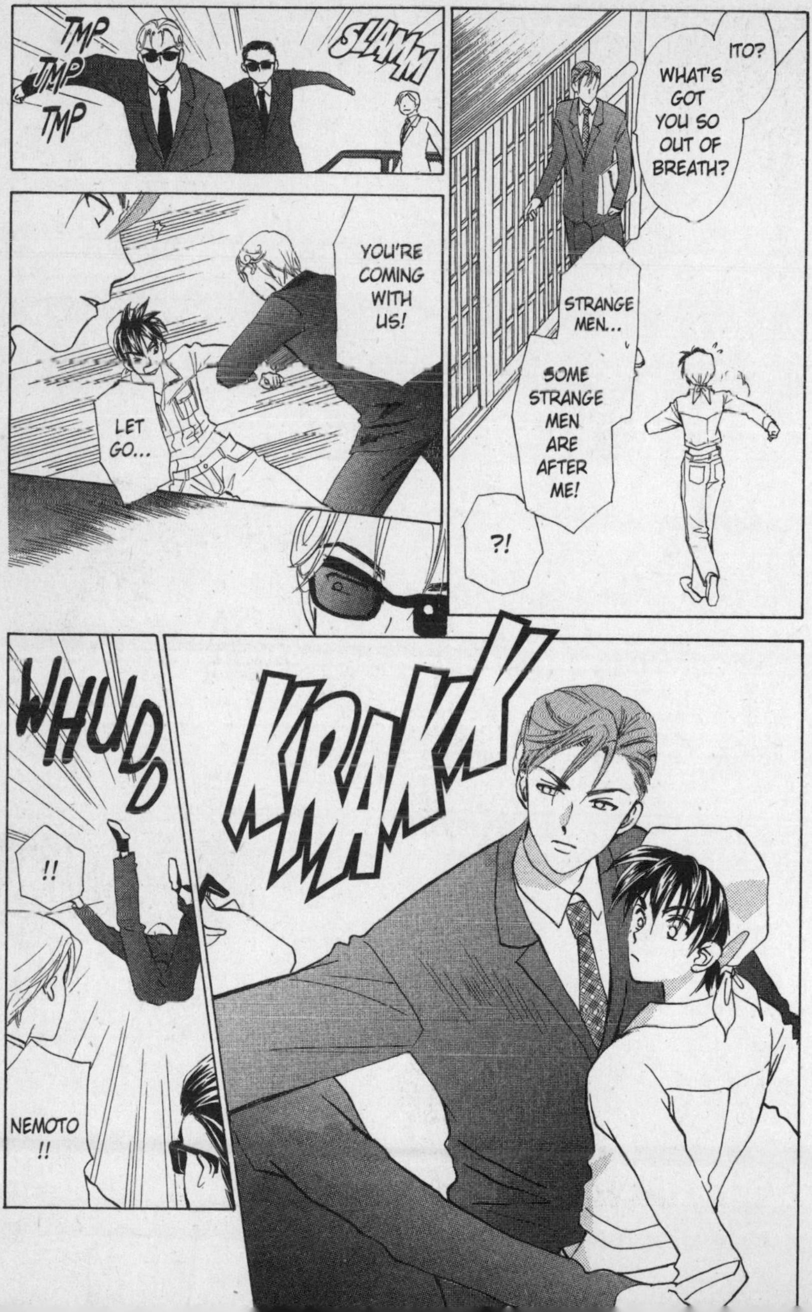
ITO? WHAT'S GOT YOU SO OUT OF BREATH?
STRANGE MEN...
SOME STRANGE MEN ARE AFTER ME!
?!
TMP
JMP
TMP
SLAMM
YOU'RE COMING WITH US!
LET GO...
KRAKK
WHUDD
!!
NEMOTO !!

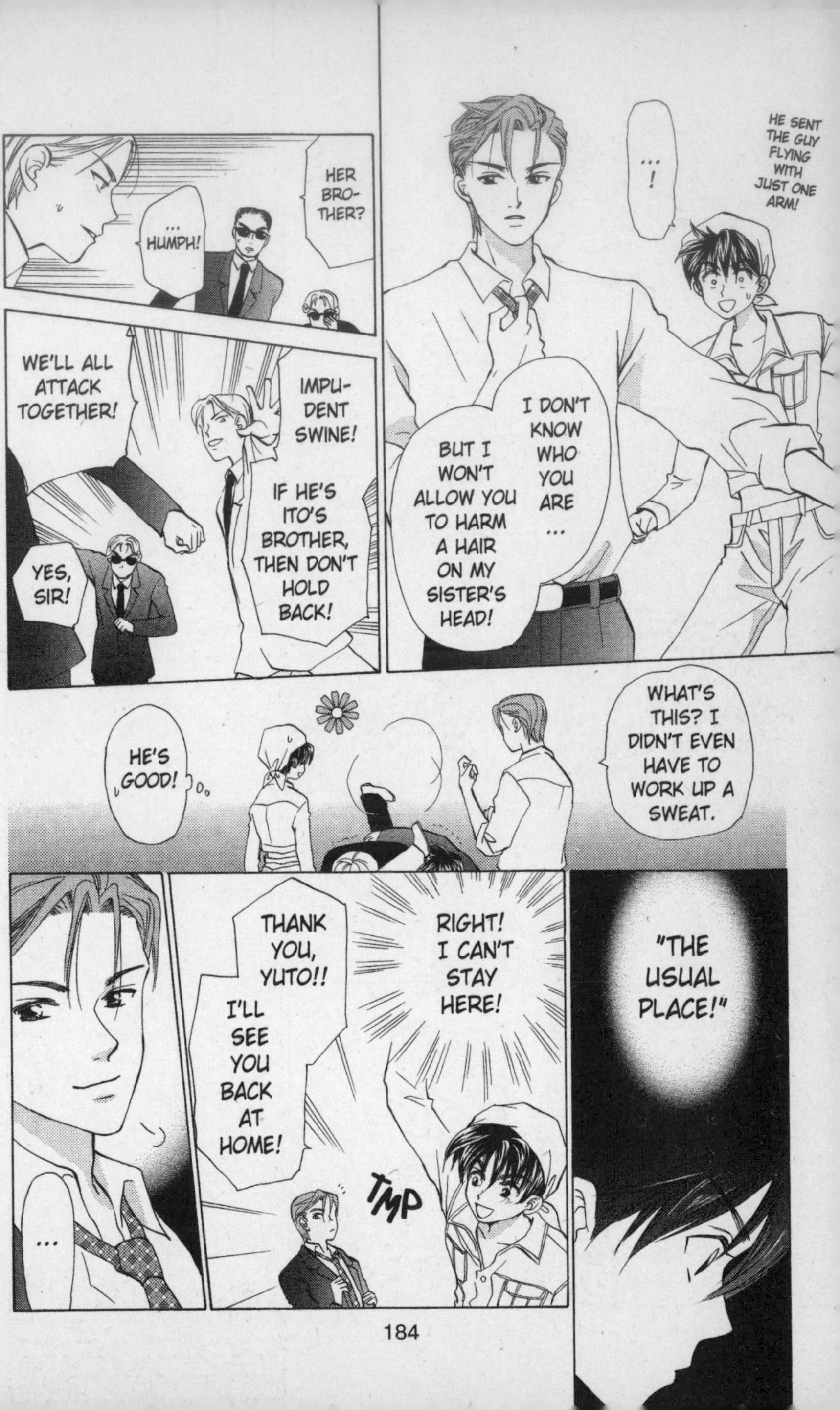
...!
HE SENT THE GUY FLYING WITH JUST ONE ARM!
I DON'T KNOW WHO YOU ARE ...
BUT I WON'T ALLOW YOU TO HARM A HAIR ON MY SISTER'S HEAD!
HER BRO-THER?
... HUMPH!
IMPU-DENT SWINE!
IF HE'S ITO'S BROTHER, THEN DON'T HOLD BACK!
WE'LL ALL ATTACK TOGETHER!
YES, SIR!
WHAT'S THIS? I DIDN'T EVEN HAVE TO WORK UP A SWEAT.
HE'S GOOD!
"THE USUAL PLACE!"
RIGHT! I CAN'T STAY HERE!
THANK YOU, YUTO!!
I'LL SEE YOU BACK AT HOME!
TMP
...

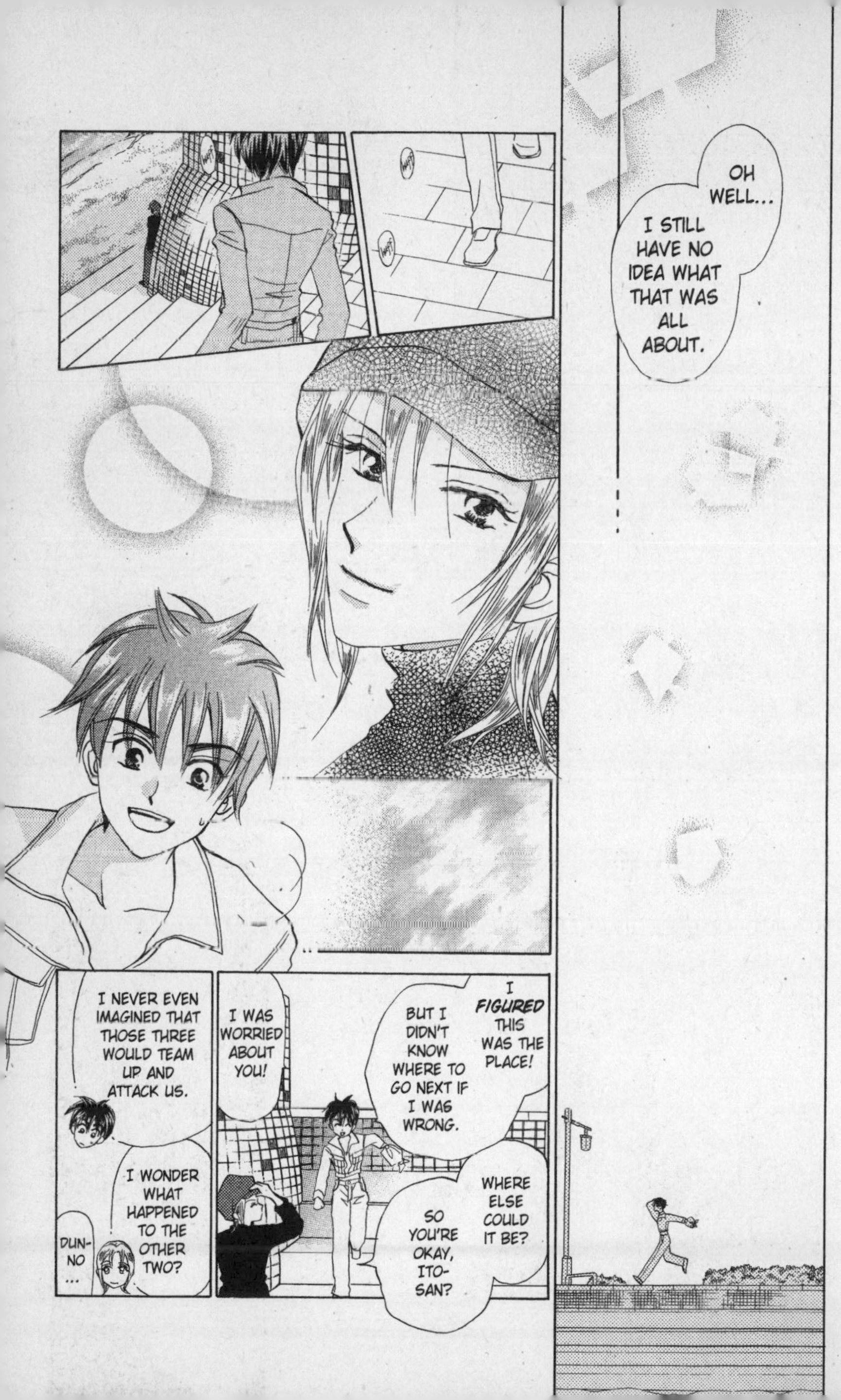
OH WELL...
I STILL HAVE NO IDEA WHAT THAT WAS ALL ABOUT.
I *FIGURED* THIS WAS THE PLACE!
BUT I DIDN'T KNOW WHERE TO GO NEXT IF I WAS WRONG.
I WAS WORRIED ABOUT YOU!
WHERE ELSE COULD IT BE?
SO YOU'RE OKAY, ITO-SAN?
I NEVER EVEN IMAGINED THAT THOSE THREE WOULD TEAM UP AND ATTACK US.
I WONDER WHAT HAPPENED TO THE OTHER TWO?
DUN-NO ...

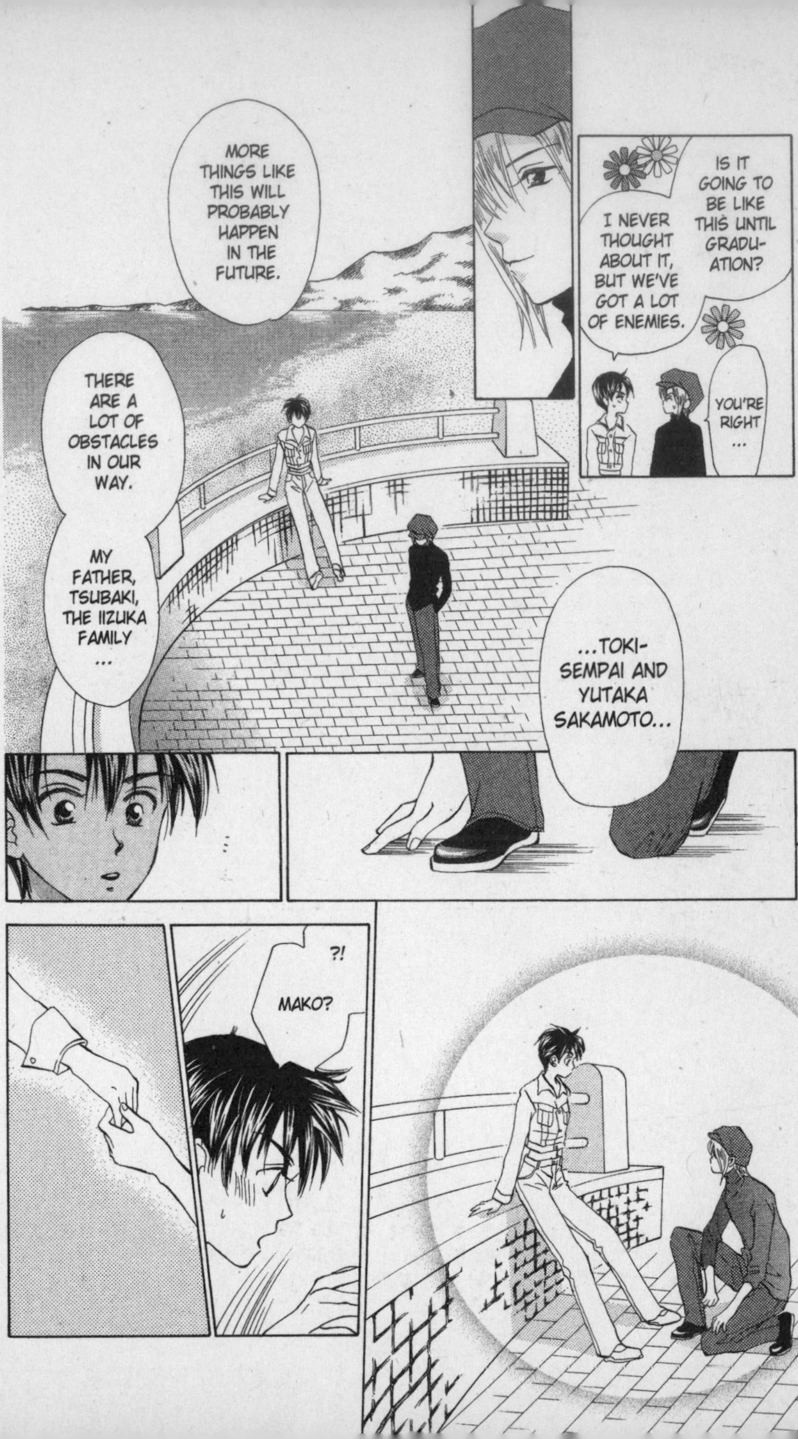
IS IT GOING TO BE LIKE THIS UNTIL GRADUATION?
I NEVER THOUGHT ABOUT IT, BUT WE'VE GOT A LOT OF ENEMIES.
YOU'RE RIGHT ...
MORE THINGS LIKE THIS WILL PROBABLY HAPPEN IN THE FUTURE.
THERE ARE A LOT OF OBSTACLES IN OUR WAY.
MY FATHER, TSUBAKI, THE IIZUKA FAMILY ...
...TOKI-SEMPAI AND YUTAKA SAKAMOTO...
...
?!
MAKO?

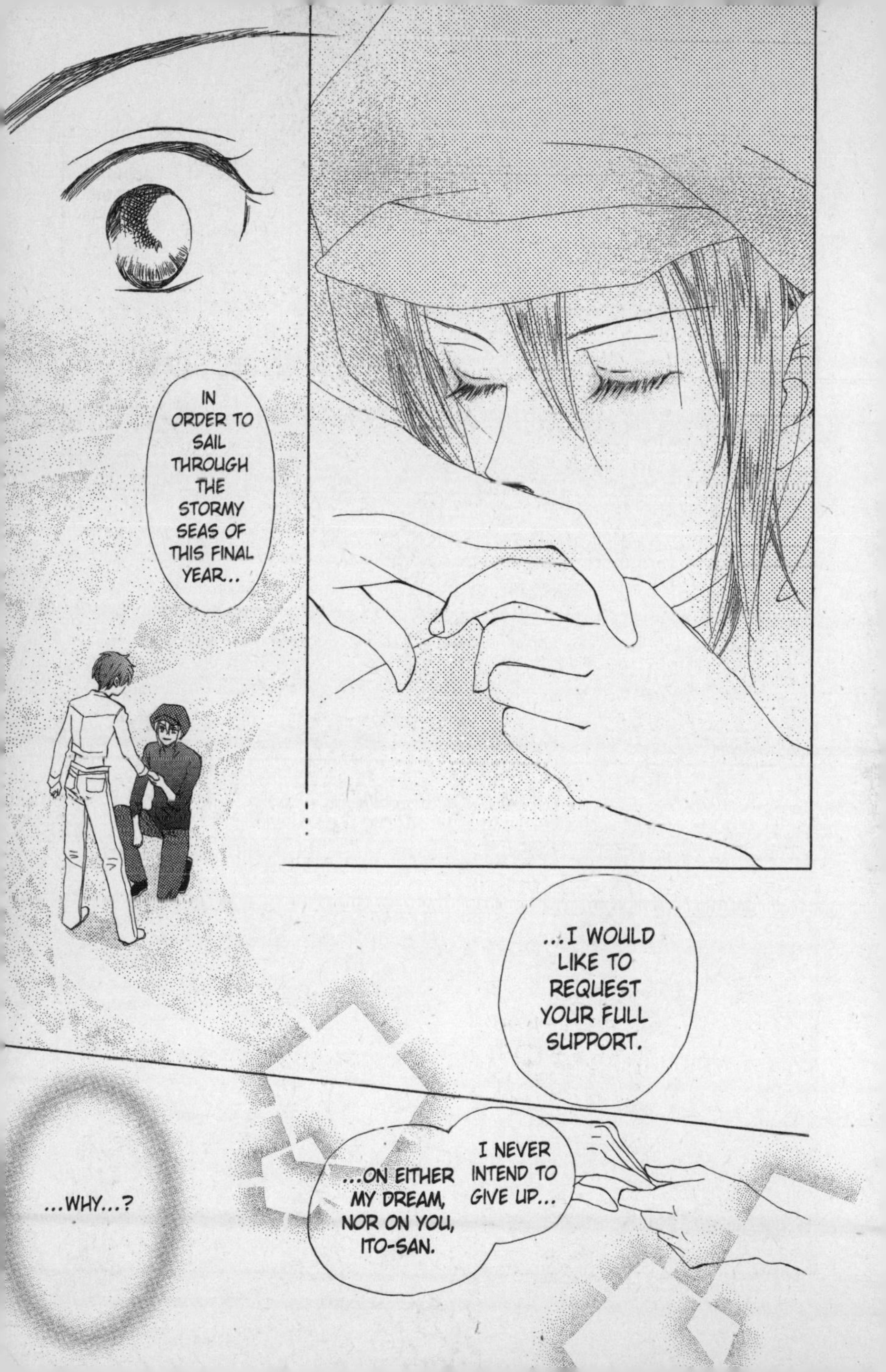
IN ORDER TO SAIL THROUGH THE STORMY SEAS OF THIS FINAL YEAR...
...I WOULD LIKE TO REQUEST YOUR FULL SUPPORT.
I NEVER INTEND TO GIVE UP...
...ON EITHER MY DREAM, NOR ON YOU, ITO-SAN.
...WHY...?

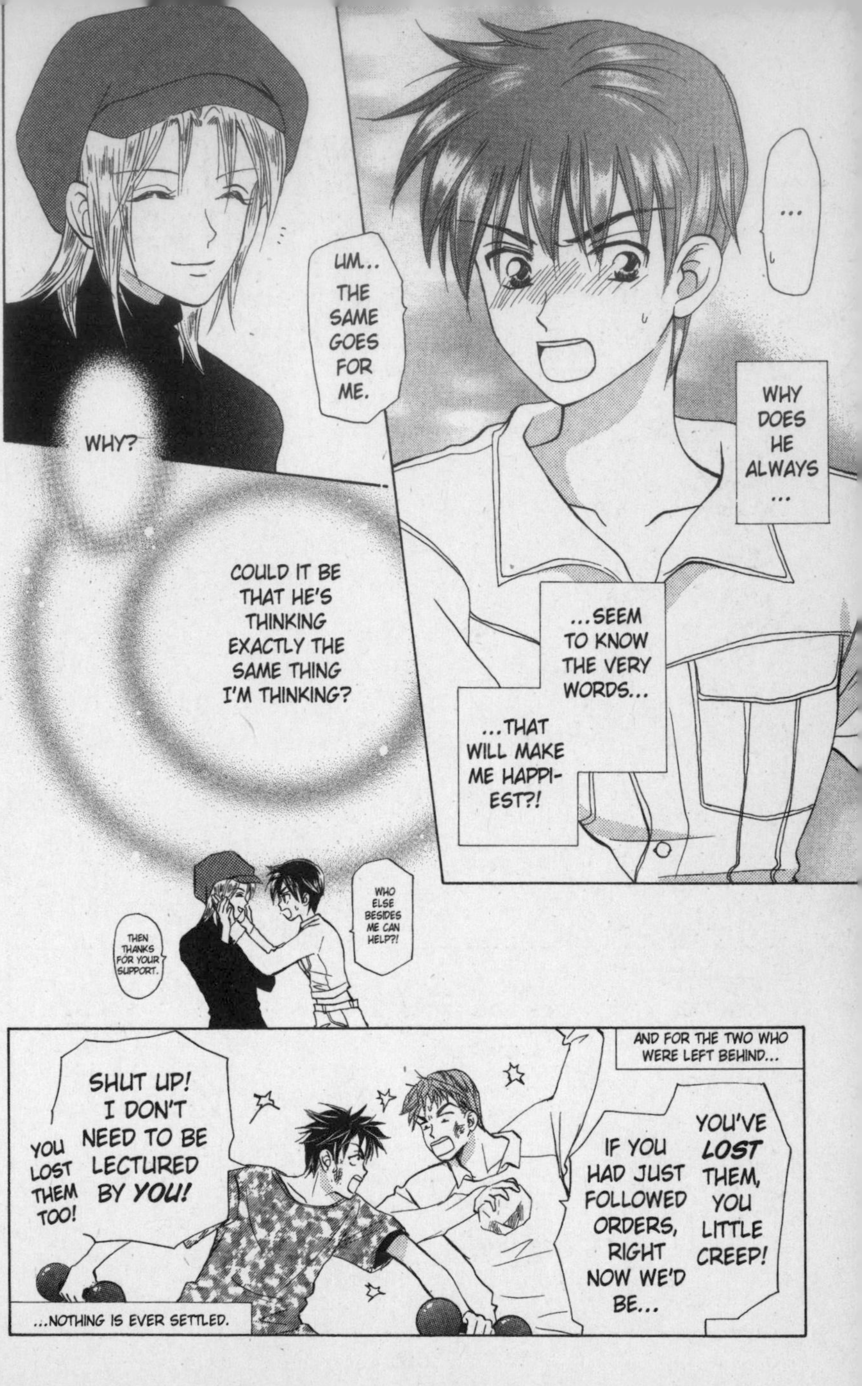
...
UM... THE SAME GOES FOR ME.
WHY DOES HE ALWAYS ...
...SEEM TO KNOW THE VERY WORDS...
...THAT WILL MAKE ME HAPPI-EST?!
WHY?
COULD IT BE THAT HE'S THINKING EXACTLY THE SAME THING I'M THINKING?
WHO ELSE BESIDES ME CAN HELP?!
THEN THANKS FOR YOUR SUPPORT.
AND FOR THE TWO WHO WERE LEFT BEHIND...
YOU'VE ***LOST*** THEM, YOU LITTLE CREEP!
IF YOU HAD JUST FOLLOWED ORDERS, RIGHT NOW WE'D BE...
SHUT UP! I DON'T NEED TO BE LECTURED BY ***YOU!***
YOU LOST THEM TOO!
...NOTHING IS EVER SETTLED.

THE VOLUME-ENDING AFTERWORD MANGA!

Behind the Scenes

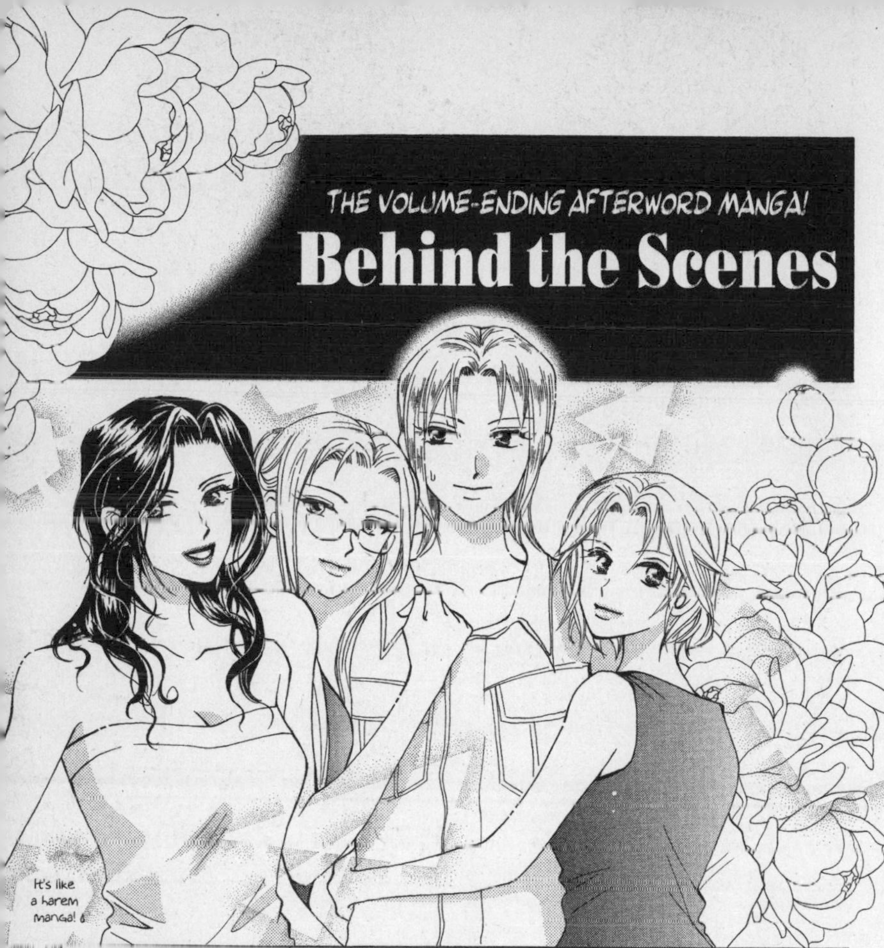
It's like a harem manga!

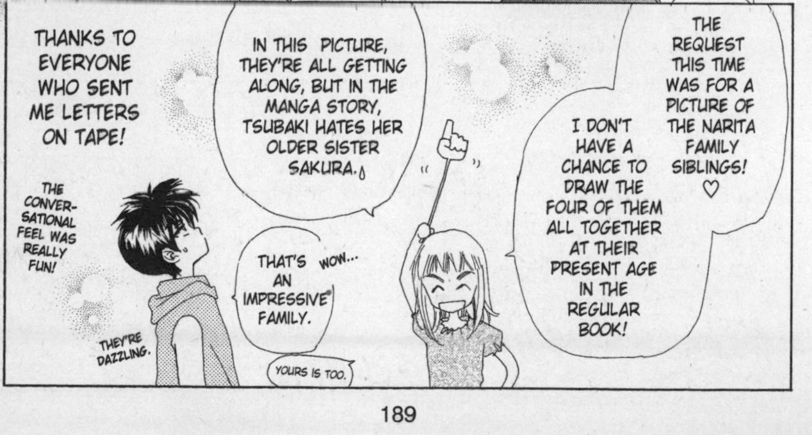
THE REQUEST THIS TIME WAS FOR A PICTURE OF THE NARITA FAMILY SIBLINGS! ♡
I DON'T HAVE A CHANCE TO DRAW THE FOUR OF THEM ALL TOGETHER AT THEIR PRESENT AGE IN THE REGULAR BOOK!
IN THIS PICTURE, THEY'RE ALL GETTING ALONG, BUT IN THE MANGA STORY, TSUBAKI HATES HER OLDER SISTER SAKURA.
THANKS TO EVERYONE WHO SENT ME LETTERS ON TAPE!
WOW...
THAT'S AN IMPRESSIVE FAMILY.
YOURS IS TOO.
THE CONVERSATIONAL FEEL WAS REALLY FUN!
THEY'RE DAZZLING.

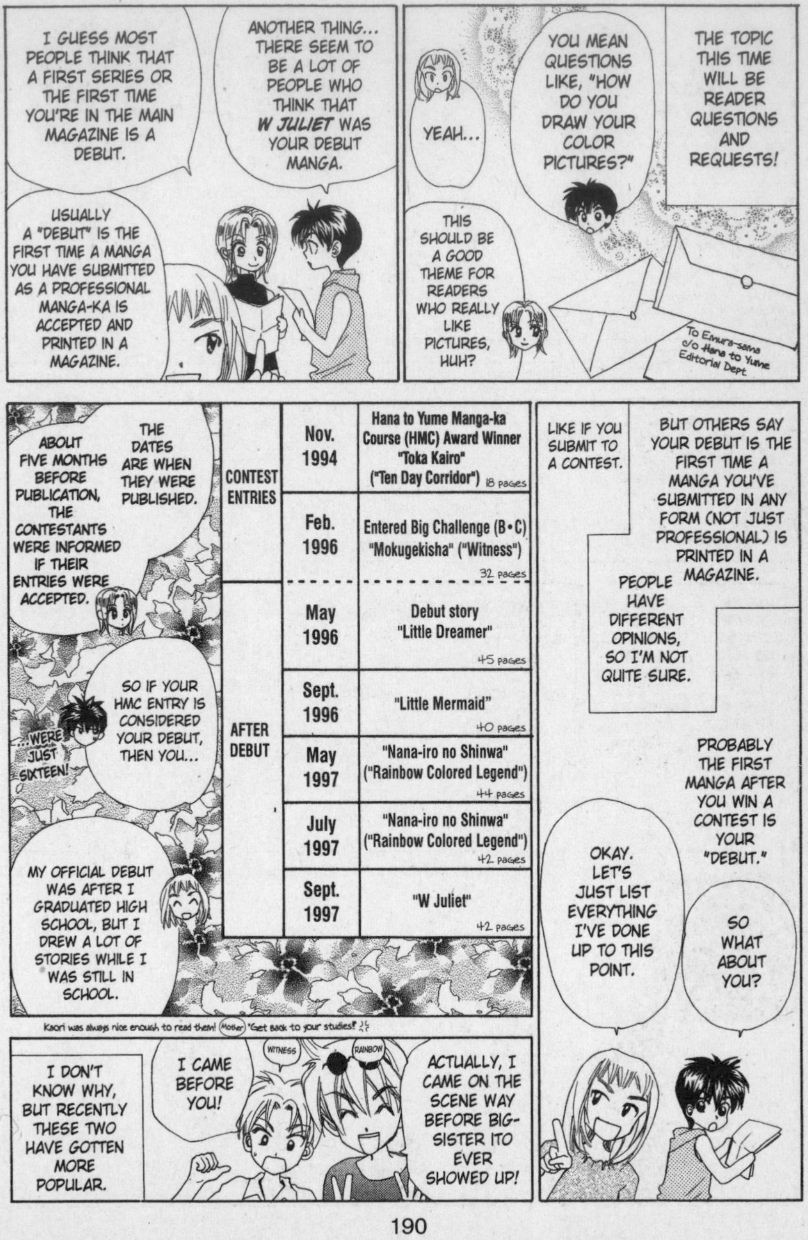
THE TOPIC THIS TIME WILL BE READER QUESTIONS AND REQUESTS!
YOU MEAN QUESTIONS LIKE, "HOW DO YOU DRAW YOUR COLOR PICTURES?"
YEAH...
THIS SHOULD BE A GOOD THEME FOR READERS WHO REALLY LIKE PICTURES, HUH?
To Emura-sama c/o Hana to Yume Editorial Dept.
ANOTHER THING... THERE SEEM TO BE A LOT OF PEOPLE WHO THINK THAT *W JULIET* WAS YOUR DEBUT MANGA.
I GUESS MOST PEOPLE THINK THAT A FIRST SERIES OR THE FIRST TIME YOU'RE IN THE MAIN MAGAZINE IS A DEBUT.
USUALLY A "DEBUT" IS THE FIRST TIME A MANGA YOU HAVE SUBMITTED AS A PROFESSIONAL MANGA-KA IS ACCEPTED AND PRINTED IN A MAGAZINE.
BUT OTHERS SAY YOUR DEBUT IS THE FIRST TIME A MANGA YOU'VE SUBMITTED IN ANY FORM (NOT JUST PROFESSIONAL) IS PRINTED IN A MAGAZINE.
LIKE IF YOU SUBMIT TO A CONTEST.
PEOPLE HAVE DIFFERENT OPINIONS, SO I'M NOT QUITE SURE.
PROBABLY THE FIRST MANGA AFTER YOU WIN A CONTEST IS YOUR "DEBUT."
SO WHAT ABOUT YOU?
OKAY. LET'S JUST LIST EVERYTHING I'VE DONE UP TO THIS POINT.

CONTEST ENTRIES	Nov. 1994	Hana to Yume Manga-ka Course (HMC) Award Winner "Toka Kairo" ("Ten Day Corridor") 18 pages
	Feb. 1996	Entered Big Challenge (B•C) "Mokugekisha" ("Witness") 32 pages
AFTER DEBUT	May 1996	Debut story "Little Dreamer" 45 pages
	Sept. 1996	"Little Mermaid" 40 pages
	May 1997	"Nana-iro no Shinwa" ("Rainbow Colored Legend") 44 pages
	July 1997	"Nana-iro no Shinwa" ("Rainbow Colored Legend") 42 pages
	Sept. 1997	"W Juliet" 42 pages

THE DATES ARE WHEN THEY WERE PUBLISHED.
ABOUT FIVE MONTHS BEFORE PUBLICATION, THE CONTESTANTS WERE INFORMED IF THEIR ENTRIES WERE ACCEPTED.
SO IF YOUR HMC ENTRY IS CONSIDERED YOUR DEBUT, THEN YOU...
...WERE JUST SIXTEEN!
MY OFFICIAL DEBUT WAS AFTER I GRADUATED HIGH SCHOOL, BUT I DREW A LOT OF STORIES WHILE I WAS STILL IN SCHOOL.
Kaori was always nice enough to read them! (Mother) "Get back to your studies!"
ACTUALLY, I CAME ON THE SCENE WAY BEFORE BIG-SISTER ITO EVER SHOWED UP!
I CAME BEFORE YOU!
WITNESS
RAINBOW
I DON'T KNOW WHY, BUT RECENTLY THESE TWO HAVE GOTTEN MORE POPULAR.

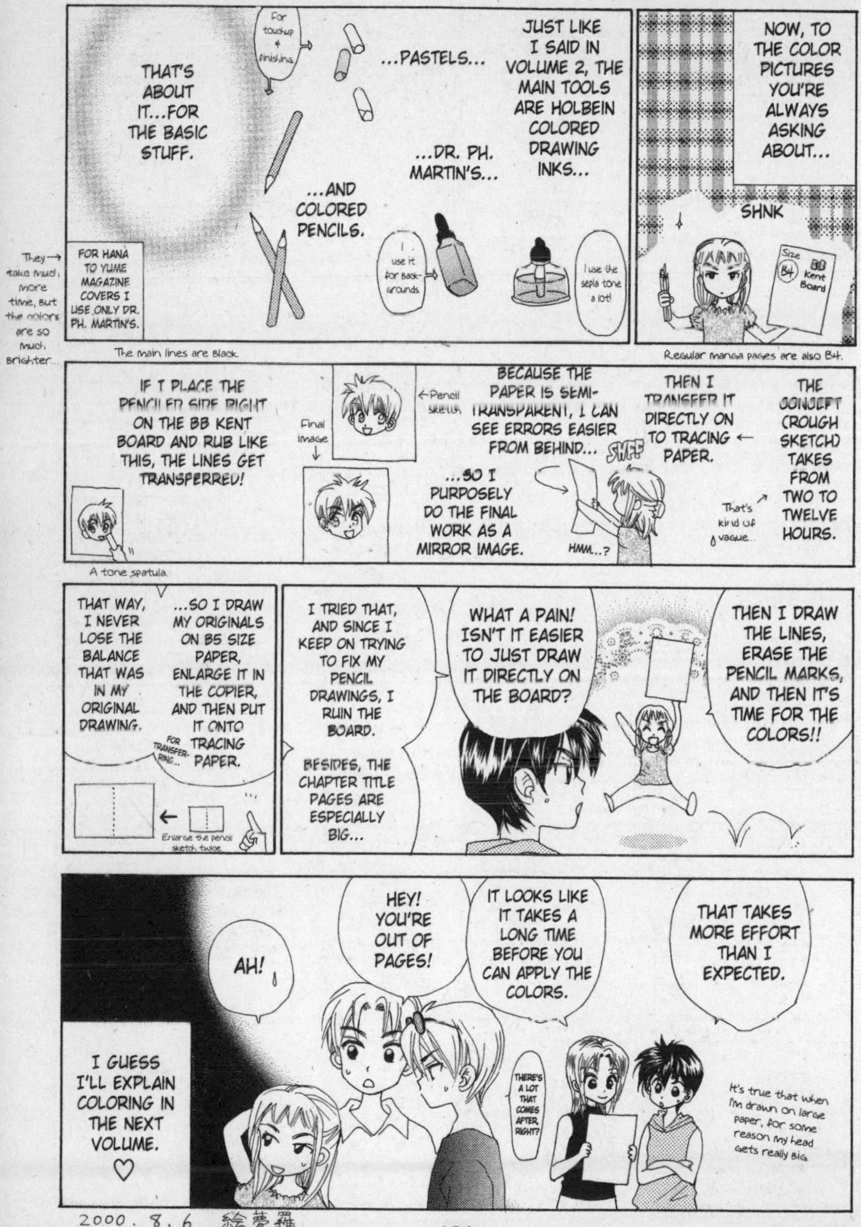
NOW, TO THE COLOR PICTURES YOU'RE ALWAYS ASKING ABOUT...
SHNK
Size B4 BB Kent Board
Regular manga pages are also B4.
JUST LIKE I SAID IN VOLUME 2, THE MAIN TOOLS ARE HOLBEIN COLORED DRAWING INKS...
I use the sepia tone a lot!
...DR. PH. MARTIN'S...
I use it for back-grounds.
...PASTELS...
For touchup & finishing
...AND COLORED PENCILS.
THAT'S ABOUT IT...FOR THE BASIC STUFF.
FOR HANA TO YUME MAGAZINE COVERS I USE ONLY DR. PH. MARTIN'S.
They take much more time, but the colors are so much brighter...
The main lines are black.
THE CONCEPT (ROUGH SKETCH) TAKES FROM TWO TO TWELVE HOURS.
That's kind of vague...
THEN I TRANSFER IT DIRECTLY ON TO TRACING PAPER.
SHFF
HMM...?
BECAUSE THE PAPER IS SEMI-TRANSPARENT, I CAN SEE ERRORS EASIER FROM BEHIND...
...SO I PURPOSELY DO THE FINAL WORK AS A MIRROR IMAGE.
Pencil sketch
Final image
IF I PLACE THE PENCILED SIDE RIGHT ON THE BB KENT BOARD AND RUB LIKE THIS, THE LINES GET TRANSFERRED!
A tone spatula.
THEN I DRAW THE LINES, ERASE THE PENCIL MARKS, AND THEN IT'S TIME FOR THE COLORS!!
WHAT A PAIN! ISN'T IT EASIER TO JUST DRAW IT DIRECTLY ON THE BOARD?
I TRIED THAT, AND SINCE I KEEP ON TRYING TO FIX MY PENCIL DRAWINGS, I RUIN THE BOARD.
BESIDES, THE CHAPTER TITLE PAGES ARE ESPECIALLY BIG...
...SO I DRAW MY ORIGINALS ON B5 SIZE PAPER, ENLARGE IT IN THE COPIER, AND THEN PUT IT ONTO TRACING PAPER.
FOR TRANSFER-RING...
THAT WAY, I NEVER LOSE THE BALANCE THAT WAS IN MY ORIGINAL DRAWING.
Enlarge the pencil sketch twice.
THAT TAKES MORE EFFORT THAN I EXPECTED.
It's true that when I'm drawn on large paper, for some reason my head gets really big.
IT LOOKS LIKE IT TAKES A LONG TIME BEFORE YOU CAN APPLY THE COLORS.
THERE'S A LOT THAT COMES AFTER, RIGHT?
HEY! YOU'RE OUT OF PAGES!
AH!
I GUESS I'LL EXPLAIN COLORING IN THE NEXT VOLUME. ♡

2000. 8. 6 絵夢羅。 E mura

Cultural Notes

The Magazine
[Reference page 130]
The magazine the banner refers to is **Hana to Yume** ("Flowers and Dreams"), a biweekly manga anthology magazine in which each **W Juliet** installment was originally published.

-sempai
Used to address more senior members of an institutionalized organization. In a school, students senior to the speaker would be addressed with -sempai, as would more senior employees in a company.

-sensei

Reserved to address people of certain professions such as teachers, doctors, and artisans. (Sometimes used for people playing the role of a teacher, doctor, etc.)

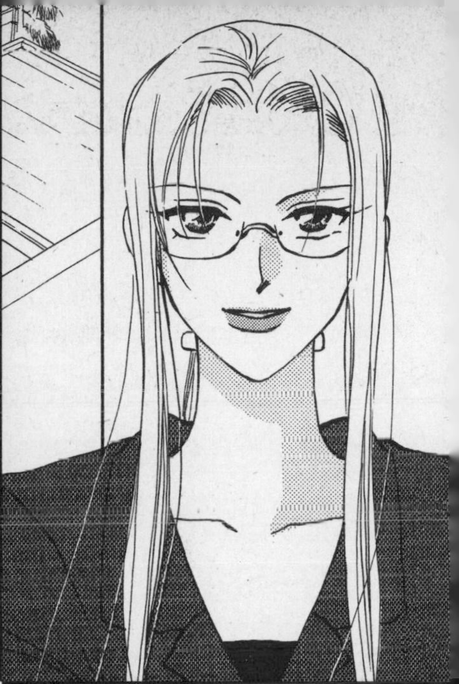

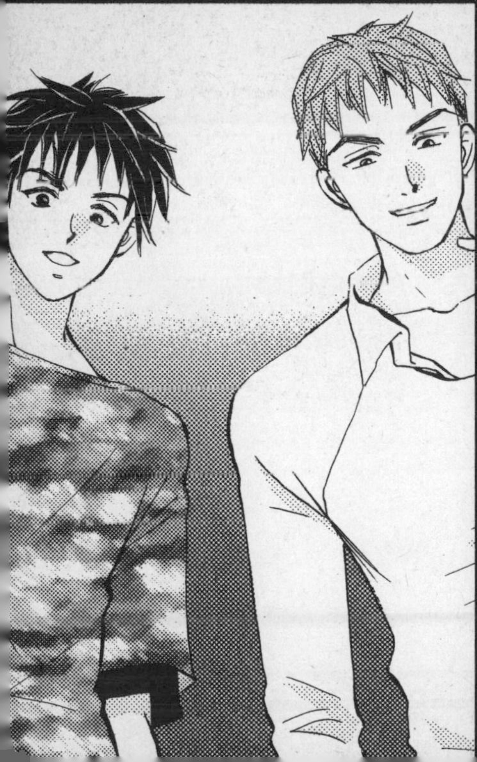

Sempai/kohai relationship

Since **W Juliet** takes place in a school club, the sempai/kohai relationship is a crucial aspect of the life of club members. It is much like the Western mentor/protégé relationship, but on a institution-wide scale. Sempai, the senior members, are expected to look after the interests of their kohai and guide them, help them with their problems, give them referrals, and be a counselor. Kohai are always expected to respect their sempai, do chores or menial tasks, follow orders, and learn whatever the organization teaches.

EDITOR'S RECOMMENDATIONS

If you liked W Juliet, *here are three more tasty shojo titles chock-full of high school hijinks.*

© 2004 Rie Takada/Shogakukan, Inc.

Happy Hustle High

Hanabi's just your average 16-year-old tomboy until her world gets turned upside-down: her all-girls school merges with a high school for boys! Going to school with the opposite sex turns out to be a lot more fun than Hanabi anticipated—and a lot more trouble. When the guy of Hanabi's dreams doesn't pay her any mind, she decides to join the new student council to get his attention.

© 2002 Kaho Miyasaka/ Shogakukan, Inc.

Kare First Love

Karin Karino always thought of herself as a wallflower, and so did all of her friends, including bossy Yuka. Then Karin meets Kiriya, the handsome guy that Yuka's been crushing on. An amateur photographer who lives alone, Kiriya seems to see an inner beauty in Karin that she never knew existed. Soon she's falling for him—hard. But domineering Yuka is determined to get in the way...

Ouran Koko Host Club
© Bisco Hatori 2002/HAKUSENSHA, Inc.

Ouran High School Host Club

Haruhi, a scholarship student at exclusive Ouran High School, can't even afford a proper girl's uniform! When she accidentally breaks an $80,000 vase that belongs to the mysterious all-boy "Host Club," Haruhi, with her men's pants and short hair, is mistaken for a boy and forced to work for the club to pay back the damages. Along the way she gets to know the intimate secrets of the school's richest and most handsome boys!

What happens when the hottest guy in school is a girl?!?

Hana-Kimi

For You in Full Blossom ™

Mizuki will do anything to get close to her idol, Izumi Sano – even transfer to an all-boys high school! Now, Mizuki must disguise herself in the classroom, locker room, and even her own bedroom. How will everyone react to the new transfer student who looks like a very pretty boy?

Only $9.95!

Hana-Kimi

1 story and art by HISAYA NAKAJO

Start your graphic novel collection today!

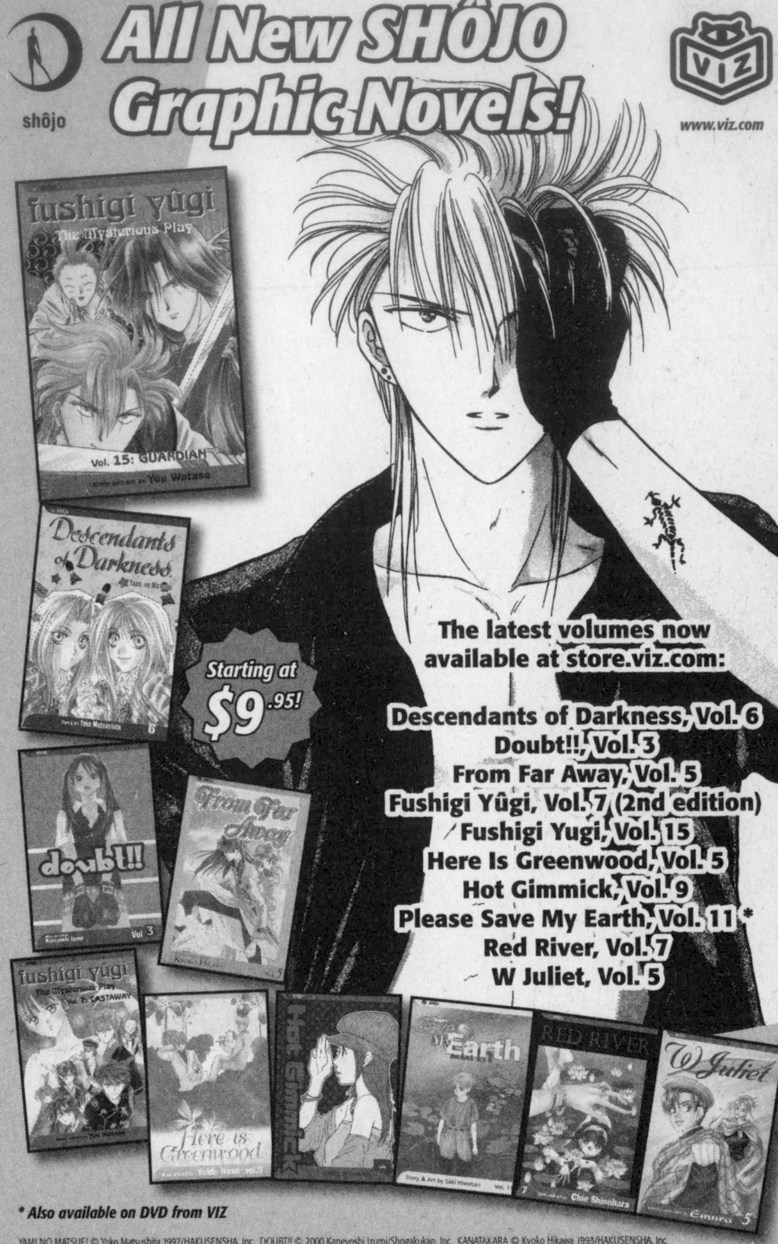

shôjo
All New SHÔJO Graphic Novels!
VIZ
www.viz.com
Starting at $9.95!
The latest volumes now available at store.viz.com:
Descendants of Darkness, Vol. 6
Doubt!!, Vol. 3
From Far Away, Vol. 5
Fushigi Yûgi, Vol. 7 (2nd edition)
Fushigi Yugi, Vol. 15
Here Is Greenwood, Vol. 5
Hot Gimmick, Vol. 9
Please Save My Earth, Vol. 11 *
Red River, Vol. 7
W Juliet, Vol. 5
* Also available on DVD from VIZ